Preparing a Nation's Teachers

Preparing a Nation's Teachers

MODELS FOR ENGLISH AND FOREIGN LANGUAGE PROGRAMS

EDITED BY

Phyllis Franklin

David Laurence

AND

Elizabeth B. Welles

THE MODERN LANGUAGE ASSOCIATION OF AMERICA

New York *1999*

Supported by grants from The Pew Charitable Trusts and The National Endowment for the Humanities

Sarah Michaels's essay, "Stories in Contact: Teacher Research in the Academy," and a version of Deborah K. Woelflein's essay, "Great Expectations, Hard Times," both appeared in the Spring 1999 issue of the *ADE Bulletin*.

Library of Congress Cataloging-in-Publication Data

Preparing a nation's teachers : models for English and foreign language programs / edited by Phyllis Franklin, David Laurence, and Elizabeth B. Welles.
p. cm.
Includes bibliographical references.
ISBN 0-87352-374-1 (pbk.)
1. English teachers—Training of—United States. 2. Language teachers—Training of—United States. 3. English philology—Study and teaching (Higher)—United States. 4. Language and languages—Study and teaching (Higher)—United States. I. Franklin, Phyllis. II. Laurence, David Ernst. III. Welles, Elizabeth B.
PE68.U5P74 1999
428′.0071′173—dc21 99-22216

Printed on recycled paper

Published by The Modern Language Association of America
10 Astor Place, New York, New York 10003-6981

CONTENTS

Preface: The School Reform Movement and Higher Education ix
PHYLLIS FRANKLIN, DAVID LAURENCE, AND ELIZABETH B. WELLES

Introduction: What Happens Next? and How? and Why? 1
DONALD GRAY

I *Model Programs*

REPORTS FROM ENGLISH DEPARTMENTS

ILLINOIS STATE UNIVERSITY 17
Renewing the Nexus: Strengthening Connections across the English Education Program

INDIANA UNIVERSITY, BLOOMINGTON 49
Watch This Space; or, Why We Have Not Revised the Teacher Education Program — Yet

NEW MEXICO STATE UNIVERSITY, LAS CRUCES 65
Defining the Secondary School English Education Camel

NORFOLK STATE UNIVERSITY 80
Preparing Secondary School English Teachers

UNIVERSITY OF IOWA 104
Educating Teachers of English

UNIVERSITY OF VIRGINIA 126
Fit Teachers Though Few

REPORTS FROM FOREIGN LANGUAGE DEPARTMENTS

ARIZONA STATE UNIVERSITY, TEMPE 145
Teacher Education Program Reform: A Case in Point

CALIFORNIA STATE UNIVERSITY, LONG BEACH 160
Creating Teaching Communities: A Model for Reform and Ongoing Renewal

UNIVERSITY OF GEORGIA 183
The Perils of an Integrated Curriculum; or, How a Team Talked for One Year and Almost Communicated . . .

UNIVERSITY OF NORTH CAROLINA, GREENSBORO 198
Integrated Perspectives: An Exemplary Program

UNIVERSITY OF SOUTH FLORIDA 221
A Curricular Response to a Market Survey of Teachers' Needs

UNIVERSITY OF VIRGINIA 241
Teaching and the Open Horizon

II *Assessment Issues*

Assessment: A Blessing or Bane for Teachers of English? 257
EDWARD M. WHITE AND VOLNEY S. WHITE

Issues for Foreign Language Departments and Prospective Teachers 284
JUDITH E. LISKIN-GASPARRO

III *Unresolved Questions*

Changing Teacher Preparation for a Changing Student Body 319
REED WAY DASENBROCK

Connecting Universities and Schools: A Case Study 332
HAROLD H. KOLB, JR.

Great Expectations, Hard Times 353
DEBORAH K. WOELFLEIN

Stories in Contact: Teacher Research in the Academy 360
SARAH MICHAELS

Facing Our Professional Others: Border Crossing in Teacher Education 373
BOB BROAD

Closely Reading Ourselves: Teaching English and the Education of Teachers 380
JAMES MARSHALL

Challenges of Teaching Literature: Reflections on the MLA Teacher Education Project 390
DAVID A. FEIN

Teaching Literature in the Foreign Language Classroom: Where Have We Been and Where Do We Go Now? 398
DORIS Y. KADISH

Appendix: Baseline Studies 412

PHYLLIS FRANKLIN, DAVID LAURENCE,
AND ELIZABETH B. WELLES

Preface: The School Reform Movement and Higher Education

A Nation at Risk is now fifteen years old, and the national debate about schools and schooling that Secretary of Education Terrel H. Bell provoked continues to command the attention of parents, reformers, politicians, journalists, foundation heads, state and federal policy makers, entrepreneurs, and teachers. Out of this debate came the six national education goals that the president of the United States and the governors adopted in 1990 for the nation to achieve for the twenty-first century: "ensuring that children start school ready to learn, raising high school graduation rates, increasing levels of education achievement, promoting science and mathematics achievement as well as literacy and lifelong learning, and freeing schools of drugs and violence." To these goals, in 1994, Congress added "improvements in teacher preparation and increased parental involvement in schools" (Campbell, Voelkl, and Donahue 1). Each year since the goals were adopted, the National Education Goals Panel has monitored progress toward them in the *National Education Goals Report: Building a Nation of Learners,* and the United States Department of Education, private foundations, the White House, the governors, Congress, state legislatures, and organizations of school and college administrators, faculty members, schoolteachers, and parents have participated in federal, state, and local initiatives to make achievement of the goals possible.

The question of how our schools might be improved has attracted relatively little attention among MLA members. Reasons come easily to mind. The public laying of blame that marked most arguments about the schools in the mid-1980s and early 1990s had a political edge that may have encouraged academics to view reform as more hype than substance. And the reformers' early focus on assessment through objective tests may also have been off-putting. Not only was assessment irrelevant to the intellectual concerns of a fair number of MLA members, it also suggested the devaluation of those aspects of a humanities education that objective tests could not measure. Moreover, at the time, leaders of the reform movement were impatient with academics who expressed doubts about either the direction or pace of the reform effort. Besides, MLA members had their own problems. The culture wars preoccupied the attention of many, and challenges to tenure, the growing use of part-time faculty members, and a relentlessly poor job market worried others. Finally, and perhaps most important, was an old habit among MLA members of leaving conversations about the schools and teaching to colleagues in the field of education.

Fifteen years is a long time, and the school reform movement has evolved. Initially school reform focused on quantitative changes, for example, more time in school, higher requirements for students and teachers, more tests (Choy, Chen, and Ross 1–2). Then the decentralization of schools was seen as important (Louis 21). The next stage aimed at qualitative improvements, the development of standards "that define both what students should know and be able to do and how teachers should instruct students to achieve those standards." Attention was therefore given to creating curriculum frameworks, "new instructional methods and materials," and new approaches to assessment (Choy, Chen, and Ross 2). Although each stage brought some improvements in student performance, none has produced the degree of change that reformers anticipated. Consequently, in 1996, the National Commission on Teaching and America's Future concluded: "After a decade of reform, we have finally learned in hindsight what should have been clear from the start: most schools and teachers cannot produce the kind of learning demanded by the new reforms – not because they do not want to, but because they do not know how, and the systems in which they work do not support them in doing so" (3).

From this insight came the current focus on strengthening the preparation of undergraduates for teaching and on rethinking training for teachers already in the field. There is a growing sense of urgency about education goals, because states will soon be seeking to hire large numbers of teachers as the student population rises; once employed, these teachers will be in their classrooms for many decades. In a statement titled "One America in the Twenty-First Century: Forging a New Future," the advisory board to the President's Initiative on Race points to the need for all students to have access to "high-quality teachers" and links high-quality teachers to the effectiveness of teacher education ("Education's Role"). In short, the school reform movement is now looking to us for help.

The situation in higher education and the field has also changed over the past fifteen years, years that have not been kind either to the academy or the humanities. Funding has become an issue, in part because the national priority that favored the growth of higher education in the post-sputnik period faded with the disappearance of the Soviet Union, in part because the political mood has shifted to a desire for less government and lower taxes. At the same time, other demands on the resources of the nation and the states—for improved schools, health care, Social Security, Medicare, and prisons—are competing with the needs of higher education. Not only is funding being constrained, the value of the humanities is being questioned. As the cost of higher education rises and as a significant share of that cost shifts to parents and students in the form of tuition, there is growing demand that fields of study justify themselves by demonstrating direct and immediate benefits to graduates' earning power and ability to get better-paying employment quickly after graduation—when student loans come due. Similarly, the anticipated financial benefits of distance education has made the humanities seem less relevant to the education of both undergraduates and those reentry students who seek career advancement. The culture wars also cast doubt on the merit of work in the humanities.

These trends have led MLA members to a rare consensus on the need to reach an audience outside the academy in order to promote a better public understanding of how the humanities and especially the study of language and literature contribute to society, prepare students for careers, and enrich people's lives. From a pragmatic point of view, then, the call to participate in school reform by strengthening undergraduate and graduate programs that serve teachers of English and foreign languages could not come at a better time.

What are we being asked to do? First, to pay particular attention to content, the subject matter we include in the courses we teach and in the programs we configure for undergraduates preparing to become high school teachers and for teachers in the field who enroll in graduate courses and programs. In an informative report on the professional development of teachers that was sponsored by the National Governors' Association, Thomas C. Corcoran points to reformers' recognition of the importance of subject-matter knowledge. The school reform movement wants teachers to function more as coaches than conveyors of facts, and the teachers who can play the role of coach most effectively are those who have a thorough grasp of the disciplines they teach (vi, 13). A similar focus on content is also important in professional development. Corcoran writes, "Current [state] policies do not encourage teachers to acquire deep understanding of subject matter through graduate education nor do they recognize the value of collegial interactions and professional activities" (13).

Therefore we are being asked to ensure that the courses and programs we offer "have rigor, depth, and coherence," that these courses and programs give students who wish to become teachers, and teachers who wish to continue their education, the opportunity to gain confident command of the knowledge base that defines the field as an area of academic study. In addition, we are urged to engage all students intellectually and to give special attention to the preparation of teachers "who serve the most vulnerable students." Corcoran argues, "Although high-quality opportunities should be accessible to all teachers, those who have been underserved in the past and who face the most difficult educational challenges should receive priority" (22, 44).

We are also being asked to invent opportunities for involving new and experienced secondary school teachers in the rethinking of our courses and programs and to collaborate with the schools and school systems as well. Corcoran asks higher education and professional associations to play a "larger role" in professional development (44). He reports:

> One of the common complaints among school reformers is that they do not receive enough assistance from higher education. Critics charge that higher education is not examining its admissions standards, not working hard enough to improve undergraduate education, not paying enough attention to the quality of teacher education, not adjusting [its] professional programs to fit the changing situations in schools, not offering the kinds [of] courses that practicing teachers need or not making the courses accessible, and not helping schools implement reforms. (40)

In June 1998, the Education Commission of the States released a survey titled *Transforming Postsecondary Education for the Twenty-First Century: Views of the Governors,* which noted that 91% of the governors felt that providing "linkages" between teacher education and primary and secondary schools was important in addressing the critical challenge facing their states. It is also noteworthy that when the governors were asked about the likely responsiveness of the various sectors of higher education in their states to meeting state-identified needs, "less than half the governors found public research universities or four-year colleges 'very responsive' or 'responsive' to meeting fundamental state needs; 17% and 12% found them 'somewhat unresponsive' in meeting state needs" (7, 6). There may be a connection between a reluctance in some states to fund higher education and the perception that higher education ignores state needs.

There are now important reasons for us to break our old habit of tuning out discussions of what happens in the schools. Preparing English and foreign language secondary school teachers has long been our community's particular responsibility. The link between the public image and representation of our community and the work we do—or choose not to do—in teacher education is now explicit in the arenas where decisions about the funding of higher education are made. Because the schools and the student population are changing and because more is now demanded of teachers, a fresh look at how we fulfill this responsibility seems in order. It is difficult to imagine a more effective long-term investment that we, as individual members of English and foreign language departments, can make in the effort to strengthen the quality of schooling in the United States. Each knowledgeable, intellectually lively teacher we educate will affect the lives of thousands of young people.

Convinced of the importance of a field-wide consideration of teacher preparation, in 1993 the MLA Executive Council authorized the development of the Teacher Education Project. Funds from the National Endowment for the Humanities and the Pew Charitable Trusts enabled the MLA to invite six English and six foreign language departments to establish teams of faculty members, local secondary school teachers, and representatives of schools of education to review the departments' courses and programs that prepare undergraduates for careers as secondary school teachers. In addition to planning on campus, the twelve teams met at two national conferences, which the MLA organized. At the first meeting, the teams learned about the school-reform movement, compared notes about what their studies of their departments' programs had revealed, and discussed possible improvements. At the second conference, project participants concluded that what they discovered from studying their programs, departmental attitudes, and institutional barriers to collaboration with colleagues in the schools would be useful to others in the field. An editorial committee was established to shape a publication. *Preparing a Nation's Teachers: Models for English and Foreign Language Departments* grew out of the committee's belief in the value of the Teacher Education Project. Part 1 contains the reports from the English departments and from the foreign language departments. In part 2, two essays discuss assessment issues for teachers of English and for teachers of foreign languages. In part 3, eight teachers reflect on their experience in schools and higher education and make suggestions for the future of school reform.

The departments that participated in the MLA project began with studies of their courses and programs in accordance with the self-assessment document that appears in the appendix to this volume. In each department, the process of self-study led to unexpected insights about how prospective teachers fared in the department, what individual faculty members and courses contributed or failed to contribute to students' experiences, and where connections between the department and the school of education had eroded and needed to be reimagined. In most, but not all, departments, useful changes—administrative and curricular—were implemented and new connections were made with teachers in local schools and with alumni. Although teaching programs in the United States have much in common, each department's account is unique and reflects local and state circumstances, a particular institutional history, and the influence of committed individuals. Taken together, these accounts demonstrate that creative rethinking of the way we prepare future teachers is possible and that there are rich personal and professional rewards for contributing to an enterprise that can change the lives of the next generation of students.

WORKS CITED

Bell, Terrel H. *A Nation at Risk.* Washington: US Dept. of Educ., 1983.

Campbell, Jay R., Kristin E. Voelkl, and Patricia L. Donahue. *Report in Brief: NAEP 1996 Trends in Academic Progress.* NCES 97-986. Washington: Natl. Center for Educ. Statistics, 1998.

Choy, Susan P., Xianglei Chen, and Michael Ross. *Toward Better Teaching: Professional Development in 1993–94.* NCES 98-230. Washington: Natl. Center for Educ. Statistics, 1998.

Corcoran, Thomas C. *Transforming Professional Development for Teachers: A Guide for State Policymakers.* Washington: Natl. Governors' Assn., 1995.

Education Commission of the States. *Transforming Postsecondary Education for the Twenty-First Century: Views of the Governors.* June 1998.

"Education's Role Cited in Closing Racial Divide." *Chronicle of Higher Education* 2 Oct. 1998: A35.

Louis, Karen Seashore. "'A Light Feeling of Chaos': Educational Reform and Policy in the United States." *Daedalus* 127 (1998): 13–40.

National Education Goals Panel. *National Education Goals Report: Building a Nation of Learners, 1998.* Washington: GPO, 1998.

DONALD GRAY

Introduction: What Happens Next? and How? and Why?

What happens next of course depends on what's already there. The idea of the MLA Teacher Education Project is that university and college faculties in departments of English and foreign languages must take a self-conscious role in the education of students who will teach our subjects in secondary schools. As the essays of this volume attest, that responsibility has been accepted and exercised very differently. But these essays also show that, whether teacher education exists as a visible, marginal, or ghostly presence in the consciousness of university and college faculties, the ways in which that presence is established and maintained are common to all departments. Collectively at least, we know how to do it. Those of us who are backward in the work can learn from more practiced colleagues the tactics and politics of educating teachers both before and after they graduate from our classrooms.

But why? We members of the MLA have all been educated to use as one pure measure of professional achievement the presence of our names in the pages of *PMLA* or on the program of the MLA Annual Convention. Why should we hunch into a desk chair at the back of a tenth-grade classroom and listen to a student panel talking about *I Know Why the Caged Bird Sings,* or to a teacher laying out the vocabulary of *les sportifs* and the conventions of the comparative adjective? Why should we, trained to explore and talk to one another about questions of literature and culture that we sometimes think too recondite to take even into our undergraduate classrooms, make it part of our profession to attend to questions about the reading and writing of high school students? Our higher educations took us into the MLA and the company of literary critics and scholars. Why should we—indeed, why should the MLA—connect with a community of teachers in the schools, with students who aspire to be teachers, and with colleagues whose profession is the education of teachers?

I find the question of why difficult. I know answers to it, some of which I have learned by reading the essays in this volume. But I wonder about the force of the answers. Everyone who teaches undergraduates teaches prospective teachers. But unless more of us really know that, and are persuaded to give thought to what prospective teachers learn from us, the next steps of many of us will not put the important and interesting question of the education of teachers very much closer than it is now to the center of our profession.

I put aside the question of why for a space to consider what we can do, if we find reason to do it. Three lessons shine out from the accounts in this volume. All have to do with connections. First, we should make a durable connection with those faculty members in schools and departments of education from whom prospective teachers learn the matter and methods of their profession. Second, we should connect with teachers in the schools. And third, we should consider the connection—or, rather, the lack of connection—between the mostly literary education prospective teachers get in our departments and the nature and demands of the subjects they teach in the schools.

Practices and Politics of Collaboration

In my experience, relationships with colleagues in education and with teachers in secondary schools are easier to start than they are to sustain. The most obvious difficulty is that collaboration takes time. Not only must busy people find time—and for teachers in secondary schools that means after school or in the evenings and on weekends—to talk to one another, they must also give these conversations a regular and enduring place on their calendars, give them time and space in which to root and grow. Right now, for everyone involved in the education of teachers, collaboration is nobody's principal business. Teachers in secondary schools work very hard just to manage the unrelenting daily requirements of five or six classes and a hundred or more students. The faculties of schools of education and departments of education include relatively few people whose responsibility it is to attend to prospective teachers of particular subjects; at my university one colleague teaches and looks after the eighty or ninety undergraduates who certify as secondary school English teachers each year. And most of us, members of MLA, do not think of teacher education as part of our professions at all. It is easy enough to field a pickup team for an occasion like the MLA Teacher Education Project. But when the project is over, it is just as easy to return to our well-fenced plots in the field of teacher education and work them diligently without looking over to see what other people are doing, or without even being aware that teacher education is what we are working at.

There is another, less obvious but equally powerful difficulty. For most of this century we have been telling teachers in secondary schools that we are disappointed in their graduates and telling our colleagues in education that their programs and practices are vacuous. This history inflects our offers to help. For a long time, maybe since the Committee of Ten in 1893 set up a canon of literary texts for high school English, our idea of help has often been to tell other teachers what to do.

I was not surprised, therefore, that when my colleagues at Indiana and I used the MLA teacher education initiative to ask high school teachers how we ought to revise our teacher education program, they were at first skeptical and, even at the end, not that forceful and particular in their suggestions. They had learned from us that we thought the matter and purposes of our courses to be pretty much up to us. Nor was I surprised by how hard it was to work our changes through the curricular bureaucracy of the Indiana University School of Education. They had learned to resist the ideas of people like me, to say, We know what we are doing, because people like me so often told them that they didn't. Certainly in a university like mine—and in this climate of budgetary constraint and accountability there are many universities like mine—economic reasons exist for these territorial skirmishes. Faculty members in the School of Education, coveting the enrollments of English courses in children's literature and young adult literature, lay claim to any course whose title contains the word *teaching*. But I think that history offers its own strong reasons for resistance. While we have neglected or even disdained teacher education, it has become a discipline to whose principles and imperatives we must now accommodate our own.

Finally, I need spend little space in a rehearsal of the familiar politics within departments of English and foreign languages that inhibit attention to teacher education and make difficult our collaboration with colleagues involved in it. For example, to what account will the writing and publication of an essay such as this one be credited? Probably, in my department, it will be considered a contribution to teaching. Maybe to service; certainly not to research, the account that pays the largest dividends, even though most of my colleagues in English would have to do a little research to find out what my reference to the Committee of Ten means. This bias toward the study and teaching of the topics that we define as the heart of our disciplines is almost universal in academic departments. The bias shows in departments like mine in which no one is commissioned to think of teacher education as part of the profession. The bias is perhaps even clearer in departments that explicitly accept teacher education as one of their responsibilities and then segregate it by assigning its exercise to one or two faculty members. In consequence, in seasons when something like the MLA project encourages some teachers to talk to one another, the conversations are more likely to connect people already interested in teacher education than they are to enlist the energies of colleagues who are busy doing something else.

Some of the essays in this volume suggest that the answer to this cycle of attention and neglect lies in the creation of structures that make collaboration among teachers of the same subject in different places one of the purposes of the institution rather than the occasional creature of opportunity or whim. The Faculty on Teacher Education and the Teacher Education Program Committee at Arizona State University, for example, appear to provide a durable nexus through which colleagues in education and the academic departments can connect whenever their interests in teacher education move them. The English Teachers Collaborative at Indiana University, Bloomington; the Center for the Liberal Arts at the University of Virginia; the agreements with school districts about courses and the common resources center created by the foreign language departments at California State University, Long Beach—these structures too, if they are supported by the university, if they become as much a part of the institution as, say, the programs that place student teachers in secondary schools, can provide continuous opportunities for connections among secondary-school teachers and faculty members in various departments who have become aware that they all teach teachers.

At universities like Illinois State and Norfolk State, still self-consciously and honorably lodged in their traditions of teacher education, such instruments and habits of connection seem to come easily. I think that the rest of us must learn these habits. Somebody must devise something within each of our institutions that says that teacher education is everybody's business. Until we do, unless we do, the effects of the MLA Teacher Education Project will flourish and fade like other initiatives that promised to involve teachers of academic subjects in the education of teachers in secondary schools. (Remember Project English? the NEH summer institutes when they were organized not as graduate seminars, around some professor's idea of a hot topic, but as vehicles to consider the commonalities of our subjects?)

Not everybody will awaken to the interest of the fact that prospective teachers sit in all our classrooms. But the work of connection and collaboration does not need everybody. It needs continuity, structures of relationship that will be available to interested teachers in seasons of engagement and that will survive the disengagement of those teachers by attracting others. Such structures must be paid for in the coin institutions use to make it clear that the work of collaboration counts: money, offices, titles, released time. The MLA cannot by itself make teacher education consistently and effectively matter to its members, but its Teacher Education Project has opened and illuminated some promising paths. Those of us who are attracted by these paths must now tell our chairs, deans, provosts, and presidents that we want the kind of help only they can give in our journeys away from home.

Connections at Home

Home means departments of foreign languages and English and, for my purposes here, the courses we offer to undergraduates. How does what prospective teachers learn in our classrooms connect with what they want students to learn in their own? Many of the essays in this volume suggest that the connection is imperfect. The theme of a disjunction between the education of teachers and the requirements of their teaching perhaps shows most clearly in the essays on the education of foreign language teachers. Again and again teachers remark the difference, for example, between the artifacts of culture students learn about when they study a foreign language in the university (culture as inscribed in a literary canon) and in secondary schools (information about *les sportifs* and other everyday practices). But surely I am not the only English professor former students have told that although they liked a course on, say, Dickens, they had a hard time putting it to use when confronted with a reluctant ninth-grader who had not yet read an entire book or an eager eleventh-grader who wanted to know what to read next. My students have not always figured out how all the analyses and personal response papers I made them write prepared them to help someone learn about subject-verb agreement and when, how, and why sentences are satisfactorily formed.

Here we do not need the help of deans or provosts, or of the MLA. The remedies of this disjunction lie almost entirely within our precincts.

The moves of some departments toward connection are explicit. For example, Illinois State University's gateway course in English studies, the senior seminar in professional issues, and the plan to integrate that seminar into a "professional semester" offer students chances to look ahead to applications of their learning and, just as important, to look back at the logic and coherence of their undergraduate education. Faculty members in several departments of foreign language have suggested that the inclusion of courses on the instructional uses of technology invites colleagues as well as students to think about how to teach what they have learned of the language and literature of another culture.

But to a degree these integrating moves are also disjunctive. They verge on a teacher-education track, on courses that are a distinct version of what we teach: English for Teachers or French for Teachers. They may enlist the interests and talents of some faculty members, but they also permit the rest of us to figure that the responsibility is being met and we need not put our minds to it. In academic departments that have retained the course in teaching methods, the one or two people who teach it tend to pay nearly the whole bill in the matter of teacher education.

That result is not a reason not to make the moves; it is a sign that they are not sufficient. We need to ask another question, not just, Whom do we assign to take care of teachers?, but also, How does the undergraduate curriculum of the department serve the purpose of teacher education? The curriculum does lie at the center of the department. A solid core of faculty members must therefore ask, first, whether teacher education is a purpose the department wants to serve and, second, how it can serve that purpose while providing and pursuing what it thinks to be a liberal study of language, literature, and culture.

If the faculty of an academic department decides to give thought to the education of teachers, how should it proceed? A frequent argument is that we should just keep doing what we have been doing and say that we serve as models. We therefore enact our pedagogical lessons. I am not persuaded by this argument. I know from experience that what I do in a university classroom does not work in the tenth grade—or, if it does, that I thrive there only briefly as a novelty. The purposes, rhythms, and physical conditions of teaching in secondary schools differ markedly from those in higher education, and the students are different too: younger (you have to be there to know how much that matters), more diverse in their abilities and interests, and in school, even if they like it, because the state requires their attendance. We can help prospective teachers learn to read, to write, and to understand language as social and cultural expression. We can help them enjoy this learning, get them to participate in our celebration of our subjects. But they cannot import the tactics of our classrooms into their own without learning, somehow and somewhere, to adapt them to the peculiar climate and circumstances of secondary schools.

So, another argument goes, we will further teacher education by helping prospective teachers learn such adaptations. I won't teach Dickens; I'll teach Teaching Dickens or Dickens for Teachers. My colleagues in the School of Education have a point when they bridle at the introduction of such titles into the catalog of the English department. I really do not know enough about the curriculum of secondary schools and the learning styles and habits of adolescents to teach such topics, and most of the people I know in departments of English and foreign languages know less than I. More important, my colleagues in my department will not welcome such courses. What we do, what we are good at, is Dickens. In our courses, students learn how Dickens writes, and by attending to his craft they practice and extend their own craft as readers. They learn something about Victorian society and how a cultural monument like the Victorian novel functioned as an expression of and an agent in its culture. They test and refine their understanding of literary texts by learning about Dickens's life, about contemporary reviews of the novels, about the current commentary on them. In short, we teach students to think about Dickens. We invite them to a speculative, liberal pursuit whose pedagogical purposes will only be confused by the introduction of instrumental, practical means and ends, even if we know enough to instruct prospective teachers in them.

But suppose, rather than convert my course to an academic version of an educational methods course or trust students to make their own adaptations (the two extremes), I systematically and self-consciously call attention to the methods of my teaching. Suppose I explain why I chose the novels by Dickens I put into the course, why we will read them in the sequence I have arranged, how Monday's task and topic fit with Wednesday's, how what happens in the third week prepares for what I want to happen in the sixth week. I can enlarge my students' awareness of their reading practices by asking a couple of students from time to time to map the class discussion of a vexed point so that we can all reflect on how meaning gets negotiated and how discussion is regulated. I can ask a colleague skilled in such observations to come to a couple of class meetings and write a description of them that I can use as a text in the course to talk about not just what but also how we are learning about Dickens.

Prospective teachers will not learn how to teach *Great Expectations* in a twelfth-grade honors course, or even why they should. But they and everyone else in the class will learn something about the tactics of teaching and maybe even more about the habits of learning, their own and those of other students.

Why?

I return to the question I had put aside: Why should faculties in English and foreign languages accept the education of teachers as one of their responsibilities? The reasons are political, social, economic, and professional. Departments of foreign languages and English are departments of literacy. Literacy confers, among other gifts (one of them being pleasure), command and understanding: command of the symbolic processes by which high school as well as university graduates will make their livings, understanding of the multiple discourses among which they will live and of the diverse people who express and promote themselves in those discourses. Literacy in more than one language compounds these gifts and offers a particularly useful kind of citizenship in a world that is increasingly international and in a country that has become determinedly multicultural and, in places, effectively multilingual.

English and the foreign languages are our subjects. We are in some measure responsible for how they exist in secondary schools and for making accessible the economic, social, and intellectual benefits they promise. Further, the existence of our subjects in secondary schools is their most public manifestation. If we want, as some of us say we want, to make visible the worth of our disciplines—to teach English, French, or Japanese in public—then we should have a presence in spaces that are more public than our own and become colleagues to counterparts who every weekday, and all day, perform our subjects to audiences more diverse and democratic than those most of us know.

Two other reasons lie close to home. We will learn something new about our subjects when we study how they exist in secondary schools. Most of us assume that the purpose of high school English or high school French is to prepare students for us. We expect secondary schools to provide a rudimentary literacy—the ability to read a poem, to shape a sentence and make a paragraph, to understand a conversation about *les sportifs* or get around Madrid or Miami. When students come to us, we will introduce them to inquiries about how a discourse cooperates with large systems of meaning to inculcate and maintain an ideology. We will give them exercises that extend the competencies learned in reading a newspaper to understandings of how a novel expresses and alters its culture. Let secondary schools perform their traditional tasks of educating citizens in the discourse of their culture so that they can fit gainfully into it. Ours is the yet more interesting task of teaching students how to interrogate the premises of their culture so that they become skeptical citizens of it.

The hierarchy implicit in these formulations makes the differences between high school and university uninteresting. The conversation degenerates into familiar recriminations and resentments—teachers in secondary schools are not doing their jobs; teachers in the universities and colleges don't understand the jobs secondary school teachers are required to do.

The conversation becomes interesting and fruitful when our subjects in secondary schools are seen not as preceding us but as intellectual and pedagogical constructions that have their own reasons for being. English and foreign languages in secondary schools exist as complicated responses to political ideas and constraints, social ambitions and liabilities, and the belief in the worth of reading intelligently, writing clearly, and knowing another language. College and university teachers who enter a high school classroom will learn something about how their students have learned and perhaps how to teach their subject. But that practical result is not the whole point. They will also learn a great deal about our subjects as social and political institutions. One reason for giving thought to our subjects in secondary schools is that we can ask about them the same questions we ask about other social and intellectual formations through which the imaginative discourses we study do their work.

The last and best reason is that thinking about the education of teachers helps us think about the education of all the undergraduates who, in different ways and for different reasons, learn in our courses. Teacher education intersects in very interesting ways with general and professional education. In their reach toward professional education, undergraduates who study a foreign language or English with us can also learn how they learn and how we teach. Our departments do offer courses that, because they engage issues of the learning and teaching of our subjects (e.g., young adult literature) or because they identify and enlarge abilities fundamental to an understanding of those issues (any introduction to literary analysis, any course in the nature of language), are particularly useful to prospective teachers. These courses need not be described as courses for teachers; they are courses in which prospective teachers can learn something pertinent to their purposes as well as central to ours. By specifying these courses as part of our contribution to the education of teachers, we in effect mark a path through our departments that leads toward professional education. We promise explicit attention to how students learn our subjects rather than, as is now common in most lists of academic courses required for teacher certification, to what they learn in them.

More important, at the other end, in the relation of teacher education to the general or liberal education of undergraduates, we can put our minds to how an education in our subjects fits our students not for the work they will do but for the learning they must undertake when they enter that work. We promote study in foreign languages and English, and in the humanities in general, as portals to a diversity of careers. As John Henry Newman said: "I lay it down as a principle, which will save us a good deal of anxiety, that, although the useful is not always good, the good is always useful" (117). By thinking about how my course in Dickens helps prepare teachers—or lawyers or management consultants or who knows what else (most of our undergraduates don't yet know)—I could become an honest advocate of this hopeful proposition. When I claim not only that a liberal arts major is intrinsically worthy but also that it provides useful knowledges and skills, what are these knowledges and skills? What exactly do we do that endows undergraduates with the habits of inquiry and reflection that prepare them to learn by themselves? If we begin by asking how the study of our subjects helps prepare prospective teachers, we can end with a better understanding of the value and uses of a liberal education.

Any discussion of what happens next begins in the consciousness that the faculties of foreign language and English departments teach teachers. That consciousness might take some of us beyond our courses and even off our campuses to work with teachers in secondary schools as part of their—and our—continuing educations. It should certainly prompt many of us to a close scrutiny of who sits in our classrooms and of what they take away from them. As the authors of the essay on the University of Virginia's foreign language program put it, we must begin to see the "invisible minority" of prospective teachers in our courses. We must no longer assume, to paraphrase a sentence in the essay on the English program at New Mexico State University, that the needs and interests of all our students are like those of the undergraduates we once were. Chances are, when we look for prospective teachers in our courses, we are going to find a lot of students whose motives and interests differ from ours, differ from those of their contemporaries who want to be teachers, and differ from one another. I like those chances. For by giving thought to the learning of prospective teachers, we might not only get good at teacher education. We might also get better at undergraduate education.

WORK CITED

Newman, John Henry. "Discourse VII: Knowledge Viewed in Relation to Professional Skills." *The Idea of a University*. Ed. Frank M. Turner. New Haven: Yale UP, 1996. 108–26.

I

Model Programs

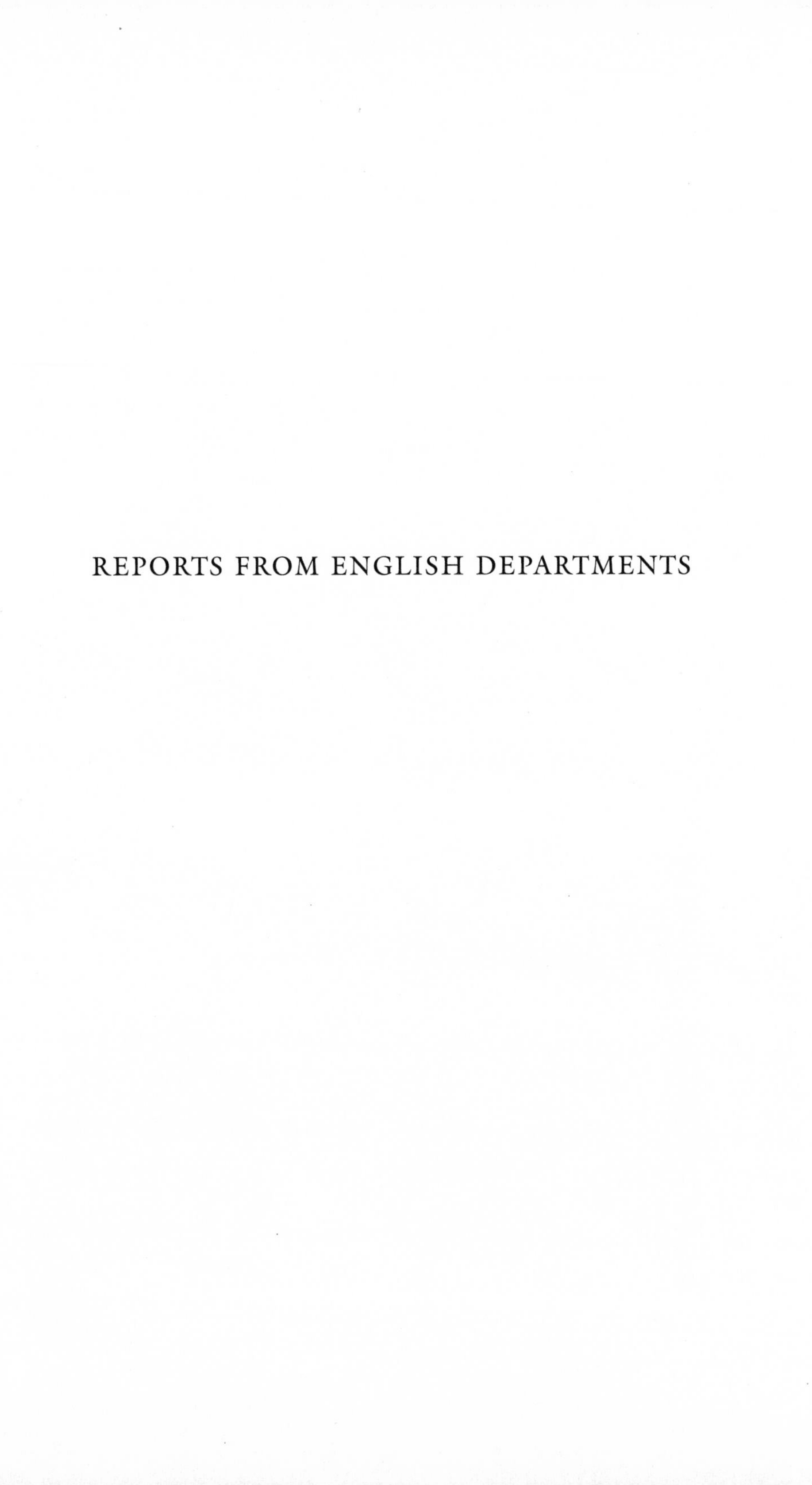

REPORTS FROM ENGLISH DEPARTMENTS

ILLINOIS STATE UNIVERSITY

Renewing the Nexus: Strengthening Connections across the English Education Program

Illinois State University was founded in 1857 as Illinois State Normal University, a teachers college. This origin has marked the institution indelibly with a commitment to teaching. Even as the university has moved in recent decades toward the values and practices of a research-oriented institution, concerns for students and their learning still dominate the daily life of faculty members. This university-wide culture of learning presents a most helpful background for our department's efforts to prepare future teachers of English.

The university's board of trustees has held Illinois State's enrollment just under 20,000 for the past several years; in 1996–97 enrollment was 19,409. About 85% of those students are undergraduates, and the rest are graduate students. The university employs approximately 950 full-time tenure-line faculty members, of whom 48 work in the Department of English. The English department has attempted to keep the use of part-time and temporary faculty members at a minimum; during the 1993–94 academic year it employed three part-time or temporary faculty members. That same year the number of English studies majors was 500, of whom 258 were English education majors (i.e., English studies majors pursuing the sequence of requirements for certification to teach secondary English).

To begin the process of envisioning an exemplary program to prepare future teachers of English at Illinois State, our team indulged in an orgy of utopianism. We listed everything we might possibly wish for in our program, with little or no regard to constraints of economics, politics, or expediency. Once that list was complete, we attempted to thematize and categorize the goals and possibilities we had generated. The six main sections of this report reflect that original effort at thematization, an effort that was expanded and refined through discussions with others participating in the MLA Teacher Education Project. Over time, a hint of pragmatism may have crept in; not every dream we originally dreamt is represented here. Still, we have tried to sustain the visionary spirit that infused our early discussions.

A word about how we have organized the results of our inquiry may assist readers. The first two sections present the two core principles of our program: "The English Studies Model" explains how our students become English studies majors, while "Literacy and Democracy" describes how English studies majors become English teachers. The next four sections contain our treatments of issues key to our teacher-preparation efforts: "Cooperation between the Department of English and the College of Education," "School-University Collaboration," "Technology in English-Teacher Preparation," and "Assessment in English Education." Each section of the report offers three modes of reflection. First, a section lays out strengths of the program as currently conceived and practiced; second, it identifies problems and possibilities; third, it proposes specific actions that would strengthen the program.

The English Studies Model

At Illinois State University, we have attempted to navigate the roiling political and ideological waters of today's profession by developing, deliberately and over a long period of time, what we've come to call the English studies model. Through careful faculty recruitment and systematic curricular change, what had been primarily a literature department has evolved over the past decade and a half into a department that, in its scope and variety, comes close to reflecting the current state of the profession. Along the way we complemented our strong traditional literature curriculum with comprehensive and up-to-date courses and programs in literary theory, rhetoric and composition, technical writing, creative writing, cultural studies, TESOL, linguistics, children's and adolescent literature, language arts, English education, pedagogical theory, and, most recently, literary publishing.

Of course, the simple addition of new courses and new faculty members, as Gerald Graff has argued (*Professing*), need not result in fundamental change. Indeed, the field-coverage curricular model, which continues to dominate in most departments and which mirrors departmental organization, successfully absorbs even the most threatening innovations by making it easy to add new courses but difficult to reconceptualize and reconstruct an entire curriculum. The English studies model as we conceive it required a change not just in the faculty and the curriculum but also in the department culture. It's not a pluralistic model in the "You do your own thing, I'll do mine" sense of *pluralistic,* what Gary Waller calls "polite pluralism" (qtd. in Graff, *Wars* 188), nor is it a model based on synthesis, on the idea, that is, that somehow the various segments of the field can always be reconciled into a unified, totalized whole. The English studies model as we have conceived it does more than recognize differences; it is based on them—on what Graff calls the "conflicts" and on the acknowledgment that, broadly conceived, the discipline(s) of English studies incorporate(s) a range of knowledges, pedagogies, and methodologies. We've tried, that is, to develop at the curricular level—but also within the departmental culture—something akin to what Fredric Jameson has called "a new mode of relationship through difference" (31). In this system, traditional scholars—and our department contains a number of highly productive traditional scholars—are as important to our goal as are faculty members committed to newer directions in the field. What we try to provide our students with, in other words, is a picture of the profession as it exists today, with all its pressures and diversity and controversies intact. We also try to teach them how to theorize these differences, something that, quite frankly, some of our faculty members are themselves unable or disinclined to do.

Over a period of a decade and a half, the department has recruited new faculty members with the English studies model in mind. We've been generally successful in appointing people who, in addition to having expertise in a specific field, are able to think synthetically, in terms of the profession's big picture, so that they are able to help move the department's culture in the direction of English studies. As a result of this cultural shift over a five-year period of negotiation, studied compromise, and productive conflict, we have transmuted the undergraduate literature major into a balanced and integrated program in English studies.

Before the new English studies major was designed, however, its goals and objectives had to be formulated. Like most university English faculty members, we shared a somewhat general and entirely tacit agreement about our curricular values, but we had never bothered to write them down. In a series of department meetings, we articulated twenty-seven goals, described as either abilities, knowledge, or attitudes, that we wanted our English majors to achieve. While we couldn't figure out a better way to present these goals to our students than in list form, we added the following caveat:

> We would like you to understand that, in spite of the fact that we have separated the goals into categories in order to clarify them, we see the categories themselves as well as the individual goals as interdependent: we hope, in other words, that as you become more and more accomplished, you will learn to bring all your abilities, knowledge, and attitudes to bear *simultaneously* on the language situations that your courses and your life outside the classroom may place you in.

A living document, this "Statement of Goals for the Majors in English and English Education" was recently amended to reflect the role of rhetorical history and theory in the undergraduate curriculum. A copy of the statement is included in appendix A of our report.

To help ensure that students achieve a large proportion of these goals over the course of their baccalaureate degree, the new English studies major includes several key components. For example, the department replaced the traditional required introductory courses in close readings of literary texts with a single gateway course entitled Introduction to English Studies. This course introduces students to the broad range of subjects that make up English studies and to some of the analytical processes most commonly employed by students and professionals in the field. Expansive and inclusive in its approach to the discipline, Introduction to English Studies is meant to serve beginning English majors and minors by providing them with what they *must* know if they are to do well in the upper-level courses in the major and with a challenging sense of what they *should* know by the time they finish the program. The course is intended to give our students a workable, entry-level understanding of the ideas set forth in the "Statement of Goals." A sample syllabus for the gateway course is provided in appendix B.

Another key revision in the new major is the replacement of the standard literary distribution requirements (four courses in British literature, two before and two after 1800; two courses in American literature, one before and one after 1865), a holdover from the coverage model, with requirements that ensure a broad-based approach to the field of English studies. All students, not just those in the teacher-certification sequence, are now required to enroll in a language or linguistics course (teacher-certification students must take two courses in this area); all students are required to take at least one advanced writing course. Additionally, students in the teacher-certification sequence must take at least one course in multicultural or noncanonical literature as well as two teaching methods courses—one in the teaching of literature, one in the teaching of writing—both taught by English department faculty members.

Finally, all English majors are required to enroll in three of four courses that focus on literary genres (poetry, prose, and drama) or on rhetorical theory and its applications. Each of these four deals with the nature and historical development of rhetorical theory or of the genre being studied. While faculty members are free to select their own texts, their selections must reflect historical distribution and some range of national literatures. (Most of the works assigned are English texts, but some translations are included, e.g., classical precedents for rhetoric and drama.)

At the end of their course work, when the major requirements are fulfilled, students are required to enroll in the Senior Seminar, an English major capstone course that uses portfolios and other methods to assess the degree to which candidates have come to understand the English studies model. Writing assignments for the seminar are designed to encourage students to examine consciously their progress as students of English, including the degree to which they have achieved the goals for the major, and to think about the personal and professional significance of their past and current work in the major. Because the seminar also seeks to help them solidify and extend their grasp of English studies, students are assigned classroom texts that take a metatheoretical and integrative approach to the field, so that they can continue to develop the theoretical frame they use to organize and understand the variety of their reading, writing, and thinking experiences. Appendix C provides a sample syllabus for the Senior Seminar. For an extended discussion of the development of this course, see the essay by Charles Harris.

The newly designed undergraduate English major, though authorized, has only just been put into practice. Just as the Senior Seminar required modification as we began to offer it, the new major will no doubt require monitoring and modification as it works itself out. Students entering the program will need to be prepared for an approach to English that is different from what they have experienced before. Well-informed advisement, provided within the Department of English, will play a key role in effecting this transition. Exit exams and portfolio assessment will be used to determine how successfully the new major helps students achieve the goals informing the program. On the basis of this ongoing assessment, the department is prepared to redesign the model or portions of that model as deemed necessary.

Literacy and Democracy: From English Majors to English Teachers

To be qualified to teach English in secondary schools, candidates need a body of knowledge, abilities, and attitudes that extends beyond those required to understand and appreciate English studies as a discipline. They need to understand how to foster in others the same kinds of understandings of English studies they themselves have achieved. This body of knowledge beyond the disciplinary is what qualifies English studies majors to be called English education majors. In a phrase, we could summarize this extended knowledge as an understanding of the relations between literacy and democracy.

Beginning with Jeffersonian ideals and strategies for building democracy, literacy learning has always lain at the heart of Americans' conceptions of democratic culture. In this century educational theorists such as Antonio Gramsci, John Dewey, Paolo Freire, and Henry Giroux frequently focus on literacy as they explore how education can promote—or contravene—democratic political structures. The watershed English Coalition Conference refreshed the literacy-democracy connection in 1987 by making its central theme Democracy through Language. And within the past year, Illinois State University as a whole named the core value binding together its diverse teacher education programs as realizing the democratic ideal. Meanwhile, the English studies model openly seeks to attend more seriously to the diversity of our field than have most other models. Our national and intellectual history, our discipline, our university, and our department therefore all urgently demand an answer to the question How do we teach English to foster democracy?

The English education program at Illinois State University answers that question with three core theoretical, practical, and pedagogical commitments: to reader-response theories of literary study, to writing-process models of composition, and to teacher-research conceptions of professional development.

READER-RESPONSE THEORIES OF LITERARY STUDY

Focusing on works by Louise Rosenblatt, Robert Probst, and Nancie Atwell, the course The Teaching of Literature explores what reader response might mean for the secondary English classroom. Reader response stands most dramatically as an alternative to objectivist approaches to literature that would fix meaning in a text or in an author to the neglect of the reader. Contrary to some representations of it, however, reader response does not constitute subjectivism, solipsism, or relativism in textual interpretation; it holds readers accountable to the communities in which those readers work, making acceptance for their interpretations contingent on following explicit criteria. Like the larger field of English studies, then, reader response approaches resolve the timeworn dichotomy between subjectivist and objectivist theories of knowledge and meaning by attending to social contexts for literary study. The popular classroom technique often called "literature circles" embodies the dynamic and creative tensions within reader response between the variability of readers' interpretations and the communal processes by which a group deliberates which readings are best.

The importance of reader response to the democratic teaching of literacy should be clear. It eliminates the ground for any reader to claim preemptive, total, or final authority for any interpretation. It allows differences among students' identities and backgrounds to make literary study not only more accessible and exciting but also more intellectually and morally compelling, without surrendering standards for evaluating interpretations. As democratic rule gives citizens the right and responsibility to debate and implement judgments and decisions for the good of the community, reader response gives readers the right and responsibility for formulating, strengthening, testing, and refining their interpretations of texts.

WRITING-PROCESS MODELS OF COMPOSITION

In the recent history of the teaching of writing, writing process has helped to broaden the focus of students and teachers of composition on written products to include the processes and strategies by which those products are generated. Our course The Teaching of Writing engages teaching candidates in the study of theory, pedagogy, and research in composition, with special attention to writing processes. Lester Faigley's "Competing Theories of Process: A Critique and Proposal" helps show how dynamic and diverse is the debate within the field of composition around writing processes; Faigley advocates special emphasis on a social (as opposed to expressivist or current-traditional) conception of writing processes. Nancie Atwell's *In the Middle* offers extensive theoretical and practical material based in the work of one teacher of writing (and literature) to show how writing processes might be taught and fostered through use of the writing workshop. Patricia Bizzell and Bruce Herzberg's *The Bedford Bibliography for Teachers of Writing* adds important historical background and organizes future teachers' access to the wealth of scholarship in composition and rhetoric. Selected essays by Maxine Hairston, James Moffett,

Peter Elbow, Ann Berthoff, and other scholars provide important background on such topics as grammar and assessment and such specific rhetorical considerations as audience, purpose, and occasion.

TEACHER-RESEARCH CONCEPTIONS OF PROFESSIONAL DEVELOPMENT

That teachers must be not only consumers but also producers of knowledge is a widely accepted principle of teacher education and teacher development. Our methods courses promote the professional habit of identifying, developing, articulating, and researching the questions and problems that candidates encounter in their classrooms and communities. We require that their plans for instruction, their research articles, and their plans for classroom research all reflect high-quality research techniques, and many classes publish sourcebooks composed of student work. These sourcebooks often serve as required readings for students in subsequent years' classes. Dixie Goswami and Peter Stillman's *Reclaiming the Classroom* provides theoretical and methodological guidance to students, most of whom have never designed an empirical inquiry. We broaden their understanding of research to include the rigorous naturalistic methods often best suited to classroom studies.

Professional conferences are by far the most common and most important forums for the exchange and production of teachers' professional knowledge. While we encourage our teaching candidates to publish scholarship in professional journals—and a number of them have done so—we also work to instill in them the inclination to attend and present at conferences. Toward this end the department provides transportation to the annual Illinois Association of Teachers of English (IATE) conference and hosts the annual Heads of Illinois Secondary English Departments (HISED) conference, at which our student teachers serve as session chairs and at which some also present talks, papers, and workshops. We strongly promote candidates' membership in state and national professional organizations such as IATE and the National Council of Teachers of English (NCTE). Where feasible, we also support and encourage our students' attendance at NCTE conferences, including recent conventions in Chicago and Nashville. As an ideal and as an everyday reality, the teacher as researcher helps democratize professional knowledge and thus helps empower and energize our future English teachers' engagement with scholarship broadly defined.

This three-strand conception of English teaching provides a strong and flexible core for our preparation of future teachers. It is idealistic enough and informed enough by the scholarship of literacy to set the highest standards for the teaching of English; at the same time, it is firmly rooted in the practices, struggles, and issues that occupy practicing teachers of English. Through this blend of resources, contexts, and orientations we teach our candidates what it means to teach English for democracy.

We also see that the three-strand core needs a bit of updating. In the realm of theory, we want to strengthen our candidates' grounding in post-structuralist theories of textuality and broaden our analyses of writing processes to include theories of composition that are more socially and rhetorically oriented. In curricular and logistical arenas, we see a series of other useful changes and connections waiting to be made. One such change involves the overall design and structure of the methods courses.

Currently, three departmental methods courses—The Teaching of Literature, The Teaching of Writing, and the Professional Issues Seminar—top off the professional education of English education majors, providing field-specific knowledge and skills necessary to foster secondary-school literacy. The first two courses are offered in the semester preceding the student-teaching experience. The third runs immediately before, during, and after student teaching. We like the strength of requiring two three-credit courses in English education methods where many programs require only one, and we also value the weaving together of the Professional Issues Seminar with the student-teaching experience. The seminar provides important team-building activities among each year's forty to fifty student teachers and features numerous guest speakers addressing such issues as discipline, professionalism, teachers' unions, censorship, and diversity.

The first opportunity we see to improve our methods courses is to integrate the first two into one. Since we believe that the study of literature and composition can and should be closely linked and mutually supportive, we propose combining the two three-credit-hour courses into a single six-credit-hour course, to be taken in the fall semester preceding student teaching. Emphasizing the productive interplay of learning literature and composition, the proposed synthesis also supports the English studies model.

A bolder move we envision is to integrate the entire professional year (the academic year in which students take their methods courses and Senior Seminar in the fall and conduct student teaching in the spring). Under this plan, teaching candidates would spend thirty-six weeks rather than twelve working with a cooperating teacher in a professional-development school. Methods course work and professional issues would be taken up in that compelling school-world context for which our aspiring teachers clamor. We firmly believe that all the learning our English education majors currently acquire during the professional year would be rendered more meaningful and more useful if they learned it as they simultaneously studied and taught.

Meanwhile, our department will work to increase opportunities for prospective teachers to join professional organizations. Currently, the Illinois Association of Teachers of English provides a free year of membership for first-year teachers, and NCTE provides a discounted membership for prospective teachers. The department will seek free IATE memberships for prospective teachers, including subscriptions to *Illinois English Bulletin*. Making membership in these professional organizations more accessible would enhance and extend our ongoing efforts to bring students to regional and national professional conferences and to encourage them to submit their research and writing for publication in professional journals.

Cooperation between the Department of English and the College of Education

Professional Studies in the College of Education takes a multidisciplinary approach to teacher preparation in keeping with the unified theory of differentiation that characterizes English studies. The Council for Teacher Education, the governance body for all teacher-education programs, recently adopted the theme Realizing the Democratic Ideal: Teacher Education at Illinois State University. The statement of values and beliefs confirms that "the democratic ideal unites caring and knowing: the more voices we elicit and the less fettered the mutual exchange among those voices becomes, the truer our convictions and conclusions will be." *Caring* and *knowing* are defined in a set of moral and intellectual attributes, reflecting the English department's commitment to preparing teachers who are public intellectuals, that is, public servants as well as scholars of English studies.

Whereas the English department prepares teachers in the content and pedagogy of the discipline, the College of Education prepares teachers for the whole secondary school environment and for entry into the profession of teaching. Teacher education across the university is accredited by the National Council for Accreditation of Teacher Education (NCATE); all programs are currently preparing folios for national review by professional discipline-centered organizations, under the auspices of NCATE. Standards of English education come from the National Council of Teachers of English. NCATE standards help ensure the quality of teacher education at Illinois State University. Within the state of Illinois, teacher education programs are accredited by the Illinois State Board of Education and by the Illinois Board of Higher Education. Illinois State University as a whole is accredited by the North Central Association.

Before student teaching, all teacher education candidates complete a minimum of a hundred clock hours of clinical experiences; many of those hours are spent at the Illinois State University laboratory schools—Thomas Metcalf is a pre-K–8 building, and University High School houses grades 9–12. In these settings, as well as in public school settings throughout the region, students observe and participate in classrooms where theory and practice are united. Through purposeful admission decisions, the laboratory schools assemble a student body that mirrors the ethnic and socioeconomic patterns of the state. This unusual admissions policy provides our candidates teaching experiences with a more representative range of students than the cultural and economic patterns of central Illinois would otherwise allow. Staffing policies are similarly innovative: laboratory school faculty associates often teach university-level classes, while university faculty members participate in action research and teach in the laboratory schools. Here again, we attempt to unify groups of educators and students usually separated by institutional habits and cultures.

All teacher education candidates take either Educational Psychology or Child Growth and Development, studying theories of learning and assessment strategies for evaluating the intellectual, social, and physical development of learners. These theories are then applied in professional studies courses as well as in clinical experiences.

Teacher candidates also take an Educational Foundations course, choosing from among historical, philosophical, and sociological approaches. Regardless of which course they choose, however, students learn about the moral, social, and political dimensions of classrooms, teaching, and schools. Each course covers the impact of technological and societal changes on schools; each includes inquiry and research, as well as aspects of school law and educational policy. Most important, each course treats in depth professional ethics and the responsibilities, structure, and activities of the profession.

All teacher-education candidates who will be certified to teach in grades 6–12 take three courses that make up the professional sequence offered by the Department of Curriculum and Instruction. In Secondary School Reading, teacher candidates learn the importance of literacy throughout the curriculum and acquire specific techniques and strategies for teaching students with diverse abilities and backgrounds. Curriculum and Organizational Issues in Secondary Schooling focuses on current issues in secondary education. Students prepare research reports on such topics as technology, multiculturalism, special needs, school reform. They also undertake clinical experiences, often in public school settings, including large inner-city schools. In Secondary Education, a general methods course, students learn daily and unit planning, and they implement those plans in extended, coherent clinical experiences at the university laboratory schools.

In each of these professional-sequence courses, students learn a full range of theories and applications. The breadth and depth of their preparation further ensures that Illinois State University teacher education graduates can make enlightened professional choices based on knowledge across the educational spectrum.

School-University Collaboration

Cooperation and articulation with teachers in public schools, private schools, and community colleges have historically been an important part of the mission and activities of the English department at Illinois State University. For over thirty years, the department has sponsored the Heads of Illinois Secondary English Departments conference, a meeting attended by two to three hundred English department chairs and their colleagues each April. Funded primarily through the thirty-five-dollar registration fee and secondarily by our English department, this conference brings in classroom teachers—many of them cooperating teachers who mentor our student teachers—as both presenters and attendees. HISED provides professional enrichment for cooperating teachers as well as for our student teachers who participate in the conference as chairs and occasionally as presenters.

The English department secured several grants, from both state and federal sources, that featured formal cooperation between secondary school teachers and the department. Among those have been two National Endowment for the Humanities education grants for summer institutes and follow-up workshops, a state assessment grant, and three grants from the National Writing Project, all featuring not only short-term courses but also the department's extended commitment to ongoing cooperation with teachers and administrators in the secondary schools. These various grants have established a vital and continuing relationship between the English department and secondary schools and teachers, who ultimately provide the placements for student teachers.

Other, less formal articulation has occurred through numerous in-service workshops provided by staff for various Illinois schools, North Central Organizational Assessment commitments, and meetings with cooperating teachers and school administrators. All these contacts have served to keep English department staff and middle and high school personnel connected and in conversation about educational matters. Finally, the department sponsors an end-of-the-year banquet for university supervisors, cooperating teachers, and student teachers. The banquet congratulates student teachers on surviving and prevailing, and it thanks cooperating teachers for their devotion as mentors.

We propose increasing articulation with secondary schools by providing organized support for first-year teachers, so they will remain in contact with the department through meetings to discuss problems and achievements. A formal mentoring system for new teachers would assure them of departmental support in their first year, with articulation continuing through contacts between mentors and secondary school department chairs. As a culmination of this experience, a retreat for first- and second-year teachers would be held annually to encourage face-to-face discussions. In these ways, we wish to reach out to our newest and most vulnerable colleagues.

Cooperating teachers and university supervisors could increase mutual understanding by exchanging personal and professional profiles before the student-teaching experience so that the student teacher would feel a firmer bond between the university and the cooperating school. This system would contribute to cooperating-teacher recruitment and enhance the matching of student teachers and cooperating teachers. While the director of English education has initiated voluntary and informal exchanges of such information, more-formal communication could ensure a greater likelihood of success for the student teacher. The department also intends to establish a statewide network of cooperating teachers through the World Wide Web as well as through other contacts.

Technology in English-Teacher Preparation

The ability to use computer technology in English instruction is becoming a critical qualification for prospective teachers. Fortunately for students graduating with a degree in English education from Illinois State University, the English department's investment in instructional computer technology over the past decade has been comprehensive. Although many graduates' first jobs will not provide them with resources comparable to those for which we prepare them, we believe in preparing students for the optimum and allowing them to scale back as their circumstances require. This approach not only guarantees that their understanding of technology and its uses will never fall short of the performance their positions demand, it also creates a basis from which they can grapple with the proliferating technology in English education inevitable in the coming decades. Prospective teachers who are prepared to teach in computer-equipped classrooms are more attractive to nearly all employers, because even schools that currently lack the relevant technology see that our graduates will be able to help them as they move forward.

In the current program, students enroll in a minimum of three courses that require the use of computer hardware and software: Language and Composition 1, Advanced Exposition, and The Teaching of Writing. Beyond these courses, students may enroll in a computer-based elective in literature.

Language and Composition 1 and Advanced Exposition are writing courses and provide students with the opportunity to learn what, from the students' point of view, are the best uses of computer hardware and software. They have access to advanced word processing, drawing, spreadsheet programs, and *Daedalus,* a LAN program that provides support for invention-and-revision instruction and facilitates collaborative work. The computers in these classrooms connect to the university mainframe, which gives students access to the Internet and the World Wide Web. In The Teaching of Writing, prospective teachers are able to view the uses of technology from the perspective of the instructor. The course emphasizes a process approach to writing instruction and provides students with the opportunity to study how the theories of that approach translate into practice. In developing and teaching lessons using the software described above, they draw on their experiences as students in Language and Composition 1 and Advanced Exposition to explore how the computers might have been used more effectively or differently to assist them to become better writers.

Preparation for using computer technology to teach literature has been less programmatic than we would have liked. But beginning in the fall semester of 1996, the English department established a computer-equipped classroom dedicated to literature courses. This step increased the number of literature electives taking advantage of computer technology and provided a computer-equipped site for the courses Teaching Literature and Writing in the Middle School and The Teaching of Literature, the primary courses designed for instruction about the teaching of literature. Some of the computer applications to be included are networking software to set up discussion groups outside class, hypertext software that will allow course projects to be submitted as electronic documents, Web-browsing software to support the exploration of literary texts and secondary resources available online, CD-ROMs consisting of literary texts and related critical material, and software programs containing fiction in hypertext. Once this classroom is operational, students in the English education program will be exposed to the uses of computers in English instruction in at least a quarter of their courses.

Beyond the classroom, the English department maintains two e-mail discussion lists to assist in the preparation and ongoing support of our students in the English education program. The student teaching list provides a means for student teachers and university supervisors to communicate while student teaching is under way. The English education list sustains this communication beyond student teaching, focusing on such issues as job openings and the graduates' interests and needs once they have secured positions.

As the English education program continues to explore the uses of computer technology in the preparation of secondary English teachers, we envision several new directions in which our efforts are likely to go. First, we anticipate establishing a World Wide Web site that would make teaching materials available from institutional settings across Illinois. Second, a distance-learning initiative could enable prospective secondary English teachers to view high school teachers at work in various educational settings around the state. At the same time, it could allow the department to offer courses for credit on various aspects of the teaching of English to teachers already in the field. Third, an online journal could publish articles by teachers throughout Illinois who in their classrooms are doing work of interest to prospective and practicing teachers. Finally, the program for preparing secondary English teachers would also look at assisting teachers in developing their own software. The emergence of such programs as *HyperCard, Toolbook,* and *Visual Basic* make programming relatively easy.

Such a feature in the teacher-preparation program not only would ensure a good match between the software teachers use and the specific challenges of learning to write and learning to read literature, but it also would provide teachers with a unique way to explore and demonstrate how they understand their subject matter and how they translate this understanding into lessons likely to help their students learn.

Assessment in English Education

Current assessments of student teachers' achievements and abilities include a departmental requirement of a 2.5 grade point average for all courses and for English courses, a C or better in Language and Composition 1 and in Language and Communication, and the passing of College of Education measures such as the Pre-Professional Skills Test before student-teaching candidates are admitted to the teacher education program. In addition, student teachers' achievement as English studies majors is assessed using a portfolio in the Senior Seminar capstone course. As to their abilities as future teachers, candidates are assessed through their English education methods courses; through courses in the professional sequence, taught in the College of Education; through pre-student-teaching clinical experiences, supervised by both the College of Education and the English department; and through direct supervision of their student teaching by the assigned cooperating teacher and the university supervisor, a faculty member in the English department. The university also requires all students to pass the university writing examination before graduating.

The English department has used portfolio assessment in writing courses and in the Senior Seminar. Currently, the department is developing its portfolio assessment of English studies majors to evaluate the program as well as individual students. This pilot evaluation of the program has been approved by the department for use next year. As the program moves into place, the portfolios will expand to include more courses and more examples of student writing. They may become a base for candidates' teaching portfolios as our students begin their careers and may serve as a long-term measure of program success.

We believe the university writing examination should in time be replaced by an authentic assessment that asks seniors to present portfolios of writing generated in their major departments, based on the model of the English department capstone course. The current exam provides a static snapshot of a student's writing in a single sitting. What we need is a portrait of writers' complex and multicontextual performances. A redeeming value of the exam for students in general is that no one fails the exam without multiple opportunities to present more evidence about writing achievement and to work with tutors if need be. Thus an ad hoc approximation of a portfolio system is in place for the university writing examination, but a full-fledged portfolio system would send a valuable political message to the university community about the importance of assessing each student's writing performance and potential by authentic means. (For a rich discussion of authentic assessment, see Wiggins.)

Currently, cooperating teachers and supervising professors from the department evaluate student teachers, both at the midterm and at the end of the student-teaching experience. Assessment by the preprofessional skills test of student teachers' readiness to teach is under review by the university's Council for Teacher Education, which is seeking assessment techniques that register the personal and situational complexity of what makes a good teacher. More extended use of observations, interviews, and teaching portfolios could greatly improve the predictive validity of our assessments.

Finally, the English education program's success can also be assessed by gauging the professional success of its graduates. Currently, a large percentage of English teachers in Illinois and many leaders in the field of English education are graduates of the program. They continue to praise their experiences in the program in response to questionnaires mailed one, five, and ten years after graduation. These responses provide important information, but an overview of the data collected could be more systematically integrated into program evaluation and revision.

We entitled this essay "Renewing the Nexus" for two related reasons. First, we believe that interconnections of many kinds—for example, across departments in our university, between the university and secondary schools, between content and methods of teaching, between learning and assessment, among student teachers scattered across central Illinois, and among the subdisciplines that constitute the field of English studies—make our program vibrant and vigorous. Thanks to those connections, our teaching candidates' futures as English teachers are rich with possibilities.

Second, we see that new interconnections—for example, between secondary school teachers and university faculty members jointly shaping the future of the program, between the teaching of literature and the teaching of writing — mark the areas in which our most important future work lies. As English educators we live and work across a web of knowledge and power that presents us with intense struggles and conflicts as well as potent solutions. We spin and rest, then spin again, continually renewing the nexus for the sake of our future teachers of English and for the sake of their students.

Bob Broad, *Department of English, Illinois State University*
Ron Fortune, *Department of English, Illinois State University*
Charles B. Harris, *Department of English, Illinois State University*
Janice Neuleib, *Department of English, Illinois State University*
Barbara Nourie, *Department of Curriculum and Instruction, Illinois State University*
Kay Parker, *Normal Community High School*

WORKS CITED

Atwell, Nancie. *In the Middle: New Understandings about Writing, Reading, and Learning.* 2nd ed. Portsmouth: Boynton, 1998.

Bizzell, Patricia, and Bruce Herzberg. *The Bedford Bibliography for Teachers of Writing.* 4th ed. Boston: Bedford, 1996.

Council for Teacher Education. *Realizing the Democratic Ideal: Teacher Education at Illinois State University.* Normal: Illinois State U, 1996.

Faigley, Lester. "Competing Theories of Process: A Critique and a Proposal." *College English* 48 (1986): 527–42.

Goswami, Dixie, and Peter R. Stillman, eds. *Reclaiming the Classroom: Teacher Research as an Agency for Change.* Portsmouth: Boynton, 1987.

Graff, Gerald. *Beyond the Culture Wars: How Teaching the Conflicts Can Revitalize American Education.* New York: Norton, 1992.

———. *Professing Literature: An Institutional History.* Chicago: U of Chicago P, 1987.

Harris, Charles B. "Mandated Testing and the Postsecondary English Department." *Profession 93.* New York: MLA, 1993. 59–67.

Jameson, Fredric. *Postmodernism; or, The Cultural Logic of Late Capitalism.* Durham: Duke UP, 1991.

Wiggins, Grant P. *Assessing Student Performance: Exploring the Purpose and Limits of Testing.* San Francisco: Jossey-Bass, 1993.

APPENDIX A

Statement of Goals for the Majors in English and English Education at Illinois State University

Preface to the Student

English is a huge academic discipline—and it's getting bigger every day, as more and more writing comes into our world and as the discipline itself expands its borders by addressing questions and using analytic techniques that used to be thought of as the exclusive domain of other fields of study. If you look at the list of undergraduate English courses in the ISU catalog (or that of any other university), you will see something of the dimensions of the subject—from ancient literature through contemporary film, from the syntax of the English language through literary criticism and theory, from freshman composition through advanced creative writing, et cetera: a total of some eighty or more courses offering ways of looking at and approaching the phenomenon of written language as it has been used and is now being used by human beings. Beyond the English department's pages in the catalog, there are hundreds more courses—in political theory, history, philosophy, social theory, psychology, et cetera—that are all part of "English" in its richest, most vigorous and engaged sense: that is, English understood as a way of knowing oneself and the world. Obviously, you can't take them all. We know that.

In fact, the major in English, you may have noticed, calls for a modest forty credit hours of course work, and the teacher-certification sequence calls for only forty-six credit hours. The wide range of apparently unrelated courses within the discipline, the ways in which English makes use of other fields of study, the relatively small number of required hours, and the differences in the two degree programs—all these features might be confusing or might lead you to believe that there is no necessary center to a degree in English (or that English and English education differ substantially in their goals). But the English faculty would like to encourage you to think otherwise. In our view, there is a core body of goals that ought to preside over and permeate a major in English (or whatever kind), and the teacher-certification sequence is best seen as one of many possible specialized variations on that core—specialized in that it involves *additional* goals rather than substitute goals. And we would encourage you to believe that working toward achieving the core goals of a major in English can and should influence your work in other disciplines as well. From its center to its edges, English is about the social and cultural uses of written language, past and present, and because of this fact, it is both dependent upon other disciplines and, at the same time, capable of enriching and supporting your work in a number of other disciplines. The following pages, which, in their simplest form, are merely the faculty's attempt to articulate the overall goals of the English major and the teacher-certification sequence, also reflect, we hope, our belief that the study of English can be a means of understanding a good deal more than the rules of subject-verb agreement.

We have pointed out the contrast between the two established programs listed in the catalog in order to make a more general point about the English program here: while we believe that there is an identifiable body of abilities, knowledge, and attitudes (see the listing below) that characterize the most successful ISU English and English education majors, we also believe that it is possible and desirable to tailor the major here so as to make it responsive to the specialized needs of certain kinds of students (of which the English education majors are an example) and at the same time keep it responsible to the core body of attributes that identify a successful English major. We encourage you to read and think about the following statement of goals in that same spirit of discipline and flexibility: we encourage you, in other words, to take seriously:

1. your own individual needs, plans, and desires;
2. the concept of English in its most extensive, cross-disciplinary, and richest form; and
3. our description of the capabilities and knowledge that in our view ought to belong (to a greater or lesser degree) to all majors who successfully complete the program here. If you are an English major, use the curricular flexibility to make the program work for you, and at the same time use the following statement of goals to keep a sense of unity and proportion in your pursuit of your degree. If you are in the teacher-certification sequence, use the required and suggested courses in your program to develop your professional abilities, and use the statement of goals to keep yourself reminded of the main claims of your "home" discipline while you pursue the additional goals of the English education program. And no matter which program you are enrolled in, keep in mind that the borders of your discipline do not stop where the English pages stop in the catalog.

The statement of goals can also be of practical use to you, we hope: we encourage you to study the following pages carefully, so that you can use the statement to help you select your courses wisely and to monitor your progress in the major. As you read the goals, ask yourself which of them you have and haven't mastered at this point in your degree program. Then choose your courses and govern your work with a view to gaining the competence you need. If you bring a critical awareness of these goals into all your work in or out of the major, then no matter what the emphasis of a given course, the goals will all be present and actively pursued. And we would like you to understand that, in spite of the fact that we have separated the goals into categories in order to clarify them, we see the categories themselves as well as the individual goals as interdependent: we hope, in other words, that as you become more and more accomplished, you will learn to bring all your abilities, knowledge, and attitudes to bear *simultaneously* on the language situations that your courses and your life outside the classroom may place you in.

One final note: the goals that we have designated here as "abilities" and "knowledge" are both descriptive and prescriptive—that is, they are *descriptions* of the capabilities and knowledge of past English majors who have been, in our view, the most successful, and they are, at the same time, *standards* that we are willing to prescribe as characteristics of successful work in the major here. But the goals in the attitudes section are not so much standards for you to meet as they are issues about which we urge you to discover and develop beliefs. In the main, the most successful English majors seem to us to have been comfortable with the discipline-specific attitudes we have listed here, but it is perfectly possible (and welcome) for you to contest these beliefs, to believe their opposites, and to argue vigorously that, for example, reading is no longer the important personal or social ability that it once was, or even that reading, writing, and books are all obsolete. Even those students who do not "believe *in*" the statements in this section, however, will need to have strong beliefs *about* the claims that are embedded in the statements. In order to arrive at informed positions about these issues, you will need to take seriously not only your work in English courses but also your work in other disciplines. And we think English, instead of distracting you from work in other fields, can be a part of that work, just as that work can and should be a part of English.

Goals of the Major in English at ISU

ABILITIES

1. The ability to read a familiar or an unfamiliar text in any of several genres (including not only traditional belletristic forms such as poetry, fiction, and drama but also such nonfiction forms as the essay, the autobiography, and the personal letter) and from any of several cultural or historical origins in such a way that the act of reading incorporates literal comprehension, aesthetic responsiveness, informed awareness of the tradition(s) and context(s) within which the text may be most productively read, rhetorical and logical analysis of its argument, and critical reflection on the implications of its origins, tradition, aesthetics, rhetoric, and argument
2. The ability to write about various kinds of texts in such a way that one's own writing articulates and embodies the multiple dimensions of the complex act of reading described above (i.e., literal comprehension, aesthetic responsiveness, awareness of tradition and appropriate context, rhetorical and logical analysis, and critical reflection) in clear, accurate, and effective prose
3. The ability to use reading and writing (as described in numbers 1 and 2 above) as a means of enabling the reading and study of other kinds of texts and situations and of producing other kinds of writing—that is, as a means of understanding and writing about a wide variety of topics, problems, and issues (e.g., personal experiences, topics in academic courses outside English,

social issues, films and other kinds of media, administrative problems within an institution or business, political campaigns) that demand skills in critical reading-observation and effective writing in appropriate forms

4. The ability to articulate a critically informed, carefully reasoned position about the social and philosophical value of the various components of English as a field of study
5. The ability to find (in a textbook, library, or elsewhere) the kinds of information that are relevant to the problem or issue being addressed in the writing situations described in numbers 2, 3, and 4 above and to integrate that information into one's own written work in a manner that both supports one's own rhetoric and argument and does justice to the source of the information

KNOWLEDGE

6. Usable familiarity[1] with a wide variety of works in various forms by British writers of various periods
7. Usable familiarity with a wide variety of works in various forms by American writers of various periods
8. Usable familiarity with a wide variety of works in various forms by writers from outside the British and American literary traditions
9. Usable familiarity with the history and grammatical structure of the English language and with linguistic theory in general
10. Usable familiarity with the history of rhetoric and with modern and contemporary theories of rhetoric
11. Usable familiarity with analytic techniques, bodies of information, and theory drawn from work in other academic disciplines
12. Usable familiarity with a wide variety of works in various forms by members of American minority groups
13. Usable familiarity with such linguistic concepts as "correct" usage, usage levels, and the dialects that make up American English—and of the social and cultural implications of the differences in language use that such concepts point to
14. Usable familiarity with such rhetorical concepts as rhetorical situation, rhetorical appeals, theories of invention, audience and forum analysis, and elements of style and argumentation
15. Usable familiarity with such backgrounds to English and American literature as the Bible, mythology, and folklore

[1]The phrase *usable familiarity,* which appears in each of the items in the two knowledge sections, is understood to mean (1) accurate memory of a number of features of the text(s) and/or bodies of information, and (2) the ability to use one's accumulated knowledge as a means of beginning a process of reasoning that results in the effective use of information as a dimension of critical reflection, analysis, rhetoric, and argument.

ATTITUDES

16. Belief in the personal and social importance of reading as a complex and culturally significant act
17. Belief in the personal and social importance of performing well in a variety of writing situations
18. Belief in the centrality of language to human endeavor in all areas and therefore in the usefulness of English as a means to achieving valuable personal and social abilities
19. Belief in the importance of aesthetic responsiveness to language as it is used in a variety of expressive and communicative situations
20. Belief in the importance of analysis and critical reflection as language-based activities—that is, activities both required and enabled by language
21. Belief in the interdependence of all the dimensions of language activity—reading, writing, listening, speaking, and thinking

Additional Goals for the Teacher-Certification Sequence in English at ISU

ABILITIES

22. The ability to read student writing in such a way that the reading process incorporates a sympathetic awareness of the complexities of the writing process as that process is manifested in students' work, recognition of the features of good written discourse (such as substantial and relevant content, clear and effective organization, specific sense of audience, verbal and conceptual clarity, appropriateness of tone, and accuracy in mechanics and usage) as they do or do not appear in the students' work, and a detailed analytical understanding of the strengths and weaknesses of the students' work
23. The ability to prepare comments on student writing that articulate and embody the complex act of reading described above and that communicate effectively to the students

KNOWLEDGE

24. Usable familiarity with the formal characteristics of the major belletristic and nonfiction genres as they have developed over time
25. Usable familiarity with at least two systems for describing and analyzing the grammar of the English language
26. Usable familiarity with a body of literature judged to be suitable for adolescents
27. Usable familiarity with the instructional materials and curricular patterns commonly used in secondary school English programs and with the role of English in the total secondary school program
28. Usable familiarity with ways of teaching English in the secondary schools—ways, that is, of selecting and adapting methods and materials for the various

interests and maturity levels of the students, of developing a sequence of assignments, and of guiding and stimulating the students' intellectual and social growth through language

29. Usable familiarity with the history of high school English teaching in the United States and with the issues in our nation's history that have influenced various pedagogical models

APPENDIX B

Introduction to English Studies

TEXTS

Barnes, Djuna. *Ladies Almanack.* 1928. Normal: Dalkey Archive, 1992.
Carlyle, Thomas. *Sartor Resartus.* 1833–34. Oxford: Oxford UP, 1987.
Melville, Herman. *Moby-Dick.* 1951. Oxford: Oxford UP, 1988.
Reed, Ishmael. *Mumbo Jumbo.* 1972. New York: Scribner, 1996.
Shakespeare, William. *Richard III.* 1593. New York: Dover, 1995.
Tey, Josephine. *The Daughter of Time.* 1951. New York: Scribner, 1995.

Davis, Robert Con, and Ronald Schleifer, eds. *Contemporary Literary Criticism: Literary and Cultural Studies.* 3rd ed. New York: Longman, 1994.
Gilbaldi, Joseph. *MLA Handbook for Writers of Research Papers.* 4th ed. New York: MLA, 1995.

COURSE OVERVIEW

Eng 100 is the department's gateway course into the major and the minor. It is an introduction to the broad range of subjects that make up English studies and to some of the analytic processes most commonly employed by students and professionals in the field. It is expansive and inclusive in its approach to the discipline and is meant to serve beginning English majors and minors by providing them with what they *must* know if they are to do well in the upper-level courses in the department and with a challenging sense of what they *should* know by the time they finish the program. It is intended to give our students a workable, entry-level understanding of the ideas set forth in the department's statement of goals.

COURSE GOALS

There are three main goals in this course. The first is to introduce students to the disciplines that rest under the English studies umbrella. Broadly, these are literature, rhetoric, and language. More specifically, they include the following—under literature: literary criticism (the study of British, American, world, other-culture, and children's literature), film and other media criticism, cultural studies, literary theory, and literary pedagogy; under rhetoric: the theory and practice of composition, including academic, technical, and creative writing, and writing pedagogy; and under language: linguistics, language usage, and the pedagogy of language. The second goal is for students to become familiar with some of the basic issues that are connected with the various disciplines of English studies. These include the questions of authorship, the role of the reader, the nature of text, the function of language, the connections between culture and language, and the possibility of meaning. The third goal is that students develop cognitive strategies for interpreting and understanding a variety of types of literary and extraliterary texts and organizational and rhetorical strategies for writing about them. These goals will be pursued through the rigorous analysis of literary texts. Students will explore such issues as the writing situations out of which these literary texts were produced, the ways readers make sense of and understand the texts they read, and how language both manifests and seeks to change the culture in which it is situated. These goals will also be pursued in the students' writing. For each assignment, a specific writing situation will be defined, and students will be asked to consider how their writing choices are affected by that situation.

GRADES

Your grade will be based on how well you demonstrate your achievement of the course goals. You will have the opportunity to do so in the following: a midterm exam and a final exam, primarily essay questions (10% each); four 5–7-page papers, each requiring a conference with your instructor (10% each); an annotated bibliography (10%); an informal class presentation (10%); weekly or biweekly one-page position papers (10%); class participation (10%). There is also a possibility of quizzes. Be aware that your grade in this class will be based on your performance. Failure to participate in the class (missing classes, not participating in discussions, not handing in ungraded assignments) can negatively affect your grade to the point of failure, regardless of your graded work.

GROUND RULES

There are no excused absences in this class. I will note your presence or absence for each class meeting. I will also note late arrivals, early departures, and mid-class disappearances. Should you be present less than 90% of the course (3 missed classes), I will become concerned about the quality of your performance. Should you be present less than 80% of the course (6 absences), I will judge that you have failed to participate in the class. Assignments handed in after the due date will be lowered a full grade (A to B, B+ to C+, etc.). After one week, no papers will be accepted. You cannot pass the course with missing graded work. Naturally, cheating and plagiarism in any form are unacceptable. Any evidence of cheating or plagiarism will result in failure of the test or assignment and may result in failure of the course.

Syllabus

WEEK 1: INTRODUCTION: WHAT IS ENGLISH STUDIES?

WEEK 2–4: AUTHORSHIP, HISTORY, AND TEXT

William Shakespeare, *Richard III*

T. S. Eliot, Viktor Shklovsky, Michel Foucault, and Stephen J. Greenblatt in *Contemporary Literary Criticism*

Josephine Tey, *The Daughter of Time*

Thurs. Feb. 6: Annotated bibliography due

Tues. Feb. 18: Paper 1 due

WEEK 5–7: THE READER, RHETORIC, AND TEXT

Thomas Carlyle, *Sartor Resartus*

Stanley Fish and J. Hillis Miller in *CLC*

Tues. Feb. 25: Midterm

Thurs. March 6: Paper 2 due

WEEK 7–12: CULTURE AND LANGUAGE

Barbara T. Christian, Patrocinio Schweickart, Raymond Williams, Edward Said, and Jonathan Culler in *CLC*

Ishmael Reed, *Mumbo Jumbo*

Elaine Showalter, Barbara Johnson, Laura Mulvey, and Michael Warner in *CLC*

Djuna Barnes, *Ladies Almanack*

Thurs. April 17: Paper 3 due

WEEK 13–15: LANGUAGE AND INTERPRETATION

Herman Melville, *Moby-Dick*

Jacques Lacan, Catherine Belsey, Roland Barthes, Paul de Man, Stuart Hall, and James Clifford in *CLC*

Thurs. May 1: Paper 4 due

Final Exam: Thurs. May 8, 10:00 a.m.

APPENDIX C

English 300: Senior Seminar, Spring 1995

REQUIRED TEXTBOOKS

Richter, David H., ed. *Falling into Theory: Conflicting Views on Reading Literature.* New York: St. Martin's, 1994. [DR]

Scholes, Robert, Nancy R. Comley, and Gregory L. Ulmer. *Text Book: An Introduction to Literary Language.* New York: St. Martin's, 1988. [TB]

Wofford, Susanne L. Hamlet: *William Shakespeare.* Case Studies in Contemporary Criticism. New York: St. Martin's, 1994. [WS]

In-class handouts.

COURSE OBJECTIVES

In the largest sense, the goal of this course is to provide you with the opportunity for achieving conscious control over our resources as an English major. By *resources,* the department means the abilities, knowledges, and attitudes you bring to bear on the language situations in which your courses and your life outside the classroom may place you. You will spend some time looking back over what you have accomplished and some time looking ahead to see how much can still get done—how much more you can learn, how much sense you can make of the courses you have taken, how much use you can make of the knowledge and abilities you have accumulated in the worlds beyond the classroom. To a large extent, then, the content of this course is English as a field of study; the process of the course is your process of discovering and articulating your relation to that content area.

The purposes of this course are:

to solidify and extend your grasp of English studies by giving you an opportunity to identify and develop the theoretical frame(s) you use to organize and understand the variety of your reading, writing, and thinking experiences in and outside of the English major

to develop your understanding of the history of English studies in America and of the current issues and controversies in the field

to add to the reading, writing, and thinking experiences you have accumulated through your experiences in the major

to assist you in preparing a portfolio of your writing that best represents your career as an English major

WRITING REQUIREMENTS

One major formal paper (20–25 pages). You will be expected to present orally a condensed version of this paper to the entire class during a colloquium scheduled for the fourteenth and fifteenth weeks of the term.

Four shorter papers (2–5 pages)

Regular informal writing assignments, both in and out of class (e.g., responses to your own earlier work, responses to assigned readings, critical summaries of arguments and discussion questions, in-class impromptu writing tasks)

A portfolio of writings from your tenure at Illinois State University, including writings from this class, with an introduction. Details about this assignment, which is a requirement for graduation and a central element in this class, are forthcoming.

Two essay examinations

Attendance policy: Because of the emphasis placed on class participation in this seminar, regular attendance is mandatory. I reserve the right to reduce your grade by one letter for each unexcused absence beyond two class meetings.

Course Schedule

WEEK 1. HOW WE GOT HOOKED ON ENGLISH STUDIES

Tues., Jan. 17 Course introduction and overview

Thurs., Jan. 19 Read Vendler (27–36) and Graff (36–43) in DR.

Writing assignment: Using these essays as models, write a brief essay (3–5 pages) describing how you "got hooked" on English studies. Be prepared to discuss (not read aloud) your essay in class.

WEEK 2. ENG 300: CHRONICLE OF A COURSE

Tues., Jan. 24 Read the following handouts for discussion:

Harris, "Mandated Testing and the Postsecondary English Department"

Fortune, "Assessing Assessment: Implementing a Portfolio-Based Assessment Program for English Majors"

"Statement of Goals for the Major in English and English Education at Illinois State University"

Thurs., Jan. 26 What Is English?

Read "Why We Read" (13–26) and "Eagleton" (44–54) in DR, and the Rogers handout, "Where Do English Departments Come From?"

Assignment: Complete the following two-part exercise, due Tues., Jan. 31:

1. Prepare a list of all the college English courses that you've taken and are now taking. First, list the courses chronologically by the semester in which you took them. Then, try to relate the courses to the statement of goals for the major in English. Obviously, some courses will fit under more than one goal, and some may not have been met by any course you've taken. Then, write at least a paragraph describing the extent to which you believe the courses you have taken have helped you meet the departmental goals. We'll return to this question more than once this semester.
2. Prepare a list of all the papers that you've written in English courses. Place as many of these papers that you can find in a folder for safekeeping. In listing the courses, use the following format:

Title	Course Name/No.	Sem./Year	Length

We'll do more with these papers later.

WEEK 3. REVISION AND THE WRITING PROCESS

Tues., Jan. 31 Read Rich's essay "When We Dead Awaken: Writing as Re-Vision" and the poems on the handout.

Due today: list of courses, with paragraphs relating these courses to goals statement, and list of papers you wrote as an English major

Thurs., Feb. 2 Read Flannery O'Connor's "The Life You Save May Be Your Own" (handout).

WEEK 4. SITUATED KNOWLEDGES

Tues., Feb. 7 Read the handout "Situated Knowledges" by Haraway. To help you prepare for class discussion, write an informal summary of Haraway's argument.

Thurs., Feb. 9 Read "How We Read" (205–17) in DR, and "Reading Texts" (3–31; by McCormick, Waller, and Flowers; handout).

Writing assignment: Choose an old paper in which you analyzed a text. In a paragraph or so, try to deduce the "repertoire of assumptions" that led you to ask the questions you asked of that text. That is, try to describe the "complex (and perhaps never fully analyzable) set of expectations, desires, prejudices, and former experiences (both literary and non-literary)" (RT 14) you brought to your reading of the text. Describe both your personal repertoire and your literary repertoire as defined in RT. Later, you will be asked to rewrite this paper in light of your current repertoire of assumptions, which has probably developed further as a result of your subsequent classroom and life experiences.

WEEK 5. WHAT WE READ: THE CANON WARS

Tues., Feb. 14 Read "What We Read" (107–18) in DR. Everyone is responsible for reading the additional essays listed below, but you will individually serve as a "specialist" for the essay listed for your group.

Group 1: Howe, "The Value of the Canon" (handout)
Group 2: Altieri (131–43) in DR
Group 3: Tompkins (119–28) in DR
Group 4: Said (193–203) in DR

Write a 1–2 page single-spaced critical summary of the argument of your group's assigned essay plus two "synthetic" discussion questions that connect your group's reading to the other groups' readings. Bring copies for all members of your group, one copy for me, and three copies for each of the remaining groups.

Major paper topic due Thursday, Feb. 23

Thurs., Feb. 16 Group discussions again, with same guidelines:

Group 1: Donoghue (144–52) and Gates (173–81) in DR
Group 2: Robinson (152–65) and Sedgwick (181–86) in DR

Group 3: Kolodny (278–85) and Smith (187–93) in DR

Group 4: Will (286–89), Greenblatt (289–90), and Dickstein (129–30) in DR

Writing assignment, due Thursday, March 9: Rewrite old paper you chose for the February 9 assignment. For the purposes of this assignment, the older the paper, the better. *Rewrite* means that you should address the same topic and the same problems from the point of view of who you are now (in point of knowledge, ability, and attitudes). Accompanying your rewrite should be a preface or afterward that comments on how your changing repertoire of assumptions led to the revisions you made in your rewrite of the old paper. (Review our discussion of Rich and O'Connor's revisions in week 3.) Be sure to turn in a copy of the old paper along with the rewrite and preface or afterward.

WEEK 6. HOW WE READ

Tues., Feb. 21 Group discussions again, with same guidelines and writing assignments as last week:

Group 1: Rabinowitz (218–21) and Barthes (221–26) in DR

Group 2: Fish (226–237) in DR

Group 3: Dasenbrock (238–48) in DR

Group 4: Booth (249–55) in DR

Thurs., Feb. 23 Essay examination

Begin reading the play *Hamlet* in WS for next week.

Major paper topic due today

WEEK 7. APPROACHES TO *HAMLET*: FEMINISM AND DECONSTRUCTION

Tues., Feb. 28 Read "Feminist Criticism and *Hamlet*" (208–20) and Showalter (220–40) in WS. Write a critical summary of Showalter's essay.

Thurs., March 2 Read "What Is Deconstruction?" (283–96) and Garber (297–331) in WS. Write a critical summary of Garber's essay.

WEEK 8. APPROACHES TO *HAMLET*: MARXISM AND THE NEW HISTORICISM

Tues., March 7 Read "What Is Marxist Criticism?" (332–48) and Bristol (348–67) in WS. Write a critical summary of Bristol's essay.

Thurs., March 9 Read "What Is the New Historicism?" (368–80) and Coddon (380–402) in WS. Write a critical summary of Coddon's essay.

Rewrite of old paper due

WEEK 9. SPRING BREAK

Tues., March 14 Travel safely!

Thurs., March 16 Wear lots of sunblock!

WEEK 10. APPROACHES TO *HAMLET*: PSYCHOANALYTIC CRITICISM

Tues., March 21 Read "What Is Psychoanalytic Criticism?" (241–56) and Adelman (256–282) in WS. Write a critical summary of Adelman's essay.

Thurs., March 23 Essay examination

WEEK 11. INDIVIDUAL CONFERENCES

Tues., March 28 Individual conferences in STV 345 (no regular class) to discuss final paper and portfolio

Thurs., March 30 Individual conferences in STV 345 (no regular class) to discuss final paper and portfolio

WEEK 12. THE LANGUAGE OF METAPHOR

Tues., April 4 Read 47–79 in TB.

Come to class prepared to discuss the poetic uses of metaphor in the poems on 74–79.

Writing assignment, due April 13: choose either (1) an editorial from a newspaper or magazine in which metaphor plays an important part, either because many metaphorical expressions are used in it or because the whole piece is based on one or more metaphorical concepts, or (2) two advertisements from a magazine for a particular type of product, such as designer perfume, cigarettes, beer, or luxury automobiles. Write a brief (2–5 pp.) essay analyzing how metaphors are presented to influence the reader's or consumer's response by appealing to the audience's often unacknowledged prejudices, ideologies, and desires.

Thurs., April 6 Read Lakoff and Johnson, "Concepts We Live By," 80–91 in TB.

Major paper proposal, including working bibliography, due today

WEEK 13. THE LANGUAGE OF METAPHOR

Tues., April 11 Read 92–103 in TB.

Thurs., April 13 Read 121–28 in TB.

Writing assignment on metaphor due today

First draft of major paper should be finished.

WEEK 14. COLLOQUIUM

Tues., April 18 Oral presentations of major paper

Thurs., April 20 Oral presentations of major paper

WEEK 15. COLLOQUIUM

Tues., April 25 Oral presentations of major paper

Thurs., April 27 Oral presentations of major paper

WEEK 16. COMPLETE FINAL DRAFT OF MAJOR PAPER

Tues., May 2 No class, work on major paper

Thurs., May 4 No class, work on major paper

Final draft due by 5:00 p.m. Friday, April 5

WEEK 17. FINAL EXAM WEEK

Tues., May 9 3:10 p.m.

Portfolio due

INDIANA UNIVERSITY, BLOOMINGTON

Watch This Space; or, Why We Have Not Revised the Teacher Education Program—Yet

The story we are about to tell is not exemplary in the way we at first imagined it would be. We had thought, in the beginning, that we would give an academic year to reading and talking about what English teachers should know and how they can learn it. Mostly, we would talk: among ourselves, with other participants in this project, with our colleagues in the Department of English and the School of Education, with teachers in the secondary schools, with our students. We would, we imagined, emerge from these conversations with a scheme that would serve as a prompt and model, for ourselves and maybe for others, of one way to educate English teachers, both before and after they enter their own classrooms.

We have done that. We have decided the purposes, and much of the content and sequence, of a program in which, if it works, undergraduates will learn enough about their subject and craft to know how to keep on learning. We have inaugurated a series of collaborations in which practicing teachers are helping plan ways to continue their own learning as well as helping us refashion the education of new teachers. Our collaborations with one another have awakened some long-dormant affiliations between the faculties of the School of Education and the Department of English. We have even set afoot among our colleagues in the Department of English the idea that teacher education is one of their responsibilities.

The plan that has emerged from all this thinking and talking does not fully represent all that we have learned, or adequately acknowledge all that we have yet to do. A curriculum is at best a conversation rather than a set of rules. But for at least a decade that conversation has lapsed on the Bloomington campus. Our recent attempts to renew it have made us freshly aware of the structures and habits that discourage collaboration even among faculty members on the same campus, to say nothing of cooperation among English teachers in the university and in secondary schools. We have only begun to press against these inhibitions, to test the resistances of colleagues who teach courses we want to change, who reign over territory on which (from their point of view) we want to encroach, and who think about English in ways we want to complicate or contest. We have not yet evolved those institutional ligatures—standing committees, advisory boards—among teachers in English, education, and secondary schools that are necessary to sustain any purpose and program in a big university like Indiana. We have, in short, made a map of course requirements and elections that we think right for prospective teachers of English. But we have only begun the journey. There is a lot of space to be traveled before anything is really changed in how teachers of English are educated at Indiana.

More important, there is also a lot of space yet to be explored on the map, traverses and portages from course to course that must be decided by the students themselves. Despite its size—indeed, because of its size—there are few faculty members at Indiana University who think it their job to offer advice and direction to these students. Like their counterparts at other large research universities, the sixty-five faculty members in the Department of English find their identities and reckon their distinction by contributing to the knowledge of their discipline and educating undergraduates and a couple hundred graduate students. Of the more than five hundred majors in the department, only about thirty each year intend to teach English in secondary schools. It is therefore easy for faculty members in English to leave teacher education to the School of Education. But faculty members in the School of Education have their own research projects to pursue, specializations to practice, and graduate students to induct into the advanced reaches of their studies. At Indiana only about a third of the faculty members in education are involved in teacher education at the undergraduate level. The direct responsibility for educating the ninety or so preservice teachers (including about thirty English majors) who graduate each year certified to teach English is left to one—just one—of our colleagues; the member on the MLA team who teaches the one—just one—course in English education currently required for certification.

So at a university like Indiana any initiative for change must struggle against an institutional inertia, which serves mostly to keep our outdated program solidly in place. We recognize, for example, that our current program sustains a bifurcation that, in practice as well as on paper, divides English studies into the "content" provided by the Department of English and the "methods" learned in the School of Education. Even within the Department of English content is sorted out in our course descriptions (and in the state certification requirements) into the historic trinity of literature, composition, and language; that division, of course, is also a hierarchy, with literary studies on top. Shaped in and by an institutional culture that offers few occasions and incentives for faculty members to talk to one another across these divisions, descriptions of the undergraduate teacher education program in English at Indiana now express current conceptions of English studies about as accurately as grammar drills and the five-paragraph theme were once thought to describe composition.

If preservice teachers do graduate with a coherent conceptual framework for learning and teaching English, it has not been by our design. Undergraduates who are studying to be teachers of English will presumably continue to find their own ways and make their own connections in a rich curriculum offered by strong departments of English and language education. What we want to do is to educate their choices. We want to furnish not just a map but also a compass that will give prospective teachers a sense of direction and an idea of destination as they track a path from course to course. If they learn how to do that, they will be prepared to teach as amply as we can prepare them. They will be ready to adapt what they have learned in the university to the circumstances and priorities of their own classrooms. They will know how, and when, and why to move on to learn something more, to continue their journey beyond the routes and boundaries we mapped out for them.

Much, and almost everything that is really interesting, has yet to happen in our story. If our account of how we came to this beginning has an exemplary force, then, it will be because it is the story of how we learned what we have to do next.

Three Defining Structures

At the start we entered a field defined by three structures whose foundations are deep. One structure is the set of state requirements for certification, recently revised. The second is the set of requirements in professional education, a block of courses and field experiences that can absorb nearly a third of the hours required of undergraduates for graduation. This complex of requirements has been in place for more than a decade. The third and most important structure on the field is that of the English major, whose requirements until last year had not been substantially changed in over twenty years.

CERTIFICATION

In the state of Indiana, certification requirements are expressed not as a number of credits to be earned but as knowledges to be attained. The newly formulated *Standards for Teachers of English/Language Arts* (1998) stipulate that the preparation of English teachers of adolescents and young adults should include reading and understanding a "wide variety of literature by multicultural and international authors and authors of both genders," "a diversity of American literature," "a variety of British works and their relationship to the history of the English language," and "a wide diversity of contemporary literature." Teachers should know and understand "theories of writing and of the writing process and how these relate to sound writing strategies," and they should possess the "ability to model writing well in a variety of forms." They should know and understand "language theory, including the language acquisition and language development processes, the history of the English language, and the changing nature of language and its different and variant forms," as well as "accepted rules of grammar and syntax and usage" (*Standards* 22).

The state board that administers the requirements leaves it to each university and college to translate these broad directives into credit hours and course names. The latitude of the new directives—especially the inclusion of the study of language and media and of the skills of speaking, listening, and nonverbal communication—is accompanied by a call, or maybe a hope, for integration. To quote the *Standards* again, prospective teachers should learn to use language arts "(reading, writing, speaking, and listening) in creating and interpreting texts" and to use "themes [i.e., writing] for this integration" (22).

PROFESSIONAL EDUCATION

Prospective secondary school teachers of English must complete eleven courses in the School of Education. Some of the courses are general (multicultural education, the teaching of reading, microcomputing, educational psychology) and some particular (a methods course in teaching English in high school and middle school, a course in teaching reading).

Like their counterparts in the Department of English, these required courses reflect a coverage model of curriculum, in which students are "exposed" to an array of topics and issues and left to their own devices as they try to assemble a batch of discrete courses into a coherent idea of teaching and learning. Right now the faculty in the School of Education is thoroughly overhauling its programs in elementary and secondary school certification. These revisions offer chances to remedy certain disjunctions, principally the separation of the English methods course from almost everything students learn in the Department of English.

THE ENGLISH MAJOR

Students seeking secondary school certification in English have two routes open to them. They may earn certification while completing a bachelor of arts in the College of Arts and Sciences or while completing a bachelor of science in the School of Education with a subject-matter specialty in English.

Students who major in English must complete thirty hours (ten courses). The recently revised major stipulates eighteen of these hours (six courses): an introductory course in the practices of literary interpretation, another course in the methodologies of literary and cultural criticism, and courses in the writing of four of the conventional periods of British and American literature, and world literature in English.

English majors who also want to earn certification as a secondary school teacher will complete thirty-six hours in their subject area, not all of them in the Department of English. In the new program, recently approved by the School of Education, undergraduates must complete a course in literature for young adults, two courses in writing, a course in the teaching of writing in middle and secondary schools, and one or two courses that fulfill the state requirement of study in the English language. We plan to develop special versions of the courses in literary interpretation and literary criticism for prospective teachers. We also want to invent a kind of fourth-year seminar in which prospective teachers are invited to reflect on the ways in which they have been taught and enabled to understand them not as functions of the styles or personalities of individual teachers (she lectured a lot; he put us in groups) but as constituting a repertory on which they can draw and in which each tactic has its own reasons and makes its own effects.

Students who take their degrees in education rather than in English and the College of Arts and Sciences also complete thirty-six hours in English. Their course elections are not all that different from those of students who complete an English major, because both are constrained by how the Bloomington campus has interpreted the state certification requirements. The principal difference is likely to be that prospective

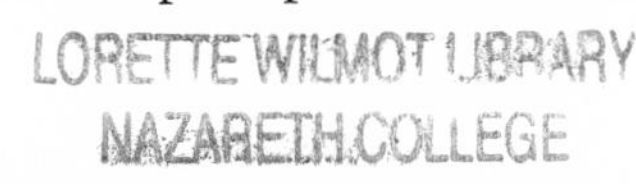

teachers who are not completing a major in English are likely to spend their elections of literature courses in space (a variety of national and ethnic literatures) rather than in time (required courses in British and American literature through the nineteenth century).

Students who earn their degrees in education are also not required to complete the foreign language requirement of the College of Arts and Sciences (two years of study of the same language). They are encouraged instead to be certified in a minor area as well (usually twenty-four hours).

Difficulties: Separation and Incoherence

We see two principal difficulties in the field defined by these three structures of requirements: separation and incoherence.

To describe professional education and the English major as separate structures is not just a convenient metaphor. It signifies a real separation. The cost is sometimes precise, as in the isolation of the methods course, and its teacher, from the faculty, courses, matter, and methods of the English major. Sometimes the cost is more general. A few faculty members in English and education met in the early 1980s to negotiate the translation of the state certification requirements into course requirements. Until recently, there has been no occasion on which they have met again to look comprehensively at the pieces of a prospective teacher's education to see whether some of the courses that make it up have changed in the past decade, and to consider whether the pieces still fit together. Unless we learn how to continue talking about how we educate teachers, in ten years, maybe even five years, our brand-new program will look as inert and antique as the one we are trying to refashion.

The separation is evident in one of the most telling findings of our recent study. We discovered that no one has a clear idea of how many prospective teachers follow a route to certification through English and the College of Arts and Sciences and how many through education. Faculty members in the School of Education have assumed that far more students seek certification through English. Faculty members in English believe that far more students seek certification through education. Our best guess, based on an analysis of the most recent graduating class, is that more students graduate each year having certified as English teachers through the School of Education (about sixty) than through the College of Arts and Sciences (about thirty).

However the proportions sort out, the important finding is that in any recent year English and education share perhaps as many as three hundred undergraduates who intend to certify as middle- and high-school English teachers. We have not been careful about, we seem not even to be cognizant of, our joint responsibility. On each side of the divide between English and education, we are often not only ignorant of what is happening on the other side, we don't even seem to have a clear idea who is over there.

The separation contributes to, or at least permits, incoherence. Consider the preparation of an English teacher in composition, which is where most undergraduates begin in English. Because most students satisfy the basic composition requirement at Indiana University in a number of different ways, teachers of advanced writing courses that prospective teachers enroll in must expect a range of different answers to common questions: What do they know? What can they do? What have they done? Where to begin?

Even when these questions are answered, in the advanced writing course most often chosen by students to fulfill a requirement in the study of writing, prospective teachers do not really study writing. As it is in most big research universities, at Indiana University the course is usually taught by faculty members and graduate students trained in literary studies. The course has therefore evolved into an exercise in literary or cultural studies, where writing is not the subject of study but a means of studying something else. Practice in how to read their culture is likely to be apt and exciting for undergraduates. But prospective teachers in the course are left to wonder how its topics and writing assignments will work in middle and high schools, where writing is still often expressive rather than persuasive or analytic.

Finally, students learn nothing about the methods of teaching writing in an advanced writing course offered by the department of English. Nor is there now a methods course in education given to the teaching of writing. Prospective teachers are expected to figure out how to teach writing on the basis of their experience as students—an experience, for all the reasons cited above, that at its best might make them good writers without giving them an idea about how and why their improvement happened.

The content of the courses that most students take to fulfill the certification requirement in language study is more settled than that of the composition courses. These courses in linguistics or the English language deal primarily with the structure of language (grammar, phonology, morphology, syntax) and to a lesser extent with questions of dialect, the history of the English language, and linguistic issues (e.g., the English First movement). More advanced courses introduce students to broad theoretical approaches to language study, usually including psycholinguistics, transformational-generative grammar, and sociolinguistics.

Prospective teachers come to these courses expecting to learn "grammar," to master "correct usage," just as newly arrived English teachers are expected by parents and principals to teach inflexible rules of grammar and conventional usage. Students are often disappointed and confused when the courses instead offer matter and ideas that complicate traditional understandings of language and, as one instructor put it, "disabuse students of language myths." The separation of these courses from the course in methods of teaching English also means that students have little chance to connect ideas about grammar and usage to the teaching of writing and reading. Nor do they spend much time talking about how to connect relatively sophisticated ideas about language to the traditional textbooks and syllabi still common in secondary schools.

Finally, most of the mysteries and incoherences of our teacher education program are contained in the courses in literature taught in the Department of English. It is likely (this is another of the things we don't yet know) that students who move to certification through the School of Education elect somewhat different courses in literature from those enrolled in by English majors who also seek certification. But these differences are surely small compared to the differences piled up as students following either route to certification roam among the more than sixty courses in literature offered by the department and encounter the manifold purposes and methodologies that may be practiced in any one of them.

Students who enroll in some of the courses required for the English major start off at least on some common ground. The different sections of an introductory course in literary interpretation are usually organized around purposes like that described in one recent syllabus: "to develop through a variety of interpretative strategies an idea of how texts can be made to mean, how such texts can be said to work in or on the world." But then students choose among four survey courses: literatures in English to 1600, 1600–1800, 1800–1900, and 1900 to the present. The second and third of these courses will certainly include American as well as British writing; the fourth will include literature in English written in countries all over the world. Because a prospective teacher majoring in English may substitute any course in an appropriate historical period for any one of the survey courses, some students may choose a course in nineteenth-century American literature and graduate having read Whitman but not Tennyson; others may choose a course in Victorian literature and end with Tennyson rather than Whitman. Students can also meet the new requirements for the major by putting together courses in nineteenth- and twentieth-century American literature and skipping completely British literature of the last two centuries, or they can make a sequence of three courses in eighteenth-, nineteenth-, and twentieth-century fiction and miss both Whitman and Tennyson. In short, the new requirements decrease the likelihood that students will graduate in English having studied a common set of texts and writers. But the new requirements also increase the possibility that prospective teachers will organize a sequence of learning that will serve them well when they take it to their own classrooms.

This miscellany of matter is almost matched by the variety of ways in which students learn as they study to be teachers. Because faculty members in the Department of English don't think of themselves as teachers who teach teachers, they pay little explicit attention to questions of pedagogy. But to the extent that teachers will do with (or to) their students what was done with (or to) them, the pedagogies that are enacted in these courses may be models as powerful as those explicitly laid out in the methods course. When recently about half the sixty-five faculty members in English were asked what students do in their classes, they replied that mostly they listen as their instructor provides a setting or background for texts, poses problems, summarizes discussion, or models acts of understanding. Then, in descending order of frequency, the students read (mostly outside class), write (also outside class, and primarily in response to reading), talk (sometimes in small groups, usually as part of a discussion involving the entire class), do research, and, very occasionally, teach the class themselves as they present the findings of research, offer an interpretation of a text, or sometimes even perform in a group reading or an exercise in role playing.

These faculty members in English were also asked what they want students to know and be able to do as a result of their education in English. Even in a relatively distilled form, the list is long, nearly two dozen statements of intention or hope, ranging from a mastery of a particular domain of knowledge (Shakespeare, American literature) to habits of reading. In between, the purposes settled around a few very large ambitions. When students read, their instructors want them to learn to make meaning for themselves, using a variety of critical addresses or methodologies. They want students to understand how meaning is informed or enabled by relations among texts and by the place of text and reader in a particular time and culture. They want students to see that acts of literary understanding are connected to the rest of experience, to recognize that reading literature calls on and enlarges the same powers of interpretation exercised in reading the world. When students write, university English teachers want them to use conventions of the discipline as well as grammatical and rhetorical conventions. More important, they want students to learn how to use writing to explore and arrive at meaning and to make a case and persuade others. Finally, these teachers want students to learn that learning is fun, to take pleasure in looking things up, finding things out, making sense of something.

Finding a Path

Once we had this rich tangle of requirements, tasks, purposes, and methods before us, our job was very much like the job we had set for our students: How to find a path through the tangle that connects some of the separations and ends in an idea about English.

We began by ignoring the difference, at least for a time, between students who certify through the School of Education and students who certify through the departmental major in English. Instead, we set three goals for the education of all of them. First, we wanted to help them think about themselves as teachers while learning in courses in English and think about themselves as teachers of language and literature while learning in courses in education. Second, we wanted to provide them with a logic of English that made manifest the reason for requirements and would inform and harmonize the choices offered to them. Finally, we wanted them to graduate knowing how to adapt whatever they learned in our classrooms to very different circumstances and how to figure out for themselves what they needed from the university in order to continue their learning.

How can we help students think of themselves as teachers? One way, we think, is to make their experience as writers in school a deliberately enunciated part of their education as teachers. We therefore plan to introduce a new course in methods of teaching writing in the School of Education. In this course students will spend time discussing and reflecting on how people write and learn to write—at least as much time as they now spend learning the grammars and structure of the English language. At the same time, we will make available a couple of sections each semester of a revised version of the course in advanced expository writing that is required for certification. In this course students will be asked to think, talk, and write about themselves as writers: what helps and what frustrates, what they are good at and why, what they were not as good at before, and how and why they got better. The course will supplement the new methods course in writing by, in effect, making each prospective teacher his or her own student.

We also want to give students a chance to put all they have learned as readers to work on books like those they will talk about as teachers. We want to let them engage questions about the psychological and social culture in which books do their work in the schools. To this purpose we will add a requirement of a course in literature for young adults. This kind of writing—the novels of Katherine Paterson, for example, poems by Shel Silverstein and Ted Hughes, some of Annie Dillard's prose—is intrinsically worthy of study and self-evidently appropriate. Equally important, such a course raises questions interesting to all readers and central to teachers. Are middle or high school students ready for *Catcher in the Rye* or *Weetsie Bat*? Are their parents ready? Why do we want people to read a given book at age 11? 17? Ever?

How can we provide an explicit logic for the education of English teachers? To aid our second purpose, we plan two other courses. One is a gateway course to be required of prospective teachers early in their time in the university, perhaps as early as their first year. In this course students would learn about the matter and motives of English: what English is, how it is studied now, why it has been studied, how different styles of literary address converge to aid understanding, how a knowledge of rhetoric and language assists in literary study, and how in turn a knowledge of literature enriches the study of rhetoric and composition.

We imagine the second course, in which students will enroll during the year that they do their student teaching, as a kind of capstone course, a valedictory commentary on learning as an English or English education major. Its topic and matter will vary; in fact, its matter will be whatever students have taken from the curriculum. But in all its forms the course will ask students to think about how they have learned to read and write in the university. We intend this course, like the gateway course, to be an invitation to self-consciousness as students begin to claim their professional lives as teachers. Especially in the second course, they can begin to practice the adaptations and mount the expeditions of discovery that they will need to make as teachers when they confront possibilities not predicted in their university training—for example, all those adventures-in-reading courses now common in the schools.

Braced by the framework of these two courses, students can, we hope, move more confidently and effectively than they now do among the array of courses in education, English, and other schools and departments that can be used to meet one or another of the certification requirements.

Suppose, for example, that we redefine the stipulation of study in the literature of a minority as a requirement of diversity, a study of the writing of difference. We then will open a range of options that includes not only African American writing but also writing by women, ethnic American literatures, gay and lesbian writing, and self-consciously postcolonial literature. The idea is that by means of such courses students will learn to see in these choices something of what is at stake in this requirement. The requirement would then acquire a reason, and the reason might persuade a student to make a coherent move to further study in, say, women's writing or Native American literatures.

At this point the constraints of arithmetic become visible. It is not necessary to do the calculations here. It is enough to say that even after a series of artful substitutions, students majoring in English will find it very difficult to complete both the major and all the courses we think important in the education of a prospective teacher. And there are some ideas on the table that would make the pinch of arithmetic yet more painful. We would like to add a course in argument to complement the courses in exposition usually offered as advanced composition. We think it would be useful to encourage students who move to certification through the Department of English to complete a course in which they read in translation (or, for that matter, in the original language) the literature of the culture whose language they are learning to satisfy the foreign language requirement of the College of Arts and Sciences.

Something has to give. We have ideas about that too. How about attaching study in the history of the English language to the first semester (Old English to Shakespeare) of the British literature survey course? How about adapting one of the courses in the large block of professional education requirements—maybe Methods of Teaching High School Reading—so that it attends to the peculiar demands of the study of nonverbal communication?

Right now these questions have no answers. They point to work in progress. We must put the questions to our colleagues in English and education and work out with them the connections between the purposes of their courses and the purposes of a revised teacher education program. The moment is propitious for such conversations and negotiations. As faculty members in the School of Education and in English have been revising their programs, some of us on each side of the divide have been poking at the pieces to make them fit with one another. Now that the pieces are almost all in place, the moment is right to ask our colleagues in English how in our new major we can teach and advise students in ways and down paths that explicitly fulfill the department's responsibility for the education of teachers.

We have also begun to move across an even wider separation by putting similar questions to practicing secondary school teachers. In the past two years, using money from a university initiative to enlarge and emphasize the university's public identity and responsibilities, we have created the South Central Indiana English Teachers Collaborative, in which teachers in the university and in secondary schools have joined to conduct common projects in teaching, research, and the continuing education of teachers. We began our collaboration by asking the teachers invited to join this venture what they now wished they had learned in the university, what they wished new teachers coming into their schools had learned, and what they thought of our proposed revision of the teacher education program in Bloomington. Their answers have mattered greatly in the work of the revision. But even more important are their answers to the next set of questions, about how we can join with experienced teachers so that they will continue to learn. Possible means range from electronic mail networks and in-service seminars to teacher exchanges, joint research projects, and perhaps the rehabilitation in the Department of English of the moribund degree of master of arts in teaching.

In a sense, everything we have learned and imagined in thinking about the teacher education program works to help us prepare teachers to continue their education. Teachers are never fully prepared: they are enrolled for life in a continuing-education program. No one in the university can get students ready for the multiple requirements and complex range of particularities that they will face in their first years of teaching. We can teach them something about English—pass on some information about language and literature, demonstrate some styles of teaching and understanding, coach their practice as readers and writers, and so on. But mostly we must teach them how to learn about English while they are in our classrooms, as they find their way through the levels, requirements, and possibilities of our courses, and when they are teaching in their own classrooms and schools. Perhaps more than any other group of students in English, not excluding PhDs, preservice English teachers are a continuing responsibility, to the university, to their teachers, and to themselves. No other group has a greater impact on the hardest question of all: How will the knowledge, abilities, and canons of judgment that make up what we call English exist and do their work in the culture and politics of our country?

What has been exemplary about our experience is not a product—an example—for others to consult and use. Rather, we have found our experience itself to be exemplary, in two senses. First, we suspect that teacher education in many universities like Indiana is troubled by the lack of coordination, the absence even of simple awareness, that confuses our program and its purposes. Second, we now think that reiterated exemplification—constant demonstrations, to our students and ourselves, of what we mean by English and how it can be learned and taught—must be at the heart of any teacher education program. We know now how rapidly an institution can lose sight of the foundation of its practices. Paradoxically, looking at a teacher education program tells us how easy it is to look away from it. Teacher education, like teachers, gets taken for granted, and on both sides of the divide. English professors are amazed to learn that the preparation of teachers is not a high priority in most schools of education. Education professors are equally dumbfounded to learn that very few English professors devote any conscious attention to demonstrating how they teach their subject.

The exposure of these empty mirror images has been a large part of our recent experience. We want to make sure that we continue really to see one another. Beyond the hard questions we have yet to ask and answer and the difficult politics we have yet to engage and survive, we want to create an education that prepares students to find their own ways in the subject of English, to take upon themselves their education-as-teachers, before as well as after they become teachers. To our students and ourselves we say, not as an empty promise of coming attractions but as a permanent motto for work always in progress: Watch this space.

Progress Report

We wrote this essay in the summer of 1996; we revised it to bring it up-to-date in the winter of 1998. In those two years we have filled in some of the space. The School of Education has approved our proposed program for prospective English teachers, and the Department of English has approved the new curriculum for its majors.

We must now figure out how to adapt one of the two required courses in critical practices—perhaps both courses—to the interests of prospective teachers so that they see some connections among the ways that English is learned in the university and in secondary schools. Or, to turn that prospect around, we need to bring some of the questions addressed by colleagues in the secondary schools—What is English? What do parents and the public want it to be? What do we want it to be? — back to the campus as issues in the contemporary practice of our discipline.

We must also decide how to define and use what we have called the valedictory or capstone course so that in it students engage questions about styles of teaching, just as in the critical-practices courses they engage questions about styles of literary and cultural understanding. Prospective teachers have spent most of their lives looking at teaching. As they begin to find their own styles, we want them to reflect on, and not simply to reflect, ours. We want them to learn that style is the consequence of choice and that each choice has its consequences. As we do that, we also will learn something about our own styles and their consequences. If we must inevitably serve as models of teaching, we ought to think carefully about the reasons for and the possibilities of the models we choose to be.

Finally, although the English Teachers Collaborative is not formally a part of the MLA Teacher Education Project, it holds at least two promises that coincide with and reinforce the work of the project. First, as the collaborative has brought together English teachers in the university and the secondary schools, it has also occasionally connected people in several universities in the state who are interested in teacher education. We plan to enlarge these connections, both within the university, so that colleagues who educate English teachers on each of the eight campuses of Indiana University start talking to one another, and also within the state, so that faculty members in English at Bloomington and Notre Dame, say, and the University of Southern Indiana help one another out in starting and sustaining collaborations with teachers in the secondary schools in their region.

More important, some of the teachers in the collaborative have used it as a base for the exploration of possibilities in their own teaching. One example: fifteen or twenty members of the collaborative have organized projects in teacher research. That is, teachers are helping one another study the effectiveness of their practices. One reason for these studies might be to validate their practices to anyone (a principal, a parent) who asks. Another might be to publish their findings or report them at professional conferences to other teachers. The best reason, however, and the one that fuels their interest and excitement, is that a carefully organized study will enable them to observe and reflect on their teaching. It is, one of the teachers said, like having another teacher in the room, someone who is there not to evaluate but to provide distance and a mode of systematic inquiry that will tell you if you are really getting done what you intended to do. This result of the English Teachers Collaborative expresses the ambition of much that we have thought about and worked for in revising a teacher education program at Indiana University that will prepare teachers to educate themselves.

Kathryn T. Flannery, *Department of English, Indiana University, Bloomington*
JoAnne Frye, *Bloomington High School, North*
Donald Gray, *Department of English, Indiana University, Bloomington*
Mary Beth Hines, *Department of Language Education, Indiana University, Bloomington*
Kenneth Johnston, *Department of English, Indiana University, Bloomington*
Joan Pong Linton, *Department of English, Indiana University, Bloomington*

WORK CITED

Standards for Teachers of English / Language Arts, Approved May 20, 1998, by the Indiana Professional Standards Board. Indianapolis, 1998.

NEW MEXICO STATE UNIVERSITY, LAS CRUCES

Defining the Secondary School English Education Camel

A camel is a horse designed by committee.

New Mexico—Land of Enchantment and, in terms of education, a few tensions. A minority-majority state, some sixty percent of its population minorities, predominately Hispanic and Native American. A state that devotes a large percentage of its annual budget to public education. A state that is one of this nation's poorest, per capita. And a state struggling to become, to use its educational system to help provide students a brighter future than their parents may have had. One of the key components of that brighter future is the thoughtful, careful preparation of future teachers. Given the importance of literacy, it is absolutely critical that we attend to the preparation of future English teachers; New Mexico State University was therefore pleased to be invited to participate in the MLA Teacher Education Project to examine our program, to discuss it with faculty members from other universities around the country engaged in similar enterprise, and to speculate about changes that might move our program toward becoming an exemplary one. This report, forwarded by the theme of constraints, presents that examination of tensions among the various elements of our program and the potential for resolution.

Our first foray into program review came in 1989, when faculty members from various departments in the Colleges of Arts and Sciences and the Colleges of Education of New Mexico State University and the University of New Mexico joined forces and spoke with one very determined voice against proposals made by the New Mexico Department of Education (NMDE) to broaden teacher licensure requirements. The department of education felt that licensure requirements were so restrictive that New Mexico's small independent school districts had difficulty staffing their classes with qualified, licensed teachers. The problem was at once simple and complex: small districts had trouble hiring and retaining qualified teachers, so they found it necessary to rely on local townspeople who could get emergency, temporary licenses; this practice took those districts out of compliance with NMDE regulations concerning licensed teachers.

New Mexico's association of school superintendents petitioned the NMDE for relief, and the NMDE's solution was to make licensing requirements so broad that nearly anyone with a college degree could get certified to teach almost anything the local school district needed. One example comes to mind. A person with a BS in economics awarded through New Mexico State University's College of Business Administration and Economics applied for a teaching license. Economics is listed as one of the social sciences on the NMDE's list of certification areas, so this person was licensed to teach history, which is also one of the social sciences on the NMDE list. The problem was that the person had never had a history course in his college career, or a course in government, or a course in any of the other social sciences, save economics, and he did not have any of the professional education courses required for licensure. Out of sheer necessity, then, faculty members in competing colleges (Arts and Sciences, Education) and in competing universities (New Mexico State University, the University of New Mexico) banded together and developed a set of courses that were then fought through the approvals necessary for adoption by the NMDE.

The job of those of us involved with secondary school English education is to prepare students to enter the English classroom in such towns as Cimarron (population 600), Las Cruces (population 80,000) and Albuquerque (population 450,000); that job is probably very similar to what is required of every other teacher education program in America. But where we in New Mexico may part company with others is that by mandate, negotiated with the NMDE as outlined above, we have to prepare each language arts teacher to enter either the middle school (grades 6–8) or high school (grades 9–12) classroom and do any or all of these things: teach literature; teach composition, from remedial through advanced; teach creative writing and produce a literary magazine; teach journalism and produce a school newspaper; teach debate and sponsor debate teams; direct the junior or senior play(s). Ideally, each school district should be able to hire five or six teachers to fulfill these varied duties. Economics dictate otherwise. New Mexico does not compare well to most states in per capita expenditure on pupils or in teacher salaries. While large districts in the state can actually hire teachers who are specialized in their training, smaller districts cannot. So our charge has been to prepare teachers for whatever they may confront on entering the classroom, whether in Albuquerque, Las Cruces, or Cimarron. The impact of NMDE mandates on our language arts education program? We have a program that is a collage, providing a little something for everybody. That collagelike nature accounts for the title of this essay: we have a program that is like the horse designed by committee; we have a camel.

New Mexico State University

New Mexico State University presents its faculty and staff with a number of constraints that we try to encounter as opportunities. Located in Las Cruces, the second largest city in New Mexico, the university serves a broad range of constituents, many of whom come from largely rural areas, many of whom do not count English as their first or even second language. We are forty miles north of El Paso, Texas, which has a population of 650,000, and its immediate neighbor, Ciudad Juarez, a city in Mexico of some 750,000. Such borderland issues as NAFTA and the *maquila* industry (international manufacturing efforts on the border) are topics of considerable interest to us. Surrounding public school districts, which send us a fair number of students, have large minority enrollments. Las Cruces public schools, for example, have a minority enrollment of 62 percent; Gadsden schools, situated on the border between New Mexico and Texas, have a minority enrollment approaching 95 percent.

Our university enrolls a total of 16,500 students, 40 percent of whom are minority. Many of these are first-generation students. That is, they are the first of their family to attend a university, and graduation ceremonies are true celebrations of their accomplishments. There is an inordinate sense of pride evident as these students walk across the stage to receive their diploma.

As a state-supported, land-grant school, New Mexico State University works to fulfill a tripartite mission: to serve the educational needs of a student body of various ages, interests, and cultural backgrounds; to be continuously involved in basic and applied research, creative endeavors that enhance the quality of life, and all other activities that involve the extension, application, or dissemination of knowledge; and to provide specialized assistance and information to the state and general public where unique resources exist within the institution to do so.

Part of the service orientation that characterizes many programs at NMSU involves the preparation of teachers. Prospective teachers fulfill licensure requirements primarily by taking course work in the College of Education and in the College of Arts and Sciences, eventually earning a BS in education. Those seeking preparation to teach secondary school language arts take from the College of Education a major in secondary school English education, while the majority of the courses they take in the content field of language arts is offered by the Department of English, in the College of Arts and Sciences.

Thus NMSU students who wish to become teachers must bridge not only two departments but also two colleges. Earning a degree from the College of Education while taking content-area classes in the Department of English, they must correlate two very different visions of the profession of English. The students themselves must create connections between departments that do not share faculty members, curricula, training, goals, or philosophy. In short, the secondary school English education degree forces students to create connections where few exist. This split vision of secondary school English education students—do they see themselves as education or English students or somehow both?—could easily be considered a weakness in our program. When starting to review our teacher training program for the MLA project, we hoped to turn this weakness into a strength, building on the connections we were asking our students to make for us. A healthy first step here involves the Department of English and the Department of Curriculum and Instruction (in the College of Education) consciously working to develop a better talking relationship, one that would be marked by more frequent discussion of the matters detailed in this essay.

Department of English

The English department has long viewed itself as one of the mainstays in the humanities at NMSU; indeed, it is the flagship department of the humanities. We see ourselves as a department with a broad range of responsibilities, including the preparation of future teachers, though most of our faculty members think our primary purpose is to provide a coherent set of courses for our majors, our secondary purpose to provide service writing courses for the entire university community, and only then to provide courses for English education majors. This view is one that is probably held by most if not all English departments in American universities. But it is a view that creates tensions as we work to educate secondary school

English education majors, because it seems that English faculty members have assumed that the needs of these students are the same as those of English majors whose plans may include graduate study in literature or creative writing but usually do not include teaching in public schools.

The English department is among NMSU's largest, generating the second largest number of student credit hours in the university. English faculty members are committed to quality instruction, and the department has earned the reputation as being one of NMSU's best teaching departments. Our teaching tends to be dynamic and student-centered; that is, we try to involve students in as much give-and-take discussion and debate as possible, both in class and in individual conferences outside class, and every class we teach is writing-intensive. That we can do this derives, in part, from class size: the largest literature classes (sophomore- and junior-level surveys) we offer enroll a maximum of 36 students, while our largest writing class (first-year composition) enrolls a maximum of 25.

The English department has approximately 140 undergraduate majors and an additional 140 graduate majors. Undergraduate majors take a 42-credit-hour major program (described below), while graduate students enroll in one of four master's programs—American and English literature, creative writing, rhetoric and the teaching of writing, or technical and professional communication—or in our doctoral program in rhetoric and professional communication. Finally, we offer three 18-hour undergraduate minors: English (a literature-based minor), creative writing, and professional writing. In addition, our teaching responsibilities include two writing courses required of all undergraduates. Clearly, our faculty members are at work in a number of arenas, so many that they are spread entirely too thin. Teaching is accomplished by a three-tiered faculty, which is one kind of constraint.

TENURE-TRACK FACULTY MEMBERS

We currently have 25 tenure-track faculty members in 24 lines. (Several years ago, we hired a couple to fill one fiction-writing position, with each person listed in the department's budget as 0.5 FTE.) Our tenure-track faculty had modest growth over the last two years, in that a proposal to increase its number was accepted by the administration. Continued growth is in doubt at present, however; NMSU's president decreed a hiring freeze, and we did in fact lose a poetry line following review of our request to fill that line.

Tenure-track faculty members embrace a range of specialties, for example, medieval studies, twentieth-century literature and criticism, feminist studies, rhetoric, fiction writing, poetry writing, and technical and professional communication. Each holds a terminal degree, whether the PhD or the MFA. A number of our faculty members have national reputations as scholars and writers, and several have held national offices in professional organizations. We sponsor many extracurricular activities: the Southwest High School Creative Writing Awards Program, now in its thirty-eighth year; *El Ojito,* our undergraduate literary magazine; La Sociedad para Las Artes, a reading series that brings writers of local, regional, and national stature to campus; *Puerto del Sol,* a nationally recognized literary magazine; the New Mexico State Writing Project, a National Writing Project affiliate site; and the *New Mexico English Journal,* the journal of the New Mexico Council of Teachers of English. In short, we see ourselves as a dynamic entity, one marked by considerable energy and enthusiasm for professional interests, but especially for those that involve our students, as each of the extracurricular activities listed above does.

Tenure-track faculty members primarily teach courses for our majors; that is, there are very few tenure-track faculty members who regularly teach first-year and sophomore writing courses and such junior-level literature courses as Literature for Children and Adolescents or Southwestern Literature, although we offer several sections of these courses each semester and although the children's literature course is required for many education majors. But this situation is necessary, for our tenure-track faculty is simply not large enough to do more than offer the courses required for both our undergraduate and graduate major programs. Each of us teaches a 3/3 load; each is required to engage in research and publication; and each works on various departmental, college, and university committees. Finally, two of our tenure-track faculty members handle the pedagogical courses (three senior-level courses, one in teaching writing, one in teaching literature, and one in grammar) offered by the department for English education majors, but neither of these two is dedicated to teacher preparation full-time.

COLLEGE FACULTY MEMBERS

We employ ten college faculty members, which is NMSU's designation for non-tenure-track faculty. These teachers hold regular positions; that is, they are eligible for benefits and are employed to teach twelve hours each semester. While they may serve on departmental committees, they are not required to conduct research and publish. They hold an MA and have as their primary teaching responsibility required sophomore- and junior-level writing courses as well as the children's literature and southwestern literature courses noted above.

GRADUATE ASSISTANTS

We employ about seventy-five graduate assistants each semester; their responsibilities include teaching one section of a required writing course and then fulfilling four to eight contact hours per week in such capacities as tutoring in our writing center or serving on the editorial staff of one of our three creative writing publications. Our cadre of graduate assistants is far and away the largest for any department at NMSU, and we employ them out of necessity. Our ability to staff courses for our various emphases in English would be diminished severely were we to require tenure-track faculty members to teach such courses as first-year composition. And so we have developed an extensive graduate program for a department our size, which has further removed tenure-track faculty members from required writing courses.

FACULTY CONSTRAINTS

Because of the breadth of our major teaching responsibilities — our undergraduate, master's, and doctoral major programs; our three undergraduate minors; our commitment to staff the required writing courses — we are under considerable stress to get everything done, which includes providing course work for English education majors. That we can dedicate only .50 FTE tenure-track faculty members to English courses designed specifically for English education majors adds to the stress.

Curricular Constraints

THE ENGLISH MAJOR

Our English curriculum is not entirely traditional. That is, we offer a variety of courses, some that are mainstream or canonical (e.g., courses specifically in Chaucer, Milton, Shakespeare), others that allow students to study a revised and emerging canon. The English major comprises 42 credit hours (14 courses at 3 semester hours each) beyond first-year composition, and it offers a blend of required and elective courses. Students have the latitude to select courses within certain parameters and in consultation with our undergraduate adviser. For example, the major requires 6 senior-level courses: 1 in American literature, 1 in either Chaucer or Milton, 1 in Shakespeare, and 3 additional courses, which may be fiction or poetry workshops, courses in rhetoric or technical communication, or additional course work in literature. The purpose of such parameters is to ensure that students enroll in a range of core courses but also have the opportunity to individualize their undergraduate curriculum, insofar as possible. The same opportunity is available at both the sophomore and junior levels. The only courses that all English majors take in common are Writing about Literature (English 301) and Practical Criticism (English 302).

THE SECONDARY SCHOOL ENGLISH EDUCATION MAJOR

In addressing revised requirements for teacher licensure in language arts, the New Mexico Department of Education relied on a set of competencies developed by the National Council of Teachers of English for students seeking language arts certification, and our job was to develop what we felt would be a coherent program of study that would also meet these competencies. This we did, adding an additional competency so that students could develop an ancillary interest if they wished to. Currently, our requirements for students taking a secondary school language arts certification exceed NMDE requirements. Our language arts broad-field endorsement area comprises 42 credit hours of courses in English, journalism, theater, or communication studies, while the NMDE requires only 24 credit hours in language arts for licensure. In addition, all education majors in the state of New Mexico take a 55-credit-hour core of general education courses. As part of curricular reform in the late 1980s, the New Mexico legislature mandated changes in the state's teacher-training programs, requiring a core of courses designed to broaden the liberal arts background of future teachers—courses in English, sciences, mathematics, history, and so on. Following the approval of the curricula submitted by the faculty at the various institutions involved, the changes in both general education requirements and broad-field licensure requirements were implemented, and the present structure of teacher education in New Mexico was established.

In sum, then, students majoring in secondary school English education at New Mexico State take 136 hours, distributed as follows, to earn a BS in education: general education courses, 55 hours; professional education courses (including student teaching), 39 hours; language arts courses, 42 hours. Of the 42 hours in language arts, 36 are taken in common; the remaining 6 taken as "required electives" are designed to give the student more background in one of the four areas defined by the NMDE as constituting the field of language arts—English, communication studies (formerly speech), journalism and mass communications, and theater arts.

The first 36 hours of course work are required in 4 departments: English (8 courses, 24 hours), communication studies (2 courses, 6 hours), journalism (1 course, 3 hours), and theater arts (1 course, 3 hours). Of the English courses listed in this section, only 5 are literature courses; the remaining 4 are pedagogically-oriented courses, including the teaching of composition and of literature. The next 6 hours offer options, enabling students to gain a slightly broader or deeper experience in language arts courses, depending on their selection. For example, students electing to broaden their experience in theater could take theater arts courses in preparation to teach theater or drama in addition to English. Students wishing to strengthen their qualifications to supervise a high school newspaper or yearbook could devote the 6 additional hours to journalism courses, while students wishing to prepare to supervise debate activities could take communication studies courses. Students wishing to add depth to their literature background could take more senior-level literature courses.

ENGLISH VERSUS ENGLISH EDUCATION: A STUDY IN TENSIONS

Setting the English education requirements against those for the English major reveals a discrepancy of 12 hours, or 4 courses. That is, given the NMDE-accepted requirements, a secondary school English major may take as few as 8 courses in English (not counting first-year composition and another writing course required by the university's general education program), whereas the English major will take 14 courses in English (again, not counting the 2 university-required writing courses). A more serious discrepancy is evident when we consider that of the 8 English courses a secondary school English major will take, only 5 will be in literature. We have questioned whether these education majors leave our program with a background in literature comprehensive enough to support their teaching adequately, and we have decided that they do not. We are constrained by NMDE requirements; we are also convinced that these requirements are so limiting that they work against quality teaching in the public school language arts classroom. Teachers need a substantial grounding in the content of their subject area to support their work in the classroom. For the English teacher, that content involves literature and writing, and although our English education students leave our program with sufficient course work in writing and the teaching of writing, their grounding in literature is not sufficient.

A second tension derives from the kinds of courses English majors take as requirements that English education majors do not. In their 42-hour program, English majors take a minimum of 27 hours (9 courses) in literature and may elect an additional 15 hours (5 courses) in literature, which many do. As noted above, English education majors take far fewer courses in literature than do their English major counterparts. But the biggest problem noted by English faculty members primarily responsible for literature offerings was that English education students were not well prepared to read, discuss, and write about literature. In the late 1980s, the English major was amended to require 2 junior-level courses in literary criticism—Writing about Literature, Practical Criticism—and students are now required to take them before enrolling in any senior-level literature course. The goal of this requirement is to provide them with the skills necessary to analyze literature and to write papers discussing that analysis in the kind of depth we expect of senior literature students. After these courses were offered enough times so that all English majors enrolled in senior literature courses had taken them, some English faculty members expressed concern that English education majors were not writing well—not from any deficiency in writing ability but because they had not had the course work that English faculty members deemed foundational. By not requiring these courses of secondary school English majors, we felt we were privileging English majors. We wanted to ensure that all students in those senior-level literature courses were on an equal footing.

A third curricular constraint involves the question of whether the purpose of the English major is truly compatible with the needs of education majors. Like many English majors, ours is designed primarily to teach students how to read and write about literature on increasingly sophisticated levels. So far, so good—public schools teachers obviously need to know how to read and respond to books. The tension here comes from our teaching students who are moving toward graduate study in English rather than students who will have five or six classes of, say, eighth-graders with widely varying levels of reading, writing, and thinking abilities. Our literature classes are not aimed specifically at supporting education majors in their future work as public school teachers but instead seem designed to maintain the English profession's dedication to literary criticism and to point students toward graduate school, despite the fact that most English majors do not continue with graduate study. To what extent should courses designed to satisfy major requirements in English take into account a nonmajor clientele? To what extent should assignments in English courses be shaped to prepare education majors for the public school classrooms they will eventually enter? To what extent should educational theory and methods courses provide specific instruction to help students apply course work in English to the public schools classroom? To what extent should English faculty members model specific teaching approaches that education majors can adapt to their teaching of those eighth-graders? These questions were raised when we reviewed our program for this MLA project; they remain unanswered and largely undiscussed. Yet they must be answered, must be addressed, if we are to work to provide as comprehensive and responsive a secondary school English major as possible.

Toward a New Curriculum in Secondary School English Education

CURRICULAR CHANGES

When our team met to discuss the various issues involved with teacher education at New Mexico State University, we agreed that a revision of current requirements was in order. Our discussions were at times spirited and included consideration of advice offered by a number of local secondary school English teachers. When asked what English education majors needed to strengthen their background for teaching, practicing teachers said most frequently that it was more work in literature and writing and less in professional education courses. At the same time, they saw a need for course work in education dealing with issues and practice in teaching secondary school reading. Education course work is so tightly prescribed that little change can be effected there. But we felt we had a bit more latitude in changing the course work required of students in language arts. We will recommend a new set of course requirements that strengthen students' background in literature but at the same time keep open options for courses in the other language arts disciplines.

Under our current requirements, English education majors may take a minimum of 8 courses in English, and only 5 of them need be in literature. Our recommended program stipulates 12 courses, 9 in literature and 3 in methodology—teaching literature, teaching composition, and grammar. The additional 4 courses this new requirement represents increases not only the number of hours required but, more important, also the range of courses students will take, thus strengthening their background in literature. Further, we would require that English education students take English 301 (Writing about Literature) and English 302 (Practical Criticism), which should make them better literature students—better equipped to read, discuss, and write about literature.

To address both the spirit and letter of the NMDE mandate that language arts students be prepared broadly, we will also recommend that students be allowed to elect 6 hours either in communication studies, journalism, or theater arts courses. This new requirement would fulfill the in-depth competency requirement of the current degree structure, but it would mark a change, in that English courses would be deleted as an option—they would already be required in the new major core.

CLUSTERED COURSES AND FIELD EXPERIENCE

In addition to proposing a revised set of language arts courses, we propose a cluster component for the secondary school English teacher education program that will include a semester-long field experience with a professional development teacher, a public school teacher who volunteers to mentor a team of future teachers. This teacher will enable future teachers to interact with secondary school students and will provide practical insights to assist them in their professional growth. While the science of teaching can be addressed at the university, the art of teaching is developed through an apprenticeship with classroom teachers in real-world situations. A team of two or three NMSU secondary school English students will spend three hours per week in a public school classroom actually working with secondary school students, preparing and implementing lessons, working with individuals and small groups, assisting with authentic assessments, and supporting the classroom teacher. These college students will be supervised in the field by faculty members from the Department of English and the Department of Curriculum and Instruction.

These supervisory faculty members will also be involved in clustered courses, so that secondary school English majors are immersed in related methods courses during given semesters. We propose these clusters:

FALL SEMESTER
English 470 (Approaches to Composition)
Reading 356 (Reading in the Content Fields)
Education 460 (Secondary English Methods)

SPRING SEMESTER
English 416 (Approaches to Literature)
English 451 (Practicum in Grammar)
Reading 356 (Reading in the Content Fields)

Our goal is to enroll the same students in the three courses at a time listed above for each semester, so that they take them as a block and so that the courses support their field experience. Students enrolled in this cluster-and-field-experience component should be able to make the obvious connections between the classroom and course work in English and education. (Note that Reading 356 is listed twice. It is a course required of all education majors and so needs to be offered in both semesters to meet student demand. Our recommendation will be that secondary school English education majors take this course during their first semester in the block sequence.)

CONTACT WITH LOCAL TEACHERS

We will continue having discussions and meetings with local public school teachers. In our meetings with them, we found a real need for these meetings, because public school teachers do not often have the opportunity to meet and talk with one another. We found great interest among them in building a stronger sense of community and in articulating teacher expectations and goals for their students and for their language arts programs. We plan to meet at least once a semester and will also use follow-up meetings of past participants in the New Mexico State Writing Project as a forum for discussion. Although sponsored by the writing project, these meetings will be advertised through the public schools and be open to all who wish to participate.

Questions in Search of Answers

As we considered the shape of our program in secondary school English education, our committee members developed several questions worthy of consideration. We offer them by way of closing, not so much to provide answers as to foster discussion about the nature and purpose of an English education program and its relation to an English program.

Whom do we serve? For whom are our English courses geared? For whom should they be geared?

How are the purposes of an English program and an English education program different? Which differences can be reconciled? How? Which cannot be reconciled? Why not?

What is the shape of the ideal English education program? What is it that future teachers should know? What kinds of experiences should they have as part of their preparation to enter the secondary school classroom?

What are the characteristics of the student population our future teachers will teach? How well does our curriculum relate to their needs and interests?

Should the English curriculum for English education majors differ from that for English majors? If so, why? And how?

In what ways beyond student-teaching supervision can public school teachers take a greater part in professional development and training for future language arts teachers?

What are some authentic assessment strategies, in addition to portfolios, for English education majors in field experiences and student teaching?

What methodologies, beyond lecture and written response, can be used in university English classes as models for English education majors?

While we have only begun to consider these questions, we think they are important, because they promise to open dialogue among colleagues and departments that often do not engage in such discussion and debate. That dialogue is fraught with possibility, for by responding to the questions we just may discover ways around current constraints, ways to resolve the tensions that now mark our efforts at teacher preparation. And our camel may become less a camel and more a horse.

Postscript

We have undertaken several of the activities outlined in the planning section of our essay. First, a committee has been formed in the Department of English to study the English portion of our secondary school English education curriculum and recommend changes. When this committee submits its report to the department, we will discuss it and then submit it to our colleagues in the College of Education for their review and comment. Second, we admitted three students to our new MA track in English that will lead to teaching licensure for its graduates. This program was initiated after discussion with our colleagues in the College of Education, because a third of the student's course work will be taken in that college.

Other activities have occurred that show growing commitment to teacher preparation. In 1997, the Department of English hired two new faculty members with specialties in literacy and composition. One of these, Amanda Cobb, serves as chair of the curriculum committee, and the other, Rebecca Jackson, serves as the department's writing-center director. Both these faculty members work with courses in the teaching of writing.

In 1998, the New Mexico Council of Teachers of English instituted an award for excellence in student teaching. The council has asked faculty members who supervise student teachers in the language arts to nominate students for this award. The first award was made at the council's 1998 annual conference in October.

Finally, following the hiring of a new president, the hiring freeze has been lifted, and we are seeing tenure-track lines restored. We now have 25 tenure-track lines in the English department, and we hired a poet in 1998. We anticipate receiving at least one more new line within the next two academic years, so the hiring situation now seems stable.

Bill Bridges, *Department of English, New Mexico State University, Las Cruces*

Reed Way Dasenbrock, *Department of English, New Mexico State University, Las Cruces*

Mark Dressman, *Department of Curriculum and Instruction, New Mexico State University, Las Cruces*

Sherry T. Hulsey, *Oñate High School*

Thelma A. Kibler, *Department of Curriculum and Instruction, New Mexico State University, Las Cruces*

Cheryl Nixon, *Department of English, New Mexico State University, Las Cruces*

NORFOLK STATE UNIVERSITY

Preparing Secondary School English Teachers

In this report we present an overview of Norfolk State University and of the role and scope of its English department and the secondary school English program. We describe the work of the university-MLA team and some of the key issues that undergird the team's proposed program. We conclude with a description of the team's proposed exemplary program for preparing secondary school teachers of English.

Norfolk State University, a comprehensive urban university with an enrollment of more than 8,700 students, is the nation's fifth largest historically black college or university. As a state-supported institution, it receives twenty-seven percent of its funding from state allocations. Other funding, at seventy-three percent, comes from tuition and fees, grants and contracts, auxiliary enterprises, and other sources.

From its inception in 1935, the university has maintained a historical mission of providing educational opportunity to students who, because of social, educational, or economic disadvantage, have not had ready access to such opportunity. The university also promises delivery of a quality education to all its students and affirms expectations of achievement and productivity by its students and graduates. Additionally, the mission provides for the expansion of educational opportunity into areas where the student population has been underrepresented, and for service to the community in areas of expertise available at the university.

The department's mission, in consonance with the university's mission, aims to provide a high-quality education that will equip student majors and nonmajors with effective communication and critical thinking skills, aesthetic appreciation, multicultural understanding, and knowledge and skills of the discipline of English language and literature sufficient to prepare them for graduate study and a variety of language-based services and careers, including teaching.

The model of the secondary school English educators that we at Norfolk State University have derived from our university and departmental missions and from the conceptual framework of our teacher education program is that of creative and continuously developing professionals who have a strong knowledge base in the discipline; pedagogical skill and variety of instructional approach; oral and written language fluency; sensitivity to cultural, linguistic, and values differences; commitment to the inclusion of diversity in the canon; and a passion for promoting their students' and their own lifelong engagement with language and literature. This model, intended to produce the "caring, competent, cooperative, and creative" novice teacher-educators that the School of Education endorses, is the goal of the Norfolk State University teacher education program in secondary school English (Norfolk State University 8).

The Department of English offers two degrees, a bachelor of arts in English and a master of arts in communication. For the bachelor of arts, the following emphases are offered: elementary school education, secondary school education, speech communication, theater, African American literature, speech pathology and audiology, Spanish literature, and French literature. The last three concentrations are recent additions resulting from the university's restructuring efforts in response to state productivity guidelines. The master's degree in communication has concentrations in speech communication, language studies, public relations, intercultural communication, and rhetoric and composition.

For the 1995–96 academic year, the department had 42 full-time faculty members and 8 to 12 adjunct faculty members. Of the full-time faculty members, 40 served in the English area of the department and two served in foreign languages; 8 to 9 adjunct faculty members served in the English area and 3 in foreign languages. The department has no teaching assistants.

During the fall semester of 1995, the department served 8,272 students in 7 general education English courses: Communication Skills 1, Communication Skills 2, Techniques of Vocabulary Building, Advanced

Communication Skills, Introduction to World Literature, Professional and Technical Writing, and Principles of Speech. During the 1995–96 academic year, 178 students matriculated as English majors; 65 of these (37%) registered in the secondary school English teaching concentration.

The department has maintained a stable faculty with a core of seasoned teachers and a cadre of developing professionals. This faculty is characterized by diversity of race, ethnicity, geography, age, and scholarly specialization and interest. Although the number of the faculty has remained constant, general education enrollment in the department has declined, while the number of majors has gradually increased. For example, the number of full-time faculty members has averaged 42 over the past five years, and the number of part-time faculty members has consistently ranged between 8 and 12, depending on need. General education enrollments in the department have declined from 12,881 in fall 1992 to 8,272 in fall 1995. This decline can be explained by the university's reduction of general education requirements in response to the state's restructuring mandate to reduce total required credit hours in order to reduce time to graduation. As a result, the department's 15-hour share of the 51-hour general education core in 1992 was reduced to 9 hours in the restructured 42-hour core in 1995.

At 178, the department's 1995–96 enrollment of English majors is the highest in the five-year period since 1991–92. This number reflects the department's continuing dynamic growth and the appeal and viability of the English major, despite the tepid job market for liberal arts majors in general and the English major in particular. Interestingly, though, there has been a shift within the major from a majority who pursued the straight liberal arts degree in 1991–92 (42%) to the majority who chose the secondary school teaching concentration in 1995–96 (37%). The greater availability of jobs in secondary school teaching, as contrasted with the relatively stagnant market on the collegiate level and the corresponding decline in graduate fellowships, in large part explains this change in trend.

A mutually reinforcing partnership has long existed between the Department of English and the School of Education in the training of secondary school teachers of English. Although the two units have some discrete responsibilities—the English department is responsible for curriculum and instruction in the content and skills of the discipline; the School of Education is responsible for providing courses and instruction in the professional curriculum—cooperation between them exists at every level throughout the program. Dual advisers from English and education are provided to students from the time of their admission to teacher education through program completion. Both the English department and the School of Education participate in the assessment of students during their admission to the teacher education process, and both units jointly supervise the students' field experiences. In addition, the English department and the Education school provide both separate and joint on-campus seminars for prospective teachers during their practicum experiences. The School of Education also keeps the department informed of state curricular and certification requirements.

The Center for Professional Laboratory Experience through the Office of Student Teaching maintains chief responsibility for assignment and placement of prospective teachers to one of several local school divisions and to one or more cooperating teachers. The program is divided into two eight-week teaching periods, to provide experiences at different school sites. These experiences are scheduled during the student's senior year, typically the second semester. The student's responsibility is viewed broadly and may include not only the role of a teacher in a classroom setting but also civic, community, and related school activities. The program involves continuous supervision and direction, since the directed-teaching component is viewed as a joint venture of cooperating secondary school and university personnel.

As a national leader in the production of African American teachers and of a large number of white teachers as well, Norfolk State University has demonstrated a history of commitment to teaching, both in the practice of our own faculty members and in the preparation provided to our students intending to teach. Because teaching has been one of the few professions that have historically been open to African Americans and because of the value placed on teaching and education for the liberation and advancement of the African American community, teaching has enjoyed a respect and support at Norfolk State University that may not be typical of institutions deriving from different cultural histories. The School of Education at NSU is the university unit charged with the responsibility for providing leadership, coordination, and evaluation of all preservice and in-service programs for the preparation of teachers and other professional school personnel. The professional-development phase of the directed-teaching component was initiated in 1965, and the preparation of secondary school English teachers began in that year.

While all faculty members in the English department may at some point teach secondary school English majors, since their degree is in liberal arts, three normally teach the English-specific core teacher-preparation courses, while four education faculty members teach the education-specific core. The areas of specialization of the three English faculty members are rhetoric and writing, literature for children and young adults, and literary criticism and theory; for the education faculty members the areas of specialization are curriculum and instruction, guidance and counseling, educational psychology, and educational assessment and evaluation.

The potential for school improvement through the national and state reform movements has generated considerable discussion among faculty members and students. We have given more careful attention to program reviews, assessment activities, and student follow-up. Further, we have increased our role in initiating new partnerships with K–12 educators. Evaluations of the true effect of the reform movements are yet to be designed. Faculty members from our department will be available to work with other university and school personnel in determining the success of various reform efforts.

The university, in response to state mandates for greater accountability, has redesigned its retention and recruitment programs. In the department, faculty advising of majors is measured: faculty members are required to report at four yearly intervals or cycles the number of students advised, the number retained from cycle to cycle, and any problems, academic or otherwise, impacting retention. This accountability initiative has also encouraged more creative use of space (e.g., the installation of laboratory features — computers, conference corners, etc. — into some classrooms to enhance both in-class and after-class student use) and technology-assisted teaching to improve effectiveness. The trend is "to do more with less," but the department knows that time will be the only judge of the results of financially-based accountability. Meanwhile, accountability for student satisfaction, student performance levels, and student marketability upon graduation forms a primary focus in departmental policies.

Preparing the NSU Preservice Teacher for the Secondary School English Classroom

At NSU there is a slogan — Where Dreams Become Reality — that refuses to go away. Despite repeated efforts to replace it with a newer slogan, it just keeps popping up in publication after publication. There must be a reason for the immortality of that slogan, and the reason is clear to anyone acquainted with our tradition: the slogan defines the spirit of the university and captures its commitment to its mission. For turning dreams into reality is what we do daily at Norfolk State. Our participation in the MLA Teacher Education Project has provided us with another opportunity to dream: to conceive and visualize our desired program for preparing secondary school English teachers. The conversion of that dream into reality will be for us an ongoing process.

Having shared in the university's long and successful history of preparing teachers, the English and foreign languages department welcomed the chance in 1994 to apply for participation in the MLA project. We wanted to be involved because this was an opportunity to take concrete steps not only to enlarge the university's national stature in teacher education but also to enhance significantly our departmental program in secondary school English teacher preparation. Given current and projected realities in secondary schools (the increase in minority populations, the decrease in test scores and basic academic skills, the decrease in minority teachers, the increase in violence, the proliferation of technology, negative influences of popular culture, etc.), we consider the mission to train future teachers a moral imperative.

From the beginning of our participation in the project, the NSU team took seriously its responsibility to study our current program, keep our faculty members informed of and involved in our activity, and begin to envision an enhanced or exemplary program suitable for the university's needs and goals. The team set about on a rigorous schedule of team and faculty meetings, information-gathering activities, and report preparation. Meeting an average of every two weeks for two to three hours, at a conference table as well as by telephone and chance encounters in halls and offices, the team had ample opportunity for spirited and fruitful discussions; it examined our current program, pinpointed areas where strengthening was indicated, and tried to reach consensus on how best to improve weak areas or incorporate new and needed features. Reaching consensus was not always possible (perhaps not even desirable), but the exercise was valuable, helping us as individuals and as a group to clarify our perceptions, philosophies, and rationales for the various program components that we considered.

A review of program goals and assumptions in the light of the university and departmental missions was a key initial activity, for these missions, together with our position on basic intellectual, philosophical, and practical issues, shaped the program we envisioned for students and graduates of our secondary school English preparation program.

The following were the goals we agreed upon:

1. To provide a curriculum and instruction that arm prospective teachers of secondary school English with the traditional matter of the discipline and the specialized components appropriate to the secondary school curriculum
2. To provide theory and models of classroom practice that effectively facilitate learning
3. To foster appreciation of and sensitivity to diversity through exposure to culturally diverse literature and language
4. To provide academic experiences and academic support services that help prospective teachers master and model excellent oral and writing skills
5. To promote the reading habit for lifelong learning and preparation for change
6. To provide training and experience necessary for enabling prospective teachers to make effective use of technology in the classroom
7. To continue and to enhance the cooperative relationship between the Department of English and the School of Education for effective coordination of academic and professional preparation
8. To cultivate an ongoing partnership among the Department of English, the School of Education, and area secondary school teachers for the effective training of secondary school English teachers
9. To facilitate the transition between college preparation and on-the-job experience in the secondary school classroom through the integration of field experiences into the early and ongoing curricular experiences of prospective secondary school teachers
10. To prepare prospective teachers of English for ongoing scholarship, professional activity, creativity, sensitivity, and enthusiastic commitment to teaching and learning

These goals were guided by the following underlying assumptions:

1. That there is value in the traditional literary canon
2. That diversity is also an important value and must be reflected in the curriculum of those who plan to teach
3. That the African American perspective is not only a defining element of our majority student population, both historically and contempo-

raneously, but also an important if underrepresented perspective in the traditional English curriculum

4. That standards for admitting works to the canon must be under continuous review to ensure inclusion and quality
5. That learning is facilitated by active involvement
6. That students tend to model practices that are modeled to them
7. That it is important to cultivate reading as both a professional and a personal habit
8. That a cooperative partnership among the Department of English, the School of Education, and area secondary school teachers is vital for the effective training of secondary school English teachers
9. That technological literacy and use are requisite for teachers of the future
10. That integration of subject matter and skills within and between disciplines promotes learning, retention, and a useful lifelong approach to learning
11. That the literature and learning styles of young adults are important elements in the curriculum of secondary school English teachers
12. That mastery of the matter and methods of the discipline by students preparing to teach secondary school English is the best way to ensure the establishment and maintenance of standards of excellence in the schools
13. That early and continuing field experience for the English major enhances the preparation and transition of the secondary school English teacher
14. That a learning environment that is nurturing and encouraging but provides for and demands quality performance is most desirable for a secondary school English preparation program

Our baseline study, compiled during the first year of the project, was illuminating and valuable, for it confirmed many of our expectations, revealed areas that needed strengthening, and provided an objective basis for some of the elements of our proposed program. The exemplary program that we propose has several components, which we have grouped under four headings: (1) enhanced curricular and professional development, (2) enhanced teaching practices, (3) enhanced preparation for field experience, and (4) enhanced assessment of learning and program effectiveness. The proposed enhancements derive from a set of values and perspectives, reflected in our assumptions and goals, that we share as a university and as a department committed to our respective and mutually supportive missions.

"The foundation of every state is the education of its youth." So stated Diogenes in the fourth century BC, and his words still resonate with amazing relevance and urgency as we rapidly approach the twenty-first century. The urgency, we believe, is in the critical need for those of us who educate educators to discharge our awesome responsibility of providing an appropriate and effective educational program that will meet the needs of the students and the age and of preparing the cadre of new teachers to implement that program. John Goodlad observed in his book, *Teachers for Our Nation's Schools,* that "the education of teachers must be driven by a clear and careful conception of the educating we expect our schools to do [and] the conditions most conducive to this educating as well as the conditions that get in the way" (4–5).

Our reflections on three issues related to secondary school English teacher preparation clearly illustrate the kind of educating we want our schools to do and the conditions that most facilitate and impede that goal. These issues, among others, helped guide our thinking as we sought to determine the shape and substance of our enhanced teacher education program.

THE ISSUE OF THE MINORITY PRESENCE (AFRICAN AMERICAN AND OTHERS) OR ABSENCE IN THE TEACHING RANKS

Nationally, approximately twelve percent of the teaching force in public schools is minority, with approximately eight percent African American. But approximately thirty-three percent of students are minority. The forecast of increasing numbers of minority students and decreasing numbers of minority teachers is even more unsettling. What is the significance of these statistics? In a very real sense they may determine the educational and socioeconomic opportunities and achievements that a large number of American youth will or will not claim. If, as psychologists such as Erik Erikson believe, identity formation is a defining process that reaches crisis proportions during adolescence, the identity that is projected, perceived, molded, or confirmed in the classroom can reasonably be expected to affect both opportunities for learning and actual achievement. Goodlad, for example, notes the lessened opportunities for lower socioeconomic minority students to learn the "high-status subject matter required for success in college" (21) because of their systematic assignment to the lowest tracks. Erikson further argues that one's personal identity is bound to one's cultural identity. If either or both are not validated by the teacher and total school environment, the educational experience may fail to achieve its potential. Given the already dismal economic picture (and the prospect of that picture's worsening) for persons without high school diplomas or for low-skilled or low-achieving high school graduates, the consequences of this failure may be personally and socially catastrophic.

Thus while it is not assumed that only teachers that share the ethnic or cultural origins of minority students can provide the positive identity validations that increase the likelihood of educational success, the absence of such teachers might well have a negative influence. We have all heard the horror stories of African American students in predominantly white classroom and school environments being denied the opportunity to learn about the contributions of African American writers, scientists, artists, and other achievers during African American History Month or Martin Luther King Jr. Day because their teachers or their school refused to acknowledge these events as significant. We have all heard about teachers who denigrate the black dialect of their inner city students instead of finding in it an opportunity to celebrate diversity and learn about language differences. A representative presence of minority teachers in the secondary schools is essential to ensure the commitment to inclusion and cultural validation that is vital to the encouragement of learning for all children.

But minority teachers are needed not only for the personal and cultural validation of minority students, they are needed also to provide balanced and equitable educational opportunities for all students. Since teachers, like most other human beings, understand, interpret, and convey experiences through the prism of their backgrounds and experiences, nonminority teachers will often fail to understand or appreciate the lifestyles, cultures, values, experiences, points of view, and learning styles of minority students, whose backgrounds differ from theirs. This gap in understanding and accommodation creates learning inequities not only for minority students but for others as well: nonminority students, too, receive a false, incomplete, and unbalanced perspective of the curriculum and the world because of the teacher's inability to relate to the experiences and lifestyles of some of their students.

Thus both the minority presence and the minority perspective must be sufficiently represented in the teaching force. In our program for prospective secondary school English teachers, we take seriously the obligation to provide the presence by recruiting and training minority teachers—a concern that has been addressed by Elaine Witty ("Increasing," *Prospects*), Sabrina King, and others—and the perspective by building a knowledge base of, sensitivity to, and appreciation for the contributions of diverse cultures. The fulfillment of this need is critical to guarantee genuine and equitable learning opportunities for all children.

THE ISSUE OF CURRICULUM CONTENT

What should be included in a curriculum intended to prepare highly qualified teachers of English for today's and tomorrow's secondary school classrooms? Surely we make no attempt to answer this question in any ultimate sense on the universal, national, or even local level. Although we have come to agreement on some basic components, we have certainly not settled this question in all its details; we continue to debate specifics. But considering the question has forced us to contemplate the product we would like to see emerge from our program and what curriculum components we think will contribute to the realization of that goal. Any answer to the question of curriculum appropriateness must be program-specific, taking into account the needs and resources of the situation as well as particular program goals.

Of course, there are some broad outlines that most of us can readily accept. For example, our team agreed that our curriculum should contain the courses and instruction necessary to provide a substantive command of the literature and language of the discipline. But consensus about which literature and which language was not reached so easily. In view of our program goals "to arm students with the traditional matter of the discipline and the specialized components appropriate to the secondary school curriculum" and "to foster appreciation of and sensitivity to diversity through exposure to culturally diverse literature and language," we agreed that our canon must be inclusive. It must reflect both the diversity that we celebrate (and want our students to appreciate in their secondary school classrooms) and the tradition that we value. But we have not yet agreed on the specific works of traditional literature or the African American and other multicultural texts that should be included. For example, in an American literature survey course (from 1895 to the present) in which instructors are permitted a choice of readings beyond a required core, consensus was fairly easily reached on such writers as Mark Twain, Henry James, Robert Frost, T. S. Eliot, W. E. B. Du Bois, Langston Hughes, and Gwendolyn Brooks. There was no consensus, though, on whether to require Twain's *Huckleberry Finn* or instead permit instructors (or students) to choose from among Twain's less racially sensitive works. Also, while it was generally agreed that Frost is an important poet of the modern period, some instructors preferred Frost's darker "Out, Out—" and "Design" to the more familiar "Stopping by Woods" and "The Road Not

Taken." Du Bois's *Souls of Black Folks* was virtually unchallenged, but there was considerable debate about the relative literary, as opposed to sociological, value of Booker T. Washington's *Up from Slavery*. Instructors' choices beyond agreed-upon selections seem to reflect, among other things, instructors' and students' sociocultural sensibilities, adherence to a personal or group literary standard, a desire to expose students to a wider range of selections by traditional authors, and a desire to expand the range of ethnic texts. There is no agreement about which literature is most appropriate for secondary school students or about the extent to which, given state- or district-mandated curricula, teachers should be free to implement their choices.

THE ISSUE OF WHO HAS RESPONSIBILITY FOR PREPARING SECONDARY SCHOOL ENGLISH TEACHERS

Historically at Norfolk State University there has been tacit and operational agreement that the responsibility for training secondary school English teachers is jointly shared by the Department of English and the School of Education, the English department preparing teachers in the content of the discipline and the School of Education, in partnership with public schools, preparing them for professional education and experiences.

Because the arrangement has worked, and continues to work, so well, we did not feel the need to reexamine our underlying assumptions or practices. Our involvement in the MLA project, however, has afforded us an opportunity to rethink this issue. And because we do not subscribe to the "If it's not broken . . . " school of thought, we have been free to consider how even an unbroken system might possibly be strengthened. The project has caused us to give more thought to how the English department, in its teaching of discipline content, can reinforce the pedagogical focus emphasized in the School of Education. We all accept the need for our curriculum to retain a strong general education component, approaches to pedagogy, and professional knowledge components, but discussion still proceeds about how and by whom pedagogy should be taught, and the relative value, in a lean curriculum, of courses in professional knowledge versus courses in the discipline. We have long prided ourselves on being good teachers, and student and peer evaluations continue to confirm that perception, but are we modeling, to the extent that we should, the variety of teaching approaches and strategies for engaging students in learning that our students will need to guide the learning experiences of secondary school students? Shouldn't we raise pedagogy to a more conscious level and provide prospective teachers in our classes more opportunities, under our guidance, to practice the craft of their future profession? These are the questions that continue to engage our thinking.

Our consideration of who has responsibility for preparing secondary school English teachers has also heightened our awareness of the need to engage secondary school teachers more regularly and more actively in partnership with us in the preparation process. Common sense demands that we do this. Just as training programs for doctors, lawyers, accountants, and social workers require ongoing collaboration with practicing professionals, so should programs for preparing teachers—not only to ensure curriculum relevance and currency but also to maintain a vital reality check on the university training program.

These issues are just some of the philosophical and intellectual questions we have entertained and will continue to ponder as we seek to define the parameters of our enhanced secondary school English program.

Some Highlights of Program Elements

ENHANCEMENTS IN CURRICULUM AND PROFESSIONAL ACTIVITY

To our existing program, with an already strong traditional curriculum and a distinctive infusion of the African American perspective, we envision the addition of several other courses and curricular emphases—including courses in contemporary literature, young adult literature, multimedia technology, postcolonial literature, and total immersion minicourses (limited enrollment, single-focus, highly interactive courses offered in two-to-three-week concentrated sessions in which the topic under consideration provides the focus for all scheduled activity)—to address student needs and interests in research skills, creative expression, and grammar. In addition, we propose increased curricular emphases in areas that we think are crucial for our graduates' professional success. Although our baseline study indicated that faculty members regularly include oral language and writing experiences in their classes, it also indicated that these activities should be increased in frequency to provide more opportunities for students to practice and perfect skills and for instructors to intervene or provide follow-up response at appropriate times. Such intervention-response is particularly useful for students whose prior language experiences have not been in the communication styles characteristic of the professional world they are preparing to enter.

Because we hope that our students, graduates, and future teachers will become avid, independent, and wide-ranging readers of literature as well as of works of scholarship and social-political discourse, we propose increased required reading and the encouragement of elective reading, including extensive additional reading in African American (see appendix A) and in other minority literature. We know that our graduates will bear much of the responsibility for promoting African American and minority literature and cultural sensitivity in the secondary schools where they teach. Therefore, increased reading in this area serves a practical as well as motivational aim, for we believe that students' identification with literature will also encourage the reading habit and, together with active professional participation, develop a pattern for lifelong learning.

Lifelong learning is a necessity if our future teachers are to remain intellectually vibrant, professionally current, and instructionally effective. Our plan to encourage supplementary reading lists for all classes and the formation of reading-discussion groups among departmental majors aims to provide prospective teachers with many opportunities for formal and informal exploration of authors, works, and ideas that expand their knowledge of the discipline and the profession beyond the boundaries of particular course content. The department will promote reading-discussion groups also through its student majors' clubs and through the student majors' collaborative activities with the faculty Book Review Committee. Participation in such groups, although voluntary, will be encouraged by instructors through exhortation, through the incentives of extra credit in their classes in which participating students are enrolled, and most important, through the instructors' inspirational example of reading and sharing.

Patterns of lifelong learning are also developed by professional activity and an ongoing preservice and in-service program, both of which will be enhanced for our secondary school teachers.

ENHANCEMENTS IN TEACHING PRACTICES

In NSU's exemplary program for training secondary school teachers, we propose enhancements in at least three areas of teaching practice: (1) use of technology, (2) use of effective learning practices, and (3) faculty modeling of effective teaching practices. The intent of the third is to have instructors at every level become more conscious of their roles as teaching models, given the likelihood that students will imitate them when the students are student teachers and when they take regular positions in secondary school English classrooms. A plan to include practicing secondary school teachers in early and continuing mentoring relationships with our students is envisioned as an extension of the modeling process.

Learning theorists from John Dewey (*Democracy* and *Experience*) to

Jean Piaget (see Ginsburg and Opper) and much pedagogical literature (e.g., Bonwell and Eison) support the notion that learning is facilitated by the learner's active involvement with the subject. Much of the literature also supports the value of collaboration in the learning process. For these reasons we wish to enhance faculty use of collaborative activities and activities designed to get students meaningfully engaged with the content being taught. While a number of faculty members in the department already use collaborative and other activities—a variety of discussion, writing, presentation, and peer-editing activities; drama; interactive online drafting, revising, and editing—to engage students in learning, the use of these activities in some classrooms could be increased, and significantly increased in a few, especially those where the lecture and the lecturer tend to dominate. That said, we hasten to add the caveat that, while we are all aware of the limitations of the lecture method as the dominant or sole method of instruction, we are also aware of its benefits, appropriately used. Active, engaged learning is the goal; the means are varied.

As common sense, experience, and research repeatedly tell us, we learn more readily and with greater retention when we are able to see links or make connections among ideas, experiences, information, and events. Therefore, through our own teaching practice we want to expose our future secondary school teachers to techniques of creating learning links that optimize students' learning opportunities by enabling them to relate and connect ideas in meaningful and memorable ways. The creative juxtaposition of intra- and interdisciplinary subject matter and experiences and the use of intra- and interdisciplinary teaching teams are two ways we hope to achieve this goal.

An area of teaching practice that we intend to enhance significantly is the expanded use of technology for teaching and learning. This emphasis is dictated as much by current social, political, economic, and academic necessity as by the pedagogical efficacy of the computer. Given the dramatic and pervasive reach of technology into virtually all facets of contemporary American society and in much of the global community, no educational institution can afford not to prepare its students to negotiate the technology that drives the institutions and operations of our lives. Our prospective student teachers must be able not only to negotiate the technology for their own use but also to assess and use it to empower those they will teach. The potential for using computer, communications, and multimedia technology in the acquiring, generating, and publishing of information in myriads of ways for myriads of purposes is enormous. That technological competency is one of the five major strands of the Virginia

Standards for English Language Arts at all grade levels further attests to its importance in a curriculum for training secondary school English teachers.

ENHANCED PREPARATION IN PRACTICAL EXPERIENCE

One of the most practically beneficial ways in which we can enhance the preparation of our secondary school majors is through cooperative programs and field experiences that provide ongoing opportunities for students to interact with secondary school students and teachers in real classrooms and to confront issues that are important to the secondary school classroom and to the profession. To achieve these goals, our program will involve a triad partnership among the Department of English, the School of Education, and area secondary schools. We know that teaching and learning do not occur in a vacuum. A variety of social layers, such as the home, family, peers, neighborhood, public and private schools, the college community, and the larger culture surround the learners and the teachers. Therefore, teacher preparation as part of the educational system is influenced and shaped by changes in society and culture. To prepare our candidate teachers to teach effectively and sensitively in the conditions and context of the times, and for us also to visualize how these times will soon change, university-school cooperation is indispensable.

A day-long symposium, Beginning a University-Community Dialogue on the Preparation of Secondary English Teachers, held in spring 1996 with approximately sixty participants from the English department, the School of Education, and area secondary schools was an important step for our team in advancing this alliance. Symposium participants were preassigned to one of six groups formed to discuss questions raised by the team and considered to be issues of importance to everyone (see appendix B for the list of group questions). Each group had a designated discussion leader and a recorder-reporter and was given one of the questions to discuss in detail and to report on in the plenary session after lunch. All groups were also asked to discuss other questions, as time permitted, and to share their insights or special concerns regarding them. Discussion was so spirited that most groups refused to take the ten-minute break planned to provide relief during the three-hour discussion period. The highly interactive reporting session was frequently punctuated by affirmations of the value of meetings and discussions like these. Session notes received from reporter-recorders were compiled and summarized by the team and distributed to all participants.

The success of the symposium, as documented in the enthusiastic evaluation responses and the almost universal appeal for more such collaborative meetings, attests to the need of such efforts. The triad of English department, School of Education, and area secondary schools will undertake a mentoring and field-experience program that permits our secondary school majors to have early and continuing exposure to secondary school classrooms, teachers, and teaching. We believe that no textbook or theoretical orientation can substitute for the laboratory experience of the classroom. The students' experiences will include observation, lesson-plan construction, preparation of teaching-learning aids, service as teacher's aide, teaching, and shadowing the mentoring teacher as that person performs numerous other roles and responsibilities.

ENHANCEMENT IN ASSESSMENT

The final component of our program is assessment. Already an established element of the university-wide assessment program, the assessment program in the English department aims at the achievement of educational goals and quality. Multiple measures of assessment are either in use or planned to determine student achievement in knowledge and skills of the discipline, program effectiveness, and student and employer satisfaction with the department and program. For the secondary school English major, these measures will include a writing and field-experience portfolio that contains analytic accounts of classroom activities, lesson plans, self-evaluations, student evaluations, and evaluations of mentoring and supervising teachers; a comprehensive examination, with essay; and a senior project based on classroom research into some significant curricular, pedagogical, experiential, or philosophical matter that has engaged the attention and interest of the student. The learning activities reflect faculty adoption of standards by the National Board of Professional Teaching Standards. Another assessment measure will be a senior exit interview-questionnaire to gauge student satisfaction with the program. The department will also participate on a cyclical basis in the university's general survey of graduates, employees, and graduate schools for feedback on the effectiveness of our program.

We referred to the School of Education's description of the "caring, competent, cooperative, and creative" novice teacher as both a model and a goal for its teacher educators. The program that we have outlined shows clearly how we plan to prepare our secondary school English teachers for competency and cooperation in the discipline and in the profession. The caring and creative components are more subjective but equally important. Literature and life, from Socrates to Anne Sullivan, abound with examples of the positive influence on learning of a caring teacher. A caring teacher is especially important for minority and disadvantaged youth, whose self-esteem, self-worth, motivation, and preparation may have been damaged, possibly with a resulting negative attitude toward and an unsatisfactory preparation for schools, teaching, and learning.

We believe that the most important factor in developing caring teachers for secondary school classrooms is the caring, nurturing teachers at every level of the students' educational and professional preparation, teachers whose expressions and behavior let students know that they are valued, that they can succeed, and that they can depend on their teachers to guide and encourage them along their journey. The Department of English at Norfolk State University is fortunate indeed to have a faculty that is caring and competent, that offers a nurturing atmosphere of encouragement, and that develops and sustains an environment both stimulating and demanding. This perception among students of the English faculty is expressed in annual student evaluations of faculty members, in senior exit interviews, and in casual conversations with students at every level. Prospective teachers come to appreciate the self-fulfilling prophecy of an instructor's high expectations and incorporate that powerful technique into their own teaching styles. A careful faculty selection process that involves participation by departmental faculty members, department head, dean, academic vice president, and president of the university has historically insisted on the caring factor as a necessary element in a candidate's qualifications.

Creativity is also a value in the design and delivery of instruction. Although we have no structured program for encouraging or cultivating this quality, we want to highlight it as a most desirable element in the effectiveness of secondary school English teachers, as it is for teachers in any discipline and at any level. Creativity consists not only, or necessarily, in the ability to generate poetry, drama, fiction, or nonfiction in powerful and memorable concepts and language; it is also expressed in approaches to thinking and doing that inspire learning or productivity, including one's own. Such creativity is particularly desirable for people preparing to teach in contemporary and future school settings, given the increasingly dynamic character of the educational process and the increasingly diverse composition of students in the classrooms. If the assumption that "one size fits all" was patently in error when school populations were much more homogeneous than they are today (especially in the public schools), such an assumption—or, worse, acting on such an assumption—will be educationally disastrous for future teachers. Through the example of our own creative faculty and through our encouragement of innovation and experimentation, we hope to stimulate our prospective teachers to be creative teachers, learners, and members of the profession and society.

Postscript

In keeping with our goals to cultivate ongoing partnership opportunities with area secondary school teachers and to provide training to enable prospective teachers to make effective use of technology in the classroom, the English and foreign languages departments, in collaboration with the School of Arts and Letters' Title III Integrated Media Program, sponsored the second spring symposium for secondary school English teachers in May 1997. The symposium was held specifically to foster dialogue on the academic preparation of college-bound students and on the professional training of English education majors and to provide a forum for interschool dialogue among English teachers on issues of concern to practitioners. The symposium theme, Computer Software Technology as a Pedagogical Tool, sparked lively discussion among the participants, who were professors from NSU's English and foreign languages departments, area secondary school English teachers, and NSU English and secondary school education majors. A media specialist, Peter Dublin of Cambridge, MA, president of Intentional Educations, addressed the group and provided a hands-on workshop in using and creating software for use in the English classroom.

Less structured but valuable to our program is an informal partnership that we are cultivating with a neighboring secondary school whose English department head is a 1982 graduate of our baccalaureate English–secondary school education program. This partnership, which we expect to lead to increased opportunities for field experiences and mentorships for our majors, to some instructional exchange, and to frequent informal discussions between the two faculty groups, is viewed by our faculty as a promising prospect.

Perhaps most encouraging of all has been the increased interest among our faculty members in improving teaching technique, particularly as it relates to increased use of technology. This interest has been expressed in faculty presentations during departmental meetings to share successful techniques and approaches and in proposal-writing activity that focuses on instructional approach. One instructor demonstrated a computer-generated instructional game, *Vocabulary Jeopardy,* based on the popular television game show, that he used to teach vocabulary in some of his classes. Another faculty member demonstrated through a *PowerPoint* and *Lotus Freelance Graphics* presentation how images from several sources can be integrated to help students link knowledge and respond critically to text. Other faculty members have developed proposals for using technology to enliven teaching and encourage active learning. Our hope is that as the university's fiscal condition stabilizes and workloads improve, more attention and energy can again be directed to the implementation of other features of the NSU enhanced teacher preparation program.

Gladys C. Heard, *Department of English and Foreign Languages, Norfolk State University*
Deborah Goodwyn, *Department of English and Foreign Languages, Virginia State University*
Rosalie Black Kiah, *Department of English and Foreign Languages, Norfolk State University*
Thelma L. B. Thompson, *Academic Affairs, Norfolk State University*
Brenda G. Williams, *Bayside High School*
Elaine P. Witty, *School of Education, Norfolk State University*

WORKS CITED

Bonwell, Charles C., and James A. Eison. *Active Learning: Creating Excitement in the Classroom.* ASHE-ERIC Higher Education Report 1. Washington: George Washington U School of Education and Human Development, 1991.

Dewey, John. *Democracy and Education.* New York: Macmillan, 1924.

———. *Experience and Education.* New York: Macmillan, 1938.

Erikson, Erik H. *Identity: Youth and Crisis.* New York: Norton, 1968.

Ginsburg, Herbert, and Sylvia Opper. *Piaget's Theory of Intellectual Development: An Introduction.* Englewood Cliffs: Prentice, 1969.

Goodlad, John. *Teachers for Our Nation's Schools.* San Francisco: Jossey-Bass, 1990.

King, Sabrina H. "The Limited Presence of African-American Teachers." *Review of Educational Research* 63 (1993): 115–49.

Norfolk State University. "Continuing Accreditation Report, Submitted to the National Council for Accreditation of Teacher Education." 1996.

Witty, Elaine P. "Increasing the Pool of Black Teachers: Plans and Strategies." *Teacher Recruitment and Retention.* Ed. Antoine W. Garibaldi. Washington: Natl. Educ. Assn., 1989. 39–44.

———. *Prospects of Black Teachers: Preparation, Certification, and Employment.* Washington: ERIC Clearinghouse on Teacher Educ. (ERIC Document Reproduction Service No. ED 213 659), 1982.

APPENDIX A

Suggested Readings in African American Literature for English and English Education Majors

Reading from a wide range of literature in many genres helps build understanding of the ethical and beautiful dimensions of the human experience. This list is a starter and not intended to be all-inclusive. (Special thanks to the Black Caucus of the NCTE for the compilation of the greater portion of the list.)

Angelou, Maya. *I Know Why the Caged Bird Sings.* Bantam, 1971. Autobiography.

———. *Wouldn't Take Nothing for My Journey Now.* Random House, 1993. Essays.

Austin, Doris Jean. *After the Garden.* NAL-Dutton, 1988. Fiction.

Baldwin, James. *Go Tell It on the Mountain.* Dell, 1985. Nonfiction.

Bambara, Toni Cade. *Gorilla, My Love.* Random, 1981. Short story collection.

Bell, Derrick. *And We Are Not Saved.* Basic, 1989. Fiction.

Bontemps, Arna. *American Negro Poetry.* Hill, 1974. Poetry.

Brooks, Gwendolyn. *Selected Poems.* Harper, 1982.

Brown, Sterling A. *The Collected Poems of Sterling A. Brown.* Comp. Michael S. Harper. Another Chicago, 1990.

Childress, Alice. *Rainbow Jordan.* Avon, 1982. Fiction for young adult and older.

Comer, James P. *Maggie's American Dream.* NAL-Dutton, 1988. Autobiography.

Cooper, S. California. *The Matter Is Life.* Doubleday, 1991.

Cortez, Jayne. *Coagulations: New and Selected Poems.* Thunder's Mouth, 1984.

Davis, Angela. *Women, Race, and Class.* Random, 1983. Nonfiction.

Davis, Ossie. *Langston: A Play.* Delacorte, 1982.

Douglass, Frederick. *Narrative of the Life of Frederick Douglass.* NAL-Dutton, 1968. Autobiography.

Dove, Rita. *Mother Love.* Norton, 1995. Poetry.

Dunbar, Paul Laurence. *Life and Works: Containing His Complete Poetical Works, His Best Short Stories, Numerous Anecdotes, and a Complete Biography.* 1911. Kraus, 1980.

Evans, Mari. *I Am a Black Woman.* Morrow, 1970.

Gaines, Ernest. *A Gathering of Old Men.* Random, 1984. Fiction.

Giddings, Paula. *When and Where I Enter: The Impact of Black Women on Race and Sex in America.* Morrow, 1984. Nonfiction.

Giovanni, Nikki. *Spin a Soft Black Song.* Farrar, 1987. Fiction.

Golden, Marita. *Long Distance Life.* Doubleday, 1989. Fiction.

Haley, Alex, and Malcolm X. *The Autobiography of Malcolm X.* American, 1970.
Hamilton, Virginia. *The People Could Fly.* Knopf, 1988. Young adult folktales.
Hayden, Robert. *Collected Poems.* Liveright, 1985.
Huggins, Nathan Irvin. *Black Odyssey: The Afro-American Ordeal in Slavery.* Random, 1990. History.
Hughes, Langston. *Selected Poems.* Random, 1990.
Hull, Gloria T. *Give Us Each Day: The Diary of Alice Dunbar-Nelson.* Norton, 1985. Nonfiction.
Hunter, Kristin. *God Bless the Child.* Howard UP, 1987. Fiction.
Hurston, Zora Neale. *Their Eyes Were Watching God.* Harper, 1990. Fiction.
Johnson, Charles. *Middle Passage.* Macmillan, 1990. Fiction.
Johnson, James Weldon. *God's Trombones.* Viking, 1976. Poetry.
Jordan, June. *Things That I Do in the Dark.* Random, 1977.
Kelly, William Melvin. *A Different Drummer.* Doubleday, 1969. Fiction.
Kendrick, Dolores. *The Woman of Plums: Poems in the Voices of Slave Women.* Morrow, 1989.
Lane, Pinkie Gordon. *I Never Scream: New and Selected Poems.* Lotus, 1985.
Lester, Julius. *To Be a Slave.* Scholastic, 1986. Nonfiction.
Lightfoot, Sara Lawrence. *Balm in Gilead.* Addison-Wesley, 1988. Biography.
Madgett, Naomi Long. *"Octavia" and Other Poems.* Third World, 1988.
Madhubuti, Haki. *Black Men: Obsolete, Single, Dangerous?* Third World, 1990. Essays.
Mandela, Nelson. *Long Walk to Freedom.* Little, 1994. Autobiography.
Marshall, Paule. *Praisesong for the Widow.* NAL-Dutton, 1984. Fiction.
Mathis, Sharon Bell. *Teacup Full of Roses.* Puffin, 1987. Young adult fiction.
McKay, Claude. *Selected Poems.* Harcourt, 1969.
McMillan, Terry. *Disappearing Acts.* Viking, 1989. Fiction.
Moody, Anne. *Coming of Age in Mississippi: An Autobiography.* Dell, 1980.
Morrison, Toni. *Beloved.* NAL-Dutton, 1991.
Parks, Gordon. *The Learning Tree.* Fawcett, 1987.
Petry, Ann. *The Street.* Beacon, 1985.
Randall, Dudley. *The Black Poets.* Bantam, 1985.
Reed, Ishmael. *Flight to Canada.* MacMillan, 1989.
Sanchez, Sonia. *Homegirls and Handgrenades.* Thunder's Mouth, 1984. Poetry.
Sanders, Dori. *Clover.* Fawcett, 1991.
Shange, Ntozake. *Sassafras, Cypress, and Indigo.* St. Martin's, 1983.
Southerland, Ellease. *Let the Lion Eat Straw.* NAL-Dutton, 1980.
Taylor, Mildred. *Roll of Thunder, Hear My Cry.* Bantam, 1984. Young adult fiction.
Thomas, Joyce Carol. *Bright Shadow.* Avon, 1983. Young adult fiction.
Toomer, Jean. *Cane.* Norton, 1987. Poetry.

Walker, Alice. *The Color Purple.* Harcourt, 1982.

Washington, James Melvin. *Conversations with God: Two Centuries of Prayers by African Americans.* Harper, 1984. Essays.

Washington, Mary Helen. *Memory of King: Stories about Family by Black Writers.* Doubleday, 1991.

Williams, John A. *The Man Who Cried I Am.* Thunder's Mouth, 1985.

Wright, Richard. *Black Boy.* Harper, 1989. Autobiography.

APPENDIX B

Questions for Secondary School Teachers Symposium Sessions

Issues and Problems

What do you see as the most important issue(s) facing secondary school English teachers?

What is your biggest problem as a secondary school English teacher?

Teaching Strategies

What teaching strategies have you found most successful in your secondary school classroom? Least? How did you acquire the strategies you have found most successful?

To what extent was pedagogy emphasized in your education courses? English courses? How valuable was it?

Teacher Preparation

How well did your teacher-training program prepare you for the curriculum that you actually teach?

How could your undergraduate teacher preparation have prepared you better?

Did your undergraduate teacher preparation program prepare you to cope with change (curricular, pedagogical, philosophical, sociological, political, etc.)? If so, how were you prepared?

University-School Cooperation

How can our teacher-preparation program at Norfolk State University serve you better? What are your expectations of us?

In what cooperative ways can we assist one another in training secondary school English teachers? In what ways would *you* like to be involved?

Standards

How do you feel about the new Virginia Standards of Learning? What do you see as their chief strengths, weaknesses, benefits, disadvantages for secondary school students or for teachers?

Do you feel prepared to teach to the standards? Why or why not?

Diversity

How important is training for sensitivity to diversity—cultural, academic, linguistic, racial, socioeconomic, etc.—for the secondary school classroom?

How sensitive to diversity are the faculty and administration in your school?

UNIVERSITY OF IOWA

Educating Teachers of English

Debates about how high schools should prepare students for college and about how colleges should prepare teachers for high schools have raged for at least a hundred years now—or at least since the invention of the public high school at the turn of the last century. It was in 1890 that President Charles Eliot of Harvard, speaking to a meeting of the National Education Association, complained of a "wide gap" between the common schools and the colleges, "very imperfectly bridged by a few public high schools, endowed academies [. . .] and private schools, which conform to no common standards and are under no unifying control" (Sizer 24). He was right, of course, but it could hardly have been otherwise. Public high schools, born of an uneasy marriage between the classical traditions of the Latin prep schools and the more entrepreneurial assumptions of modern trade academies, were from the beginning marked by an ill-defined mission. Few students were attending high schools when Eliot made his observation—only seven percent of those between the ages of fourteen and seventeen were enrolled in 1890 and only a little over eleven percent in 1900. And the majority of those enrolled were women, who had little chance of finding a purchase in the rapidly expanding universities. Still, Eliot foresaw rightly that a clearer and more stable relation between the public schools and the colleges had to be forged if the interests of both were to be served.

In many ways, universities and high schools have been trying to design that relation ever since. To heal the gap that he first observed, Eliot himself set in motion a series of professional discussions that in 1893 resulted in the *Report of the Committee of Ten,* a still remarkable document, authored almost entirely by university-based scholars, that established a secondary school curriculum in both the traditional and modern subjects. Since 1893, there has been a long series of colloquia, task forces, conferences, and blue-ribbon reports that attempt to articulate the appropriate roles of secondary schools and universities in the teaching of the various subjects. In the teaching of English, such attempts have included the range of NDEA institutes in the early 1960s that followed in the wake of sputnik and were funded by newly available federal monies; the Dartmouth Conference of the late 1960s, which grew from wide-ranging interest in British models of language and literacy learning; and, more recently, the English Coalition Conference of the late 1980s, which was in some ways a response to the rhetoric of educational reform generated by *A Nation at Risk.* In each of these cases, university and public school teachers sought to articulate their relationship to the subject of English, to their students, and to one another. For the sake of the students they both served, those involved knew they had to sustain a relationship with one another. They came together in times of change and even crisis precisely because they saw, as Eliot had seen a century ago, that there was a gap that needed tending, that would not be healed.

There are at least two dimensions to the relation between public schools and universities, and both have been the source of professional disagreement. Secondary schools have from their inception been expected to prepare students for the university. Universities usually want students who are ready to learn what universities are ready to teach, and so they design admission requirements and set standards that students must meet before they come to the university. These requirements exert an extraordinarily powerful pressure on the high school curriculum. Students are often advised to take particular courses because they are required for college admission, and the fear of not being admitted to the "right" college drives the study habits of many adolescent students.

But preparing students for college work is a manageable task only when there is some agreement about what college work entails — and here is the second and more problematic dimension of the university-school relation. To state the hopelessly obvious, contemporary academic disciplines within the university are seldom defined by stable borders and well-established conventions of inquiry. In fact, they are undergoing, especially in the humanities, a kind of Heraclitean transformation, in which change seems the only constant and in which the appearance of new kinds of knowledge and new kinds of knowledge making have become a sort of tradition. The scale and the direction of these transformations needn't be rehearsed here, but it seems clear that many university disciplines—and perhaps especially literary study—have undergone massive changes in the last quarter century, and that these changes themselves may create unprecedented challenges for university-school relations. At the very least they raise a series of important questions about how within a discipline undergoing enormous change we can prepare teachers for secondary schools, where such changes are unlooked for and perhaps unwelcome.

Of course, any teacher education program housed in a university represents an institutional attempt to bridge the gap between the university and the secondary schools. In what follows, we describe our efforts at the University of Iowa.

The Department of English

Virtually all undergraduates preparing to teach secondary school English at the University of Iowa are English majors in the College of Liberal Arts. There are presently just over one thousand English majors—an increase of more than a hundred percent in the last ten years—although there has been no corresponding increase in the size of the English faculty. The department now has about forty FTEs, with an increasing plurality in the junior ranks. The last decade has seen a host of retirements and a range of new hires, with strong representation in literary theory and cultural studies.

As the *Handbook for the Iowa English Major* makes clear, the undergraduate major requires thirty-three hours of courses in or cross-listed with English. Of these, at least three hours must be in readings courses (designed to give students intensive practice in close reading and interpretation), at least three hours must be in authors courses (which give in-depth study to one or two authors), and six to seven hours must be in literature, culture, and cultural study courses (which focus on the cultural contexts in which literature is written and read and on other cultural aspects of literary study—ethnic, feminist, regional, popular, and interdisciplinary). In addition to these requirements, majors must take at least nine semester hours in literature written before 1800. Only nine hours of creative writing may be applied toward the thirty-three-hour total.

Nearly all undergraduate English courses are taught by full-time faculty members in the Department of English: part-time teachers are hired as seldom as possible, usually to fill in for faculty members on leave. Enrollments in the courses are most often "discussion-sized"—twenty-five to thirty students in rooms with movable desks. A handful of courses are smaller (e.g., honors proseminars) and a few more than a handful are somewhat larger (Shakespeare and several of the literature and culture courses). In general, however, English majors at Iowa have many opportunities in their courses to participate in discussions with faculty members and peers and many opportunities to have their written work read carefully by their teachers. Large, impersonal lecture classes, taught by a faculty member with discussion sections led by graduate assistants, are largely absent from the undergraduate curriculum—a matter of continuing pride to a department that takes its teaching mission quite seriously.

The English Education Program

Since all those preparing to teach English are English majors at Iowa, all those teaching English at Iowa are involved in English education to some degree. The task of orchestrating the program that prepares teachers, however, falls specifically to three faculty members—two jointly appointed in English and the College of Education and one full-time in the College of Education. All three have teaching experience in public schools, and all three focus their scholarship on language and literacy in school settings.

Students wishing to become secondary school teachers of English have three program choices: (1) they may enter the undergraduate teacher education program (TEP) as early as their sophomore year, fulfilling the requirements for the English major and the state requirements for teacher certification as part of their undergraduate work; (2) they may enter the credential-only program (CO) after they have completed their BA in English, taking only those English and education courses that are required for state certification; or (3) they may apply to the master of arts in teaching program (MAT) after they have taken their BA in English. The MAT program requires eighteen graduate hours in English in addition to the courses required for state certification; students enrolled in it must have completed an undergraduate degree with strong grades in English and must take the Graduate Record Examination. Those who finish the program receive a graduate degree as well as state certification to teach English in secondary schools. Since Iowa's English education program is certified by the state to prepare public school teachers, students who meet the requirements of any of these three plans automatically receive teaching credentials from the state department upon presentation of the appropriate paperwork.

Students who would enroll in the undergraduate TEP program must have completed at least six hours of course work in English with grades of B or better. They must also have a cumulative grade point average of at least 2.5 in their other courses, must submit a personal statement about their reasons for choosing teaching as a profession, and must include at least two letters of recommendation with their application. Students applying for the credential-only and the MAT programs must have completed substantial undergraduate course work in English (almost always as a major) with grades averaging B or better. They must also submit a personal statement and letters of recommendation. As mentioned above, MAT students must also take the GRE.

Applications for the three programs are reviewed three times a year—in fall, spring, and summer. Students who meet the basic requirements are almost always admitted, but about twenty to twenty-five percent of each applicant pool do not meet those requirements and are denied admission. On average, about twenty-five students are admitted in each admission review. At the time of this report, about one hundred students were enrolled in the combined TEP and CO programs, about thirty in the MAT program.

All students who are to be certified to teach English through Iowa's teacher education program must take the following English courses, in addition to the courses that may be required for the English major:

a course in Shakespeare
a course in nineteenth- or twentieth-century British literature
two courses in American literature
a course in writing
a course in approaches to teaching writing

Students in the program must also take three courses that are cross-listed in English and education. These are:

Language and Learning
Teaching Literature to Adolescents
Methods English

Finally, they must take an array of courses required by the state for certification and offered through the College of Education:

Educational Psychology
Foundations of Education
Mainstreaming

Human Relations for the Classroom Teacher
Microcomputing
Methods of Teaching Secondary Reading

In addition to their course work, students preparing to teach must complete two practica in schools. The first, Introduction to Teaching English, places students in secondary schools for a half day every day for about ten weeks. There they observe one or more teachers, help with small-group work and tutoring, and read and grade student work under a cooperating teacher's direction.

When all their course work has been completed, students student-teach, which places them full-time in schools for a full fourteen-week semester. There, working again under the direction of a cooperating teacher and university supervisor, they take increasing responsibility to plan and orchestrate instruction throughout the school day.

At the center of our program are three courses that engage students in examining their three primary concerns as teachers of English: the teaching of literature (Teaching Literature to Adolescents), the teaching of writing (Approaches to Teaching Writing), and the development of language (Language and Learning). Each of the courses asks students to explore the conventions governing the teaching of English, to examine the research that analyzes and critiques those conventions, and to write extensively about their developing view of the profession. Assignments support students in their exploration of praxis; students consider theory and use it to create practical pedagogical designs. Taken together, the courses provide students with a space to read, write, and reflect on the assumptions that inform the teaching of literacy and on their own experience as students in English classrooms.

A Closer Look

Curricular overviews of the English major or of the teacher education program, of course, can tell us only so much about the lived life of those who are preparing to teach—and of those who are teaching them. To understand more fully the complexities of an education in English, we undertook a study of the English courses our undergraduate TEP students take most frequently. What follows is an attempt to describe what we found.

THE COURSES

In order to determine the kinds of English courses our TEP students most frequently take, we began our study by analyzing the transcripts of the seventy-nine undergraduates currently enrolled in our program, making a simple count of the courses they had taken that were listed or cross-listed with the department of English.

Given the common professional interests of these students, we were somewhat surprised by the wide range of English courses they had taken as part of their major. Of the 91 courses on the transcripts, 62 had been taken by five or fewer students and 17 had been taken by only one. The courses themselves went from Introduction to Feminist Criticism and Irish Literature and Culture II (one student each) to Shakespeare (59 students) and Classical and Biblical Literature (38 students). The range can be explained at least in part by the different points at which students decide to enter the teacher education program: those who enter relatively early may move quickly toward the courses required for certification, while those who enter later may sample from a wider range of offerings before confronting the requirements.

Not so surprising, given Iowa's long-standing commitment to the teaching of writing, were the number of TEP students who enrolled in writing courses. Nonfiction Writing, Poetry Writing, and Fiction Writing were the fourth, fifth, and sixth most frequently taken courses.

A simple count allowed us to determine the English courses that had been taken by at least ten students. These courses are shown in the table, in course-number order.

All but one of them meet at least one of the requirements of the English major or the teaching certificate or both. All these courses are taught frequently—at least once a year and sometimes, when summer session is included, three times a year. The combination of necessity and opportunity, then, make the courses likely choices for these students. The only course frequently taken but not required is Literature and Philosophic Thought—a class taught by one of the most popular instructors at the university.

A list like the one we've constructed can tell us something about how many of our students negotiate a fairly complex set of curricular requirements, but it's important to remember that the majority of our teacher education students have not taken most of the courses listed. With the exception of the course in Shakespeare, which was taken by fifty-nine students and is quite specifically required for teacher certification, no one course was taken by even half the students in the sample. The focus on the courses most frequently taken, then, should not occlude the larger pattern of variety and individual discretion in the undergraduate careers of these students.

Enrollment in English Courses of at Least Ten Teacher Education Program Students

COURSE	ENROLLMENT
Literature	
Classical and Biblical Literature	38
Reading Novels	18
Reading Poems	11
Reading Short Stories	20
American Literary Classics	15
Chaucer	11
Shakespeare	59
Selected American Authors	27
Selected Modern Authors	10
Literature and Culture of the Middle Ages	12
Literature and Culture of 18th-Century England	15
Literature and Culture of 19th-Century England	11
American Ethnic Literature	14
Literature and Culture in America before 1800	10
Literature and Philosophic Thought	10
Writing	
Creative Writing	14
Nonfiction Writing	23
Prose Style	12
Fiction Writing	21
Poetry Writing	23

THE SYLLABI

After we had determined the courses our students most frequently take, we asked the faculty members teaching those courses to supply us with the syllabi they gave their students. Because undergraduate writing courses are often not taught by tenure-line faculty members and because we wanted to focus our analysis on patterns across a range of courses, we did not ask writing instructors for syllabi. Some of the faculty members we would have contacted were on leave, and some of the courses our students frequently take were not being offered during the semester of the study. In the end, we received thirteen syllabi from twelve colleagues who were teaching or had recently taught ten of the courses most often taken by our students. (One colleague taught Selected Modern Authors and

Reading Novels and thus supplied two syllabi. Two courses, Shakespeare and Selected American Authors, were represented by two instructors each, who taught different sections of the course.)

The syllabus for any course represents the first text to be read and interpreted by the students. Like almost any other text, a syllabus for a literature course is interpretable because it abides by conventions of form, supplies information in predictable categories, and meets at least some of the expectations of its readers. In the following, we examine the language of the syllabi in three categories: the statement of goals, the reading for the course, and the writing for the course.

Statement of Goals. Our analysis of only thirteen syllabi for undergraduate literature courses indicated a fairly remarkable range in the kind and amount of information instructors provided about goals. At one end of the scale were those syllabi that did not mention goals at all. The syllabus for Reading Poems, for instance, lays out the schedule of assignments and remarks briefly on the kind of writing expected but does not offer a perspective on what the larger purposes of the course might be. The same is true of the syllabus for Reading Short Stories and of the even briefer syllabus for Literature and Culture of Nineteenth-Century England. At the other end of the scale are syllabi that go to great length to spell out the instructors' goals and to specify how they might be achieved. One of the two syllabi for the Shakespeare course, for instance, mentions five large purposes:

1. to master twelve of Shakespeare's major plays
2. to exercise skills in visualizing and feeling the dramatic point of dialogue and episode and in conceiving the structural relations among parts
3. to formulate and communicate the result of insight by talking, writing, and portrayal
4. to understand and use the historical contexts in which Shakespeare live, worked, and wrote
5. to learn to value personally and to judge aesthetically the enduring work of these plays

The syllabi that articulate goals include, at the very least, statements about what students will do in the class: thus students will "read novels written in various literary periods" in Reading Novels, and they will be "introduc[ed] to some of the major works of Melville and Twain" in Selected American Authors. They will "consider the intertextual relations among the fictions" of Jean Rhys and Jamaica Kincaid in Selected Modern Authors, and they will "explore" questions and "[go] through the works in chronological order" in American Literary Classics. In fact, the verbs that carry the action within goal statements are fairly standard: *read, explore, consider, discuss, exercise.* Quite often—more often than not—the subject who will be doing that reading and exploring is a *we*—a *we* that embraces both teacher and students and that emphasizes the joint nature of the work to be undertaken.

Goal statements serve to invite students into a semester-long conversation for which the course will provide a space. Thus, on the syllabus for one of the Selected American Authors classes, students were told that the class would "focus on two of the most influential African American writers from the contemporary era: James Baldwin and Toni Morrison," and in American Literary Classics they were asked, "What is a literary 'classic'? And what makes a literary work distinctively American?" There is an enthusiasm about such language: it is a beckoning (albeit of a rather shy, academic sort) meant to engage students, to enliven their interest, to make them curious and glad they are taking the course. Sometimes this is quite explicit. In the syllabus for Literature and Culture of the Middle Ages, the instructor said happily, "I can't wait to introduce you to three texts seldom read by undergraduates: The Latin *Walthari poesis,* the Russian *Prince Igor's Campaign,* and the Finnish *Kalevala.* A marvelous diversity of cultures!"

Reading. Not surprisingly, each of the thirteen syllabi we studied specified the texts students were to read during the semester. The Shakespeare syllabi named the plays that would be read in and out of class; the Chaucer syllabus named the tales that would be discussed; the syllabus for Literature and Culture of the Middle Ages named the epics that students would study. Even the syllabus for Reading Short Stories and Reading Poems, where texts are usually short, were quite specific about what students should prepare to read. Only one of the syllabi—for one of the two sections of Reading Short Stories—did not name precisely which stories would be read. Instead, students were told that they would be reading "Hemingway stories" or "Mori stories" at different times during the semester. The edition of Hemingway stories and the edition of Mori stories that students were to purchase were, however, specified clearly on the syllabus. Students must either buy or borrow the books they will need for a class, so the listing of required texts in a syllabus seems perfectly understandable. Only two observations are worth making about this standard feature of course syllabi.

First, we note the specificity in the reading required. In Reading Poems, students will read Dickinson's "The Bustle in the House" and "Because I could not stop for death"; in one section of Reading Short Stories, they will read James's "The Beast in the Jungle" and Joyce's "Araby"; in American Literary Classics, they will read *The Awakening* and *As I Lay Dying*. Even the edition of required texts is usually specified—and if not, then often it is specified silently, because it was the edition ordered from the bookstore. The net effect is to foreground the reading of particular texts in particular material forms: all the students will, quite literally, be on the same page when they study a given text.

Second, we note that almost all the texts required in these literature courses are, in fact, literature—at least as it has been traditionally defined. They are novels, stories, poems, plays, and epics. There are a few instances of nonfiction with literary credentials: Hurston's *Of Mules and Men* in one of the short story sections; Baldwin's *The Fire Next Time* in a section of Selected American Authors. But only three of the syllabi require reading that is, again by traditional definition, nonliterary. In one of the sections of Reading Short Stories, the instructor builds the course around the way stories are structured in speech and in writing and thus requires Walter Ong's *Orality and Literacy*. In the other section of Reading Short Stories, the instructor asks students several times to read criticism related to the stories being discussed. After reading James's "The Beast in the Jungle," for instance, students are asked to consider Eve Sedgwick's essay "The Beast in the Closet: A Gender Critic Reads James's 'The Beast in the Jungle.'" And in Selected Modern Authors: Jean Rhys and Jamaica Kincaid, the syllabus states that students will read "historical materials concerning the Caribbean region and its literary movements [. . .] and some critical essays on the writers and their works." These materials are on reserve in the library, however, not named in the syllabus itself.

These two features of reading requirements—the specificity of the work and its edition; the privileged position of literature—are such conventional ways of organizing our instruction that their effects may be invisible to us. But taken together, they make a powerful if implicit case for one kind of teaching instead of others, one kind of textual study instead of others. Such a case is made equally clear by the kind of writing assignments described in the syllabi.

Writing. Descriptions of required writing, like lists of required reading, were a standard feature of the syllabi we collected: the only significant variation seemed to be in the amount of information provided about the writing to be done. All mentioned the number of papers to be turned in, and most mentioned the length that the papers were expected to be. The number ranged from "one paper with thesis, argument, and evidence" to seven two-page papers with far more specific guidelines. Not surprisingly, the number of papers expected was inversely proportional to the number of pages expected. Generally, students were asked to write between twelve and twenty pages for a course—more when no midterm or final was planned, less when there were other sources of evaluation.

Perhaps the most revealing feature of these descriptions of writing is how little description there actually is. This is due in part to the fact that specific assignments will be handed out as the course moves along. But it suggests an assumption that the student readers already know what a paper means: an argumentative essay with thesis and textual evidence that the instructor will evaluate for its clarity, coherence, and adherence to the conventions of the genre. Interestingly, only the syllabi for Reading Poems and Reading Short Stories—courses designed for students near the beginning of their work in the major—spell out what students should do. The description of the writing required for one section of Reading Short Stories is very specific. For each of the seven two-page papers, students are asked, "Choose a topic that intrigues, fascinates you most and that you consider central to a discussion of the work. Move from a precise analysis of two or three passages to wider, more general implications while still pointing out specific passages. Quote only short, important passages from the text." The directions specify that students should, in their introduction, "briefly state [their] thesis"; they should remember that they will not "convince through generalities and vagueness, but through close analysis of the text." In the syllabus for Reading Poems, students are told that the idea of their last paper will be "to present a clear, useful, and sophisticated essay intended to explain how [they] go about reading poems." For the other section of Reading Short Stories, the instructor lists as one of three goals, "to develop writing skills, grammatically, syntactically, analytically—in other words, holistically."

Outside the reading courses, very little is said in the syllabi about what form papers are to take—except, that is, when the papers are not close analytic readings with thesis and evidence. In one section of Selected American Authors, the instructor describes the parodies that she wants students to write: "Two [. . .] will be due during the semester—one of Baldwin and one of Morrison. Each will be no more than one single-spaced typed page. I will offer a list of suggested 'scenarios,' and you will mimic the style and thematic concerns of each author in presenting that scenario." In the Shakespeare courses, both of which ask students to think of the plays as scripts to be performed, students are told that their writing will "uncover" specific scenes in the play and show how those scenes fit within the larger concerns of the play as performance.

Papers of the sort we usually assign are an especially obvious feature of our teaching, but we would like to argue that it is precisely the obvious we need to notice, for it is the obvious features of our teaching—the elements we take most for granted—that have the most powerful, cumulative effect on our students. The evidence from these syllabi, unsurprising as it is, suggests an approach to literary study that has come to seem natural to us and probably to our students. The question to be addressed here is how natural or appropriate such an approach might be in a high school classroom populated by a much wider range of students than those found in the university.

The Curricular Conversation

Because university classrooms and public school classrooms are so clearly not alike, because students preparing to become teachers must negotiate borders that have been only sketchily mapped, we are trying in our teacher education program to engage students in an ongoing conversation about those differences—and thus about schooling as they have experienced it. This conversation extends across classes, takes particular shape in classes, and finally defines the intellectual space within which we hope our students will move with increasing confidence and grace. The discussion opens with an issue that is easy for our students to see if difficult for them to resolve: the differences between the conventions and cultural norms of the English department and those of the College of Education. How are the teaching, reading, and thinking different in the two departments? How are the students different? What are the consequences, as an English major, of naming oneself a future teacher?

We might begin with this last question, because it is surely where our students begin. What are the political dimensions of their decision to teach? Though English departments seldom take a direct interest in the future vocations of their students, we often hope that our best students—

those who are especially skilled in the kinds of reading, talking, and writing we privilege—will themselves go into the trade, will attend graduate school, write books, become something like us. All the evidence must be anecdotal here (to our knowledge, this portion of departmental culture has never been studied systematically), but we'd have to guess that those same best students are seldom encouraged to go into public school teaching. On the contrary, if such students display an interest in teaching they are likely to be told that they are too good for such a future, that they might waste themselves there, that they should try for something higher. There are undoubtedly exceptions to this attitude, but there is a very strong sense among students going into English teaching that they are working against some fairly sturdy cultural expectations—and those expectations are not limited to university English departments.

To take only the most obvious example, talented young women who decide to become teachers must not only resist the hopes of their English advisers, they must also resist the now widespread assumption that talented young women will not become teachers—that teaching is an occupational ghetto from which women have happily escaped. A woman who teaches school in the late twentieth century is voluntarily choosing a role that was mostly involuntary for professional women only a generation or two before. It requires some degree of conviction to overcome the stigma. Deciding to be a teacher, in other words, is not easy—especially if one possesses the very talents and commitments we most want teachers to have.

But once the decision is made, the differences between English and education continue to challenge the student moving back and forth between the two. In their English courses, students are often engaging in close readings of literary fiction in the search for meaningful patterns; in their education courses, they are scanning nonliterary nonfiction in the search for useful information. In their English courses, students are usually writing analytic essays parsing the themes of particular texts; in their education courses, they are often imagining teaching scenarios, integrating information from a range of texts, or responding to the arguments for one kind of teaching, one version of reform. The practices are different enough to call on different strategies, and in our classes we attempt to help students become self-conscious about those strategies—for their own learning and for the learning of their students.

The most central change for students moving between English and education, however, is the shift from the authority of the text to the authority of experience. In English, it is largely the text that answers questions, that settles debate. The issues addressed in almost any discussion finally involve textual meanings: What does the text say? How do we know what it says? What alternatives are possible? In education, the emphasis shifts to practice, to activity, to instructional work in particular contexts. The experienced teacher and not the text becomes visibly authoritative, becomes through the knowledge of classrooms and students—not through the knowledge of books—the answerer of questions. The books most read and cited by students in education are usually those by teachers writing about their teaching; the conversations to which students most attend are those orchestrated by teachers who make frequent references not to books but to their own classroom lives. Our classes ask students not to choose between these two sources of authority but to recognize them for what they are—to name them and examine their value.

This exploration of the most obvious tensions between English and education only begins the conversation. Through the two years that our students study with us, we attempt to engage them in three different kinds of investigation—each related directly to their ongoing experience as learners in the university.

In the first of these investigations, we invite students to inventory their histories as readers and writers. What they will take most for granted is what they have known firsthand. Part of our job as educators is to help them "know their knowledge," as Coleridge put it—to help them represent to themselves the opportunities and constraints that have shaped their lives in school. This autobiographical project takes different shapes in different classes. In Language and Learning, students are asked to reconstruct the literacy practices in their homes as they were growing up. What magazines, newspapers, and books could they remember seeing? What did they remember about their parents' reading and writing? Were the students read to as children? Encouraged to read or to pretend to read? Were there encyclopedias, children's books, posters about books, tapes of books? Was there time for reading? Space and light for reading? Were skill in literacy and excellence in schoolwork held up as ideals? What was the family's implicit and explicit assumptions about their futures? This exercise is completed in conjunction with a reading and discussion of Shirley Heath's *Ways with Words,* probably the most frequently cited ethnographic study of literacy in the United States. Heath's work provides both a model and a rationale for the students' investigation, because she shows so convincingly that literate skills and attitudes are shaped well before individual literacy is achieved. Our students' autobiographical work can help students see their pasts more clearly and help them as well to remain open to the influences of the home lives of their own students.

Comparable projects are assigned in almost every English education course we offer. In Teaching Literature to Adolescents, students are asked to write a reading autobiography. Beginning with a time line on which they place lists of the authors and books they read at various points in their past, students first orally rehearse the stories of their reading lives in small groups and then write those stories—remembering everything they can about what and when and how they read, about the times they read a great deal and the times they read almost nothing. They are asked to notice what seem to be high points of reading, moments when reading mattered a great deal to them, and low points, when they always could find something else to do. Perhaps most important, they are asked to explore the relation between the reading they did outside school and the assigned reading they did for school. In Approaches to Teaching Writing, students are asked to write a sketch of a teacher who affected their writing a great deal—for good or ill. They are asked to remember what powers that teacher seemed to have, what the teacher said or did that made such a lasting impression; they are asked to articulate what they have learned about teaching and about writing from their experience with the teacher. They are also asked to write an analysis of their own writing processes—to take the reader through a writing project from the generation of an idea, through the panic and procrastination, to the drafting and revision, to the feeling of relief or anxiety that comes with completion. Again, the emphasis is on learning what we already know, representing what we already do. This as a way for a student to find a usable past and an identity as a teacher.

Finally, in their English methods classes, students are asked to reconstruct their histories as students of English—to go back to junior high and work up to the present, remembering what they read for their English classes, what they wrote, what they resisted, what they loved, what they ignored. Some of this reconstructing is done in discussion, but all the students are encouraged again to note high points and low points, to appraise their commitments honestly, to say aloud where they still need encouragement, to ask their still unanswered questions. We believe strongly that our students cannot go forward until they've systematically inventoried the baggage they carry with them, and the projects we assign are one way of getting that work done.

If one kind of investigation in our program asks students to look back, another asks them to look around. We want our students to become informed and critical consumers of classroom practice, and so we begin early in their time with us to ask them questions about what they see and hear when they enter schools. During the program, students have the opportunity to observe three kinds of classes—their university English classes, their education classes, and the public school classes that they visit as part of their practicum. Though they are clearly participants in all three contexts, we want them to be spectators as well—to look for patterns, sequences, conventions, rhythms, shape, intention, meaning.

In Language and Learning, students are asked to tape-record what is said in a given instructional setting—a teacher-led large-group discussion, a students-only small-group discussion, a writing conference, a tutorial—and to analyze what they hear. Who talks the most; who the least? What are the general patterns of turn taking? What kinds of questions are asked? What kinds of knowledge are exchanged? What levels of abstraction are reached? How can we tell if an exchange was successful or not? This exercise complements ongoing efforts in class to explore together the conventions that govern classroom discourse in different settings. We bring in transcripts of real large-group, small-group, and one-on-one discussions and ask students to interpret them as texts. We ask them further to interpret in the same way the teaching they are seeing as students. What kinds of questions do their English teachers ask? What are the turn-taking patterns in their Shakespeare class? their modern poetry class? their advanced composition class? Why do they think those patterns obtain? What would it mean to alter them?

Using their observations of university classrooms as a baseline, students in their practicum are able to contrast the patterns they have found with those they see in public school classrooms. What are the differences and similarities between eighth-grade discussions of literature and university discussions? How are the roles of teacher and student different in the two settings? How are the expectations different, and how are those expectations communicated? Obviously, the observing in public schools can be more systematic than the observing we can manage in university classrooms. The practicum is designed specifically to encourage observation and reflection about teaching in secondary schools, but no comparable opportunity is available to study university teaching. Once the process of inquiry is initiated, students become quite skilled at asking questions about conventions and patterns and can use the lenses through which they have learned to see to investigate discourse in a fairly wide range of instructional settings.

Finally, we want our students to be more than intelligent observers of others' teaching; we want them to be deeply reflective students of their own teaching. As they move from our classrooms into their own, we hope that from theory they will move not to practice but to theory-shaped thinking about practice. We hope, in other words, that the conversations about teaching that we have initiated through the first two kinds of investigations will be continued as students investigate their own teaching decisions, their own teaching lives.

Beginning with English Methods, which students take the semester before student teaching, and continuing through the seminar that accompanies student teaching, students are consistently asked to represent some aspect of their teaching practice (an assignment, a sample of their students' work, a videotape of a class discussion, an audiotape of a student-teacher conference) and to reflect on why that practice took the form it did; what theories, hunches, or wisdom informed its shape; and how and why it might be revised. We want students to get better at not just the doing but also the thinking about the doing.

To this end, students are asked as part of their student teaching to prepare a professional portfolio that contains much of the writing that they have completed in the program — the autobiographical essays and the observational investigations, for example — and some artifacts of their teaching and samples of their teaching on tape. The portfolio is meant to provide students with a representation of who they are and what they can do — a representation that we hope will help them find work as teachers. But more important even than that, the portfolio is meant to give students an occasion for reflecting on their practice — and to begin a professional lifetime of such reflection. The portfolio is concluded by an essay in which the student overviews the portfolio's strengths and weaknesses, notes themes of growth and change, and honestly appraises what remains to be learned. Students leave our program, we hope, with as many questions as answers, but with a practiced feel for how answers might be found.

These are the ways in which our program is trying to help students move from the university to the public schools. We have only begun to implement some of our ideas, and so our success, if we have any, will not be visible for some time. Still, thorny questions remain about the relations between university English departments and public schools, and we'd like to close our report with those questions.

Should Teachers Teach As They Were Taught?

There is a kind of folk tradition that suggests that we should teach as we were taught. In fact, a pervasive, popular view is that those who would teach well need only be in the classrooms of those who teach well. Thus Rita Kramer, in her attack on professional teacher education, argues, "How to teach English literature should be the concern of professors of English, not experts in curriculum and instruction. [. . .] Everything you need to know about how to teach English—that can be taught didactically—can be learned within the framework of an undergraduate English major" (219).

Such views may be hard to counter, since we have a substantial body of research that suggests that the teaching we witness will powerfully shape the teaching we practice. Dan Lortie, in his 1975 study of teachers, pointed to our "apprenticeship of observation" (61): twenty or more years of watching teachers perform cannot help but influence new teachers as they make their way into the profession, and that influence will, almost by definition, pull instruction back in a conservative direction—to the way it was done before. The voices of teachers past inhabit us—and perhaps haunt us—as we find our own voice in the classroom and, in a Bahktinian sense, we may find ourselves speaking their words with our mouths, reproducing the speech genre that is instructional discourse each time we lead a discussion.

And yet, though both folk tradition and systematic research point to the difficulty of change, we find ourselves at a point where change must be undertaken. The kinds of teaching suggested by the English syllabi we studied here has been with us for at least fifty years now. In the first edition of that founding document of the New Criticism, *Understanding Poetry*—in an introduction directed significantly "To the Teacher"—Cleanth Brooks and Robert Penn Warren gave us the words that still inform and justify much of our work in classrooms. "The poem in itself," they taught us,

> remains finally the object for study. One must grasp the poem as a literary construct before it can offer any real illumination as a document. [. . . In the teaching of literature] the treatment should be concrete and inductive, [and] the poem should be treated as an organic system of relationships. (iv, xv)

Such approaches (as Richard Ohmann, among others, has argued) served us well both theoretically, because they were consonant with the scholarship we were doing, and practically, because they allowed us to teach an increasingly larger population of college students. The practices were useful, they worked, and thus they became the standard. And through the process of observational apprenticeship—for about three generations now—they have constituted the taken-for-granted script, the all-but-invisible convention that governs what seems possible in our classrooms.

Our scholarship has moved well beyond that point in the 1950s when the New Criticism was new and all but imperial. But our teaching, all dissatisfactions and exceptions acknowledged, seems to have remained there. Unless we are willing to rethink self-consciously our practices and our assumptions, we may find ourselves slipping into the default mode of unconsidered, long-standing procedure. Part of the problem, of course, is that we have talked about our teaching so seldom that we have little theoretical leverage with which to imagine alternatives. We look in one another's classrooms if asked, if there's a problem, if a promotion is in the offing, but in general the language we use to describe our teaching is impoverished—full of *good*s and *nice*s and *interesting*s—words that would embarrass us if we built them into our scholarship. It is almost as if we consider our own and our colleagues' teaching something private, something we're not quite comfortable discussing in meetings among strangers, something best left behind closed doors.

We need to enrich the language that we use to describe our teaching. We need to consider what our teaching is teaching our students about our work. We need to study our colleagues who are trying something new, and we need to learn how our professional culture keeps others from trying. We need to ask what kinds of knowledge and what ways of knowing we are fostering in our classrooms, and we need to ask whether that knowledge and that knowing are what we want after all.

We are not just teaching literature, we are also teaching how to teach. And that fact of our professional lives raises several important questions:

If the field of literary studies is exploding with new and contested developments—newly available texts, theoretical perspectives, ways of reading—how are high school teachers to negotiate the emerging terrain? Gerald Graff has argued that university faculty members respond to changes in their discipline with a kind of cellular growth in their departments: when a new specialization comes into its own (Anglophone literature, cultural studies, queer theory), we simply, if not always easily, add a new faculty line. The department, then, has got the area "covered," although individual faculty members do not have to change much. High school teachers, however, though they usually work in departments, do not specialize. They are, each one of them, responsible for all the literary study that 120 to 150 students will receive in a year. They cannot count on a colleague to cover an area; they must cover it themselves. Like Walt Whitman's poet, they must be large, they must contain multitudes.

Or maybe high school teachers aren't supposed to change, aren't supposed to keep up. Have we, without thinking about it much, relegated to high schools the responsibility for teaching the canon so that we can teach the interesting material more closely related to our scholarship? In this view, we may want students to read *Gatsby* and *Great Expectations* and *Huck Finn,* just as long we don't have to do the teaching. According to recent research (Applebee), the ten most frequently taught texts in high schools are heavily canonical: four plays by Shakespeare and six of the other usual suspects (*Huck*, *Gatsby*, *Great Expectations*, . . .). To what extent does our teaching implicitly assume—or at least hope for—an acquaintance with literature that we are less than eager to teach ourselves?

Is teaching students how to make arguments about literature the best way to teach them how to think about literature? Constructing an argument usually involves the selection of one possibility over others, but the best arguments set that range of possibilities into conversation with one another. In fact, the best arguments are seen as part of a larger discussion about an issue, text, or author. But students reading a text for the first time are unlikely to see a range of possibilities; they sometimes have difficulty seeing even one. Is it possibly premature to ask them to narrow the range of their interests about a text, to stake a claim for one reading above others before they have explored those others? What if we asked students to multiply possibilities in their writing, to generate a series of possible readings, to draft dialogues among different points of view, to reach for a more spacious sense of a text's meanings instead of nailing just one? Constructing arguments for one another is how we live our professional lives, but students are not us and are not likely to become us. By privileging argument in our teaching over other forms of discourse, we may block our students' sense—our own sense—of how reading makes us rich.

Do the material conditions under which most high school teachers work—the student load; the daily, hourly classes; the absence of time, office space, and privacy; the curricular power of administrators—contrast so sharply with the material conditions under which

> college faculty members work that the two practices must be seen, finally, as different in kind, calling on different skills, different investments, different modes of intelligence? If the freedom to choose is one of the defining characteristics of the professoriat, how realistic is the assumption that high school teachers, operating with conspicuously less freedom, can learn in our context how to teach in theirs?

Such questions shape our continuing reform agenda.

Paul Diehl, *Department of English, University of Iowa*
Miriam Gilbert, *Department of English, University of Iowa*
James Marshall (chair), *Department of English, University of Iowa*
Janet Smith, *Iowa City Community Schools*
Bonnie S. Sunstein, *English Education Program, University of Iowa*

WORKS CITED

Applebee, A. N. *Literature in the Secondary School.* Urbana: NCTE, 1993.

Brooks, Cleanth, and Robert Penn Warren. *Understanding Poetry.* New York: Henry Holt, 1938.

Graff, Gerald. *Professing Literature.* Chicago: U of Chicago P, 1987.

Heath, S. B. *Ways with Words.* New York: Cambridge UP, 1983.

Kramer, Rita. *Ed School Follies: The Miseducation of America's Teachers.* New York: Free, 1991.

Lortie, Dan. *Schoolteacher: A Sociological Study.* Chicago: U of Chicago P, 1975.

Ohmann, Richard. *English in America.* New York: Oxford UP, 1976.

Sizer, Theodore. *Secondary Schools at the Turn of the Century.* New Haven: Yale UP, 1964.

UNIVERSITY OF VIRGINIA

Fit Teachers Though Few

More than once during the MLA Teacher Education Project, we felt like strangers in a strange land. Unlike many of our colleagues at the other institutions participating in the project, we in the English department at the University of Virginia do not devote much of our time or attention to the deliberate, mindful training of secondary school teachers of English. Several of us do work individually with secondary school teachers, as we describe below, but two features of teacher training at the University of Virginia have combined to keep that training outside our collective attention. First, students who want to be secondary school teachers constitute only about five percent of the English majors that graduate each year. Second, those students enroll in a five-year program administered by the Curry School of Education, which remains separate from the Department of English, although students in the five-year program must fulfill the requirements of an English major.

Despite these differences between our program and some of the others, the teacher education project gave us an opportunity to review teacher training at the University of Virginia and to discover that for the most part the English department serves this small population adequately albeit often unconsciously. At the end of this report, we have specific suggestions for enhancing the role played by English department faculty members in teacher training, but we begin by describing aspects of our university, our department, and the Curry School of Education that bear most directly on the training of teachers of English. Then we consider what we learned from conversations both with graduates of the five-year program and with area high school teachers. The suggestions we make follow directly from these conversations.

The University of Virginia is a public research university. According to *University of Virginia at a Glance* in the university Web site, the university offers 48 bachelor's degrees in 46 fields, 98 master's degrees in 68 fields, 6 educational specialist degrees, 2 first-professional degrees (law or medicine), and 55 doctoral degrees in 54 fields. The total student enrollment is approximately 18,000: 12,000 are undergraduate students, 4,000 graduate students, and 1,700 law or medicine students.

For public higher education in Virginia, the 1990s have meant drastic financial cuts. According to *Some Virginia Higher Education Facts* (1995), the university receives only 12% of its funding from the state, as opposed to 27% in 1989 (State Council of Higher Education for Virginia). In 1989, Virginia ranked twenty-ninth in the country in state appropriations per student; as of 1995, it ranked forty-third. While these cuts have had a variety of effects on the Department of English, some of which are harder to isolate and quantify than others, we can point to one effect as a clear example. Because the budget for teaching assistants has not increased to keep up with inflation over the last several years, we are staffing fewer courses with discussion sections led by graduate instructors. ENAM 311 (American Literature before 1865) used to consist of two lectures a week given by a professor and sections taught by graduate students. Now it consists only of a professor's lectures; graduate students handle the grading of papers and exams but do no teaching. Since students in the five-year teaching program take several large lectures, which we discuss below, this change affects the quality of their education. Other factors, such as growth in class sizes, our inability to offer competitive fellowships to successful graduate applicants, and the stagnation of faculty salaries, also have an undeniable effect on our undergraduate program, but they are indirect and do not lend themselves easily to analysis.

Despite the diminishment of state aid to the university, the Department of English has managed to maintain its national reputation. According to a report released by the National Research Council in September 1995, in a survey of faculty quality the graduate program in English at Virginia ranked fourth overall and fifth in educational effectiveness. Although the department has strengths in all the traditional periods of English and American literature, as well as in many other areas that reflect recent theoretical and methodological developments in our discipline, it is especially strong in nineteenth-century British literature, bibliography and textual editing, and creative writing. The faculty consists of 38 professors, 13 associate professors, 7 assistant professors, and 8 lecturers, for a total of 66. The usual faculty teaching load is four courses a year, only one of which should be a graduate course and at least one of which should be either a 200- or 300-level undergraduate course. With 330 graduate students in residence during the fall of 1995 and 281 undergraduate majors receiving degrees during the winter, spring, and summer of 1995, the English department has the largest graduate and undergraduate programs in the College of Arts and Sciences.

Although its reputation rests largely on the research of its faculty members, the English department devotes considerable time and attention to the teaching of teachers, both its graduate instructors and schoolteachers throughout the Commonwealth of Virginia. Recently the English department began offering two new graduate courses, Teaching the Introductory Literature Course and Teaching Methods. Both are one-credit courses aimed at beginning graduate instructors, the former focusing on 200-level literature courses, the latter on the required composition course. Before students teach composition, they work with the director of writing programs in a course called Academic and Professional Writing, in which they run their own weekly sessions for small groups of undergraduates. In addition, they meet weekly with the director of writing programs to discuss pedagogical matters. In 200-level introductory literature courses, graduate instructors have the opportunity to work in teams of six or seven with a faculty member. Together the faculty member and graduate instructors discuss various possible approaches and construct a common syllabus. During the semester of teaching, the graduate instructors meet regularly with the faculty member to discuss whatever practical and theoretical issues arise.

With the founding of the Center for the Liberal Arts in 1984, the department began making regular contributions to the professional development of Virginia schoolteachers. Members of the English faculty frequently travel throughout the state to give presentations to teachers at high schools during the academic year, usually in a series devoted to a particular topic selected in consultation with schoolteachers or their representatives. Some recent topics have been "Foundations of the Modern in Literature and Art," "New Texts, New Voices: Asian Literature and Culture," "Contemporary Southern Literature," "New Issues in British and American Texts," "Contemporary Literature and Culture," and "Contemporary Women Writers." During the summer, English department faculty members have led two- and three-week seminars for teachers in Virginia Beach, such as Rethinking the Role of Grammar in the English Curriculum; Modernism and the Novel in the Twentieth Century; The Doom of Romance; World Literature: Studies in Contemporary South American Fiction; and a seminar on Shakespeare. Alternatively, teachers can apply to come to the University of Virginia for residential institutes, such as Reading, Understanding, and Teaching Poetry or Forms and Practices of Fiction. According to a summary provided by the center, since 1984 its programs have served 8,235 teachers and involved 351 arts and sciences faculty members, 217 of whom teach at the University of Virginia. The center has received state and national awards and recognition for "leadership in the rejuvenation of secondary and elementary education" (*Standards of Learning*).

Since all students in the five-year teacher education program, which we describe more fully below, must also fulfill our requirements for an English major, we should call attention to recent changes in those requirements. During the 1994–95 academic year, the department voted to adopt several changes which took effect in the fall of 1998. Before, a student planning to major in English had to earn a grade of C or better in one of the specially designated 200-level seminars. Once the student had fulfilled this prerequisite, he or she needed to complete thirty-two hours of course work at the 300 level or higher. Although a student could substitute designated courses for either or both parts of the required eight-hour survey of British literature (ENGL 381-382), the basic requirements were these: ENGL 381-382; any medieval or Renaissance course except Shakespeare; a Shakespeare course; any eighteenth-century course or a course in American literature to 1865; a course in a so-called nontraditional subject, such as Women's studies, African literature, Caribbean literature.

The new requirements for the major lengthen the required survey to three semesters: ENGL 381 (British Literature before 1660), ENGL 382 (English and American Literature, 1660–approximately 1870), and ENGL 383 (Literature in English, approximately 1870–Present). These changes resulted from extensive discussions both about the place and significance of American literature in our curriculum and about the importance of introducing students to literature in English that does not come from Great Britain, Ireland, or the United States. In the past, apparently we assumed that since most English majors took at least one course in American literature anyway, we did not need to require such a course. In addition, our old requirements made it clear that the people who established them assumed that the primary story that needed telling in an

English department was the story of English literature, while the story of American literature constituted a subplot of local interest and importance. In changing ENGL 382, which focused on eighteenth- and nineteenth-century English literature, to a course that includes American literature of the same period, we have acknowledged that the story of American literature is too important to be left to a casual aside.

Meanwhile, in introducing ENGL 383 in the fall of 1998, a course that focuses on twentieth-century literature written in English throughout the world, we have acknowledged our responsibility to show students the range of such literature and to include that literature in the story of the literary production of a century that is coming to a close. Since both ENGL 382 and 383 demand of lecturers a breadth and depth of expertise that exceeds what most of us feel comfortable claiming for ourselves, initially we are teaching these courses in teams of two. In most of the large classes offered by the department, lecturers tend to come forward voluntarily from the ranks of the senior faculty.

Since we are adding a required course to our students' load, we have voted to simplify additional requirements to a Shakespeare course; one course in literature before 1800; one course in American, nineteenth-century British, or twentieth-century British literature; and one 400-level seminar. The introduction of this last requirement reflects our feeling that students should not graduate as English majors without taking an advanced course that provides the benefits and rigors of a small group. The 400-level courses are small seminars for approximately fifteen students. These courses tend to rely heavily on discussion and to emphasize student writing.

Those few English majors who are also prospective teachers of English, usually about ten to fifteen students a year, enroll in a five-year program during which they earn both a Bachelor of Arts degree in English and a Master of Teaching degree. The College of Arts and Sciences and the Curry School of Education share responsibility for the BA-MT programs. The Curry School oversees program admissions, field experience (including student teaching), assessment at the completion of the program, and certification requirements. Meanwhile, individual departments in the College of Arts and Sciences, along with the special-subject faculty members of the Curry School, determine content area requirements in their respective fields. The College of Arts and Sciences also determines the general studies requirements. Additional requirements are stipulated by Virginia state or national accreditation agencies. That these requirements have been changing rapidly lately places an added burden on advisers in the college and the Curry School. The state requirements have become more flexible, whereas those of the college have become more specific. The Virginia program follows the guidelines prepared by the National Council of Teachers of English (NCTE) special Committee on Teacher Preparation and Certification (*Standards for the English Language Arts*).

Students in the BA-MT programs are first and always students of the College of Arts and Sciences, then simultaneously members of the college and the teacher education program (in their second through fourth year), and then (for the last half of their fourth and all of their fifth year) graduate students in teacher education, provided they meet the criteria set for grade point average, Graduate Record Examination, and field performance. They do not receive their BA degree until they finish their fifth year and the MT requirements. When they graduate, they receive both diplomas at the same ceremony.

Prospective teachers must meet the requirements for an English major described above, but they must also use some of their electives to meet specific requirements of the BA-MT program: one course each in American literature (pre-1900), American literature (post-1900), the novel, poetry, and the history of the English language. In addition, each student must complete at least six credits of graduate courses in British or American literature. Strongly recommended but not required are at least one course in creative writing or nonfiction writing beyond the 100-level composition courses, women's studies, African-American and other minority literatures, as well as course work and practical experience in theater, cinema, and other visual and print media.

The required courses taught by the Education school are Learning and Development; Curriculum and Instruction; Literature for Adolescents; Linguistics for Teachers (also called Language, Literacy, and Culture); The Exceptional Individual; Instruction and Assessment; Teaching English; Teaching Composition; Seminar in Special Topics; Seminar in English Teaching; Teaching Associateship in English; Contemporary Educational Issues; and Field Project in English. Several of these courses have additional laboratory and field-experience components.

Examining twenty-nine transcripts of students who graduated between 1992 and 1995 inclusive, we discovered that there has been some discrepancy between written requirements for the teacher training program and the courses students actually take. For example, only seven students took ENLS 303 (History of the English Language), but this course is listed as a requirement in the published literature. Further investigation showed that the English department did not always offer this course. We also found that although a course in African American and other minority literatures is strongly recommended, few students followed the recommendation. In addition, we observed that few students took undergraduate courses beyond the 300 level, and no students participated in the English department Distinguished Majors Program.

Our study of the transcripts showed that the courses that students took most frequently—History of English Literature (ENGL 381-382); Shakespeare I and II (ENRN 321-322); and American Literature from the Puritans to the Present (ENAM 311-312)—are all large lecture courses, enrolling between a hundred and four hundred students. The ENGL and ENRN courses consist of two weekly lectures delivered by professors and a weekly section meeting led by graduate students. The ENAM courses also consist of lectures delivered by professors, but as we noted above, they no longer have discussion sections led by graduate students and rely instead on graduate student graders to handle most of the student writing and exams. All these courses require ten to twenty pages of writing and a final examination. Some also have a midterm examination.

After we examined the transcripts of recent graduates, we consulted a survey of recent graduates of the BA-MT program. During 1994, the Curry School of Education interviewed a sample of teachers from the first graduating class of the five-year teacher education program. The sample represented all grade levels and all program areas. The Curry School then compared the findings of these interviews with those of interviews with graduates in the field after two years, and with teaching associates in their last year of the program. Eventually the school shared the results with the self-study committees evaluating the program and making recommendations for improvements. The majority of the teachers in this sample, after five years, were teaching in suburban or rural areas.

When asked about weaknesses or recommendations for improving the teacher education program, these graduates made the following recommendations:

Greater preparation in reading for elementary school majors
More, and more practical, preparation in classroom management
Preparation for work with special-needs students
Provision of appropriate background and experience for middle grades
Better coordination and communication between the College of Arts

> and Sciences and the Curry School of Education (Curry School of Education, "Evaluation Interviews," "Phone Interviews," and "Teaching Associate Interviews").

We cite these recommendations to show that all but one of them involve matters beyond the competence of the Department of English at the University of Virginia. The call for better coordination and communication between the College of Arts and Sciences and the Curry School of Education, which we endorse, also involves changes that our department cannot make by itself, but we believe that the strategies we suggest below reflect the spirit of this call.

In an effort to identify matters or problems that pertain specifically to teacher training in the Department of English, we initiated longer conversations with selected recent graduates, usually by telephone. In these conversations, we asked them to evaluate their training as English majors. For the most part, they seemed content with courses in the department. Most admitted having fairly modest expectations regarding their courses outside the School of Education. They tended to talk about their English classes as providing "content" knowledge, whereas their classes at the Curry School provided pedagogic "theory." In other words, none had expected English classes to teach them how to teach; several, in fact, indicated that the differences between a university course and a high school course were so great that the former was in no way a pedagogic model for the latter.

What the students had unanimously expected from their English courses was an adequate "grounding" (the word most often used) in English and American literary history. An introduction to a range of canonical works; some ways of understanding and talking about these works; and a sense of familiarity with the literary and social histories into which the works fit: these are the things the Curry students said they needed from the English department. Not surprisingly, their approach was on the whole a pragmatic one. They wanted to be able to take something useful away from their college classes. In this context, *useful* invariably meant content knowledge rather than pedagogic skill or critical theory. Several expressed some passing interest in various forms of literary theory, but even these considered theory to be at best a secondary consideration.

Our conversations supported the results of our survey of transcripts, confirming that BA-MT students tend to cluster into the big survey courses, especially in American literature. Given their desire to cover a range of material, this clustering makes perfect sense. Only one student had taken a 400-level course. She thought it a very useful experience but also considered it a "supplement" to the survey courses she took. When asked whether a 400-level seminar should be required for BA-MT students, no one objected, but no one seemed especially enthusiastic. This absence of enthusiasm may well come from a lack of understanding of what can be accomplished in a seminar that cannot be accomplished in a lecture course.

The responses of students reflect both the strengths and weaknesses of most of our 300-level courses. The students wanted grounding, and most thought they got it. But with few exceptions none seemed to have been particularly inspired or challenged by these courses. Several students spoke of them solely in terms of receiving information. While receiving information is unquestionably one aspect of literary training, it is not the only one. If former students do not see the point of taking a seminar, the Department of English needs to work harder to describe and distinguish among the various kinds of courses it offers.

With respect to advising, the idea that we consolidate the BA-MT students by assigning them all a single adviser in the department received unanimous support from former students. Two of the people we spoke with had sought out particular faculty members for advice and mentoring; the others felt, to a greater or lesser degree, cut off from the department, since their relatively small number made them all but invisible in large courses. They seemed to feel like interlopers in the department and tended not to approach course instructors with requests for kinds of assignments that would more nearly meet their needs as education school students.

Having consulted our own recent graduates, we decided to add another dimension to our study by speaking with English teachers from three area high schools: Charlottesville High School, Western Albemarle High School, and St. Anne's–Belfield School, a private school. We also examined representative syllabi of English and related humanities courses taught in grades 9 through 12 in these schools. Although most of the teachers had not trained at the University of Virginia, the data gathered speaks usefully to our practices. The main goals of our investigation were two. First, we wanted to get an overview of the range of literary works being taught in local classrooms, to explore the institutional constraints (if any) under which local high school teachers operate in designing their syllabi, and to examine the correlation between the academic emphasis of the University of Virginia English major and the academic emphasis of high school curricula. Second, we hoped to gather information from experienced English teachers about the way their professional and academic training had or had not prepared them to enter the high school classroom. We also invited their suggestions about what might be done to improve the education of prospective high school English teachers.

The teachers to whom we spoke said that they could work relatively independently in designing their syllabi, although several wished they had more time to discuss curricular design and to consult with their colleagues. They generally worked within quite broad institutional guidelines. The *Albemarle County Public Schools English / Language Arts Curriculum Guide* for grades 9–12, for example, is not a particularly constrictive document; it permits instructors a good deal of freedom in deciding how its educational goals will be met and what texts they will teach. Perhaps a more significant factor informing curriculum design is the simple fact that the large majority of these students are college-bound. Some seventy percent of the students in the two public schools go on to some form of further education; at St. Anne's, it is nearly one hundred percent. The students' eventual performance on the SAT and AP tests is thus a governing issue.

The variety of content in the syllabi from just three high schools proved especially striking. Western Albemarle High School, whose curriculum seems to be the most traditional, offers its college-bound twelfth-graders a historical survey of largely British literature: selections of canonical works from *Beowulf* to the moderns. Meanwhile, ninth-graders at the same school spend a good deal of time on the Bible as literature. At Charlottesville High School, by contrast, students have the opportunity to take an interdisciplinary honors humanities course in world studies, cotaught by history and English instructors; it is a survey of world history, from antiquity to World War I, that has a certain amount of non–western European focus and is complemented by readings in world literature. The twelfth-graders at St. Anne's read an eclectic mix of nineteenth- and twentieth-century poetry and fiction; it ranges from Gerard Manley Hopkins to Sylvia Plath, from *The Death of Ivan Ilych* to *Their Eyes Were Watching God*. The eleventh-grade courses in American literature showed the most convergence across the three schools; but at Charlottesville High School the students read Barbara Kingsolver and Kaye Gibbons in addition to canonical works by Hawthorne, Melville, Hemingway, and Salinger, and the school offers an English–social studies course in American studies as well as an eleventh-grade English course on the African American experience. At St. Anne's the curriculum supplements the basic

American survey with plays by Sophocles and Shakespeare. Teachers at St. Anne's integrate world literature with American-British literature on a regular basis and also teach the *Odyssey* and *Julius Caesar* in tandem with an ancient history course.

Teachers tended to complain about time constraints on developing new curricula. This complaint was most obvious at one school, where there had been an institutional turn toward a more multicultural canon. Teachers from that school remarked that the pressures of their schedules made it difficult to explore and evaluate a wide range of possible new readings. This problem was exacerbated by the fact that their training had tended to focus on the Western canon. Interviewees from both the public schools, whose faculty members also had to design English courses for non-college-track students, wished they had a wider background in young adult literature and had received more advice about how to engage the interest of reluctant readers. Several wished that they had been encouraged to take more college courses in contemporary literature or that they had had access to courses that were organized thematically rather than historically.

There seemed to be a general feeling that in the upper grades a balance between content coverage and the ongoing development of students' writing skills was especially difficult to achieve. One teacher remarked that preparation for more-complex interdisciplinary courses seemed to cut down on time available to grade student writing: she found it difficult to comment on student work in detail. Another teacher wished she had had more instruction in how to comment on student writing. Written work in the college-prep courses in the eleventh and twelfth grades of the public schools generally seemed to be divided among quizzes, journals, and essays of the 250-word, five-paragraph variety.

In conversation, nearly every teacher suggested that prospective high school teachers should get into the classroom earlier, since extended classroom observation would give them a clearer sense of what awaited them and would bring into focus the way that pedagogical theory must necessarily be accommodated to the many variables of classroom practice. Interviewees noted that young teachers must be able to improvise and adapt to specific contexts. They also emphasized that high school English teachers are teachers of children as much as English teachers: many young teachers seemed unaware that course content would not teach itself and that they must come up with ways of communicating that content energetically. As far as the teaching of writing was concerned, teachers asserted more than once that younger teachers seemed better trained to teach personal narrative than to teach analysis or argument. One interviewee also suggested that she would have liked to have had more training on the psychology of reading—on how to unpack the mechanics of a process one has acquired by and large instinctively. There was some disagreement about the usefulness of various forms of non-teacher-centered or "active" learning. Some teachers said they would have liked more emphasis on teaching students the skills that would help them edit their own or their peers' papers. But another teacher perceived the growing emphasis on "process teaching" in her school as an obstacle to efficient communication of background information that would enable the class to move on to more sophisticated tasks.

Almost every teacher interviewed wished he or she had had more training in the material details of classroom management (matters as basic as how to use a blackboard, how to use an overhead projector) and in the paperwork of teaching (how to write up assessments and lesson plans, how to keep grade books and other records, how to organize a notebook). One teacher also suggested that beginning teachers might benefit from some pointers on how to manage parent-teacher conferences effectively.

Examining the remarks of these (not necessarily University of Virginia–trained) teachers in the light of our institutional practices suggests that the Curry School has anticipated many of their wishes in four particular areas. First, at the Curry School, distribution requirements for prospective high school English teachers do seem to foster the kind of content coverage some of the teachers found lacking in their own training. Majors in secondary school education and English must take an education school course on literature for adolescents and an English department course on twentieth-century American literature. Moreover, the English department offers a significant number of undergraduate coursesin cultural studies, women's literature, and the writings of various ethnic minorities.

Second, with respect to the teaching of writing, our secondary school education majors are required to take a course in the teaching of writing. But we might usefully encourage more dialogue between the Curry School faculty members specializing in this area and the people involved in teaching expository prose writing in the English department. Now that the Department of English has been augmented by faculty members from the former Rhetoric and Communications Department, which the university closed on the recommendation of a task force charged with discovering ways to save money, it might be a good time to call on the expertise of those teachers.

Third, the Curry School offers an elective entitled Positive Classroom

Management. Its description suggests it may be the course on classroom basics the local teachers wished they had taken. But the Curry School survey of its graduates suggests that many of them would have liked "more practical training" in classroom management. More of our BA-MT students should be encouraged to take it.

Fourth, Field Experience—a one-credit-hour course that prospective Curry School majors are asked to take in their second year—would seem to give them the early exposure to classroom situations local teachers felt to be so desirable. It would be useful to gather some information on education majors' experience in this course.

During our conversations with both our recent graduates and area high school teachers, we found ourselves thinking about the new pressures on traditionally trained teachers to understand and use various forms of computer technology. The University of Virginia offers two approaches to preparing teachers for changing conditions in the profession. One teaches about up-to-date computers, software, media, and relevant methods. The other teaches how using these new media might alter traditional ways of teaching and learning English. In both courses, it is important that the student teacher use various technologies in order to understand what they can do.

At the Curry School of Education, prospective teachers learn technological skills by using software to prepare instructional materials and lesson plans. The following courses are offered but not required of students in the BA-MT program in English: Instructional Technology for Teaching and Learning, Instructional Computing (the sequel to Instructional Technology), Software Applications in Education, Production of Instructional Materials, and Advanced Video Technology. In addition, in a *CU-SeeMe* environment, a telecommunications course, Contemporary Issues, links seven universities in the United States and Canada. In real time, the course studies six cases of cooperative problem solving. The development of a school newspaper, for example, teaches teachers what factors to consider in solving problems that professional teachers encounter.

The Department of English offers one undergraduate course in technology and the study of English. This course, Theory and Practice of Hypertext, combines discussion sections and lab sessions to train the student in authoring, editing, and maintaining a hypertext document. The course teaches students how to learn about computers by using computers. The intersection of image and text, as well as online thinking and argumentation, gets specific attention and practice. Students learn, for example, about the prominent role of software tools for using and understanding other software tools. Both the particular skills and the self-adjusting attitudes developed in this course are essential skills for teachers who will use technology in contemporary and future English programs.

Currently under consideration, a course entitled History of the Book anticipates and evaluates assumptions about traditional patterns of reading, writing, and speaking. As it instructs a prospective teacher in learning how linear print influenced writing and speaking, the course will also develop knowledge that the traditional discipline of English does not address but that contemporary high school students encounter daily, such as methods of hypertext research, interactive CD-ROM, hyperfiction, online communication, and multimedia texts.

We propose in addition the development of a third course, one that would prepare teachers for unforeseeable changes in the educational institution. An upper-level interdisciplinary seminar, The Cultural Impact of Technologies, would study the life spans of particular technologies to understand how those technologies have altered institutions and produced other technologies in their image.

In conclusion, we note with pleasure that the Curry School of Education has received national recognition for excellence in teacher preparation and that the Department of English ranks among the best in the country. Students who enroll in the five-year BA-MT program enjoy the benefits of these distinctions. Although our investigation has turned up some recommendations from recent graduates for improvement in the training students receive in the Curry School, none of the recommendations pertains specifically to the curriculum of the English department, and we do not see the need for introducing a group of new courses.

One recommendation does reflect a weakness that we have identified in our program. In desiring better communication and coordination between the College of Arts and Sciences and the Curry School, recent graduates wish for an improvement that the English department can make simply and at no cost. Instead of scattering the relatively few BA-MT students among advisers throughout the English department, advisers who may have little or no experience with such students, the department should consolidate its advising of them, assigning each new group of ten to fifteen students to a single adviser who understands their situation and can direct them accordingly. We recommend strongly that the dean of the faculty and the chair of the English department recognize the importance of this adviser by releasing him or her from other advising.

With this simple change, the adviser could help the students make better use of the courses they take and keep them from feeling like outsiders in the department. For example, an adviser could encourage students to take courses in technology, in African American literature, or in other areas, which would serve them in a high school with a strong technological, multicultural, or other focus. An adviser could also give majors more active guidance in using the resources of the department as they satisfy their education school distribution requirements in poetry, the novel, and post-1900 American literature. The adviser could bring to their attention courses that would increase their familiarity with works and authors they might eventually use in their own teaching.

In general, the adviser could encourage students to approach their professors and engage them in discussion about the teaching of literature and writing. Although students claim that they look to the English department for grounding in the content of our discipline and not for pedagogical instruction, their English courses cannot help becoming more valuable if students take advantage of opportunities to discuss with their professors how they teach what they teach.

In addition, we strongly recommend that all BA-MT students take at least one and preferably two 400-level seminars in literature. Although university teaching may appear to have little in common with high school teaching, high school teaching has far more in common with spontaneously managing the many voices heard in a seminar than it does with delivering a written lecture to two hundred or three hundred people. In their 400-level seminars, BA-MT students should make a special effort to incorporate their pedagogical concerns into their course work. For example, they might ask to give presentations, lead discussions, or orient their written work toward teaching. If none of these possibilities seems appropriate, at the very least they should meet with their professors during office hours and initiate conversation about teaching. Such conversation could enrich the study of young teachers in the English department.

Postscript

In many ways we started from further back than other teams involved in the MLA Teacher Education Project, and so we had further to go to coordinate the needs and goals of prospective secondary school teachers with the resources our English department has to offer. The two-worlds problem—education school students versus “mainstream” majors—has always been acute at Virginia. Our committee thus saw its task largely in terms of consciousness-raising among the faculty (beginning with the committee members themselves, none of whom entered this project with a clear sense of the specific educational needs of the prospective teachers in their midst). Because education school students make up a relatively small percentage of the students in most English classes, faculty members tend not to be fully aware of this particular constituency. The committee worked to disseminate among English department faculty members information both about the specific requirements imposed by the Curry School on its BA-MT students and about the different needs and expectations of the Curry students in our classes. Most faculty members, once they become aware of the issues, are more than willing to work with these students to craft assignments, projects, tests, and essays that help hone the professional skills the students will need. After consulting with faculty members in the Curry School, the committee saw no need to propose changes in the English department curriculum. The existing curriculum is adequate to the task at hand, so long as faculty members remain aware of the different constituencies they serve. The committee did recommend one structural change in the department, which was adopted in 1997. Academic advising for education school students has been consolidated, so that a single faculty member is now responsible for all such students. The results so far have all been positive. Students feel that the quality of the advising has dramatically improved and that they no longer are interlopers in the department.

Stephen D. Arata, *Department of English, University of Virginia*
Stephen Cushman (chair), *Department of English, University of Virginia*
Paul David Erb, *Saint Anne's–Belfield School*
Clare Regan Kinney, *Department of English, University of Virginia*
Joseph E. Strzepek, *Department of Curriculum, Instruction, and Special Education, University of Virginia*

WORKS CITED

Albemarle County Public School English / Language Arts Curriculum Guide. 1994; rev. 1995.

Curry School of Education. "Evaluation Interviews with Curry Grads—5 Yrs. Later." *The Communicator.* 1993. 3.

———. "Phone Interviews—2nd Year Teachers." 1993.

———. "Teaching Associate Interviews." 1993.

Standards for the English Language Arts. Urbana: NCTE; Newark: Intl. Reading Assn., 1996.

Standards of Learning for Virginia Public Schools. Richmond: Virginia Board of Educ., 1995.

State Council of Higher Education for Virginia. *Some Virginia Higher Education Facts.*, 1995.

University of Virginia at a Glance. U of Virginia. 15 Sept. 1998 <http://minerva.acc.virginia.edu/facts/glance_enrollment.htm>.

REPORTS FROM FOREIGN LANGUAGE DEPARTMENTS

ARIZONA STATE UNIVERSITY, TEMPE

Teacher Education Program Reform: A Case in Point

When the Modern Language Association first announced its Teacher Education Project, several faculty members in the Department of Languages and Literatures at Arizona State University were already initiating an effort to assess and improve the existing teacher education program in Asian languages, French, German, Russian, and Spanish. At the same time, the College of Education was engaged in an attempt to "reinvent" its programs for undergraduates and postbaccalaureate students. Our participation in the MLA project gave impetus and added credibility to our efforts in teacher education.

As part of the MLA's project, our department assessed the status quo and began the process of fomenting change in each of the five language sections. The department's team first met with section coordinators, the supervisors of graduate teaching assistants, and the advisers of education majors to review each language section's program and present the elements of our model curriculum. Each language section received specific recommendations and was asked to set priorities, goals, and timelines.

The Institutional Context

The main campus of Arizona State University is located in Tempe, a city of 165,000 in the Phoenix metropolitan area. Libraries, which house over 8 million items, and free computing facilities throughout the campus support the research of students and faculty members. Of ASU's 43,000 students, 11,000 are pursuing graduate studies.

Arizona State University is one of only eight universities in the country without a medical school or land-grant standing to achieve Research University I status from the Carnegie Foundation for the Advancement of Teaching. It was also one of only five research universities to receive a Pew Foundation grant to start the Preparing Future Faculty Program. ASU is proud of the high achievements of its undergraduates: ten Truman scholars in the past five years, more than any other public university received in that time; a 1995 Rhodes scholar; and five 1995 Woodrow Wilson fellows.

Within the College of Arts and Sciences, the Department of Languages and Literatures offers instruction to approximately six thousand students in eighteen foreign languages, including Classical Greek and Latin. Its faculty is composed of over fifty tenured and tenure-track members, several part-time and yearly-contract faculty members, and typically one to five visiting professors from various countries.

The department offers the following degrees: BA (Chinese, French, German, Italian, Japanese, Russian, Spanish), MA (French, German, Spanish), and PhD (Spanish). The French and German sections have lecturers in charge of coordinating first- and second-year teaching assistants, who carry the responsibility for teaching most of the first- and second-year classes; the Spanish section has a new assistant professor with a specialization in applied linguistics, to serve as the director of the basic language program. He currently supervises sixty teaching assistants, with the aid of a full-time assistant, two lecturers (who also teach three classes each), and two specially trained teaching assistants (who also teach one class per semester).

As might be expected, a great many Spanish students speak the language at home. In a survey of lower-level Spanish students conducted in 1995 (Guntermann, Hendrickson, and Urioste 17), nineteen percent reported that they spoke Spanish at home to varying degrees. A special program is in place for them at the second- and third-year levels, but the number of sections of these classes is limited. For this and various other reasons, Spanish-speaking students register for regular classes at all levels. Beginning in the third year, there are also many Mormon missionaries, returned from around the world, who study the languages of their host countries in order to maintain their proficiency. Because many of these advanced students opt to become language teachers, our teacher candidates tend to speak their languages rather well. (The establishment of tests to document this proficiency is still in the planning stages.)

Each year our department graduates 15–20 Spanish teachers, 6–7

French teachers, 3–4 Japanese teachers, 1–2 German teachers, and 1–2 Russian teachers. The number of French candidates may be declining. That the number of Japanese candidates is increasing causes problems for those in charge of placing students in local schools for field experiences and student teaching, since high school Japanese programs are few in the Phoenix area.

At ASU, students desiring to become language teachers receive a bachelor of arts in education with a specialization in a language; the degree makes them eligible to be recommended to the Arizona Department of Education for state certification as secondary school teachers. A foreign language major who seeks to become a teacher must gain entry into the Professional Teacher Preparation Program after the completion of fifty-six credit hours with a GPA of 2.5 or better. Students are advised for their general studies and education courses in the College of Education, and they have a faculty adviser in the department who assists them in planning their language majors.

The Professional Teacher Preparation Program is a collaborative effort between the College of Education and other colleges. There is a long history of attempts to improve communication among the various units and colleges whose majors elect teaching as a profession. From 1990 until the 1995–96 academic year, for example, the University Secondary Teacher Education Council served this purpose. Two years ago, the associate dean for teacher education in the college established the Faculty of Teacher Education, a committee of faculty members campus-wide who teach or advise education majors. As a way of facilitating decisions pertaining to curricular changes and policies, a Teacher Education Programs Committee, composed of representatives from participating colleges, was also formed. It is housed within the Division of Curriculum and Instruction in the College of Education.

THE PROGRAM OF STUDY AND STUDENT TEACHING

Like other language majors, secondary school education majors must complete 30 credit hours in the major language and 15 in "related fields"—most commonly another language, area studies, or linguistics. The preservice teacher must also satisfy the professional education sequence, which prepares the aspiring student with a series of courses and field experiences, 35–36 credit hours over four semesters. The remaining credits toward the 120-credit-hour degree requirements involve course work in general studies.

The culminating experience for the preservice candidate is student teaching, which is coordinated by the Office of Professional Field Experiences in the College of Education. While student teachers are in the field during the fifteen-week experience, they are each assessed a minimum of four times by a university supervisor. Supervisors are specialists in secondary school education but not necessarily in foreign languages. This lack is an obvious weakness in our preparation of language teachers; financial considerations have not allowed the supervision of foreign language student teachers by a specialist in their field since the mid-1980s, when foreign language enrollments suddenly skyrocketed due to new language requirements at the same time that foreign language faculty members were lost to other universities.

In addition to the Professional Teacher Preparation Program, which is designed for undergraduates, there is a special postbac program for people with college degrees who wish to become certified to teach. In foreign languages these students must meet the same requirements as the undergraduates. To expedite their pursuit of certification, the College of Education designed a set of courses to be completed in less time than it takes undergraduates to fulfill the requirements of the Professional Teacher Preparation Program. Postbac students may also opt to work toward a special master's degree in education. At this time the postbac program is being evaluated for probable revisions, to include more hands-on experiences in the schools.

DEPARTMENTAL FACULTY ACTIVITY IN TEACHER EDUCATION

Faculty members in each of the five languages provide advising and content preparation for their majors, but the Department of Languages and Literatures has only one specialist in foreign language education, who teaches a generic methods course every semester. All teacher candidates take just one methods course, although Spanish majors are also required to take Spanish Applied Linguistics, which lays the theoretical and language-specific foundation for the methods preparation. In French, a similar course is available but not required. A recently approved MA in Asian studies is designed to include special teacher preparation in Japanese and Chinese.

Since 1980, the graduate-level course Trends and Issues in Language Teaching has been taught every other year. In addition, MA candidates in French, German, and Spanish may pursue degrees in language and culture. There are other programs in Spanish linguistics and applied linguistics.

In order to ensure the best possible preparation for all language majors, language study is required through the senior year, as well as the usual literature, linguistics, and civilization courses. At the basic level, teaching assistants are required to attend three weeks of orientation before their first semester of teaching, during which they also must take a course in methods of teaching. These courses are taught by the supervisors in French, German, and Spanish, all of whom are active in the profession. The French supervisor recently completed service as president of the Arizona Language Association and now edits its newsletter; the German supervisor is pursuing a PhD in pedagogy and second language acquisition at the University of Arizona; and the new Spanish supervisor is a publishing scholar with a PhD in applied linguistics.

Several faculty members in various languages have actively participated in professional language teaching activities with local schoolteachers in several ways: taking leadership roles in state teachers' organizations; leading and supporting the (currently defunct) collaborations of language teachers across levels; serving on the steering committee of the elementary schoolteachers' association; organizing and directing numerous workshops on pedagogical topics; and participating in the Faculty Ambassadors program, in which faculty members visit high schools to work with teachers, review curricula, and speak to students.

The MLA Project

During the 1995–96 academic year, the ASU team completed a baseline self-study of our programs and designed guidelines for a model program. The team began by surveying faculty members in five languages and collecting and analyzing course check sheets and syllabi. At the same time, it surveyed current education students at the most advanced levels, many of our recent graduates (1990–95), and mentoring teachers who have worked with language education students over the years, supervising their observation and participation experiences and their student teaching.

FACULTY SURVEY

Because language teachers need a high degree of proficiency in order to teach in the language and because teachers tend to teach the way they were taught, the team examined the experience of education majors in the department's courses. Faculty members in the five languages responded with almost total cooperation by answering the questionnaires and submitting course syllabi. The findings of this self-study are not particularly surprising: our program does not differ greatly from those of similar institutions.

Language Courses. Most language instructors report that they employ student-teacher conversations, explanations of language material, grammar and vocabulary drill, and student oral presentations. A much smaller group uses peer-group activities, authentic and semiauthentic listening exercises, literary readings, and cultural activities. It is only in the smallest group that students have the opportunity to experience student-led and student-organized activities, authentic readings from daily life, prereading exercises, and in-class communicative writing practice.

Tests and quizzes are most commonly used to assess students' progress in language courses; student written tasks and oral presentations to the class are also evaluated. Portfolios are used by a handful of instructors, and oral tests are typically administered at the end of each course.

Civilization, Literature, and Linguistics Courses. That civilization, literature, and linguistics courses are usually taught in the target language exclusively provides students with considerable valuable listening experience. But there is little small-group or pair work, and students have few opportunities to experience cooperative learning activities or prereading exercises. They write several papers in the target language, and a few faculty members require them to revise their work.

There is a particular need to plan specifically for the development of language proficiency in these content courses. In our program and other traditional programs, students typically enter such courses at the Intermediate level of proficiency, which means that they can speak and write sentences in the present tense, on topics close to their personal experience, with numerous grammatical inaccuracies. Yet, in literature, civilization, and linguistics courses, they must deal with intellectual content that requires extensive vocabulary and advanced grammar and the ability to use that vocabulary and that grammar for academic purposes. What has been lacking in such courses is systematic attention to the ability to describe and narrate in past and future time, in paragraph-length, coherent discourse. Students often graduate without these Advanced-level skills, for lack of practice in them. At ASU we plan to conduct further workshops for faculty members on proficiency development and methods of measuring it (such workshops were begun several years ago but discontinued).

VIEWS OF CURRENT STUDENTS, RECENT GRADUATES, AND MENTORING TEACHERS

Current Students (N=16). Questionnaires asked for ratings of language courses, assessment procedures, literature and culture courses, linguistics and methods courses, advising, and the extent to which the studies in the Department of Languages and Literatures and the College of Education were well integrated. The responses of this group were the most negative of all the groups; forty-four percent disagreed or disagreed strongly with the positive statements.

Highest ratings were given to the linguistics and methods courses. Lowest ratings were given to the evaluation of communicative oral and written practice; teaching formats in most literature and culture classes, in that they did not model teaching practices conducive to proficiency development; integration between the College of Education and the Department of Languages and Literatures; and the use of technology. (After the opening of new language laboratory and computing facilities, combined with three consecutive summer workshops for faculty members, the use of technology has become more common.)

Students also were asked to provide written comments and recommendations. Most commonly, they criticized the relation between the College of Education and the Department of Languages and Literatures and the lack of variety and appropriateness of teaching methods in both. They asked for more preparation in methods and applied linguistics; more exposure to portfolios, oral exams, listening exercises, and prereading preparation; and more courses in area studies taught in the target languages.

Recent Graduates (N=21). This group was much less critical and more inclined (or able) to provide helpful suggestions, although the graduates gave few high ratings to language courses, assessment, or teaching approaches in the literature and civilization courses. They gave mixed ratings to advising and the linguistics courses.

Their numerous written comments noted that the linguistics and methods courses had been the most useful, even critical, to their teaching careers, and they recommended the addition of more like them as well as more opportunities to study abroad, more speaking practice, more variety of teaching methods, and a better balance between grammar and communication. They praised the usefulness of specific activities that some individual faculty members had used (e.g., oral communication activities, the use of Hispanic television for teaching and testing) and expressed appreciation for the cultural contributions made by native-speaking teaching assistants.

This group was highly critical of the advising and preparation it had received in the College of Education and the lack of coordination between the College of Education and the Department of Languages and Literatures. They would have preferred less theory and more evidence of how it is applied, more instruction on how to organize classes, and more modeling of varied methods of teaching and procedures for assessing student achievement.

Mentoring Teachers (N=13). The mentoring teachers were four in French, four in Spanish, and five who taught more than one language, the languages including Russian, German, Japanese, and Latin. In general they were quite positive about the students' preparation in the respective languages and cultures, although several recommended that all future teachers have experience in a country where their language is spoken. Many teachers also made specific recommendations about how students could receive more preparation in planning lessons and designing whole units that were stimulating and that deviated from the textbook, in order for them to see the relations among teaching techniques, goals, and test items. These teachers were particularly critical of students' lack of abilities in classroom and time management.

They felt that future teachers will need to know the national and state standards and how to reach them; need expertise with technology, with curriculum development (because of new types of schools and increased local control), and with planning and team teaching cross-curriculum courses with teachers in other subject areas; and most particularly need to be able to work with increasingly diverse student groups.

Toward a Model Curriculum

Drawing on the information from the baseline self-study, the literature on educational reform, the two Houston conferences, and our reflections on our collective experience, the project team identified five areas of teacher development and wrote guidelines for a model curriculum that includes the two areas for which the department is most responsible: language and culture, linguistics and pedagogy. The curriculum guide is given in its entirety in the appendix to this report.

Issues That Affect Implementation

As we enter the all-important implementation phase of our project, we are aware of the difficulties that may arise on several fronts.

Consensus building among faculty members is one front. Like the faculty of most universities, ours have long paid little attention to teacher education, leaving it to the College of Education and one specialist in the department. For change to occur, each language section will need to attend to its own unique situation and needs. We plan to provide each section with specific recommendations and ideas and any help that it may request.

Another difficulty is resources: time, personnel, funding. For the implementation of our recommendations, one specialist in language teaching is inadequate. Either other language sections will have to target teacher education in future hires, or the department as a whole will need to pool resources or request a faculty line together. A new position is especially important if we are to expand our master's programs for teachers.

There should be incentives for attending to teacher education, devoting time and effort to it, and welcoming change. The university now boasts a system for rewarding teaching and service. Teacher education will have to be specified as one of the areas for which faculty members receive due compensation in these two categories.

A workable action plan is needed. Since this endeavor is the first of its kind, we wish to proceed in a manner that will result in improved programs in each language section.

Our department should collaborate with the College of Education and the schools. Differing cultures, together with a lack of well-established lines of communication and a lack of mechanisms for change, make it difficult for us to work closely together to achieve what we feel is necessary so that we do not continue to offer a rather fragmented experience for our students. We must seek ways to collaborate and to provide an integrated program, through which students may move more smoothly and perceive continuity in their preparation.

Our participation in this project has brought to our attention the gap that exists between traditional teacher preparation and the realities of high school classrooms. Through this project we have also become advocates for students and the programs and courses that serve them, and we have come to approach teaching from a more scholarly perspective, as both researchers and practitioners. We must now apply what we have learned, as we proceed with the implementation phases of the project.

Postscript

Since submitting our final report for the MLA Teacher Education Project, we have instituted a few changes in our programs and made plans for other, more substantial modifications.

First, requirements for entrance to the foreign language education programs are being raised; applicants may no longer apply credits from the first two years of language study toward the thirty hours that are required for the major. We are also considering requiring of applicants a minimum 3.0 GPA in courses in the major field.

Second, the College of Education has asked the academic units that offer teaching majors to provide two methods courses instead of one; the second course is to replace one of the two generic methods courses that are currently taught in the college. This request coincides perfectly with our plans as described in our report.

At the same time, the director of our MLA project, who is also a methods instructor, has been authorized to spend a one-semester sabbatical during the spring of 1999 redesigning the current multilanguage methods course and adding a language-specific course to be taught in Spanish, to serve as a possible model for the other languages. Until these courses are in place, the College of Education will continue to provide its current level of instruction.

Since it is expected that both of the newly designed courses will include clinical work in the schools, the sabbatical project will involve secondary school teachers in the planning and implementation of the program. A final component of the project will consist of collaboration with the College of Extended Education in assessing the in-service development needs of local teachers and designing means to meet those needs, including distance learning. To carry out these plans, grant funds will be sought.

Within the Department of Languages and Literatures, faculty members demonstrate a continued commitment to work with teachers and the schools. Another of our colleagues has been elected president of the Arizona Language Association, and three others continue to serve on its board of directors or Planning Committee. This year, a group of junior faculty members is organizing a regional language fair for high school students and teachers in the spring.

In teacher education in general, Arizona universities may experience reforms in the immediate future, given that the next president of the Arizona Board of Regents has stated repeatedly that teacher education will be a major focus of her efforts. In addition, the new governor of Arizona has placed education at the top of her priorities. We are hopeful that our plans for teacher education will be more successful, with the stated interest of these officials and the expressed support of key administrators in our two colleges.

Main author
C. Gail Guntermann (chair), *Department of Languages and Literatures, Arizona State University, Tempe*

Other members of the team
John Alexander, *Department of Languages and Literatures, Arizona State University, Tempe*
Pier Baldini, *Department of Languages and Literatures, Arizona State University, Tempe*
Liana Clarkson, *Mount View High School*
Suzanne Bader Hendrickson, *Department of Languages and Literatures, Arizona State University, Tempe*
Sheryl L. Santos, *College of Education, Arizona State University, Tempe*

WORK CITED

Guntermann, Gail, Suzanne Hendrickson, and Carmen de Urioste. "Basic Assumptions Revisited: Today's French and Spanish Students at a Large Metropolitan University." *Patterns and Policies: The Changing Demographics of Foreign Language Instruction.* Ed. Judith E. Liskin-Gasparro. Boston: Heinle, 1996. 3–33.

APPENDIX

Draft Model Curriculum Guide for Teacher Education

Goals

language proficiency at Advanced level in listening, speaking, reading, and writing

pedagogical knowledge and skills invested with current theories of language learning acquisition, the diversity of today's schools and students, classroom language learning research, and up-to-date technology

cultural knowledge and skills necessary for effective, confident interaction in immersion situations broad preparation in general academic studies (for effective citizenship, intellectual development, communicative abilities, leadership, content-based language teaching)

These goals are written in accordance with the National Foreign Language Standards and the Arizona Foreign Language Standards. To meet these goals, we recommend the following guidelines.

Language and Culture

In the model program, proficiency in the language and culture is achieved by

extensive practice of language for social, travel, and classroom related activities; emphasis placed on communicative ability, appropriateness, and accuracy in real-life situations
teaching in the target language at all levels
integration of language proficiency development, cultural knowledge, and literature at all levels
cooperative learning for planning, problem solving, and learning subject-matter content in all language and content courses
individual and group presentations of other subject matter (e.g., history, science, math) in the target language
use of the audiovisual lab and taped materials from television and radio
use of the computer lab for foreign language word processing, for the use of language-specific software, for interaction with native speakers (e.g., e-mail, voice mail, chat sessions) and for searching the Internet
use of authentic print media
related course work in other areas (e.g., history, art history, geography, philosophy, music)
stress on critical thinking in comparing and contrasting both home and target cultures
use of various types of literature at all levels
maintaining a portfolio of best work throughout the program
student peer teaching, editing, and evaluation
student self-monitoring and self-evaluation
use of prereading, reading, and postreading exercises in teaching all content
close advising and mentoring throughout the program
proficiency testing at entrance to the education program for diagnosis; proficiency testing before student teaching to assess whether or not candidates have reached an adequate level (e.g., Intermediate High)

PROCEDURES, FIRST TWO YEARS

Students should

learn appropriate social behavior for functioning in the culture, taking into account varied contexts, roles, gender, age, and their place as a foreigner

practice art of "getting around"
learn geography, customs, family roles, some art, literature, and music; history, politics, sociology, economics
select general and area studies courses to learn more about the culture
select a second area to teach
begin maintaining a comprehensive portfolio
reach proficiency level of Intermediate-Mid by end of fourth semester

PROCEDURES, FINAL YEARS

Students should

take diagnostic tests in all four skills and cultural knowledge, and get feedback, at beginning of third year
learn recent and current events in country or countries where target language is spoken; relate these to areas learned in first two years
continue intensive study of the language
practice with computer technology
work intensively with popular culture
take culture and civilization courses
pursue courses in related fields to learn more about the culture and area studies
learn literary terminology and concepts and overview of literary masterpieces; take at least one in-depth literature course
achieve conscious, systematic integration of language proficiency development into all content courses
study abroad or have immersion experience
take a capstone course, with individual projects that demonstrate learning and proficiency in the language and culture
receive proficiency testing in all four skills, to demonstrate Advanced level
finish and polish portfolios

Linguistics

In the model program, proficiency in linguistics is achieved by

study of basic concepts and theories of language and language use in communication
knowledge of phonology, morphology, and syntax of the target language
knowledge of theory and research in language acquisition in general and acquisition of the target language by adults and children
comparison of the native and target languages
applications of linguistic knowledge to teaching the language and for curriculum design; some practice in microteaching pronunciation, auditory discrimination, and vocabulary

gaining information about the language learner: learning styles and strategies, attitudes, motivations, language anxiety and language beliefs, and their relation to language learning

PROCEDURES

Students should

take an introductory course in linguistics
take an introduction to linguistics in the target language
take a course or courses in phonology, morphology, syntax
take a course in applied linguistics

Pedagogical Preparation

In the model program, proficiency in pedagogy is achieved by

practice in using professional resources (e.g., journals, teachers' organizations, books and monograph series)
defining clear goals and objectives for language learning and teaching
knowledge of traditional and nontraditional methods of teaching
practice in integrating culture into language teaching; use of technology for both
knowledge of oral skill development; practice in presenting new material, designing and implementing lessons for varied functional practice in context, and using technology
knowledge of listening skill development; practice in designing lessons for comprehension of both teacher-prepared and culturally authentic materials, including the use of technology, and in finding-making-adapting materials
knowledge of reading skill development; practice in teaching sound-symbol relations, designing lessons for comprehension of authentic materials, including literature, and in using technology
knowledge of writing skill development; practice in designing lessons for providing extensive and intensive writing practice and in using technology
practice in integrating the skills in lesson plans
practice in developing achievement tests and administering proficiency tests
practice in assessing progress, products, and performances in all four skills and culture
practice in giving feedback and correcting errors
practice in promoting and defending language study, orally and in writing
an introduction to curriculum design and development
knowledge of course planning and practice in unit and lesson planning
evaluating instruction and programs
evaluating and selecting textbooks and other materials
devising supplementary materials
teaching other subject matter in the language

PROCEDURES

Students should

take two methods courses for teaching languages

do peer microteaching

attend language-specific breakout sessions led by mentoring professors in each language

hear presentations by high school teachers with current expertise

prepare lesson plans, exercises, presentations, test items, assessment procedures, communicative activities, portfolios

have service learning experiences; do supervised field observations, tutoring, case studies, and microteaching and team teaching in at least two schools with varied characteristics

do student teaching for one semester, full-time, with seminars with other student teachers, to view and critique videos of their teaching, discuss varied ways to teach the same thing, share ideas and materials, discuss problems with peer counseling, bring together theory and practice

take a final proficiency test in pedagogy

do research projects

interact with local communities of native speakers

take courses in the College of Education, to learn the issues that all teachers face: human development, diverse learners, multicultural education, classroom and time management, school law, concepts of curriculum design and development, technology in education, preparation for fomenting change

keep journals of reflections and observations on teaching language and culture

create files of ideas for future use

Recommended Strategies for Implementing the Model

1. Begin implementing change for proficiency development in language and culture courses by designing a second methods course and by applying diagnostic tests at entry and proficiency tests at exit.
2. Redesign existing courses to integrate recommendations wherever this is possible; create new courses where necessary.
4. Organize workshops for faculty development.
5. Guide students in selection of general studies courses; communicate with community colleges and College of Education.
6. Begin special advising as early as possible in the student's career, no later than fourth semester.
7. Articulate with College of Education, community colleges, and the schools.
8. Replace some College of Education courses with department courses specific to teaching languages.
9. Do not accept 200-level credits toward the thirty hours required for a teaching major.

CALIFORNIA STATE UNIVERSITY, LONG BEACH

Creating Teaching Communities: A Model for Reform and Ongoing Renewal

California State University, Long Beach, is an urban, comprehensive public university enrolling about 27,000 students and offering bachelor's and master's degrees. Besides offering a wide range of liberal arts and science programs, the university is distinguished for its professional programs in health and human services, engineering, business, education, and the arts. It is the third largest university in the twenty-two-campus California State University system. Located in Los Angeles County, the Long Beach area is one of the most ethnically and culturally diverse in the country, and this diversity is reflected in our student population.[1] In the last fifteen years, the area has seen the growth of numerous immigrant communities; within a few miles of the campus are the largest Cambodian and Vietnamese communities in the country, as well as important Korean, Chinese, Filipino, Central American, South American, and Laotian populations, to name a few. Most students are commuters, and most transfer from community colleges.

As an urban comprehensive university, Cal State Long Beach has by necessity and by destiny become the site of a process of thoughtful educational reform and, at times, of demands for change that cause uneasiness. The circumstances contributing to the current period of curricular and programmatic restructuring include an unprecedented era of budget cuts, changing demographics, globalization of the marketplace for job-hunting college graduates, and a strong demand by the legislature and the public that the role of the university be reevaluated. The battles that faculties have waged to defend their disciplines from this assault on education have left scars, particularly in higher education. Nevertheless, one can argue that these circumstances have provided an ideal context in which to reassess the mission of foreign languages in the university and to take stock of the formal preparation of future foreign language educators at the elementary, secondary, and postsecondary levels. Traditional departments have been forced to examine the way they do business and what they teach, and faculty members are beginning to understand that they can better defend their disciplines by revamping the curriculum, becoming more accountable for student outcomes, and reaching out to collaborate with departments with whom they have had little prior contact. Through this process, the conversation about the role and place in the curriculum of the study of languages other than English has reached every corner of the university. As universities nationwide revise their general education offerings, language study is holding its own, as the 1996 MLA survey shows (Brod and Huber).

The Department of Romance, German, Russian Languages and Literatures has been at the forefront of academic and professional reform on our campus since it was created as the result of a merger of three departments five years ago. We realized that each language area shares common goals for student success and, in particular, common concerns regarding the need to reconceptualize the curriculum for future teachers of foreign language. We determined that the only long-term and enduring solution to student success in teacher preparation could be found by conceiving of ourselves as part of a foreign language teacher-scholar-student community. Scrutinized from this community perspective, our programs and their underlying philosophies revealed themselves to reflect a disciplinary and social reality that was twenty-five years old and in need of serious rethinking. In addition to the merger, reduced allocations, growing student numbers (particularly in Spanish), and fewer faculty members have influenced the restructuring of language programs on our campus. Higher demands placed on faculty members in the areas of service to the department, the college, and the university; scholarly productivity; retooling and innovation through technology; grant writing; and teaching loads (twenty-four units a year) have provided an equally decisive impetus for change.

Language Study at Cal State Long Beach

In the fall of 1995, the number of students enrolled in a language course at the university was 6,489. Enrollment in most languages follows national trends; Spanish, having 150 majors and 70 minors, is one of the most popular degrees in the College of Liberal Arts, and more students would be enrolled were it not for budgetary constraints. The MA in Spanish has over 40 active students every year. French enrolls 30 students in the major program, 30 in the minor, and 12 in its MA program. German has 15 majors and 20 minors, and its MA program has 7. The Italian minor program has 20 students, and the Russian 8.

Many students majoring in French, German, or Spanish also study or minor in another language. Since each major program requires the study of at least one year of another foreign language (French requires two years), students often opt to continue their study of the second language through completion of the minor. Knowledge of Spanish is extremely important in the California classroom at every level. Not only is Spanish the most widely taught language K–12, but also a large percentage of the students are Hispanic and often speak Spanish rather than English as their first language. In the state of California, success in finding a teaching job is linked to one's ability and qualifications to teach another foreign language, ESL, or both. The French program has kept its second language requirement at two years and encourages students to study Spanish precisely because of job market considerations. When BA students in French express an interest in pursuing the single-subject teaching credential, they are immediately advised to add a minor in Spanish to their educational program if not declare a double major.

In the general education package, foreign language is one of the three areas listed (along with literature and philosophy) to complete the twelve-unit requirement for humanities and the arts. Students can take up to nine units of foreign language (the equivalent of two courses) to satisfy this requirement. Our location in southern California; our ties to Latin America, Europe, and Asia; the multilingual and multicultural nature of our student population; and the wide array of language offerings housed in our institution have been factors in the decision to make foreign languages a major component of the general education experience. Although only a few departments have a language requirement for their undergraduate or graduate degrees, in the last decade or so many professional and academic programs have been strongly recommending that their students make a foreign language their minor. University requirements concerning languages have not yet caught up with the increased demand for college graduates proficient in a foreign language.

All our language programs are staffed by permanent faculty members. These faculty members have declined considerably in number over the past seven years because of the many faculty lines in foreign language programs that were not continued after retirements. This hiring profile corresponds to national tenure-track staffing trends in foreign language departments, which the MLA has documented in its institutional surveys over the years. Though fewer in number, full-time faculty members in language programs on our campus have still been hired in the last ten years. Teaching assistants and part-time faculty members, however, have replaced some of the full-time assignments. For some degree programs in foreign language, part-time faculty members have become and will remain crucial to the maintenance of a full complement of courses.

Our department offers a wider selection of languages than any other California State University campus in the region; it also serves as a resource for universities that do not teach such languages as Russian, Italian, or even advanced German. Although these programs were generally developed with a traditional emphasis on literature, they have incorporated, as options, linguistics and language acquisition, translation studies, cultural studies, and language for business purposes. The faculty are committed to undergraduate teaching and trained in current pedagogy and proficiency-oriented instruction; they also are engaged in the development and application of multimedia-based language instruction. These shifts in curricular focus have occurred, in part, because of the fluctuating demands that students and the marketplace are making on foreign language programs. Massive demographic changes in the regional population have resulted in an explosion of urgent but unmet needs in areas ranging from the sector of health and human services to the teaching profession to global business.

The university and the Department of Romance, German, Russian Languages and Literatures face a problem that is common to most urban universities but is particularly acute here. Our permanent investment in language programs grew in response to the liberal arts and the international mission of the university. If we are to meet the human service employment needs of this region, respond to the cultures of our communities, and provide the state with qualified language teachers at the elementary, secondary, and college levels, we must stabilize existing programs, develop a more flexible and responsive curriculum, and enter into partnerships with the local schools. Serving as a resource for universities that do not teach Russian, Italian, or advanced German and providing a wider variety of courses to students in our upper-division and MA programs in French and German have resulted in the creation of FLAIR (Foreign Language Alliance Intra-regional) with our sister campus in southern

California, the California State University, Fullerton. The two universities share upper-division and MA-level courses in French and German, while Fullerton students are granted credit for our Italian and Russian courses (Fullerton dropped instruction in both languages in 1992, a year of severe budget cuts in the state university system) and our students are allowed credit for Fullerton's Portuguese program, since we do not offer this language.[2]

Preparing Teachers for the Long Beach Unified School District

Cal State Long Beach is located within the geographical boundary of Long Beach Unified School District, a large urban school district that serves over 80,000 students from kindergarten through twelfth grade. Over thirty-seven percent of the students in the district come from households receiving Aid to Families with Dependent Children, and the district-wide student transience rate is high. In addition, over one student out of every three enrolled in the district (36.1%; N = 21,130) is classified by the state of California as limited English proficient (LEP). A large number of students live in overcrowded conditions and have been exposed to a high rate of domestic and social turmoil. For too many students, the time spent in the public school classroom is the safest time of the day or night. The need for strong academic skills among this at-risk population of students has been emphasized in countless studies. With the transformation of factory jobs requiring low levels of literacy, numeracy, and linguistic and cross-cultural competencies into jobs where such skills are now prerequisites for the constant and varied retooling necessary for long-term job security, the foreign language curriculum can serve not only as a locus for language acquisition but also as a locus for the development of a student's sense of self in relation to the rest of the world. In this context many LEP students have a clear advantage that needs to be validated by the educational process. An educational environment that places high value on one's ability to communicate in languages other than English makes the educational experience of the LEP student that much richer and more meaningful.

Foreign languages have an important place in the school district's curriculum. In the 1995–96 school year, of the more than 20,000 high school students, over a third—approximately 8,600—were enrolled in a foreign language class. The breakdown by language is: Spanish, 6,510;[3] French, 1,080; German, 429; Japanese, 405; Chinese, 216; Latin, 42.

As the need of the marketplace for a bilingual and multilingual workforce grows, educational expectations K–12 will feel that need, and these numbers will certainly increase.[4]

In 1993 the state of California mandated a new type of teaching credential, one that has very specific implications for students in foreign languages. The most salient feature of the single-subject credential in foreign language is the establishment of Advanced as the ACTFL level of proficiency required of the candidate. Our ability as a department to provide our students with the means for achieving this demanding yet thoroughly laudable requirement is a direct function of the degree of consensus among the foreign language educators of Long Beach about the process and timetable of foreign language acquisition from the primary through the postsecondary level. In a community where our students become the teachers of future students, a change made anywhere in the cycle will eventually influence the cycle as a whole.

The foreign language departments of the university and of the Long Beach Unified School District have started to develop content and performance standards collaboratively for the school district; the project was completed in the fall of 1998. They have also begun formal articulation agreements for the first time. The agreements for Spanish were signed May 1997 and went into effect in fall 1997 (see appendix). Agreements for French, German, and Italian were signed September 1998.

These articulation agreements represent the culmination of the first phase of a multistep process that began over two years ago with informal discussions between faculty members from the Department of Romance, German, Russian Languages and Literatures and from the Department of Asian and Asian American Studies with foreign language teachers representing the high schools and middle schools of the Long Beach Unified School District. The meetings came about as the result of an initiative spearheaded by the dean of the College of Liberal Arts at Cal State Long Beach and the vice president of education for the Long Beach Community Partnership[5] to bring the areas of language arts, mathematics, social science, and foreign language into closer alliance K-16. Known as the Seamless Education Project, the initiative served as a catalyst for bringing educators together by discipline. The initial meetings of informal discussion among foreign language teachers soon led to plans for more serious consideration of how they might work as partners. At subsequent meetings, they compared textbooks and course outlines, competencies, outcomes, and portfolios. At this juncture the group was invited by the school district to enter into the formal process of articulation. At a June 1996 meeting, the articulation officers from the school district and the university provided the group with sample documents and timelines. French, German, and Spanish will be the first languages to articulate their programs, with Chinese, Japanese, and Russian following in a second phase.

The MLA-Required Baseline Study of the Department's Curriculum

The MLA asked our department, which was participating in the Teacher Education Project, to undertake a baseline study of its curriculum with the preparation of teachers in mind. Our team determined that our baseline study would be effective only if every member of the faculty participated. To this end, a questionnaire was prepared by team members and distributed to all full-time faculty members. Since ninety percent of them have taught every course in the curriculum in a particular language program, they were asked to respond to questions with all the course offerings in mind. They were unanimous on most questions, so we summarize their responses as representative of a departmental view.

The curriculum was determined to be traditional and literature-based. Although Spanish has created the program options of linguistics and translation over the past ten years, Spanish professors were of the view that more work on these options was necessary, particularly in the way they articulated with the core curriculum. In French and in German, where only one linguistics course is taught as part of the curriculum, the monopoly of the literature-based approach was strongly felt, although the German faculty members have rewritten many of their courses from a cultural studies perspective, which is a nationwide trend in German. All faculty members questioned the extent to which students were leaving the program with baseline competencies; they wondered how students could enter classrooms to teach when their skills were deficient. Everyone expressed the need to rethink the curriculum course by course, once desired outcomes for each program—especially programs for teacher candidates—had been established.

All our faculty members graduated from PhD programs where research was the focus. We were trained as "pure" researchers, with very little instruction, reading, or discussion on issues of pedagogy, classroom management techniques, teaching methods, learning styles, learning objectives, or syllabi preparation. Our experience in this arena was limited to participation in a teaching-assistant training course at the beginning of graduate school, if that. As this reality dawned on us, we realized the irony of a group of research types trying to train future teachers to perform in activities that they had never mastered themselves, or attempted to. Our graduate student experiences had been so compartmentalized that many of us had never even taken a course in linguistics. Since we had determined a dearth of linguistics courses to be the greatest weakness of all three programs, we were aware that the composition of our faculty presented the largest hurdle: of fourteen full-time faculty members, only one was a linguist. We humbly listened to her when delineating our needs.

From our questionnaires we identified three primary ones. First, future teachers need a wider variety of material than literature for interesting their students in languages and cultures other than their own. Faculty members agreed that culture should be taught throughout the four-year curriculum but were dissatisfied with the more facile definitions of culture, such as eating habits, dating customs, and so on. They wanted to find a way to build culture into the curriculum so that variety and continuity would be ensured. They also realized that a means of testing this knowledge had to be sought and that the area of cultural competency, content, and testing would have to be addressed by the entire department as an area for instructor-based training and development.

Second, students are trying to acquire foreign languages, but they do not possess even basic knowledge about what language is—theories of language, components of language, its social dimension, and so on. Competence in linguistics means knowledge about the structures, processes, and properties of one's own language(s) and of languages in general. It also means knowledge about language acquisition, sociolinguistics, and dialectology. We agreed on the reasons for encouraging linguistic competence in future teachers:

Teachers familiar with the linguistic properties and the sociolinguistic standing of the major dialectal groups of Spanish will be better equipped to deal constructively with the many regional varieties of Spanish in their classroom. They will understand that no dialect is superior to another and that the similarities among dialects are much greater than the differences. This is particularly important knowledge for educators in southern California and other areas that have a large and varied Spanish-speaking population.

Linguistics can give teachers insight into how contact with English changes other languages. They will appreciate the structural complexity of codes such as Spanglish and develop an inquisitive rather than a judgmental attitude toward the forces shaping United States Spanish.

Teachers who understand what it means to know a language, what processes are involved in learning a second language, and what aspects of a particular grammar are likely to present a challenge for native speakers of English will be more effective.

Linguistic knowledge can shortcut the learning of other Romance languages by serving as a road map to their syntax, phonology, morphology, and lexicon. People who have a basic understanding of the processes involved in the acquisition of a second language will know how to direct their efforts to maximize their learning. They will also be able to teach more than one language, and there is an increasing demand for such teachers.

Finally, as Steven Pinker points out, the explicit knowledge that the average educated person holds about language and linguistics is often superficial and inaccurate. Language majors, because they have chosen a language as their field of specialization, must be held to a higher standard of knowledge regarding language.

Third, we agreed on the need to improve assessment, although this turned out to be the thorniest issue. When assessment is done consistently and at precise intervals, departments and the students they serve are forced to analyze outcomes in terms of program quality, student ability, and commitment to foreign language acquisition. This kind of monitoring was almost completely absent in our programs. All programs felt there was a need to tailor syllabi in a consistent and systematic way so that they would be guides to both student and teacher, a need to chart progress from a definite beginning to a clearly stated goal or goals, and a need to justify the content and the manner of instruction as most appropriate to attain the competencies established as objectives. Impetus for an assessment program comes directly from the new California standards for teacher certification in foreign languages. Since teacher candidates must test at the Advanced level to receive their credential, the measuring of student progress toward this level should be built into programs on a year-to-year basis. It is to be expected that in the future BA programs will be judged according to the percentages of students who attain Advanced proficiency.

Systematic methods of assessing cultural and linguistic proficiencies must be established as well. At the time of the baseline study, we had not determined whether the assessment program should be developed for all three proficiencies at the same time or whether the three should be developed one by one, language proficiency assessment coming first.

Next Steps

As a result of what we learned from the baseline study, we went to work on our programs to address the problems that had been identified. The changes each program adopted are described below. In some areas, such as linguistic and cultural competencies, although the changes are described only once, they apply to French, German, and Spanish programs alike. Pedagogical approaches and course materials are similar across language sections. They include the use of film, video, and the Internet so that students can explore the Spanish-speaking, francophone, and Germanic worlds in direct and more personal ways.

SPANISH

After studying the results of a survey of students enrolled in a course for bilingual teachers, we realized that we were assuming a common cultural-knowledge base in our students that was simply absent. To address this issue, we reorganized the goals and content of our basic-core curriculum, starting with the third-year language courses. These two courses offer a review of grammar and work in the acquisition of composition skills. We altered the content to put cultural competency in a more prominent position. A new cultural-literary text was selected. Students in our second-year language courses are already using computers and the Internet to complete reading and writing assignments, so the transition has been relatively smooth. We have access to several labs equipped to handle twenty-five students at a time; all the Internet assignments, however, take place outside classroom time.

Students have to choose one of two civilization courses, Spanish Civilization or Latin American Civilization, to satisfy the requirements for the basic core. These courses combine history, geography, politics, and the arts to complement the basic cultural information obtained in the second- and third-year language courses.

Another significant change we made in the Spanish program was an expansion of the basic-core curriculum. An existing course, Introduction to Literary Analysis, was added as a prerequisite for the survey of Spanish literature and the survey of Spanish American literature. The rationale for the new course was to increase literary competence by preparing students to approach a text before they dealt with a whole literary canon. We conducted a survey about the perceived usefulness of having a prerequisite to the two literature surveys. The response was overwhelmingly favorable: more than 80% were in favor, out of 70 students surveyed. The remaining

20% assumed the prerequisite would be useful but were more concerned about the timely completion of their degree than about proficiency.

In Masterpieces of Spanish Literature and Masterpieces of Spanish American Literature, we have introduced cultural materials to provide students with sufficient information to contextualize the literary works they study. We want students who have taken the second- and third-year courses to be well equipped to integrate into their next courses the historical, geographical, artistic, and political contexts they have learned. We are aware that they need continued reinforcement and that we have to teach them actively how to make connections, how to link events, how to integrate knowledge. Our driving force for reform is based on the idea of multiple and sustained exposure to a set of cultural-linguistic-literary knowledge bases to be approached from distinct and varied perspectives.

The area of proficiency in linguistics was addressed for all languages earlier in this report, but it is of special relevance to the Spanish program, because of the variation in the linguistic capabilities of students who study Spanish in southern California. The issues of limited English proficiency, Spanish for Spanish speakers, and Spanish for first-time learners require of Spanish teachers a thorough background in applied linguistics, sociolinguistics, and dialectology.

We have made the linguistics concentration the recommended option for all Spanish majors planning careers in teaching and at the undergraduate level have replaced Spanish Phonetics and Phonology with Introduction to Spanish Linguistics as the linguistics course in the core curriculum. This new course, presenting the main issues in Spanish phonology, morphology, and syntax, is intended to provide a broader view of language than its predecessor. The philosophical orientation of the course is primarily generativist, although other schools of linguistics are briefly discussed.

FRENCH

Demographics have greatly affected enrollments in the French program at Cal State Long Beach. At one time the program enrolled primarily students of European origin with ties to France and an interest in continental Europe. Today, approximately half the students enrolled in the French program are of Southeast Asian, Middle Eastern, Hispanic, or African American origin. French has played a role in their lives, either as the language and culture of France, the colonizer, or as part of an elite education in Iran, Lebanon, or Syria. The need for the program to reflect the entire francophone world is increasingly voiced by our secondary school student teachers. Those working with predominantly African American students cite high interest in the student body for French-language African and West Indies literature.

Our diverse student population has taught us a great deal about what our expectations for cultural and literary competence should be. Many students are already part of the francophone world; they are trilingual if not quadrilingual; and they have firsthand information and experiences that give them a global perspective. We have restructured the cultural and literary components in our classes accordingly. Students graduating with a BA in French from Cal State Long Beach must be knowledgeable about the history of France, with an emphasis on cultural history; the evolution of French political history, especially the French Revolution, and France's role in modern political discourse; French theater and the fine arts; French colonialism, particularly in Louisiana, Canada, Southeast Asia, North Africa, West Africa, and the West Indies; postcolonialism and its continuing social impact; religious diversity and its history; France's role in the European Community.

A reconceptualizing of cultural literacy that widens the focus from France to the francophone world as a whole led to the following programmatic changes. Our baseline study showed that our two survey courses lacked definition and continuity, making it difficult for students to acquire and retain knowledge by any means other than rote. We chose a topic that framed those courses to ensure cultural continuity: France's self-image and the representation of the other through the centuries. By our considering France's view of herself and the other, what was once a laundry list of names, genres, and titles has acquired meaning and some parameter of qualitative comparison beyond the aesthetic that can be applied to literary study. This focus implicitly brings students to questions about political and religious institutions, their establishment and evolution, and the individual within them. Our frame also makes it impossible to ignore the francophone world. We determined that a survey course on the francophone world was of paramount importance for future teachers, who would be called on in ever increasing ways to teach their students about the world. The course is also important for international studies majors, many of whom fulfill their three-year language requirement by taking French and often add a French minor to their course of studies. We therefore instituted a new course, Survey of Francophone Literature, and a new option that includes such courses as Switzerland as a Model for European Diversity (a French-German course with a language-across-the-curriculum component) and The Literature and Culture of Quebec.

Restructuring content around social issues makes film an ideal medium for presenting content. Films such as *La reine Margot, The Return of Martin Guerre, The Night of Varennes, La grande illusion, Indochine, The Last Metro, Au revoir les enfants,* and *Hiroshima mon amour* introduce historical, religious, and sociopolitical material through music, visuals, and dialogue, which allow the student more direct access to a cultural issue than is at times possible with a book. These films are now a permanent part of the French survey course curriculum.

The introduction of a francophone survey course and a francophone option has made us aware of the need to include a sociolinguistic component in our phonetics course. The phonetics course is required by the state of California for all teachers of French. We are also developing a linguistics option in French and will advise those who are planning a career in teaching to select it. The option consists of new or revamped courses in phonetics, second language acquisition, and Romance linguistics. Second Language Acquisition has been taught on a regular basis, but before our baseline study and discussion it was never taken by students outside the Spanish program. Our linguist colleague expressed an interest in reviving and revamping Romance Linguistics, a course that had not been taught in several years. Students of French and Spanish who need more linguistics courses in preparation for a career in teaching will now have access to this course. Students of French are also able to enroll in additional linguistics courses at our sister campus, California State University, Fullerton, which emphasizes linguistics over literature.

Finally, we are developing a capstone course and an undergraduate reading list that includes works in linguistics. The capstone course and the reading list will be closely connected. The outcome expected in this course, which includes language proficiency, reflects our restructuring of the entire program's curriculum and syllabi.

GERMAN

The German program is less oriented toward teacher preparation, because of the small number of student teachers in German who complete the credential program each year. Instead, the faculty has developed German-for-business courses and is revising the curriculum to reflect a cultural studies format. Relations between our German program and high school and community college teachers of German have always been strong and have been strengthened as we work toward an articulation document.

Over the past few years, our German program has changed its curriculum from one that was solely literary to one that emphasizes cultural studies. All language programs integrate literature and other cultural components, not only in upper-division classes and seminars (by genre or period) but also in beginning and advanced language classes. In these classes, the prospective teacher experiences literature inductively as a student; at a later stage, deductively (i.e., through methodology, pedagogy) as a teaching assistant. In German, or in any language, fairy tales and myths can be used as a primer for other literary and cultural texts. Selected for easy recognition, they provide input that is comprehensive while opening a variety of cultural, sociological, and psychological discussion possibilities.

Prospective teachers learn that the reception (comprehension) of literary texts is inseparable from the student reader's activity and spontaneity (subjective interpretation, biographical affinity) but not necessarily inseparable from the teacher's mastery of the text—or from the secondary literature, either. They also learn that the objective is not to arrive at one conclusion (from a single analysis) but, rather, to allow and tolerate open-endedness, the unexpected, the surprise, and the multicultural perspective that does justice to the student's place, time, and background. Thus, the learner experiences this fundamental rule of cultural assessment: that one learns as much about one's own culture as one does about the culture being studied. It is therefore legitimate to approach literature through personal needs, wishes, desires, and expectations. The study of secondary literature, critiques, and other forms of academic interpretation have their rightful place in literature lectures and graduate seminars, providing the historical and intellectual perspectives necessary for the informed professional.

For all our students and for those going into the teaching profession in particular, new paradigms are needed in literary studies; a variety of texts should be introduced, not only literary ones. Furthermore, students should learn the differences between analyzing literature as a personal experience and as an abstract one; literature becomes the student's object as opposed to the instructor's. The benefit of the personal approach for students who have no literary experience is that it becomes a conduit to other types of literary study. We must develop and apply assessment tools that allow for polyvalence in student responses, with emphasis on the questions rather than on the answers. Literary assessment tools capable of testing for understanding at a variety of levels need to be developed.

Changes in the Teacher Preparation Program

The Department of Teacher Education at Cal State Long Beach offers professional education course work that leads to a multiple-subject credential for those wishing to teach at the elementary level (K–8); a single-subject credential for those wishing to teach at the secondary level (6–12); and a master of arts in education, with an option in either elementary or secondary school education. We recently completed a credential program that supersedes the previous one (the new program was mandated by the state in 1983). The program encompasses all subject-matter programs, is designed to meet the needs of a culturally diverse population, and places a strong emphasis on the development of cross-cultural understanding as well as on the development of language and academic skills.

The Cal State Long Beach teacher-training program for secondary school teachers is unique even among those of the other institutions in the California State University system. The teaching of courses for the single-subject credential on our campus is shared by the subject-matter department—in our case, Romance, German, Russian Languages and Literatures—and the College of Education. The subject-matter department is responsible for teaching Preliminary Field Experiences in Foreign Languages (EDSS 300F) and Methods of Teaching Foreign Languages (EDSS 450F). This partitioning of the teaching responsibility ensures subject-matter and methods currency for the credential candidate as well as maintenance of a pedagogical focus in the subject-matter department.

Given the current demands of proficiency from employers in the public and private sectors and given the new state teaching credentials, which require Advanced proficiency, we are striving to make our courses reflect this philosophy of performance and evaluation. Proficiency is not limited to oral proficiency; it should not even be limited to the four basic skills of language. It must include culture, linguistics, and literature.[6] All these areas are important, but the most crucial in terms of immediate, tangible outcomes is proficiency in language communication. As a result, we are exploring the most cost-effective ways to institute a systematic oral proficiency assessment process for all our students. We have also added an oral proficiency assessment component to evaluate the performance of teacher candidates, particularly those candidates who come to us from other institutions.

Implementing a proficiency-testing program that does not increase costs and faculty workload seems impossible to achieve at this juncture. As a stopgap measure, we have decided to advise our students of French and Spanish to take one of three government tests, the DELE (Dìploma de Español como Lengua Extranjera, offered by Spain) and, offered by France, the DELF (Diplôme d'Etudes de Langue Française) and the DALF (Diplôme Approfondi de Langue Française). As there were very few such testing venues in California, our campus will become a site for the DELE. Since our professors participate in the correction of these exams, they have an opportunity to garner firsthand knowledge about assessment of all four skill areas. French students will take the DELF in the fall at Loyola Marymount University, the first DELF site to be established in Los Angeles. We hope that these exams will give our students a goal to work toward. Teacher candidates will be required to perform well on them. Both the French and Spanish consulates have remarked on the move toward higher standards in American education and on the need to assess performance in relation to established parameters.

To maximize success in promoting and evaluating oral proficiency, we have identified the need for a process of ongoing academic advisement. Students will periodically be assessed on concrete activities designed to help them gain proficiency; they will also be allowed to draft an individual timeline for evaluation that fits their personal learning curve. The notion of seat time, often unrealistic, will be deemphasized; students will be able to repeat portions of the course under a special contract tailored to their needs (independent study). These extra units will be used as electives.

We have added to the curriculum an internship course for each language. These variable-unit courses are being set up with the collaboration of area employers, school districts, and community centers. We have already established links in the areas of education, health science, translation, and human services. The internships will allow students to improve oral and written communication and acquire a variety of professional skills. Starting in the fall of 1998, prospective teachers will be required to work as language interns in intermediate or advanced courses given by our department. The interns will be responsible for correcting student work and subsequently meeting with the students in regularly scheduled group tutorial sessions. Interns will be evaluated for their interaction with students and their ability to establish a productive student-teacher relationship. For the first time we will be able to comment, in a letter of recommendation, on a prospective teacher's interpersonal skills and readiness for the classroom. The interns will be supervised by the professor teaching the course and by either the teaching assistant or single-subject coordinator.

For many years, the Long Beach Unified School District had a science center and a social science resource center, not at the same school. Three years ago, centers for math, history, language arts, and health were set up as well. At that time, all existing centers were consolidated at one central location in Long Beach. Foreign languages were not among them.

Although Cal State Long Beach faculty members participate in meetings and workshops at the other centers, apparently they were not conceived of as the team effort of a learning community. Our proposal to establish a foreign language resource center fills an obvious gap. The center we propose is wholly innovative in conception and design. From the start, the resource center for foreign languages will be set up as a partnership of the Long Beach Unified School District and Cal State Long Beach. Once articulation agreements are in place K–16, with proficiency as the goal, all members of the community will work toward the same end. The resource center, housed on the Long Beach campus, will be equipped to conduct a variety of assessments; to provide workshops and in-service activities; to maintain an updated resource library on methodologies, linguistics, and culture, both in electronic and text form. By fostering collaboration among language professionals, the center will create both synergy in the professional community and interest in language acquisition, learning, and teaching. We have successfully applied for outside funding to coordinate the strategic planning, development, and implementation of the project.[7]

The teaching mission of our profession must become even more strongly embedded in the culture of foreign language departments. As professors we are primarily teachers and should be linked, as mentors, to students who intend to become teachers, and to student teachers as well. We have neglected for too long to promote the image of ourselves as teachers both within our programs and to the community at large. The dialogue about who we are to our students needs to extend beyond the walls of academe.

Changing expectations of the professoriat at most BA- and MA-granting institutions such as ours coincide with a need to reexamine and rethink our roles as teacher-scholars and to shift emphasis back to the teaching and teaching-related aspects of our jobs; these include mentoring, advising, and helping students plan and prepare for careers and professions in a foreign language.

Paradoxically, multimedia and distance learning have forced us as a community to pay much closer attention than ever before to learning styles, learning strategies, course and lesson design. Cognition and pedagogy have become popular topics at conferences, deans' retreats, and in departments around the academic coffeepot. Changes in our professional culture have inspired the programmatic changes we are making for those Cal State Long Beach students who will become teachers one day.

But what may be the most important realization remains subtly hidden at the interstices of curricular reform: that our profession has at some level failed to honor one of its highest responsibilities, that is, to instill in our students respect and admiration for the teaching profession. Curricular reform is the backbone of change, but we hope to accomplish a more profound act of revitalization and renewal by redefining the essence of our profession. Each of us must become the embodiment of this elusive construct: the teacher-scholar. Such a lofty goal may seem ambitious, even immodest, but we must realize that the alternative is further erosion of trust in the university's ability to prepare students for the workplace of the twenty-first century and a missed opportunity to regain the ever-threatened intellectual and ethical authority invested in all institutions of higher learning.

As the faculty has worked together on this project and on the rectification of our credential program, we have risen to the challenges facing our program. We have formed a de facto community of learners whose commitment to the preservation of each of our language programs and to increasing the visibility of foreign language study on campus gave that community the strength to see beyond the immediate obstacles and to forge a vision for the future.

We believe that the positive energy our department has brought to teacher training in foreign languages inspired the dean of liberal arts to apply to the National Language Center's Language Mission Project. Our campus was one of sixteen selected nationwide to participate in the project, and two of our faculty members will play an active role on the project as committee members. The Language Mission Project continues the work that was begun by our department in the MLA Teacher Education Project and has succeeded in engaging faculty members and administrators throughout the campus in thoughtful dialogue about the role of foreign language educators. Funding for the foreign language and literature programs that existed ten years ago may never be restored, but the College of Liberal Arts and the Department of Romance, German, Russian Languages and Literatures have rolled up their sleeves together with the Long Beach Unified School District to structure the language programs of the future and to focus on the linchpin in our relationship: the foreign language teacher.

Main authors
Clorinda Donato, *Romance, German, Russian Languages and Literatures, California State University, Long Beach*
Claire Emilie Martin, *Romance, German, Russian Languages and Literatures, California State University, Long Beach*

Other members of the team
Magdalena Andrade, *formerly of Romance, German, Russian Languages and Literatures, California State University, Long Beach*
Maria Carreira, *Romance, German, Russian Languages and Literatures, California State University, Long Beach*
Elizabeth Ann Hartung-Cole, *Long Beach High School Superintendent's Office*
Wilm Albert Pelters, *Romance, German, Russian Languages and Literatures, California State University, Long Beach*

Notes

[1]Forty-four percent are white and non-Hispanic; 21% are Asian, Asian American, or Pacific Islander; 20% are Mexican American or Hispanic; 9% are African American; 6% are Filipino; 1% are Native American.

[2]The FLAIR program was easy to set up bureaucratically, since students have been able to take courses at their home campus and at any other campus of California State University without incurring added expense, thanks to the Passport Program established by the chancellor's office in 1990. The largest hurdle we had to overcome was the reluctance of the foreign language faculties on campuses that had been rivals to set aside their competitive feelings for the good of the students and the survival of our discipline. The potential for regionalization of programs by the state university system was another concern. Faculties feared that one campus might be assigned French and another German, for example, or in a worst-case scenario, that all language programs might be moved to one of the two campuses. These fears were allayed by the administration, and we were encouraged to proceed. Areas of strength from each campus emerged, and we have been able to serve our students better. In French, Fullerton is more specialized in linguistics, whereas the Long Beach campus focuses on literature. Several students in BA and MA programs in French now take courses at the Fullerton campus if they wish to pursue linguistics.

[3]This number includes the 1,471 students who were enrolled in Spanish for Spanish speakers classes.

[4]Current California high school graduation requires that a student have ten semester credits (usually a one-year course) of fine arts or foreign language. The state's city college system has no further foreign language entrance requirements. The California State University system requires that incoming freshmen complete two years of electives from the following: advanced math, agriculture, English, foreign language, history or social science, lab science, and visual and performing arts. University of California freshmen admissions requires two years of foreign language study of the same language and recommends a third year.

[5]The Long Beach Community Partnership is a private, nonprofit corporation developed to find innovative solutions to today's problems through collaborative leadership. The partnership provides a framework for business, government, community interests, and educational institutions to work together. One of the activities of the Seamless Education initiative is to involve Cal State Long Beach

in the Articulation Council to develop three-way courses among the Long Beach Unified School District, Long Beach Community College, and the university ("Our Mission").

[6]"A student who seeks to earn the single-subject credential in foreign language should understand authentic speech in a variety of situations and contexts, demonstrate knowledge of and sensitivity to culture, demonstrate proficiency at productive skills of speaking and writing the language, and critically interpret works of literature in their specific cultural and historical context" (Sikula, Buttery, and Guyton 33).

[7]In 1998, the College of Liberal Arts received a National Endowment for the Humanities Challenge Grant. These funds will provide seed money for the heritage language programs on campus and for a resource center.

WORKS CITED

Brod, Richard, and Bettina J. Huber. "Foreign Language Enrollments in United States Institutions of Higher Education, Fall 1995." *ADFL Bulletin* 28.2 (1997): 55–61.

"Our Mission." *Update* May 1996: 3.

Pinker, Steven. *The Language Instinct.* New York: Harper-Perennial, 1995.

Sikula, John, Thomas Buttery, and Edith Guyton, eds. *Teacher Preparation in Languages Other Than English: Quality and Effectiveness Standards for Subject Matter Programs in California.* Sacramento: Commission on Teacher Credentialing, 1994.

APPENDIX

Cal State Long Beach / Long Beach Unified School District Articulation Agreement for Spanish

1. ADVANCED PLACEMENT SPANISH LANGUAGE. FULL OR PARTIAL EQUIVALENCY FOR THE FOLLOWING COURSES:

LONG BEACH UNIFIED SCHOOL DISTRICT COURSE NAME	CAL STATE LONG BEACH COURSE NAME
Option 1	
AP Spanish Language	Spanish 201A + portfolio (4 units)*
Option 2	
AP Spanish examination	
score of 3	Spanish 201A (6 units)
score of 4 or 5	Spanish 201B (6 units)

*All AP students will compile a portfolio of written/audio/video work accomplished during the course. The instructor will guide the students in assessing the value, quantity, and quality of the work to be included. This document will be used as a companion assessment tool to the student's performance in the class and/or the exams.

2. ADVANCED PLACEMENT SPANISH LITERATURE. FULL OR PARTIAL EQUIVALENCY FOR THE FOLLOWING COURSES:

LONG BEACH UNIFIED SCHOOL DISTRICT COURSE NAME		CAL STATE LONG BEACH COURSE NAME
	Option 1	
AP Spanish Literature		Spanish 410 examination + portfolio (3 units)
	Option 2	
AP Spanish Literature examination score of 4 or 5		Spanish 410: Introduction to Literary Analysis (3 units)

CONDITIONS AND STIPULATIONS

A. Students must complete the AP language or university course with a grade of B or higher.
B. Students who have completed the required courses for the articulation certificate will be notified. A list of students will be sent to the articulation office at Cal State Long Beach. The articulation officer will notify the pertinent department.
C. Students who have successfully completed the AP Spanish literature course (B or better) but have not taken the AP literature examination are encouraged to take a Spanish 410 final. If the student passes the examination with a B or higher, she or he will receive the grade earned in the examination and the three upper-division units. Students who have passed this examination will be able to enroll in most of the 300- and 400-level language, literature, and culture courses. (Some courses have other prerequisites.)

Course Competencies for AP Spanish Language (Long Beach Unified School District) and for Spanish 201A and 201B (Cal State Long Beach)

The following material has been extracted from *AP Spanish: A Guide for the Language Course,* by Jose Díaz et al.

LISTENING

Students who have successfully completed AP Spanish Language will have developed sufficient skill in listening comprehension to enable them to:

- comprehend formal and informal spoken Spanish
- follow, with general understanding, oral reports and classroom lectures on nontechnical subjects
- understand the main points and some details of conversations between native speakers

follow the plots of Spanish-language television shows and movies and understand the main ideas in character dialogues

READING

The successful AP student will demonstrate proficiency in reading nonfiction and literary texts in Spanish with good overall comprehension. The student will be able to:

understand magazine articles on various topics of general interest
separate main ideas from subordinate ones
draw inferences from material read, although recognition of subtle nuances may be limited
develop strategies for interpretation of unfamiliar words, idioms, or structures, relying on broad general vocabulary and knowledge of grammatical forms and structures
appreciate some figurative devices, stylistic differences, irony and humor

WRITING

The student will have mastered the ability to write in Spanish on topics of general interest. By the end of the course, the student will:

demonstrate good written control of most grammatical forms
employ vocabulary extensive enough to cover most topics, compensate for gaps in vocabulary by circumlocutions
write an organized narration or description several paragraphs in length, demonstrating a variety of sentence structures and good control of syntax
present and defend ideas and points of view
provide appropriate examples and draw conclusions from them
provide introductory remarks, transition, and a conclusion in an essay

SPEAKING

Students who have successfully completed the course will have attained a speaking proficiency that allows them to:

communicate facts and ideas with an accent that is accurate enough not to interfere with comprehension
discuss topics of current interest and express personal opinions, while demonstrating a good command of grammatical forms and syntactic patterns
narrate, describe, and explain, using tenses and moods correctly
have immediate recall of a fairly broad range of vocabulary in order to speak with a level of fluency and accuracy that does not impede communication

Course Competencies for AP Spanish Literature (Long Beach Unified School District) and for Spanish 410: Introduction to Literary Analysis (Cal State Long Beach)

The student who successfully completes the AP Spanish Literature will be able to:

understand lectures in Spanish and take accurate notes

participate actively in literary discussions in Spanish

perform a close reading of Hispanic literary texts in all genres

analyze the form and content of literary works both orally and in writing, using appropriate terminology

identify and discuss the elements of a narrative text: describe and evaluate the setting (geographical location, time period) and the relation of the characters to setting; summarize the plot and analyze the plot structure, including point of view, main conflicts (among characters, environment, ideologies), climax, denouement, author's techniques (foreshadowing, flashbacks, stream of consciousness); identify characters, discuss their traits and functions in the text; analyze the style, citing literary devices, tone; discuss the theme(s)

analyze a poem and discuss the interrelationship of the structure, theme, and effect: identify the form (e.g., ballad, sonnet), poetic devices (e.g., personification, simile, metaphor), rhyme, and meter; interpret the theme(s), indicating how poetic form and technique contribute to meaning; discuss the effect of the poem on the reader

analyze a drama, incorporating both dialogue and stage directions: identify the theme(s); discuss the playwright's techniques (e.g., foreshadowing, flashbacks, figurative language); identify the structure (sequence of action, metatheater); identify the use of symbols in the context of the drama; describe and analyze the characters through dialogue, actions, and interactions

analyze an essay: identify the form (narrative, poetic, dramatic), tone; enumerate the premise(s) and discuss what technique the essayist uses to reason or persuade

UNIVERSITY OF GEORGIA

The Perils of an Integrated Curriculum; or, How a Team Talked for One Year and Almost Communicated . . .

Mankind today is threatened by a number of disasters which have all been man-made: They are disasters of culture rather than the disasters of nature to which our ancestors were regularly exposed. [. . .] The only way towards survival is to become even cleverer so that the negative consequences of our cleverness can be compensated for. This demands concerted action on issues for which, unfortunately, different cultural values make people disagree rather than agree. In these circumstances, intercultural cooperation has become a prime condition for the survival of mankind.

—Geert Hofstede

Furthermore, I do not share the opinion that intellectual and systemic differences are undesirable "obstacles" to the articulation we seek between the different sectors of the educational system. Rather, they might be viewed as opportunities for an ongoing dialogue that respects differences instead of trying to erase them.

—Claire Kramsch

In his recent book *Cultures and Organizations: Software of the Mind,* Geert Hofstede argues for an acceptance of cultural differences within groups and institutions. Although his is a model designed to make business organizations aware of the need for intercultural communication in a broad sense—what we might call cultural sensitivity to those who speak different languages and have different views on propriety—we could very well take a lesson from his conclusions. In the world of education, as in the world of business, we too have created what Hofstede calls "disasters of culture" by calling whatever is wrong with our schools "their" fault and "their" problem (241). When discussing the education of future K–12 teachers of foreign languages, each group involved seems to point an accusatory finger at all the others.

After more than one year of work toward developing a model teacher education curriculum, the members of the team from the University of Georgia are trying to rise above their self-made "disasters of culture" and "embrace the conflict," as suggested by Claire Kramsch in the spring 1995 issue of the *ADFL Bulletin* ("Embracing"). This report cannot be called final, for the dialogue begun this year must continue, if we are to avoid falling back into the old, familiar, and for many of us comfortable, past conditions. We found, for example, that when we presented our model program during the MLA Teacher Education Conference held in Houston in March 1966, we had developed a new and revised curriculum for the Department of Romance Languages but, for a variety of logistical and political reasons, had not included in our conversations the faculty member from language education. Our new curriculum, although much more sensitive to the needs of teachers, is still a curriculum in Romance languages and literatures and not in linguistics or second language acquisition; our curriculum still does not necessarily meet the expectations of our colleagues in the College of Education. The challenges that we faced at the beginning are great, and perhaps the most enduring lesson from this project will be an awareness of our differences and an effort to continue the conversation. As we began developing the present essay, our different expectations and beliefs became even more apparent. Our individual and collective voices clamoring to be heard often got in the way of communication. The process itself exemplifies Mikhail Bakhtin's theory of heteroglossia ("Dialogism") better than any classroom lecture on the subject. But before we look more closely at the perils of an integrated curriculum and how we almost failed in communication, some background information is helpful.

When the MLA distributed a call in November 1994 for proposals for participation in its teacher education project, the Department of Romance Languages at the University of Georgia welcomed the opportunity to submit an application. It seemed to us that several recent events occurring in the state of Georgia in general and in the department in particular were converging and that the MLA project was exactly what we needed to focus our efforts in curriculum revision. Among the events that led the department to apply for participation in this project are the following:

In 1988, the state of Georgia adopted a Quality Core Curriculum for its public schools. The QCC was put in place as a response to low achievement by Georgia students compared with national norms in virtually every subject area. QCC presents many challenges for local schools, but the one that directly relates to our project is the College

Preparatory Curriculum proposed by the board of regents of the university system of Georgia. Primarily concerned with the preparation of precollege students, the board of regents outlined a curriculum that would be implemented as entrance requirements into all thirty-four state system institutions—including junior and community colleges. Among the requirements for the College Preparatory Curriculum were two years of a foreign language. Entering freshmen were given a two-year grace period, so that requirements began to be obligatory in 1990, making the 1994 graduating class the first to have entered the University of Georgia under the new guidelines. The new entrance requirements are now fully implemented and have created an emergency situation in foreign language teacher preparation in the state. Every school system in the state needs a foreign language teacher, and colleges of education throughout the system are not able to prepare enough qualified teachers for the available positions.

In 1990, Governor Zell Miller was elected on a platform of establishing a lottery for education in Georgia. Two years after his inauguration, the legislature and the people of Georgia voted to create a state lottery. The governor established in 1993 what he called the Hope Scholarships. These lottery-funded scholarships ensure that any Georgia student who graduates from an accredited high school with a B average is entitled to a free postsecondary education in the state, provided that he or she maintains a B average in college. Furthermore, the governor started a public prekindergarten plan, making Georgia the first—and perhaps the only—state in the country to provide free public education P–16. The scholarship program has been a boon for students, but it also has caused a rapid and unprecedented enrollment growth at the University of Georgia, the state's flagship institution. Entrance requirements have become stricter annually for the past three years, making the University of Georgia one of the most selective public universities in the country.

At the same time that the Quality Core Curriculum became a reality in the K–12 system in Georgia, the regents of the university system of Georgia appointed a new chancellor. When he announced his priorities, Chancellor Stephen Portch included outcomes assessment of all programs in all the institutions. Although outcomes assessment had been mandated by the legislature, the regents had not yet implemented a plan.

Chancellor Portch announced that one of his priorities was to change the university system from quarters to semesters. Attempts to make this change in the past had been blocked either by the faculty of the University of Georgia, who feared an increased teaching load and expressed this fear in many resolutions of the Franklin College of Arts and Sciences senate and the university council, or by the administration of smaller colleges in the state, who saw the quarter system as an advantage for nontraditional students.[1] Three years and many committee hours later, the system is currently engaged in the Semester Conversion Plan, to be fully implemented in the fall of 1998.

At the University of Georgia, many changes were also taking place. The university council began discussing a new multicultural diversity requirement that was adopted by the faculty senate of the Franklin College of Arts and Sciences for implementation in the fall of 1995.

At the department level, in 1993, Doris Kadish became the new head after a two-year period of transition during which there were two different acting heads.

During the 1993–94 academic year, then, the Department of Romance Languages not only faced the changes of a new administration but also had to adjust to external pressures, not the least of which was the increased demand for courses suitable for teacher training. The courses taught in our department were considered too traditional, too literary, and not appropriate for teachers.

During the development of the outcomes assessment plan mandated by the legislature, faculty groups in the Romance languages began evaluating current offerings at both the undergraduate and graduate levels. They spent one academic year (1993–94) discussing basic expected outcomes at each level of language and literature instruction. In October 1994, by a unanimous vote, the faculty approved the basic expected outcomes that would be measured in a senior exit interview conducted both in English (by the department head) and in the target language (by individual faculty members). An exercise of a target language interview was videotaped and evaluated by a committee of faculty members.

As the Franklin College of Arts and Sciences faculty senate discussed the multicultural diversity requirement, we discovered, much to our surprise and dismay, that our courses did not meet the university's requirement. *Multiculturalism* and *diversity,* we came to understand, were culturally coded words that had little to do with foreign languages and literatures. Indeed, the Department of Romance Languages, along with all other foreign language departments at the university, was often left out of the discussion.

As our self-study progressed, we discovered that some of the undergraduate majors who were pursuing a career in precollege teaching were not making satisfactory grades in the Teacher Certification Test, which is a requirement for teacher certification in the state of Georgia (this test will soon be replaced by the ETS Praxis Examination). Teacher training at the University of Georgia is divided between two colleges—the College of Arts and Sciences for content courses and the College of Education for professional courses and student teaching. In the 1960s there was a good bit of coordination between the two areas (indeed, some of the faculty held joint appointments). While there has been some communication between various members of the language departments and the Department of Language Education since the early 1990s, our present concerns have not been systematically addressed. The Teacher Certification Test presumably measured language skills and content areas; if students were not making satisfactory grades, the Department of Language Education tended to place the blame solely with the Department of Romance Languages for the lack of preparation of future French and Spanish teachers. It became imperative to look into the programs and courses and make decisions.

Through the years, the department has tried to maintain a balance between the preparation of precollege teachers (mostly at the undergraduate and MA levels) and the preparation of future college teachers. Our challenge, not unlike that in many other research universities, has been the articulation of these two goals. Meanwhile, the Terry College of Business at the University of Georgia began requiring the equivalent of a minor in languages for its international business degrees. Enrollments in upper-division undergraduate courses began to swell, and students have not been shy in letting the faculty know exactly what they perceive to be their needs and what they think, not always rightly, should be done. Finally, our own majors have increased in numbers; they, too, have told us what they think they need. Each year, nine to ten thousand students enroll in classes in the Department of Romance Languages, and the faculty faces the annual challenge of evaluating and meeting the real or perceived needs of all constituents.

The department has twenty-six faculty members with a professional rank, some twenty temporary instructors, and some seventy teaching assistants. Four of the faculty members specialize in linguistics; the other twenty-two specialize in literary studies. As with most traditional departments, most of the faculty members in French and Spanish fulfill teaching responsibilities and undertake scholarly pursuits in a particular genre or time period. In the undergraduate program, most French and Spanish faculty members teach the literature survey courses that best cover their particular area of interest.

The department offers a BA in French, Italian, Spanish, or Romance languages; an MA in French or Spanish literature or linguistics; an MA in Romance languages; and a PhD in Romance languages or in French or Spanish under the Romance languages. Undergraduate language students who wish to obtain a teaching certificate in French or Spanish are not allowed to major in Romance languages as undergraduates; instead, they must enroll as majors in foreign language education, in the College of Education. If they wish to pursue a major in Romance languages afterward, they may do so, upon graduation in a modified master's degree program in education that allows students to complete the necessary requirements for teacher certification. But their curriculum in language and literature courses will be in the College of Arts and Sciences.

When we learned that the Georgia team had been selected for participation in the MLA Teacher Education Project, we began a systematic self-study of courses, evaluation methods, enrollment patterns, articulation, and requirements at the state and local levels for precollege teachers. Our baseline study provided us with the first step toward establishing communication with the College of Education. We found, for example, that for the BSEd in French or Spanish students are required to take five courses in language, three courses in literature, and one course in culture. It did not come as a surprise that, given a choice, future precollege teachers opted to take courses labeled *language* or *culture* before courses labeled *literature*. Indeed, in our dialogue with in-service teachers, we hear the same request for summer courses, that there be more in language and culture. Yet most faculty members, unless they are specifically trained in linguistics, prefer to teach courses in literature. Throughout the years we have heard, and some of us believe, that literary analysis and criticism are more interesting and worthwhile endeavors than teaching courses that have been traditionally labeled as skills.

One issue we are just now beginning to confront in the Department of Romance Languages is precisely the fact that in foreign language and literature classes we are teaching language skills at every level. Even when students are native speakers of the literature that we discuss, we are still dealing with the skills of language manipulation. At the undergraduate level, when we teach foreign literature, we have the double duty of making not only the literary language accessible to the students but also the language of the text itself. Traditional language courses emphasize skills over content. Students have rightly concluded that concentrating on one level of learning is easier than trying to acquire skills and content at the same time. Comments in course evaluations in the department show that many precollege future teachers see no need for literature courses. Analyzing this situation, some language and literature faculty members have concluded that the culture courses that these students are asking for deal primarily with the activities of daily life—getting up in the morning, having breakfast, brushing teeth, and so forth—whereas for the faculty members in Romance languages *culture* means ideological issues, gender issues, race relations, or the complexities of political systems and historical underpinnings in society. When literature courses are framed within these cultural complexities, preservice and in-service teachers (in the summer classes) at times complain of the lack of culture in those classes.

The analysis of why preservice and in-service teachers make such comments in course evaluations is an example of our almost communicating with our colleagues in language education. Language education faculty members state that they *are* concerned about what gets treated as literature in the language departments. One of their specific criticisms is that much of what is defined as literature to them seems irrelevant to the curricular needs of teachers of grades P–12. That is, the question is not whether there should be literature courses; the question is what genres of literature (defined from a range of traditions) are valued and thus given attention. The language education faculty member in our team exemplified her point by summarizing that, given the purposes of foreign language instruction in grades P–12, it is unlikely that a course entitled The Spanish American Essay in the Nineteenth Century will be as relevant as a course entitled Adolescent Literature in Twentieth-Century Spain. At issue here, it seems to some in the Department of Romance Languages, is more than relevance for teacher preparation; it is the very definition of education.

On the question of what constitutes culture in a foreign language class, the faculty in our department cannot agree. Some hold the idea expressed by our colleague in language education, that what teachers want and need are courses that make explicit the cultural embeddedness of even the most mundane activities. Our colleague maintains that for teachers what is important is precisely what a day is like for adolescents in Spain or what gender issues are encountered by teenagers in Puerto Rico or what values and beliefs about youth, age, and family are constructed in the magazines, movies, and songs geared to young people there. Some faculty members in Romance languages believe that to reduce ways of defining culture to having breakfast and brushing one's teeth seriously misrepresents culture, that not all culture is daily life, and that much of it is embedded in very formal literature. This disagreement is another example of almost communicating, where each voice in the polyphony makes an argument that seems perfectly clear within that voice's context but becomes opaque when translated to the other. Such miscommunication and misconception appeared not only in our dealings with colleagues from other departments and colleges but also in our understanding of *diversity* and *multiculturalism*.

The multicultural diversity requirement that the university council proposed meant dealing with the many cultures that make up the United States, not with the diversity of cultures in the world. Yet we find in the mission statement for the University of Georgia the following paragraph:

> With its statewide mission and core characteristics, the University of Georgia endeavors to prepare the university community and the state for full participation in the global society of the twenty-first century. Through its programs and practices, it seeks to foster the understanding of and respect for cultural differences necessary for an enlightened and educated citizenry. It further provides for cultural, ethnic, gender, and racial diversity in the faculty, staff, and student body. The university is committed to preparing the university community to appreciate the critical importance of a quality environment to an interdependent global society. (*Undergraduate Bulletin* 15)

One additional element must be described in the context of the MLA project, curriculum reform, and Spanish and French teacher preparation at the University of Georgia. Shortly after the Georgia team was selected to participate in the project, our department received notification of award of a major grant from the National Endowment for the Humanities; it had applied for this grant in the fall of 1994. The project, "Integrating Culture, Language, and Literature: Strengthening Preservice Foreign Language Teacher Education through Curricular Change," has been directed by Doris Kadish, department head and member of the Georgia team. The primary goal for the project as described in the proposal was to strengthen cultural, theoretical, and linguistic education of K–12 teachers by:

> revising undergraduate and graduate curricula to include a broad range of cultural components; strengthening the theoretical and historical preparation of the faculty to develop new courses and

revise existing courses to assure inclusion of language, linguistics, literature, culture, and theory (as appropriate) at all levels of instruction

revising practices of teaching literature, culture, and language to combine the cultural emphasis with a strongly interactive, communicative approach

cooperating with foreign language professional organizations in integrating the revised curriculum to the national standards for teaching languages in K–12

taking advantage of the state of Georgia's mandated outcomes assessment program to rethink and revise the nature of the curriculum

This project provided funds for two faculty seminars that included extensive reading and discussion of topics covering these four steps. For most of the faculty members who participated, at least a portion of the readings and discussions covered material that was new because it belonged to a different discourse community. Discussions were open and, for the most part, honest. During these seminars, faculty members read a common core of texts, discussed curricular changes, and educated one another about biases, ideologies, and concerns. Perhaps most important, the grant provided them with time to reflect about the department's mission in the field of foreign language and literature education. They found their differences to be great. Claire Kramsch could be describing our faculty when she speaks of "different intellectual styles," "different research traditions," and "different political leanings" ("Embracing" 12). In our department are all the discourse communities Kramsch mentions: there are those eager to "set priorities," "set evaluation procedures," and "determine outcomes," others who represent a discourse concerned with "critical reflection," "student-centeredness," and "critical pedagogy, cultural criticism, and postmodern thought." Still others engage in what Kramsch calls the "discourse of metaphysics, literary criticism" (10). These discourses were apparent during our discussion of the core readings and perhaps even more so in the conversation on the curriculum. Our faculty members display different styles, training, philosophies, and scholarly pursuits. They belong to different professional organizations, read different journals, hold different pedagogical ideologies, and literally and figuratively speak different languages. As a faculty, we cannot reach agreement even on what writing style manual to teach our students and require of them in writing exercises: the MLA style is preferred by the literary scholars, the *Chicago Manual* or APA style preferred by the more scientific among us. We believe, as we argued in our NEH grant proposal, that to change a curriculum we first need to change ourselves. Our conflicts and differences were especially apparent as we met with six outside consultants (each representing at least one of the four languages that we teach and representing several of our discourse communities), who advised us on implementing a new curriculum.

While the entire faculty in the Department of Romance Languages went through the activities involved in the NEH grant, the Georgia team met monthly to discuss with local-area teachers some of the items established early in our conversation. The team was concerned primarily with articulation among all levels of instruction, placement of incoming freshmen in college language classes, requirements, and standards for foreign language education. The team was stimulated by the two MLA teacher education Houston meetings to continue to exert a positive influence on colleagues in the development of a model foreign language curriculum. Those members of the team who were in the Department of Romance Languages brought home to the department new ideas that helped them and others make decisions concerning the development of new curricula for the BA and MA in French and Spanish. The two projects converged, and the department reached consensus on basic philosophical underpinnings of its curricula.

The faculty approved this statement:

> The basic philosophy of the revised BA curriculum is that it will be integrative and courses will combine language, literature, culture, and theory. The curriculum takes into account the need to maintain and improve our students' linguistic competence at all levels, the need to reflect developments in cultural studies, and the need to integrate courses so that students do not necessarily have "literature" and "nonliterature" courses. (*Philosophy of B. A. Program*)

In the graduate programs, the faculty approved this philosophy:

> The graduate program will favor a contextualized and integrated approach to the study of Romance literature, linguistic, languages, and culture. "Contextualized" is taken here to mean viewing literature and language as interrelated components of a broad network of cultural, political, and economic practices and institutions. "Integrated" is taken here to mean, at the level both of individual courses and of the graduate curriculum as a whole, that the learning process will be structured in such a way as to combine literature, linguistics, culture, and theory. (*Philosophy of M. A. Program*)

Our philosophical statements were translated into curricular decisions only after the faculty agreed to separate into different language groups. Even within our own department, although the basic philosophy remained clear to everyone, the difference in cultural ideologies of the different languages became too great an obstacle to forge a common curriculum. Enrollment patterns also played a role in many curricular decisions. One question was, Can the less commonly taught languages afford to teach all courses in the target language when enrollments are low? Another question was, Can the basic communicative goal be achieved in Spanish classes when enrollments explode and there is unprecedented growth in interest?

In a recent book, the Brazilian anthropologist Ruben Oliven demonstrates through fascinating empirical research that the more we try to think globally and achieve common goals for all, the more we retreat into our own traditions, cultural values, and discourses. Oliven likens this behavior to a kind of survival instinct. To use a North American metaphor, each language group in our faculty discussions ended up circling its wagons, that is, becoming territorial and thereby at times forgetting the initial goal of the two projects—K–12 teacher preparation. The dialogue begun more than a year ago among many sectors involved in teacher training has aroused some old patterns of discourse. To quote Claire Kramsch in her response to Heidi Byrnes and Elizabeth B. Bernhardt, our discourse showed signs of the old dichotomies, "intellectual exercise versus untidy reality, the privileged few versus the student masses, lofty talk versus action on the ground, iron cage of inaction versus responsible action, local private interests versus the communal good" ("Reply").

All the vagaries described above help explain why we have difficulties in communicating and why we have encountered many obstacles in the effort to achieve a truly integrated curriculum. When we presented our model program at the second Houston meeting, 21–24 March 1996, we realized that we had not involved the College of Education in its development. To be sure, we had met, discussed, and argued about what future teachers needed, wanted, should have, and so forth. But when it came down to a decision on curricular matters, the Department of Romance Languages chose what it thought was best in terms of the pragmatic, academic, and political realities of its faculty. Twenty-two of our twenty-six faculty members are primarily literature professors who, although they care passionately for the language, culture, and ideologies represented in the texts that they teach, tend not to concern themselves with the practical implications of those texts for future teachers. In many respects, during this past year the Georgia team did a great deal of speaking to one another but not enough listening. At times they almost communicated. But they did not, because of the struggle inherent in trying to understand a different culture — a different discourse community.

On the one hand, our colleagues from language education are concerned that certain fields did not enter into the year-long conversation held by the Georgia team: second language acquisition, cognitive psychology, general learning theories, and theories that deal more specifically with the learning of other languages. Our team member from the College of Education summarized her frustration: "While much time has been spent on discussions related to such issues as course content and placement exams, no time has been spent discussing *how* one learns to read, write, interact, think, and, indeed, *learn* in another language. From the perspective of the Department of Language Education, there is a pervasive — and dangerous — laissez-faire attitude about such instructional matters." On the other hand, faculty members in languages and literatures tend to react negatively to statements that imply a lack in their preparation, a lack of concern with learning theory. And what interests faculty members in language and literature — literary theory, cultural theory — receives what might be called the mirror-image treatment from colleagues in the College of Education. We have been speaking from and through our separate discourse communities and have not thought, perhaps, that the most we may be able to expect from one another is acceptance, tolerance, and open dialogue. The solution for the "school problem" will not come from any one discourse community; it will begin when different communities attempt to communicate.

As we move toward a new calendar for the University of Georgia, we have the unique opportunity to question our positions and values. Faculty members in Romance languages must deal with questions such as, Why are our literature courses perceived as irrelevant for future teachers? More important, how can we make all our courses relevant for all students? One of the greatest challenges that we face is to rethink literature courses so that they address issues that are relevant to our students in general and to future teachers in particular. Language education faculty members will also have to question their values and expectations and devise ways to communicate with the other. The most valuable lesson from this project has been the acknowledgment from both sides of the campus that communication is difficult and at times painful. This acknowledgment in itself is the first step toward many compromises that will undoubtedly continue to be debated in future projects.

All texts have underlying cultural value that can be extracted, explained, analyzed, studied, and enjoyed, whether we read for content, discursive elements, or linguistic variations. What better opportunity to teach future teachers about foreign cultural values and judgments than by guiding them through a systematic reading of the texts from that particular culture. Paulo Freire in his *Pedagogy of the Oppressed* argues for the study and understanding of texts as a means of becoming aware of our biases through the mirror of other cultures. According to Freire, teachers cannot impart knowledge, but they can impart the ability to question cultural texts—written, oral, and visual.

It is up to us to question our teaching, our students, and our texts, so that students will come to their own definition of culture. All humans display cultural values in texts. If we are able to guide our students in the decoding of these texts, we may be able to guide them toward some intercultural understanding. Precollege teachers play an important role in the linguistic and literary development of young people today. The values that we instill in future teachers will be the values that they in turn convey to their students. Our greatest challenge—indeed, our greatest opportunity in reshaping teacher education in foreign languages—is to rethink our discourses and their implications.

We began this essay by quoting from two colleagues who argue for the acceptance of differences and for intercultural cooperation. The MLA Teacher Education Project has provided us with an opportunity to engage in debate and to join in the conversation about what is best for our schools. Perhaps the greatest outcome of this project has been to foster the conversation and to provide a safe forum for discourse communities to emerge. We have heard one another. Now it is time that we begin to listen more carefully; to discern what is possible; and, without compromising our cultural values, to cooperate toward a goal of intercultural understanding with all its complex ramifications. As our profession continually changes, our cooperation "has become a prime condition for [. . .] survival" (Hofstede 241).

Postscript

Three years have passed since the University of Georgia participated in the MLA Teacher Education Project. During this time, the faculty at the university has inaugurated a new president, completed the transition to the semester system that began in the fall of 1998, and instituted a post-tenure review system. Any one of these changes would be enough to cause some tension among faculty members and among different colleges and departments in an institution; all three at once might produce chaos. This has not been the case at our university, at least not within the structure of foreign language teacher education as described in our original report.

The Department of Romance Languages and the Department of Foreign Language Education have completely revised their curricula at both the undergraduate and graduate levels. New courses in Romance languages reflect a consensus philosophy in the department that students will be exposed to language-linguistics, literature-theory frameworks, and culture at all levels of instruction, from the beginning language class to the most advanced doctoral seminar. To this end, faculty members are committed to working together in the implementation phase of the new curriculum.

Candidates for foreign language education degrees at both undergraduate and graduate levels will no longer have separate classes in the Department of Romance Languages designed specifically for future teachers. Instead, the department wishes to offer the best in an integrative curriculum while at the same time taking individual needs into account. Indeed, the majority of the faculty in Romance languages has adopted a policy of accepting a teaching project as a substitute for the traditional critical-theoretical term paper for those students who wish to pursue teaching. Faculty members who have implemented this policy report positive results (see Kadish, this volume).

Representatives from the Department of Romance Languages and from the Department of Foreign Language Education meet periodically to discuss common goals and interests. Members of the Athens Area Academic Alliance continue to get together four or five times a year, and their discussions have been relevant to the new curriculum, to the change to the semester system, and to issues raised by block scheduling.

As our report shows, we are pursuing a conversation among departments and among faculty members. Dialogue is at times difficult, since we speak different languages and see the world from different cultural viewpoints; but despite our differences, dialogue exists and perseveres.

José Luis Gómez-Martínez, *Department of Romance Languages, University of Georgia*
Joan Kelly Hall, *Division of Language Education, University of Georgia*
James L. Jones, Jr., *Clarke Central High School*
Doris Y. Kadish, *Department of Romance Languages, University of Georgia*

Jean-Pierre Piriou, *Department of Romance Languages, University of Georgia*
Carmen Chaves Tesser (chair), *Department of Romance Languages, University of Georgia*

Note

[1]Research universities in the state wished to change the calendar so that students would graduate in May rather than in June and thus enter the job market with the majority of college graduates. Smaller schools were more interested in three entry dates.

WORKS CITED

Bakhtin, Mikhail. "Dialogism in the Novel." *The Dialogic Imagination: Four Essays.* Trans. Caryl Emerson and Michael Holquist. Ed. Michael Holquist. Austin: U of Texas P, 1981. 269–305.

Freire, Paulo. *Pedagogy of the Oppressed.* Rev. ed. Trans. Myra Bergman Ramos. New York: Continuum, 1995.

Hofstede, Geert H. *Cultures and Organizations: Software of the Mind.* New York: McGraw, 1991.

Kramsch, Claire. "Embracing Conflict versus Achieving Consensus in Foreign Language Education." *ADFL Bulletin* 26.3 (1995): 6–12.

———. "Reply to Heidi Byrnes and Elizabeth B. Bernhardt." *ADFL Bulletin* 26.3 (1995): 17.

Oliven, Ruben. *Tradition Matters: Modern Gaúcho Identity in Brazil.* Trans. Carmen Chaves Tesser. New York: Columbia UP, 1996.

Philosophy of B. A. Program. Dept. of Romance Langs., U of Georgia. 16 Feb. 1999 <http://www.rom.uga.edu/ugrad/philba.htm>.

Philosophy of M. A. Program. Dept. of Romance Langs., U of Georgia. 16 Feb. 1999 <http://www.rom.uga.edu/graduate/philma.htm>.

Undergraduate Bulletin. Athens: U of Georgia, 1998.

UNIVERSITY OF NORTH CAROLINA, GREENSBORO

Integrated Perspectives: An Exemplary Program

Background

The University of North Carolina's participation in the MLA Teacher Education Project in foreign languages provided the opportunity for our team to become resident experts on state and national performance standards while simultaneously shoring up one of the principal planks in our departmental platform: our commitment to teacher training. With the active intervention of a colleague from the Department of German and Russian, of one of our alumni as our representative from the schools, and of our undergraduate research assistant (a senior French major preparing to teach), our task turned into an exercise in collaborative learning that has laid the groundwork for what we believe will produce benefits for all concerned—students, faculty members, teachers, and administrators.

The team's journey of (self-)discovery began when we devised surveys for our colleagues, our students, and alumni who had been in-service teachers and after we analyzed catalog descriptions and course syllabi. We also attended to the prescribed reading list, visited high school classes, and interviewed experts in the field before producing our baseline study, which in turn suggested the direction in which our exemplary program would evolve. The gist of this program, which we have had occasion to present before colleagues at home, at the second MLA Teacher Education Project Conference in Houston, and at the 1996 ADFL Seminar East in Columbus, Ohio, forms the center of this report. As will be seen, our program boasts a multidimensional structure, with complex interrelations among its several parts. It is intentionally process-oriented to illustrate the need for a dynamic rather than static approach to teacher preparation in foreign languages.

The University of North Carolina, Greensboro, is a midsize, community-oriented, public institution, one of three to grant the doctorate in the sixteen-campus university system. A women's college until the 1960s, UNCG has a long-standing tradition of excellence in the liberal arts and sciences as well as a strong commitment to professional education. It has a faculty of over 700 and a student body of approximately 12,000, composed of 9,200 undergraduates and 2,800 graduate students.

The foreign language departments at UNCG form an integral part of the university's liberal arts program, which is delivered principally through the College of Arts and Sciences. These departments also are heavily involved in preparing teachers for the state's public schools. The multifaceted mission of the Department of Romance Languages stresses a commitment to excellence in teaching and research and stresses support for intellectual community and critical inquiry across the disciplines, with the professional schools, and with the public. In that department, students may earn bachelor's and master's degrees (MA or MEd) in French or Spanish, and they may study Italian through the intermediate level. The Department of German and Russian offers a BA in German, a minor in Russian, and introductory courses in Japanese. Prospective Latin teachers study their major in the Department of Classical Studies, which, like the Department of Romance Languages, now enables students holding a baccalaureate degree to earn a master's degree along with A (initial) licensure and G (graduate) licensure in record time.[1]

The recently consolidated Guilford County School System is known for its emphasis on technology and its leadership in establishing the information highway in North Carolina. Most of our students seeking licensure perform their student teaching and other field experiences in this system of 94 schools (60 elementary schools, 17 middle schools, 14 high schools, and 3 special schools). Jones School, one of the elementary magnet schools, offers a Spanish language immersion program, where many of our students have the opportunity to observe and participate. Of the 58,576 students in Guilford County schools, 44% are minorities. Special classes in English for speakers of other languages (ESOL) are offered for 1,200 students. These students represent 59 languages or dialects; the largest group is Vietnamese, the second largest Hispanic.

The table provides a snapshot of the two UNCG language departments represented on the MLA team.[2]

The number of tenured and tenure-track faculty members has been

The Two Language Departments Represented on the MLA Team at the University of North Carolina, Greensboro

	DEPARTMENT OF ROMANCE LANGUAGES	DEPARTMENT OF GERMAN AND RUSSIAN, INCLUDING JAPANESE STUDIES
Full-time tenured and tenure-track faculty members	14 (7 French, 7 Spanish)	3 (1 Russian, 2 German)
Part-time or temporary teachers	17 (4 French, 12 Spanish, 1 Italian)	5 (1 Russian, 3 German, 1 Japanese)
Undergraduate general education students	2,945	680
Majors (juniors and seniors in the spring of 1996)	28 Spanish (including 5 teaching candidates), 23 Spanish as second major (including 1 teaching candidate), 15 French (including 8 teaching candidates), 13 French as second major (including 1 teaching candidate)	16 German (including 3 teaching candidates), 19 German as second major, 7 Russian Studies major

declining, while the number of full-time, non-tenure-track faculty members has increased. We have, however, become less dependent on part-timers. All tenured faculty members routinely teach some lower-level language courses as part of their regular teaching load.

The most significant recent change has been the mushrooming enrollments in Spanish, accompanied by a drop-off in French. Russian has also declined, while Japanese—offered for the first time in 1995–96—has already attracted considerable interest.

The number of majors and second majors in French, German, and Spanish has been increasing, although Spanish alone has shown marked change. Upper-level courses tend to be fairly small, generally ranging from 10 to 15 students. In 1995–96, a larger percentage of French majors ultimately chose to pursue licensure than did Spanish or German majors; but it is too early to determine whether this increase represents a trend. Among students of Spanish and German, double (or second) majors are popular.

A few statistics may help fill out the enrollment picture in Spanish and French. In 1996–97, we had a total of 910 students enrolled in French courses (up 3% from the previous year). We had a total of 2,469 in Spanish (down 5% from 1995–96). In upper-division courses we had 72 in French in 1996–97 (up 13% from the previous year). In Spanish, upper-division enrollment reached a total of 411 (up 39% from 1995–96).

In 1987, North Carolina mandated a K–5 second language program for all children, giving them the option of continuing through grade 12. At the same time, the state adopted a K–12-only licensure in French, German, and Spanish. It is available at the A (initial) level and, for Romance languages, at the G (graduate) level. Majors who wish to teach earn a BA degree, completing at the same time the appropriate teacher education curriculum (30 semester hours). Once they have attained acceptable teaching competencies, these majors are declared eligible for licensure by the department in question. For many years our departments have relied heavily on a faculty member who has a PhD in French and holds a joint appointment in Romance languages and in the School of Education's Department of Curriculum and Instruction to ensure smooth collaboration between the two administrative units involved in preparing second language teachers. We are on the brink of a new era with the retirement of this colleague and the appointment of her full-time replacement in the Department of Curriculum and Instruction, as of 1 August 1996. Efforts have begun (such as naming a Spanish faculty member as liaison with this replacement) to find new ways to promote effective cooperation between our separate units. With the ever-increasing number of limited English-proficient students in North Carolina, there has arisen a need for more colleges and universities to provide teacher training in English for speakers of other languages. UNCG has recently reinstated its add-on licensure program (the only type currently allowed in the state), and advisers in the language departments are encouraging students to seek dual licensure, which will make students more marketable and add to the much-needed pool of ESOL teachers in North Carolina.

Students seeking licensure follow a three-semester sequence of field experiences, whenever possible in professional development schools; the sequence culminates in a full semester of student teaching at the end of the students' senior year. The Office of Teacher Education coordinates placement and tracks students' progress toward fulfilling licensure requirements; students' advisers in the language departments and in the Department of Curriculum and Instruction provide oversight. Cooperating teachers in the county schools, the methods instructor, and faculty members who teach the professional education courses play a collaborative role in the supervision and assessment of preservice teachers.

PARTNERSHIPS THROUGH PROFESSIONAL DEVELOPMENT SCHOOLS

The School of Education at UNCG began exploring the idea of professional development schools (PDSs) in the early 1990s. These are public schools where the administration and the faculty have agreed to work with a university in a collaborative effort to improve the preservice experience and to aid in the professional development of teachers. The university's elementary and middle school programs initiated a partnership with the Guilford County Schools four years ago. In our model, the elementary and middle school students are formed into cohorts of twenty-five to thirty at the beginning of their junior year. These teams remain together for two years under the guidance of a faculty team leader until their teacher education program is completed. The program is heavily field-based as students spend ten to twenty hours per week for three semesters in one of two schools before doing their student teaching. The students contribute to the educational program of the schools by tutoring, working with students in small groups, and providing time for the professional development of their supervising teachers during school hours.

The secondary education program has been developing a professional-development-school relationship with three Guilford County schools during the past two years. The secondary school student teachers have a three-semester sequence of field experiences beginning in the spring of their junior year, with a general introduction to secondary schools that focuses on technology, exceptional learners, and multiculturalism; each component has a practicum in one of the partner schools. During the fall of the senior year, student teachers enroll in their methods course, which has a ten-week observation-and-participation field experience in the high school where they will do their student teaching the following semester, and with the same teacher. As a result of this extensive experience, these students are better prepared to teach than those from traditional programs.

While the UNCG–Guilford County Schools PDS Partnership has created a living laboratory for research and development, encouraged faculty development, and fostered much stronger linkages between practice and research, it will endeavor in the future to bring about systemic changes at the classroom and school levels. What is envisioned is a process of continuous improvement designed to develop the leadership, problem-solving, and technological abilities of participants as they work as members of an interprofessional development school team. The project design will include a system of feeder schools—elementary, middle, and secondary—that build a school system within a school system. To create quality schools, a broader educational environment is needed, one that includes not only the schools and institutions of higher education but also community agencies, business and industry, and the home. The goal will be to create a continuous learning community of students, teachers, university faculty members, principals, school counselors, parents, business leaders, and community agency personnel through collaboration, professional development, and research.

IMPORTANCE OF TEACHER PREPARATION AT UNCG

The preparation of teachers has been pivotal in our institution's century-old history, from its origins as a normal school, through its days as the Woman's College, one of the three original institutions of the Consolidated University of North Carolina, to today, when it boasts an award-winning school of education among its six professional schools, which complement our College of Arts and Sciences. In recent years the North Carolina Teaching Fellows Program, which provides four years of financial assistance to successful candidates in exchange for four years of teaching in North Carolina schools, has brought excellent students our way. In addition, scholarship money has routinely been made available to UNCG students enrolled abroad, an increasing number of whom are our majors seeking teacher licensure. Significant in this regard is our spring semester in Costa Rica, the fruit of a cooperative effort by the Department of Romance Languages, the School of Education, and the Office of International Programs, which incorporates one professional education course that includes observation and participation in the schools there along with the program of Spanish studies. Recently, too, we inaugurated an exchange with the school of education at the University of Extremadura, as an addition to our long-standing summer and fall programs in Spain. Exchanges have also been arranged with institutions in France and Germany. Immersion experiences for in-service teachers of French and Spanish were held on campus during the 1980s, with funding first from NEH, then from the state of North Carolina (Governor's Language Institutes). Some of the same people who participated in these summer institutes subsequently earned their master's degrees at UNCG.

Many of the master's candidates who already held an A licensure earned an MEd, which includes G licensure. Departmental faculty members have always sought ways to collaborate with area teachers through

Academic Alliances or by working together in the Foreign Language Association in North Carolina (FLANC) and the AATSP, AATF, and AATG.

Institutional support for the activities outlined above has been buttressed lately by an influx of funds from various quarters meant to upgrade our technological resources and our ability to access them. The new multimedia language center symbolizes for us a long-term commitment to the importance of second languages and cultures on the part of the university; we interpret the center as a signal to continue our efforts to improve delivery of our programs, generally as well as specifically, to our majors, especially to those among them who will be imparting what they learn to future generations of North Carolina schoolchildren.

All the full-time tenured or tenure-track faculty members in both the Romance languages department and the German and Russian department are involved in teaching the courses required of majors preparing to teach. One lecturer, who holds a PhD, regularly teaches business Spanish, which is applicable to the major. Professional education and methods courses, as well as student teaching, are handled by the School of Education. In addition to taking courses designed to produce competency in oral-aural, writing, and literary skills, which are part of the major in every case, students preparing to teach must study phonetics and civilization. Faculty members in the language departments have traditionally been available to instruct in all these areas.

The review of the Romance languages department in 1993–94 called for us to assess our major, using multiple measures; we have now established a plan to do this. The good job market for teachers with adequate proficiency constituted another motivational factor for us, along with the need to produce students capable of scoring well on the National Teachers Examination in their subject areas. The MLA Teacher Education Project has been another powerful force. Thus, both traditional and new sources have combined to provide the impetus for change, and our responses have been framed accordingly.

The MLA Team's Recommendations

ADVISING AND MENTORING

As our team examined our current system of advising and evaluated the knowledge and skills of students nearing completion of our program, we developed a clear awareness of the need to monitor in more telling detail the progress of individual students toward the objectives of the major. To provide better advice to our students and better assessment of their performance will entail a shift from reliance on a traditionally prescribed series of courses intended to cover language, literature, and culture. Adequate completion of such courses does not, after all, guarantee the acquisition of knowledge and skills deemed essential to the well-educated foreign language major.

In devising a mechanism to provide continuous, individual assessment, the team also recognizes the need for that responsibility to be shared by departmental faculty members. Currently, students meet with their major adviser each semester for guidance on course selection, study abroad, future career options, and other related academic issues. In the future, faculty members (starting with Spanish courses, where the numbers are higher) will share the task of advising all the undergraduate majors in their ordinary academic concerns. The undergraduate advisers' role in Spanish and French will include coordinating a new mentoring process that helps each student identify an appropriate faculty mentor who will closely oversee that individual's professional development. The mentor will meet regularly with the student to assess performance and identify any problem areas and will guide the student toward completion and presentation of the major portfolio. In a one-credit, independent-study course directed by the mentor—it has yet to be formally proposed—the student will finalize this portfolio. It will be submitted for review at the end of the senior year and evaluated by at least two members of the relevant graduate faculty.

By involving several faculty members in the development over time of each student's portfolio, we hope to offer all majors and in particular the future teachers a more realistic and timely evaluation of their strengths and weaknesses than has been the rule. In addition, the work of advising (reconceived as mentoring) becomes more meaningful and is shared more equitably among more members of the department. The faculty-student ratio at UNCG should facilitate such individualized attention.

PROFICIENCY ASSESSMENT AND THE PORTFOLIO APPROACH

Prior to the inception of the MLA project, assessment of proficiency in our departments was at best sporadic. Placement exams were administered to incoming freshmen, who presented high school units in French or Spanish (UNCG has a foreign language entrance requirement for all students as well as a college requirement of proficiency through the intermediate level). These tests were homemade, home-administered, and home-scored; placement was determined internally and without regard for aural ability; no oral section was included. The most immediate advance in this respect, a direct result of study and action by the MLA team, has been the university's acquisition of the Brigham Young University Computer Adaptive Placement Examinations (CAPE) in French and Spanish. Site-tested and site-calibrated in the spring of 1996, these were first administered to new UNCG students that summer. To offset the lack of an oral component, the Department of Romance Languages supplemented the examinations, for high achievers, with oral interviews; we hope to implement full-fledged oral and written proficiency testing for such students later.

Assessment at the exit from the major in French or Spanish formerly consisted of another homemade, home-administered, and home-scored written test. It was a multiple-choice exam that covered grammar, culture, and literature. The department has agreed to replace the old exit exams with portfolio-based assessment.

The MLA team recommends that a process of continuous assessment of the five pillars of proficiency (listening, speaking, reading, writing, and culture) be implemented. Students would be asked to compile a working portfolio that begins as soon as they declare their major and continues through the senior year. During their last semester, they would convert this working portfolio into a summative portfolio. This conversion would take shape with the assistance of a faculty mentor and would be scrutinized periodically by the major adviser.

The portfolio is designed to document students' language skills and knowledge of the culture and to help the faculty mentor evaluate students' improvement as they go along, especially at certain key checkpoints. The department will determine the precise form and mode portfolio evaluation takes during the 1997–98 academic year; there is already agreement that the portfolio should contain the appropriate combination of qualitative and quantitative instruments, providing multiple means to assess various skills. Initially, the portfolio might contain a curriculum vitae with a description of courses taken in the major and relevant courses taken in other departments and disciplines. In a liberal arts statement, students might offer a synthetic narrative reflection on the relations between their program experiences and the department's goal to instill the liberal arts values that derive from the study of foreign languages, cultures, and literatures. In addition, the portfolio might include the score on the CAPE, which would be (re)administered at the threshold of the major sequence to determine readiness and to establish a benchmark. Other means (e.g., a simulated oral-proficiency interview) would be necessary to assess listening and speaking levels, perhaps at this same juncture but certainly before any student teaching experience. (With the support of college funds, the department will purchase in the coming year the materials required to begin implementing such interviews.) The portfolio might also provide evidence of students' increasing ability to make use of the target language for research and to employ it in a variety of written contexts. In addition, the portfolio would document students' growing sophistication about the target culture(s) by including reports on cultural events attended by the students, documenting some activities during their study abroad, and so forth. The summative portfolio should also contain evidence of activities related to preparation for teaching, when appropriate.

PORTFOLIO ASSESSMENT

In our efforts to make our program more student-centered, we have taken a hard look at our teaching practices and our methods for evaluating student progress. We realize we must have students participate more in the assessment of their progress toward proficiency in the four skills as well as in culture and literature. A first step is to establish knowledge and performance goals for students at each level of instruction and ways to help them meet these goals. The portfolio concept offers the advantage of allowing students to become independent, self-directed learners who have a say in what goes into the portfolio, reflect on their entries, and engage in self-evaluation. Other advantages of portfolio assessment include possible links within and across courses, both in the department and in the School of Education. Students in teacher education will include in their portfolios elements from their teaching and be expected to use the portfolios to help integrate their academic course work and their experiences in the field. The process will promote more peer collaboration as students share, evaluate, and reflect on their portfolios and the portfolios of others. Finally, portfolio assessment will enable students to learn about the learning process, since such assessment is done by them rather than to them.

Assessment at the all-important exit point would take various forms. Since expected achievement levels for graduating seniors would be well known by all, both program evaluation and appraisal of individual attainment would be in order. Multiple measures could be employed for outcomes assessment in program evaluation (standardized examinations in the content area for would-be teachers, alumni surveys, reports from employers, exit exams, and exit interviews). For individual students the definitive measure would be the completed summative portfolio.

CULTURAL STRANDS AND THE CAPSTONE PROJECT

An additional feature of the portfolio could be the inclusion of a cultural strand. Cultural strands encourage students to integrate culture and language learning by organizing instruction around interdisciplinary themes. Language majors could develop expertise in a particular aspect of the target culture by selecting and pursuing a cultural strand throughout their junior and senior years. Students' interests and professional goals should be stimulated by a variety of cross-cultural and interdisciplinary inquiries. The capstone project could focus on art and architecture, festivals and folklore, educational systems, literature, film studies, media and popular culture, or history and politics (see the appendix for a more extensive list of topics).

Language majors would consult initially with faculty mentors to determine the appropriateness and scope of the desired cultural strand as well as resources available for studying it, including courses in other content areas. In each appropriate course in the major, they would be encouraged to prepare a paper or an oral presentation related to the strand; the paper would be added to their portfolio. They could also document their use of technology to maximize their exposure to authentic materials and gain further insights into the strand. Study abroad would provide opportunities to conduct interviews and collect additional pertinent data. In the future, we envision the incorporation of a capstone project in the portfolio. The one-credit independent study currently under consideration by the department could be expanded to a full three-credit capstone experience in which the students would synthesize, evaluate, and present the results of their research to faculty members and fellow students.

Language learners in the twenty-first century will need to understand the relations among cultural perspectives, practices, and products if they are to use their knowledge of the language to interact effectively in the target culture. We anticipate that increased cultural understanding, familiarity with organizing cultural themes, unification of course work, collaboration with faculty mentors, enhanced linguistic proficiency, and utilization of technology implicit in the cultural-strands component will create teachers capable of meeting the challenge of these future students.

TOTAL IMMERSION

It is our belief that in order to speak and teach knowledgeably about another culture, it is essential that a teacher acquire firsthand experience of that culture. We also recognize that most teachers will not attain an acceptable level of linguistic competence until they have been totally immersed in the target language for a sufficient period of time. To send a teacher into the classroom without the benefit of a total-immersion experience does a disservice to both the teacher and the students. Accordingly, we recommend that all teacher education majors acquire firsthand knowledge of the target language and culture through a total-immersion experience.

Ideally, each teacher education major should participate in a study-abroad program lasting at least one semester if not a full academic year. If students' financial or personal circumstances do not permit such participation, a summer program could be substituted, provided it has an academic component judged acceptable by the major adviser. Study abroad should be considered mandatory except in rare cases. If a student is able to present compelling reasons (other than cost and inconvenience) that would preclude an extended period of residence abroad, then the student and the adviser should develop an alternative plan intended to simulate a total-immersion experience (to the extent possible) in the university or in the community—for example, volunteer work with immigrants, an internship with a foreign-owned company, pairing the student with an international student.

Whereas we can train students in other areas of teacher education (science, social science, English) using only the resources provided by the university and the local school system, students preparing to teach a second language simply cannot be expected to attain an acceptable level of linguistic or cultural proficiency without the benefit of a total-immersion experience. Because transportation expenses and the cost of living in some countries will pose a financial hardship for many of our students, the university must support this vital aspect of the language program by providing financial aid in addition to the scholarships already available.

Students interested in study abroad are encouraged to consult the Office of International Programs at UNCG. Offering information on scholarships for study abroad, exchange programs, and so on, the office is relatively new on campus, but it has had great success in expanding the role of international education at UNCG. We have more and more foreign students studying at the university, and their United States counterparts travel to many different countries. For example, last year we hosted an exchange student from Extremadura, Spain, while one of our majors was studying in the School of Education there. UNCG also has its own long-standing departmental programs: a summer program in Spain (Cáceres), a semester program in Spain (Madrid), and a semester program in Costa Rica. The Costa Rican program has a teacher education component, allowing students to take one of their education classes and visit Costa Rican secondary schools while they are in that country.

TECHNOLOGICAL LITERACY FOR TEACHING MAJORS

Electronic language laboratories have developed from rather passive, drill-based facilities to multimedia environments where students perform as self-motivating centers of activity. Instead of offering digital extensions of traditional teaching techniques, multimedia laboratories can function as valuable immersion centers for foreign languages, literatures, and cultures. The communication links to the Internet, the World Wide Web, and international libraries supply cornucopias of authentic resources to individualize and expand classroom programs.

Since 1994, these assumptions and expectations framed our team's discussions concerning the exemplary use of digital technologies in foreign language education at UNCG. It was an opportune time for the Department of Romance Languages—the largest of three foreign language departments on campus—to map out new multimedia teaching ventures, as our team's ideas and recommendations matched well with broader technology initiatives proposed by the university.

It soon became apparent that the infusion of interactive technologies was going to play a major role in reorienting the departmental teaching major as well as most other components of the foreign language curriculum. In 1995, the MLA team developed a blueprint for redesigning, restructuring, and remodeling the department's old tape laboratory. Financed through college and university funds, this restructuring was completed in the fall of 1996, and the new multimedia language center opened in the spring of 1997. The center contains twelve multimedia stations with Internet, satellite, and network connections and with software for eight foreign language programs taught in the College of Arts and Sciences.

In line with current instructional theories and foreign language methodologies, the interests and needs of students occupied center stage in our laboratory plan. Of primary importance was the design of the space itself. Students should feel at ease, be able to converse, study in groups or in private, and explore available resources at their own pace. In a nutshell, our pedagogical and technological priority was to combine hardware, software, and connectivity to foster the proliferation and integration of foreign language studies on campus.

Use of the laboratory's multimedia resources by teaching majors will range from basic language training and information retrieval to intermediate communication and research activities, and from integrating the Web as an instructional tool to the design of virtual learning environments. Two instructional models are emerging. The first is the interactive-gallery paradigm, which utilizes the multimedia features of the Web to exhibit and disseminate information for classroom use. The second is the extension of the classroom into digital domains to incorporate more-sophisticated features. Web-mediated teaching allows courses, fully or in part, to be taught over the Internet.

The integrated design of the new multimedia language center, and its combination of electronic instruction, training, research, outreach, and entertainment functions, ties the department closer to foreign language communities and schools across the region. That connection directly benefits our teaching majors. By fostering an environment of directed exploration and experimentation, the electronic laboratory is turning into a teaching hub for the three foreign language departments on campus.

To enhance our students' technological literacy and to increase teaching majors' familiarity with the changing paradigms of foreign language instruction, our exemplary program focuses on the mastery of four crucial technological skills:

Operation of multimedia learning centers. Teaching majors will receive part of their technological training by proctoring students at the department's multimedia learning center. By operating computer workstations and handling hardware connections and network configurations, future teachers will gain proficiency in the use of software applications, satellite broadcasts, Internet archives, electronic mailing lists, and digital bulletin boards. This practical training at the center will include, with the use of other multimedia teaching tools, the operation of portable computers with overhead projectors.

Use of television and telecommunication systems. Student teachers and teaching majors will operate remote-control monitors and VCRs, open Internet connections, download files, and record foreign language broadcasts. They will have privileged access to the laboratory's workstations to access programs, tape audio and visual materials, and log into telecommunication sessions. Exposure to a broad array of multimedia resources should encourage teaching majors to incorporate these materials in their classroom work and perhaps model new approaches to foreign language education.

Access to computer networks and individual accounts. UNCG's foreign language departments will provide all teaching majors with free Internet access, electronic mailboxes, and network accounts. Students will be able to use free digital storage space to download resources, customize software applications, research the Web, and publish their own multimedia materials in cyberspace. The individual accounts will allow students to explore digital domains at their own pace and document their technological proficiency in the form of virtual journals and portfolios on the World Wide Web. Portions of these electronic résumés, portfolios, or "Webfolios" will be exhibited on the Internet to demonstrate cyberliteracy and proficiency. Preparing the Webfolios will offer teaching majors valuable opportunities to master hypertext programming and Web-site design.

Use of the Internet as a global archive. During their enrollment in the department's foreign language programs, teaching majors will learn to utilize the Internet as an interdisciplinary, cross-cultural, and multilingual studies arena. As a global information archive, the Internet offers students interactive immersion opportunities unlike any other teaching tool. Preparing data files, establishing Telnet links, accessing FTP documents, and subscribing to foreign language e-mail discussion lists are essential reference skills for teaching professionals in the Internet age. Relying on these global resources will allow majors to expand their classroom experiences and find new contacts abroad through virtual role-playing and immersion activities. In these partnerships and discoveries lie the primary rewards for teaching majors to appropriate new classroom technologies.

These four skills are designed to encourage students' expeditions into the field of teaching technologies, challenge their notions of computer literacy, and offer yet another reason for their pursuit and mastery of a foreign language. As our departments cast their technological nets ever wider, the educational resources of the information age help connect native speakers and second language learners across the globe. This new connectivity can indeed play an important role in improving our teacher education programs without adding new courses or costs for our students.

What's in It for Me?

A STUDENT'S PERSPECTIVE

Today's teachers face numerous challenges both inside and outside the classroom. The increasing demands of the profession require that future teachers be part of a program that affords them a superior preparation.

Like most college students, I have not yet learned how to be my own educational advocate. At times I am unsure of what classes best suit my needs. I am not certain how to receive such help as tutoring or career counseling. Or how I will give that help as a teacher. For these reasons, the possibility of building and maintaining a relationship with a faculty member serving as my adviser-mentor appeals to me. I believe that in this situation my individual needs will be met more effectively, because I will be able to take advantage of a knowledgeable professional who is approachable, trustworthy, and interested in my success.

The cultural-strand component of the UNCG program intrigues me, because it provides the opportunity to choose an area on which to focus my studies, permitting me to gain a deeper understanding of a particular sphere of the target culture. The capstone project as well as other avenues for leadership in the target language (e.g., tutoring, assisting professors) will aid me in making the transition from learner to teacher. The summative portfolio, which will track my progress throughout the program, likewise encourages me to take personal responsibility for my education.

As a lover of the target language, I would naturally like to rely solely on it for spoken communication in the classroom. As with many other teacher candidates, however, lack of confidence in my speaking abilities makes me apprehensive about being the primary language model for my students. Therefore I am eager to study abroad, and I look forward to the total-immersion experience that is an integral feature of UNCG's program. I also want to take advantage of the opportunities available at UNCG, thanks especially to the newly equipped computer lab, to become more culturally and linguistically proficient. Most exciting for me is the prospect of creating a digital portfolio, which will, I hope, make me a more apt contender in an increasingly competitive job market.

A LANGUAGE AND LITERATURE FACULTY MEMBER'S PERSPECTIVE

Given the relatively small size of our department, many of us are called on to teach both language and literature courses, and although most of us received more preparation in literature than in language, we are willing to teach both types of courses in order to meet the needs of our students. We are also called on to teach lower-level courses on a frequent basis, and most of us accept these assignments as a necessary if not always inspiring component of our regular teaching load. While our exemplary plan does not specifically address the teaching of literature, we believe that all advanced courses—language, culture, and literature—will benefit from the changes we are proposing in our plan. Students who receive better training (through total immersion in the target language, independent research into the culture, individualized and carefully monitored programs of study, regular assessment of developing language skills, familiarization with technological resources, etc.) will be better equipped to participate in and profit from advanced courses. One of the greatest frustrations of teaching any upper-level course is that many students have not attained sufficient proficiency to handle the language component of the class. This problem is particularly acute in literature courses. We believe that if the recommendations cited in our report are implemented, we will be able to provide students with a level of preparation that will allow them to function more effectively in all their advanced courses.

AN EDUCATION FACULTY MEMBER'S PERSPECTIVE

If foreign language majors in teacher education can achieve greater proficiency in their target languages and cultures through a more student-centered program, one that provides proper placement, personalized faculty advising and mentoring, and a mandatory study-abroad experience, then the foreign language methods instructor, the university supervisor, and the cooperating teachers will be able to focus their attention on training the preservice teachers in the process of teaching rather than having to spend so much time working on their communicative skills and their content knowledge. The result will be that student teachers will be able to spend more of their time on the strategies, techniques, methods, and materials of teaching that will make them more competent teachers — masters of both content and process.

A SECONDARY SCHOOL TEACHER'S PERSPECTIVE

We secondary school teachers are often reluctant to supervise student teachers, because very few display a high level of linguistic competence. Phonetic, syntactic, and lexical deficiencies or uncertainties can disrupt the continuum of learning in the classroom and result in frustrations for all parties. The proficiency component in the proposed exemplary program at UNCG would alleviate this concern and would foster increased cooperation between the secondary schools and the university.

The improved teacher training in the proposed exemplary program would also strengthen articulation between courses and improve collaboration at the secondary level, because newly hired graduates would possess the skills necessary for dynamic, proficiency-oriented instruction. Veteran teachers would be assured that the students coming from a new colleague's classroom would have had maximum exposure to the language.

Ultimately, the proposed exemplary program would result in raised expectations for students in the secondary schools. Those administrators and teachers who currently do no more than pay lip service to teaching for proficiency would have to make radical changes in order to meet the higher linguistic demands for future university students.

A DEPARTMENT HEAD'S PERSPECTIVE

The action agenda devised by the MLA team offers our departmental leadership a blueprint for program improvement, which can be highly useful in the ongoing quest for ever scarcer resources. The process of developing the plan enlightened and energized those involved and helped forge or solidify valuable interdepartmental links. The publicity that ensued from appearances by team members at professional conferences is already bearing fruit in the form of increased expressions of interest from prospective students. The momentum generated by our activities has loosened the hold on internal purse strings when pleas have been presented in connection with the MLA Teacher Education Project. An example of that loosening is our developing multimedia language resource center. All these developments have helped in our recruitment of new faculty members. It is significant, too, that for the very first time we hired someone with a linguistics rather than a literature specialty.

Of course, not every aspect of our effort has borne such positive fruit. There are still those among the faculty who are uninterested in, unconvinced by, or downright opposed to so much emphasis on teacher education in our departments. There is concern that such a focus, with its insistence on proficiency, may spell doom for our traditional strength in literary appreciation and research. Another worry, even among the champions of our agenda, is that the new order will usher in an era of truly onerous workloads. This fear concerns not only the time that would be required to monitor students' progress properly but also the extra work that would be needed to see to the numerous items of unfinished business in the plan (the nature and form of the exit exams, to cite just one example.)

But all in all, from my department head's perspective, the agenda set out by the MLA team offers more solutions than questions, more opportunities than problems. Well informed and realistic, it has the potential of winning more converts and of making a real difference not only for prospective teachers of modern languages at UNCG but for all our students.

A DEAN'S PERSPECTIVE

The opportunity for our foreign language departments to participate in the MLA Teacher Education Project came at an important historical moment. The department-review process had already identified a number of issues and desiderata for which participation in the MLA project was highly relevant. The college and university had recently embarked on initiatives to improve the student-centeredness of all programs; to conduct meaningful outcomes assessment for all programs; to enhance the use of instructional technology; to provide enhanced training in instructional and information technologies for our students, but particularly (by state mandate) for students in teacher education programs; and to increase dramatically the number of students participating in study abroad.

So what was in it for me all along was the promise of significant progress for participating departments toward fulfillment of these goals. The MLA project team's report demonstrates that such progress is being achieved in all these areas, and I'm very pleased. This has been an excellent collaboration.

There is an additional something in it for the institution: I believe UNCG is well positioned to become the leading institution in our state (and perhaps in the region as well) in internationalized curricula, in collaborations with universities abroad, in study-abroad opportunities, and in the study and teaching of foreign languages. Our participation in the MLA Teacher Education Project has served to emphasize these possibilities.

A PROVOST'S PERSPECTIVE

The United States faces economic, ecological, political, and social challenges of enormous significance. If we are serious about successfully meeting these challenges in a competitive, global environment, then achieving educational excellence must be a national imperative as we move toward and into the twenty-first century. Our visions about what education ought to be must not be limited by what we have experienced it to be; schools and schooling will change more in the next two decades than in the past two hundred years. The task for planning for educational excellence must be approached with a sense of great responsibility and a sense of great urgency: great responsibility, because the quality of life in the United States depends on our success; great urgency, because the time to act is now.

The role of professional educators at all levels and how they conceptualize their responsibilities will change dramatically. Educators will no longer function primarily as disseminators of information; they will be responsible for teaching others how to use information to enhance their thinking and functioning abilities. To develop this new breed of educator will require universities to rethink both the liberal arts and professional curricula. It will be necessary to recruit the ablest and most imaginative students for the education professions—students who themselves aspire to be problem solvers, thinkers, and leaders.

It is my hope that the MLA Teacher Education Project in foreign languages at UNCG can serve as a model for all teacher education programs on campus as we continually rethink our teacher education curricula. The characteristics of the project—mentoring, continued assessment, portfolios, capstone projects, technology, and immersion, must be the characteristics of all teacher education programs at UNCG, if we are to maintain a leadership position in teacher education in North Carolina, the southeast, and nationally.

Postscript

We found the MLA Teacher Education Project to be a tremendously rewarding experience. The collaboration and dialogue among team members gave each person a much better understanding of the realities of the individual situations of others and a true appreciation for the challenges that they confront in their professional lives. Several members of the team have given presentations at local, regional, and national conferences and at other institutions in the state to publicize the ongoing developments and attract new students to our programs. Unfortunately, classroom visitations and other collaborative efforts have not continued. The biggest obstacle to these partnerships is lack of time: university and high school schedules seldom coincide, and professional and personal obligations limit our ability to sustain the momentum inspired by the project.

Following the conference phase of the MLA project, the modern language departments at UNCG saw significant changes in the operation of their laboratories. A new multimedia language center opened in the spring of 1997 for instruction in French, German, Greek, Spanish, Italian, Latin, Japanese, and Russian. The center boasts powerful computers that link students to foreign countries through the World Wide Web; a television system that carries the Deutsche Welle channels; new VCRs, CD-ROMs, and laser-disc players; and headphones and cassette players. The center augments the older audio lab, where students can listen to tapes and watch videos. The new lab gives students more options. They can enter chat rooms or use e-mail to write to peers abroad. For the first time on campus, students can plunge into other cultures to visit virtual museums, markets, and media sites. The lab has become a distribution center for learning materials and an intuitive environment ideal for guided discoveries in foreign languages, literatures, and cultures.

In the fall of 1997, the Spanish faculty began sharing the task of advising all their undergraduate majors, but they have yet to develop the proposed system of mentors to oversee portfolios. The use of portfolios in the Romance languages department is progressing in stages; it is beginning first at the graduate level, then will proceed with undergraduate teaching majors, and by the fall of 1999 will apply also to all undergraduate majors. Our curriculum has been revised to provide better articulation between levels and to emphasize development of all skills at each level.

These efforts have led to a few changes in the area of assessment. We are currently using the Computer Adaptive Placement Examination (supplemented where appropriate by an oral exam) for placement purposes. The CAPE has proven to be a fairly reliable and manageable tool. Additionally, we envision using it as one measure of students' progress over a period of time.

The Assessment Committee in Romance Languages is now preparing a set of guidelines for student portfolios. These guidelines suggest that portfolios should be phased in gradually, starting with a pilot group of teacher education majors. A capstone-course has been proposed. The course would carry one credit and would allow students to prepare summative portfolios. The department is participating in a college-wide initiative to assess all graduating seniors in the spring of 1998. They will be asked to evaluate both their general education and their experience in the major.

The teacher education project has left us with a sense of accomplishment and a renewed interest in improving the training of our language teachers. It has also left us with a strong awareness of problems that remain to be solved and challenges that lie on the immediate horizon. While various internal aspects of our program can be further improved—assessment; opportunities for immersion; better integration of language, literature, and culture—certain external aspects require significant attention. Specifically, we still need more articulation with secondary-level teachers and with the education faculty members who train those teachers. This articulation was presumably one of the primary objectives of the project, an objective that, for us and we suspect for most other universities, was never fully achieved. Nevertheless, the project, by virtue of its very inception and the enthusiasm it has generated among its participants, has set us all moving in the right direction.

Laura Chesak, *Department of Romance Languages, University of North Carolina, Greensboro*
David A. Fein, *Department of Romance Languages, University of North Carolina, Greensboro*
Kathleen Kish, *Department of Romance Languages, University of North Carolina, Greensboro*
Andreas Lixl, *Department of German and Russian, University of North Carolina, Greensboro*
Jane Tucker Mitchell, *Department of Romance Languages, University of North Carolina, Greensboro*
Carmen T. Sotomayor, *Department of Romance Languages, University of North Carolina, Greensboro*
Katherine White, *Grimsley High School*

Notes

[1]Students meeting admission requirements who enroll full-time can complete the option 2 MEd in French or Spanish in sixteen months. We expect the same situation to prevail after our MA and MEd degrees are consolidated into a single master's in Romance languages and literatures, with four tracks: French, French education, Spanish, and Spanish education. We anticipate that this change will go into effect in 1997–98.

[2]In the Department of Romance Languages, one of the full-time faculty members held a joint appointment, devoting half her time to the Department of Curriculum and Instruction in the School of Education. She retired in the summer of 1996. The number of part-time or temporary teachers does not include two teaching assistants in Spanish. One of the part-time or temporary French teachers was hired for the spring to replace a tenured assistant professor, who retired midyear.

APPENDIX

Sample Cultural Strands

Aesthetics
Agriculture
Archeology
Art and architecture
Biographies
Emigration and exile
Ethnicity and diversity
Fables and mythology
Family
Festivals and folklore
Film studies
Gastronomy
Geography
Gender equality
Health and ecology
History and politics
Humor and satire
Immigration
Judicial systems
Linguistic inquiries
Business and industry
Children's literature
Clothing and textiles
Economic institutions
Educational systems
Literature
Media and popular culture
Military and defense
Museums
Music
Philosophical perspectives
Radicalism and extremism
Regional studies
Religious institutions
Science and technology
Social issues
Television
Theater and performance
Transportation and travel

UNIVERSITY OF SOUTH FLORIDA

A Curricular Response to a Market Survey of Teachers' Needs

Founded in 1956 and already Florida's second largest university, the University of South Florida ranks thirteenth in the nation among all universities in enrollment. More than 34,000 students pursue 200 undergraduate and advanced degrees, including a PhD in public health and an MD. The average SAT score for entering freshmen is 1300. The student body has more than 100 National Merit and National Achievement scholars. University of South Florida students come from all 50 states and from 142 foreign nations. Nearly 1 of every 4 students belongs to a racial or ethnic minority. Concerns for diversity complement the overall objectives recently affirmed by President Betty Castor: strengthening academic programs, providing access, and attracting talented students.

The university's more than 1,900 faculty members include over 70 Fulbright scholars and 45 endowed chairs. In 1998, the university achieved Research I status in the state system, with over $135 million in annual research. National and international recognition has accrued in many research areas, including Alzheimer's disease, immunology, cancer, marine science, accounting, education, engineering, and the performing and visual arts.

The Division of Languages and Linguistics of the College of Arts and Sciences and the Foreign Language Education Program in the Department of Secondary Education of the College of Education have a long history of successful collaboration. For the last five years, faculty members from both programs have been jointly planning curriculum changes and innovations as well as new courses and course scheduling. Graduate students from foreign language education receive teaching assistantships in the language department, and graduate foreign language majors have the option to take graduate courses in foreign language education. Faculty members from both divisions serve on each other's committees and make joint program and faculty hiring decisions. In addition, several research projects involving members from both faculties are currently in progress, and courses are being team-taught with faculty members from each unit. Even for a forward-looking university, such activity is quite avant-garde.

As a department that has 25 full-time faculty members, about 17 adjunct professors, and some 30 teaching assistants; delivers instruction in 13 languages; and averages 125 undergraduate language majors, one-half to two-thirds of whom are prospective teachers, the Division of Languages and Linguistics is committed to an ongoing examination of the needs of teachers. We engaged in formal consideration of this question as recently as 1994, when we worked with the College of Education to ensure that our courses on both BA and MA levels met national guidelines as established by ACTFL and NCATE (Natl. Council for Accreditation of Teacher Educ.) and guidelines of the state of Florida. We carefully check against these guidelines each course we teach and submit a report on each of our programs to Florida's Department of Education.

Collaborative Programs and Projects

A concrete expression of the goal of collaboration between the College of Education and the College of Arts and Sciences is the planning and implementation of a joint PhD program in applied linguistics, second language acquisition, and foreign language teaching. The specialization of this program focuses on applied linguistics and second language acquisition issues as well as on foreign language pedagogy. The program also emphasizes second language instructional technology. A pilot version housed under the interdisciplinary track of the PhD in curriculum and instruction was very well received both by students and by observers from other institutions. Unique both in focus and delivery, it responds to a very special opportunity in a region and state where second language acquisition is critical. Florida's emergence as a bilingual (at least) environment makes both the study of language acquisition and the perfection of language pedagogy a high priority for the university. Evidence of the commitment to this collaborative project is that the College of Arts and Sciences has listed this degree as a priority on its master plan and that the College of Education submitted an addendum to its master plan indicating full partnership in the endeavor. (A master plan is required by the state university system when a new degree program is planned or implemented.) This joint program is a strong indication of the compatibility between both colleges and between both departments: the Division of Languages and Linguistics and the Department of Secondary Education (its Foreign Language Education Program). It is an indication also of their desire to move forward and create quality programs fitting the needs of our time.

Our department became interested in the MLA Teacher Education Project as part of our ongoing articulation with the Foreign Language Education Program faculty and as a reflection of our continued belief in, and commitment to, the role of arts and sciences departments in teacher training and in service to local school districts, both for foreign languages and for English as a second language. The Florida state university system's *Program Review of Foreign Languages and Linguistics* in both 1990 and 1998 applauded our work with our colleagues in the College of Education in this shared enterprise, describing it as a model relationship for the entire system. We were convinced that the MLA project would permit us to receive some external support for our efforts, enabling us to improve the process of our collaboration as well as provide national recognition of its value.

Like many arts and sciences departments, our unit supplies language and content area courses in support of the teacher preparation programs in our sister college. The liaison has been excellent between the two departments on matters such as scheduling of offerings to meet the needs of education students, the creation of new courses to address new state requirements for teacher-training programs, and the participation of arts and sciences faculty members in the staff development activities in the fifteen local school districts within the university's service area. The emphasis has been mainly on French, German, and Spanish but more recently also on Russian, Japanese, and Modern Greek (the last because of local community demand).

Joint collaborative projects with area public schools have involved creating some mechanisms for certification of teachers of less commonly taught languages, particularly Japanese and Modern Greek. We need to do more in the area of these languages. Another growing area of collaborative effort has been instructional technologies. If our joint doctoral program described above is approved, a large number of projects in this area may emerge. At the current time, our weakness is articulation among various courses within our curriculum, and this weakness impacts on teacher-training sequences. We also need to strengthen the proficiency (linguistic competence) of preparing teachers who are not native or near-native speakers. In particular, we need to develop more mechanisms for providing in-country language experiences, especially support and scholarships for the many students unable to participate in such programs for lack of financial resources.

Our faculty members have a number of joint grants and projects with colleagues in education, locally, nationally, and in a few cases internationally. They regularly teach in-service classes for foreign language teachers of our county and surrounding counties. They are called on often to conduct intensive workshops that use current methodology. These workshops may be sponsored by the University of South Florida or underwritten by the counties. They can be whole-day sessions for an entire week (during summers or vacation periods). One team member has programs in Venezuela and Costa Rica, where teachers are recertified in Spanish. A non–team member prepares prospective teachers in culture and civilization during summer programs in France. Teachers who cannot go to a foreign country benefit from the intensive summer conversation class "Tous les matins en français."

Current assessment procedures include interviews with students, both during their programs and when they graduate. To the degree that it is possible, we continue to obtain feedback years later through our professional interaction with area public and private schools. Our other areas of service include: career counseling, running sessions and workshops on technology and foreign language teaching, sponsoring visits to the area by such important scholars on foreign language education and acquisition as Howard Altman, Richard Brod, Stephen Krashen, and Teresa Pica.

Several of our faculty members, two of them on this team, have participated in the Consortium for International-Intercultural Education in Quebec. Other notable activities with foreign language teachers and prospective foreign language teachers are judging and administering local, state, and national contests (e.g., the AATF contest); sponsoring several annual conferences on second language acquisition; running oral proficiency interview workshops and multicultural workshops and symposia; obtaining grants from Florida's Department of Education and the federal Department of Education; creating collaborative curriculum design with Florida's Department of Education; providing numerous advisory boards, task forces, and consultations.

The university's foreign language education faculties are committed to service to the community. Particularly noteworthy is this faculty's participation in SCAAF, the Suncoast Academic Alliance of Florida. SCAAF is a collaborative composed of foreign language professionals teaching in elementary and secondary schools and in colleges and universities as well as of administrators involved in foreign languages. SCAAF, affiliated with the national organization of Academic Alliances in Foreign Languages and Literatures, has members from eight different counties. It was founded in April 1989.

The mission of the Suncoast Academic Alliance of Florida is to promote the study of foreign languages, literatures, and cultures; to seek creative solutions to professional problems and concerns; and to share knowledge, ideas, and strategies. The organization informs the community of the value of foreign language study, provides opportunities for continuing professional development, seeks support of policy makers for foreign language education, improves the language proficiency of students and teachers, and advocates and supports the implementation of foreign languages in elementary schools.

Several meetings, workshops, and lobbying efforts have been organized over the years and were extremely well attended. SCAAF was the host for the Florida Foreign Language Association's 1991 annual convention in Tampa. The association returned in 1998. The 1991 conference was the largest in the association's history. One of the workshops was "Teachers Training Teachers" and featured a swap shop that was extremely successful. The workshop was attended by about fifty teachers from five different counties as well as from the university. SCAAF provides the perfect vehicle for networking and disseminating information.

The University Reward System

We now address some of the anomalies inherent in our institution. The University of South Florida presents many of the ambiguities and inconsistencies that figure in discussions about the present state of the American university. Not the least of these ambiguities stems from a disjunction between performance standards and professional responsibilities considered in theory as well as viewed in specific circumstances. Thus, with a faculty and administration trained in large part at older universities in traditional settings, USF subscribes to deeply rooted assumptions regarding the importance of scholarly research conducted within increasingly specialized disciplines. For the most part, then, our institutional culture emulates that of universities that have quite different settings and histories.

One can only wonder, however, just how applicable to our institution, a commuter university with several branch campuses in a megalopolis, can be the structures and ambitious mission statements of institutions that are well endowed and often located in small college towns. Those of us in foreign languages and in a sprawling urban setting marked by ethnic and social diversity and major high school systems find much irony in an adherence to a prioris born in tranquil academic groves. Not surprisingly, our graduate and upper-division language courses attract a large percentage of teachers in training or already in the field who need certification in areas like language and civilization. One would think that proficiency courses and culture courses are self-evident priorities; but in foreign languages, institutional aspirations for an academic respectability defined in other times and climes maintain a reward system that prizes specialized research and professional visibility at the expense of meaningful curriculum development leading to enhanced language proficiency in local high schools and community colleges. Thus, faculty members are much more likely to be rewarded for having articles on literary topics published than they are for dealing with the challenges of proficiency-based curricula and teacher training. Professional advancement presumes the "language-literature dichotomy long institutionalized in departments of foreign languages and literatures at North American universities" (Kramsch 7). One might say that the dichotomy at the University of South Florida has in recent years become even more pronounced as we continue to develop in keeping with prevailing notions of academic prestige.

To be sure, the university reflects a set of values that has evolved not only at older institutions but also in our professional societies and associations, which have privileged academic research over pedagogic reform and encouraged the proliferation of mutually exclusive specialized pursuits. The effect, until recently, has been general indifference to the integrated approach to language teaching central to *Standards for Foreign Language Learning* (National Standards in Foreign Language Education Project). Those of us who entered the profession inspired by a generous enthusiasm for foreign cultures have long chafed under parameters that increasingly fragment literary traditions and historical movements, creating specialties ever more artificial and recondite, even to the point of sundering culture from literature. This sundering has taken place in a number of programs, including our own.

In an early meeting concerned with implementing the university's part in the MLA project, our team came to the conclusion that in order to shape a future curriculum in the best way we should ask a graduate of our program who was teaching in the area to gather some solid, data-based information from teachers in the local schools about exactly what teachers wanted and needed in their university preparation to teach foreign languages. We would then be able to examine our beliefs and principles in the light of the experience and preferences of those teachers. We were fortunate to have in Patricia Kessler, who teaches Latin and Spanish at Armwood High School in Hillsborough County, just the person to carry out this task. She designed and conducted a survey of her colleagues in the Tampa Bay area. The results of that survey are summarized as follows.

Tampa Bay Market Survey of Teachers' Needs

One of the initial steps in this project was to determine the needs of the community we serve. We sent the following questions to a representative group of a hundred teachers in the Tampa Bay area, soliciting their responses and reactions:

What were some of the courses in your foreign language teacher education that were most helpful once you were in the classroom? What, in particular, made these more helpful?

What were some of the things in your foreign language teacher education that you found not at all helpful to you in the classroom? Why?

Can you think of any areas/courses/topics that were not covered at all, or only superficially, and that should be covered more?

Thirty-one responses were received. The comments on those questionnaires were used to create final categories for the Tampa Bay Market Survey of Teachers' Needs. Questionnaires were sent out to all high school foreign language teachers in the three-county area of Hillsborough, Pinellas, and Pasco. Approximately 280 surveys were distributed; 150 teachers responded. We totaled the responses to each question by adding the raw scores for those agreeing, disagreeing, or not responding. We also computed a percentage score.

Information was also gathered from each teacher regarding years of classroom experience and universities attended. The years of classroom contact ranged from first-year teachers to teachers with thirty-nine years of service. Sixty-five teachers—43% of those responding—had done at least part of their training at the University of South Florida. Results of the final survey are shown in the table on the next page.

We would summarize these results as follows:

More time should be spent on teaching conversational skills, fluency or facility in the language, basic grammar skills, and not literary criticism.

"The following courses from my foreign language teacher program were helpful to me once I entered the classroom."

	AGREE	%	DISAGREE	%	NO RESPONSE	%
Internships/Practicums	142	95	5	3	3	2
Conversation	128	85	9	6	13	9
Methods	125	83	16	11	9	6
Current Trends in Foreign Language Education	123	82	10	7	17	11
Curriculum and Instruction	119	79	19	13	12	8
Pronunciation and Phonetics	118	79	18	12	14	9
Literature	111	74	24	16	15	10
Testing	111	74	17	11	22	15
Instructional Technology	102	68	22	15	26	17
Measurement	82	55	51	34	17	11
Foundations of Education	55	37	86	57	9	6
Statistics	51	34	86	57	14	9
History of Education	47	31	94	63	9	6

"I would have preferred more coverage of the following topics in my foreign language teacher education program."

	AGREE	%	DISAGREE	%	NO RESPONSE	%
Fluency-building strategies	133	89	9	6	8	5
Cultural characteristics (beliefs, traditions, values, attitudes, etc.)	132	88	9	6	9	6
Classroom management	131	87	10	7	12	8
Methods for teaching through instructional technology	129	86	9	6	13	9
Cultural highlights (art, music, literature, etc.)	128	85	11	7	11	7
Administrative issues (paperwork, discipline, clubs, parents)	107	71	26	17	17	12
From theory to practice (from ideal to real-world issues)	106	71	28	19	16	10
Methodology for separate subjects (e.g., grammar)	106	71	21	14	23	15
Grant writing and fund raising	87	58	50	33	13	9

> We need to be prepared to teach not only the language but also the culture of the people who speak that language. More time should be spent learning about culture with a small *c* (holidays, customs, myths, etc.) and somewhat less time about culture with a capital *C* (arts, etc.).

In addition to the topics mentioned by the survey, teachers said they would have liked more classroom experiences. Classroom experiences as early and often as possible during their undergraduate training would have made learning more realistic and authentic. They said that college professors should teach in the target language from the beginning levels onward and use teaching techniques that teachers will be expected to use themselves: cooperative learning, Total Physical Response, communicative-based approaches, and so on.

Teachers' Needs

As we interpret the results of the Tampa Bay Market Survey of Teachers' Needs, considering both information represented by the tables and concerns written by the teachers in the comment section of the survey, it quickly becomes obvious that although some types of teacher-training courses were found to be more useful than others, teachers in the field would have preferred greater emphasis on certain topics during their training program. Among these topics are modeling of good teaching, a variety of teaching techniques, instruction in the target language, applications of technology, fluency-building opportunities, surface and deep culture knowledge, classroom management skills, and exposure to methods, internships, and practicums.

Teachers seem to be telling us, "If you only lecture your students, then they most likely will emulate your sole teaching technique—lecturing." In other words, if professors want to inculcate the need for lowering the affective filter in beginning language courses, then they must lead by example. If they want to see certain behaviors in their students' classrooms, then they must provide that behavior in their own classroom. Another closely associated topic is the need to impart instruction in the target language. Here the teachers are clearly telling us that they do not appreciate those prima donna scholars who dazzle their students with all the minutiae of a specialized, narrow field but who exhibit—when forced to do so—an atrocious command of the target language. Professors who conduct a class in the target language and, regardless of specialized vocabularies and contexts, speak the language with advanced proficiency are the models to be copied by future foreign language teachers.

Teachers want to know how to apply modern technology to foreign language teaching. Why are they not shown how to activate foreign language characters or dictionaries in their computers? How can they use printers in a more effective way? How can they use e-mail to teach a class in target language composition? Foreign language teaching should not only be technologically up-to-date with other disciplines, in order to cultivate a progressive image among students; it should also facilitate specific applications to our discipline.

The study of the cultural products and behaviors of the people who speak a given language is a task that teachers find quite useful in their classrooms. They want to know not only about the values, beliefs, and behaviors found in the deep aspects of a culture but also about the food, architecture, media, and aesthetics exhibited on the surface aspects of that culture. It is plain to them, as it should be to us by now, that a work of literature can teach both aesthetics and human behavior, both artistic creativity and political history, both parody and the preterite/imperfect dichotomy. Culture, then, can act as a glue that binds the different products and behaviors of a people.

Another topic singled out by teachers in the survey was classroom management. It seems they are sent into the classrooms of America unaware that American society has decided to use its classrooms to address a number of issues that in earlier times were handled in the home, church, courthouse, doctor's office, and police station. Teachers need more than Candide's experience to cope with these societal problems and challenges.

Students can benefit from situations where they are required to engage in risk-taking and other behaviors necessary for success in developing fluency. Study-abroad programs offer distinct possibilities for fluency building; but the mere act of transporting students to a target language environment does not guarantee success. Study-abroad programs have to engage students in the life of the target language country, and they have to create among the students needs that require an interaction with natives that is intercultural and in the target language. Some of these needs can be created also among foreign language students in this country, by requiring their interaction with target language communities in the United States or overseas (by means of modern communication technologies such as fax, e-mail, etc.). This was a crucial topic for the teachers participating in the survey. We disregard it only at the profession's peril.

Finally, the teachers in the field are telling us that they want to know about methods, new and old, because they often lack a historical perspective on why we are where we are now. Why was ALM (the audio-lingual method) so big at one time, and why is it gone today? What was wrong or right with it? New teachers need internships and practicums before they are turned loose into the world of public school classrooms.

Teachers in the Tampa Bay area have given us their opinion about the training we provided for them. Indicating to us their concerns, they are challenging the profession to undertake meaningful academic reform. We at the University of South Florida think that their case is not unique in the United States. We think that they are right in feeling let down by the profession. We hope that the profession will listen.

Our Team's Assumptions and Principles

As our team met, it came to a consensus regarding assumptions and principles. We found, when our review and discussions progressed, that we agreed on six undergirding principles. Furthermore, we found that these principles were in striking resonance with the teachers' needs as identified by Kessler's survey.

The foreign language should be viewed as subject and not object.

Our team agreed with Diane J. Tedick et al. that viewing language as subject "emphasizes the communicative, dynamic, and social nature of language as well as the power of language" (71n1). While recognizing the value of scholarly study of linguistic and literary texts and the contribution of such study to language acquisition, we insist that students must use their increasing skills to act and interact with authentic materials, whether those materials be illuminated manuscripts from the Middle Ages, a current news report, or the latest rock lyrics. One team member uses a colleague's short stories to illustrate the *passé simple.* Students then incorporate the verb forms into an alternative ending to the story or create their own story. Another team member integrates visits by some fifteen Francophones per semester in her conversation class. The students, conversing with and questioning these visitors, gain in both confidence and fluency. A recent visitor, a member of the university's administration, welcomed pointed questions about the philosophical, social, economic, and political aspects of his life in a *département* in our hemisphere as well as in an African country. He concluded his visit by generously inviting the students to drop by his office and chat in French.

Teachers will teach the way they were taught.

Some of our team felt that the phrase "or will rebel completely" should be added to the above principle. But we are all intensely aware of the responsibility we have in training future teachers. Just as we hope we have retained the best in our teachers' and professors' methods, so do we wish to model successful methods to future classroom teachers. Such modeling could range from the incorporation of stimulating materials (instead of overreliance on a textbook) to our manner in the classroom, as we invite and engage the students to interact with the language and with one another—instead of overcorrecting their errors, which serves to inhibit or raise the affective filter (Krashen 116–17).

Students will learn what is relevant to them.

Our task is to choose and develop a style, materials, and procedures that inspire students. When we become aware of their interests, perhaps through oral interviews, journals, or weekly compositions, we can maximize communication strategies. The foreign language courses most often judged relevant by teachers in our survey were Conversation (85%), Pronunciation and Phonetics (79%), and Literature (74%). In the education curriculum the relevant courses were the most practical ones: Internships/ Practicums (95%), Methods (83%), Current Trends (82%), Curriculum and Instruction (79%), and Testing (74%). Instructional Technology was judged relevant by only 68% of those responding. Explanations for this unexpected result centered on the gap between the ideal world (the fantastic possibilities available) and the real world (less than adequate funding to pay for them). Over half the teachers surveyed felt the need for workshops or seminars on grant writing and fund-raising. We overwhelmingly concur, as our own department is currently in competition for a grant that would fund two-way video technology for our distance-learning network.

Variety is essential to effective teaching.

When we went to the second MLA Teacher Education Project Conference in Houston, we brought along a feature article that had just appeared in the *Tampa Tribune* about a team member, Associate Professor Carine Feyten, who teaches with passion and variety. A passage reads: "Projects are tackled in groups, lectures are broken into 15-minute morsels with activities, questions, and student presentations strewn throughout" (Cummins 3). Despite the uneven level of interest in instructional technology among the teachers in our survey, we encourage use of those resources and, just as important, the necessary training for that use. We are convinced that technology brings both variety and effectiveness to the foreign language classroom, whether the technology be videos of regional language varieties (celebrated now rather than scorned), pen pals through the medium of e-mail, discussion lists, data banks available through the Internet, or a joint class interacting simultaneously here and in the country of the target language.

Teachers need more target language exposure and practice.

On this point we took the stand that in the ideal program study abroad should be a firm requirement. At our own university, "support for internationalization comes from the top," with a president and a provost who are both "ardent internationalists" (*University*). The internationalization of our campus can provide both conversation partners in this country (in a manner organized by our English Language Institute, directed by team member Jeffra Flaitz) and encouragement to participate in the numerous overseas study or exchange programs advocated strongly by our associate director of international affairs, who happens to be tenured in our division. Language-across-the-curriculum programs, available now in a growing number of universities, can be a boon to future teachers' development of realistic and useful vocabularies, as faculty members and TAs in other disciplines share their expertise in the target language.

Proficiency is a sine qua non in foreign language teaching.

Often the ideal world and the real world are at odds. One of our team had two teachers who returned for summer language classes after being told by their principals, "You will teach French in addition to German." Despite the advice by Wilga Rivers for a teacher "who is not fluent himself in the foreign language" (210–12), these teachers preferred to go into their classrooms confident not only in their teaching ability but also in their language proficiency. Our team would emphasize Alice Omaggio's central thesis in *Teaching Language in Context:* "Instruction will be most effective if it is contextualized and oriented toward proficiency goals" (427).

The statement of philosophy in the recent *Standards for Foreign Language Learning* envisions "a future in which *all* students will develop and maintain proficiency in English and at least one other language, modern or classical" (7). Proficiency is integral to the five goals of foreign language education that are presented in *Standards* (27–63). As students are guided to communicate interpersonally, interpretatively, and presentationally (to adopt the language of *Standards*), the teacher's own proficiency is crucial. Therefore our proposed curriculum has, as an important component, several stages of proficiency assessment.

Implications

INSTRUCTION IN THE TARGET LANGUAGE

To assert that all foreign languages should be taught in the target language would seem to be stating the obvious, except that we know not all courses are taught this way. One of the most compelling reasons for using the target language as the only language of the classroom is that most college and university major programs require between thirty and thirty-eight hours, hardly enough contact to ensure the level of fluency desired by both students and instructors. Naturally, when we say the target language should be the only language of the classroom, we understand that there are exceptions to every rule. There may be certain features of a language—the category of aspect in the Slavic verbal system comes to mind—that benefit from some explanatory discussion in English. But such discussion should be brief, to the point, and designed to complement all manner of graphic examples and hands-on exercises done à la John Rassias, that is, the so-called Dartmouth Method, in which a teacher makes grammar explanations by acting them out, using appropriate props.

LANGUAGE PROFICIENCY OF TEACHERS

With fluency the paramount goal of every foreign language program, proficiency should become an exit requirement for all teachers of language. Not only will such a requirement help focus the efforts of both instructors and students, it will also move us away from the time-honored tradition of measuring progress by seat time. The availability of standardized tests, especially the Oral Proficiency Interview of ACTFL, makes the assessment of proficiency easily attainable. In addition to or in combination with ACTFL instruments, it would be highly desirable to have prospective language teachers demonstrate or exhibit their fluency through projects or performances to be worked out with their instructors.

STUDY ABROAD AS A REQUIREMENT

We used to consider studying abroad desirable; we now realize that it is a necessity. Living surrounded by native speakers provides constant contact with a language that we cannot hope to duplicate by means of regular academic courses. Furthermore, studying and living in another country exposes students to all manner of linguistic and cultural nuances that cannot be reproduced in a nonnative environment. Try as we might, we will not be able to replicate in Tampa the experience of a conversation with a French gendarme or a Moscow militiaman. For years we have hesitated to make study abroad a requirement for majoring in a foreign language because not all students are able to afford such an experience. But now that we have recognized the need for study abroad and have moved toward funding such study through various scholarship schemes, we should be able to formalize that requirement in the not too distant future.

CHANGE IN METHODOLOGY

Perhaps no other field undergoes such frequent changes in classroom methodology as foreign languages. Yet some senior instructors remain fixed in the methods they acquired several decades ago as graduate teaching assistants. It is our belief that as we cycle rapidly through what are sometimes fads, we select and keep the most effective approaches and strategies available. A vitally interactive classroom that involves the students directly with the language should be a constant of methodology. Among current assessment practices we find such things as cooperative learning, portfolios, and assessment of oral performance to be logical companions to interactive strategies. An overriding goal of both teaching and assessment should be to enable students to demonstrate their proficiency.

A CURRICULUM THAT INTEGRATES SKILLS

The titles we give courses suggest the compartmentalization of skills, as though composition, conversation, and reading were separate things. Since we know that on the contrary language skills complement one another, we should insist that these skills be integrated throughout our curriculum. Only by constant reinforcement of all the skills in each of our courses can we hope to achieve the proficiency we and our students require.

MORE OPPORTUNITY TO SPEAK IN CLASS

Second language proficiency as a sine qua non for foreign language teaching mandates the provision of abundant in-class and out-of-class opportunities for future teachers to produce natural, spontaneous speech in the target language. Nevertheless, some research studies show that in the traditional foreign language classroom students have on the average only four opportunities to speak, and that when they speak, it is usually a one-word or one-sentence response to a teacher's display question (a display question requires the learner to demonstrate knowledge of a structure rather than to react intellectually or emotionally to a concept). At the risk of failing to complete all chapters in a textbook, university-based foreign language teachers must invest as significant a portion as possible of the regular class hour in interactive tasks. While the MLA recommendation that class size be held to twenty-five is helpful, the provision of ample opportunities to speak through small-group communicative tasks is essential to promote fluency. The choice of textbook is also a critical factor in promoting increased fluency; the more interactive the text design, the less pressure there is on the teacher—novice TA or seasoned PhD—to develop original communicative activities. In short, if proficiency is expected of graduates of foreign language programs, where but in class are students to be exposed to regular, frequent, and meaningful opportunities to speak?

A CURRICULUM THAT INCLUDES CULTURE AND PRACTICAL LANGUAGE USE

In addition to giving students ample opportunity to communicate effectively in the target language, curriculum designers should bear in mind the need to expose students to a range of speech styles, registers, accents, and varieties. Not only does such an emphasis become an excellent exercise in listening comprehension but also, and perhaps what is more important, it reveals the ethnopolitical realities of major languages, because a language may be "owned" by a variety of groups that do not share significant cultural features aside from it.

Elements of culture, in fact, belong in the foreign language curriculum throughout the course of study. It is especially important that deep culture be given weight that is equal to or greater than that of surface culture. The exercise of exploring answers to the question "Why do these people behave, believe, and perceive as they do?" deepens learners' appreciation for cultural differences and also gives learners insight into the ways they behave, believe, and perceive as a product of their culture. An appreciation of cultural differences prepares students for life in general and promotes a healthier, more mature attitude toward the behavior of others, both in other cultural communities and in their own.

Indirect, abstract, and broad as these benefits may be, most learners study a foreign language for pragmatic reasons. Rare is the student who enrolls in a foreign language course solely for the love of language or literature—a love that often is the instructor's primary motivation. The resulting conflict between the student's expectations and the instructor's requires a concerted effort to reshape course work to reflect the practical as well as the theoretical nature of language study and use. This effort is called for now and in the future. While there is no doubt that studying a foreign language has the potential to round out the worldview of a university student, today's world places more people than ever before in a position to use their language skills as a means to improve their livelihood. For this reason, foreign language programs are remiss if they fail to balance the theoretical with the practical.

THE NEED FOR TEACHING INSTRUCTIONAL TECHNOLOGY THAT IS SPECIFIC

The process of considering and addressing the real-world needs of today's language learners leads us naturally as a profession into the effective production and use of new instructional technology. The prospect is not welcome to all faculty members, and students are often significantly more proficient in the use of technology than are their instructors. It is the foreign language department's responsibility to create in-service opportunities and other incentives for faculty members to develop skill as well as comfort in the application of computers, CD-ROM, two-way video, the Internet, and other technologies to classroom instruction. These technologies should not be perceived as a way to sugarcoat foreign language instruction, although learning may be made more palatable as a result of their use. Rather, it is important to understand how the new technologies illuminate certain aspects of language more effectively, assist in the delivery of foreign language instruction more powerfully, and expand the range of content more broadly than did previous instructional tools. Instructional technology offers us not just "the best way yet" but a highly effective way to immerse our students in a dynamic and rich foreign language learning environment.

A curriculum designed to prepare prospective teachers for successful careers should be discipline-specific. Therefore courses dealing with the application of instructional technology that is exclusive to the teaching of foreign languages should be created. But in many universities today, instructional technology courses have a broad and generic focus, as if technology lends itself to all content areas in the same way. The same fault exists in courses in curriculum and assessment. Drawing prospective teachers together from the full range of the curriculum certainly has the potential to develop useful insights for foreign language teachers, but that practice also reduces the possibility that they will gain the specific skills they need to exploit the benefits of instructional technology, to design curricula that reflect the state of the art in language teaching, and to develop assessment instruments that address the unique features of foreign language learning. In other words, we are making the argument that the instructional, curricular, and testing uses of technology in mathematics, foreign languages, science, social studies, and other disciplines are more different than alike and that therefore interdisciplinary course work in this area is not justified. Resources should be dedicated instead to offering prospective teachers the opportunity to explore those aspects of teaching that are most compatible with their specific discipline.

Proposed Curriculum

To meet the goals and needs discussed above, the team from the University of South Florida proposes a curriculum that retains certain staples of foreign language training (courses emphasizing oral and written communication at advanced levels; surveys of literature, culture, and civilization) while responding to desiderata of teachers in the field (courses in nonadult literature, in cinema and other media). Some courses are included (in cognitive development, global education, special education) because they are mandated by the Florida Department of Education for all approved teacher-training programs. Our team concurred that assessment, curriculum, methods, and technology courses should be specific to the discipline of foreign languages and that methods courses should be level-specific.

Perhaps the most controversial part of our proposed curriculum is the study-abroad requirement. Though widely approved, the requirement has not become a standard feature in teacher training because of the perception that many prospective teachers cannot afford study abroad. Recent changes, such as portability of student financial aid, and innovative approaches, such as the allocation of a small portion of student fees at the University of Texas to a study-abroad scholarship fund for needy students, encouraged us to make study abroad an essential feature of the curriculum.

The full realization of this curricular proposal will be one of the major collaborative efforts of the two foreign language academic units at the University of South Florida during the next five years.

In conclusion, we return to some issues addressed in the introductory part of this report. Like faculty members at many newer institutions (i.e., founded in the second half of this century), we are not sanguine about the prospects for innovation in our profession, which continues to be fragmented along fault lines that may actually be widening instead of narrowing. The demographics of the coming decades offer small basis for optimism about bridging the gulf in higher education between professors whose education and interests are directed toward maintaining a reward system that benefits highly specialized (primarily) literary scholarship and professors who must be concerned (primarily) with language, pedagogy, and teacher preparation. A discouraging aspect of the emerging profile of the profession is not that it is aging—age means inevitable turnover and new blood—but rather the programs where the new faculty is being trained. As increasing numbers of new PhDs seek a declining number of tenure-track university teaching and research posts, departments at developing institutions (usually the newer, metropolitan ones) enjoy large pools (often running to a hundred or more) of exceptionally well-qualified applicants for every advertised job. In such a buyer's market, the short list tends to be dominated by applicants from PhD-granting departments at the most prestigious schools. Yet these departments are precisely the ones whose decades-old hegemony over the profession has produced the current state of affairs. In the final analysis, both our experience and the experience shared with us by other departments participating in the project compel us to conclude that future innovation rests in the hands of those faculties and departments that contributed to this report.

The areas in our present curriculum are as follows:

Oral communication
Culture and civilization
Survey of literature
Written communication
Practicums and field experience
Special education
Cognitive devleopment
Assessment
Curriculum
Secondary methods
Student teaching

The areas we propose for our new curriculum are as follows (new areas are in italics, and starred areas are already in operation).

Oral communication
Culture and civilization
Survey of literature
Nonadult literature
Pedagogical grammar
Written communication
Cinema and other media
Language in context
Cognitive development
**Global education*
Special education
Foreign language assessment
Foreign language curriculum
**FLES Methods and second language acquisition*
Secondary school methods

**Technology and distance learning in foreign language*	Practicums and field experience
Study abroad	Student teaching

Note: areas of the above curriculum may entail one or more courses each.

Carlos J. Cano, *Division of Languages and Linguistics, University of South Florida*
Roger W. Cole, *Division of Languages and Linguistics, University of South Florida*
Carine M. Feyten, *Department of Secondary Education, University of South Florida*
Jeffra J. Flaitz, *Division of Languages and Linguistics, University of South Florida*
Warren Hampton, *Division of Languages and Linguistics, University of South Florida*
Patricia Kessler, *Armwood High School*
Victor E. Peppard, *Division of Languages and Linguistics, University of South Florida*
Richard A. Preto-Rodas, *Division of Languages and Linguistics, University of South Florida*
Christine M. Probes, *Division of Languages and Linguistics, University of South Florida*

WORKS CITED

Cummins, Cathy. "Ahead of the Class, USF's Best Teachers." *Tampa Tribune* 29 Feb. 1996, University / New Tampa sec.: 1+.

Kramsch, Claire. *Context and Culture in Language Teaching.* Oxford UP, 1993.

Krashen, Stephen. *Principles and Practice in Second Language Acquisition.* New York: Pergamon, 1982.

National Standards in Foreign Language Education Project. *Standards for Foreign Language Learning: Preparing for the Twenty-First Century.* Lawrence: Allen, 1996.

Omaggio, Alice C. *Teaching Language in Context: Proficiency-Oriented Instruction.* Boston: Heinle, 1986.

Program Review of Foreign Languages and Linguistics. Tallahassee: Florida State U System, 1990 and 1998.

Rivers, Wilga. *Teaching Foreign Language Skills.* Chicago: U of Chicago P, 1970.

Tedick, Diane J., et al. "Second Language Education in Tomorrow's Schools." *Developing Language Teachers for a Changing World.* Ed. Gail Guntermann. Lincolnwood: Natl. Textbook, 1993. 43–75.

University of South Florida 38.3 (1996): 4.

UNIVERSITY OF VIRGINIA

Teaching and the Open Horizon

The University of Virginia was founded in 1819 by a former ambassador, and that origin, reinforced by the university's proximity (less than a hundred miles) to Washington, DC, and its cosmopolitan suburbs, is reflected in the strong orientation of undergraduates toward careers in politics, foreign languages, foreign service, and international business. Of the university's six undergraduate schools, the College of Arts and Sciences is by far the largest, with approximately 9,000 undergraduates (predominantly women; one-third of the students are from outside Virginia) and 2,200 graduate students working toward the MA, MS, and PhD degrees. Majors are offered in French, German, Ancient Greek, Italian, Latin, Russian, and Spanish. There are minors in those languages and Arabic, Chinese, Hindi, Japanese, Persian, Portuguese, Sanskrit, and Urdu. Many undergraduates fulfill general education requirements in the college before transferring for the last two years to get bachelor's degrees in the Schools of Engineering, Architecture, Nursing, or Commerce.[1] Students preparing for a career in primary or secondary school education at the university begin by enrolling in Arts and Sciences and after two years seek admission to the five-year combined BA-MT program at the Curry School of Education. Once admitted to the program, they are concurrently enrolled in the college and the school for the next three years. Upon successful completion of the five-year program, they obtain a BA from the College of Arts and Sciences and an MT from the School of Education.

The number of undergraduates at Virginia planning to teach foreign languages is relatively small. In 1996, for instance, eight students received the BA-MT with a foreign language speciality. With the exception of physical education, this five-year program is the only path for undergraduates to obtain licensure as secondary school teachers at the University of Virginia, although college graduates may apply to the Curry School for a separate graduate degree in education leading to licensure.

When a team assembled at the university in 1995 to heed the MLA's call to study the preparation of future language teachers, the five-year joint program was the focus of the team's study. Our team consisted of a representative from each of five language departments; a member of the Department of Curriculum, Instruction, and Special Education from the Curry School; and two high school teachers, one in Spanish and one in French.[2] The five-year program had existed since 1985. Given the relatively small numbers of students in modern languages planning on teaching careers, our first two questions as a team were: Who are these students? and How should their education in the College of Arts and Sciences differ from that of any other undergraduate? We freely admitted to one another that future teachers were a largely invisible minority among our majors (only the future Latin teachers in the classics department were not invisible). University faculty members in foreign languages for the most part have not been consciously involved, when they teach undergraduates, in contributing to the way foreign languages are taught at the primary or secondary school levels. But since 1984, they have collaborated with schoolteachers in the workshops and seminars of the Center for the Liberal Arts (about which more below).

Since the language departments are also and, from the point of view of their senior faculty members, most of all departments of literature, future teachers currently take a standard major with emphasis on literature and—in French, Spanish, and German—cultural history. The departments do offer introductory courses in language, through which students fulfill the language requirement for the arts and sciences BA and in which some students begin a second or even third foreign language. However, we concluded that the introductory language courses were irrelevant to our study. Very few BA-MT students take these courses, since most BA-MT students, who are in Spanish or French, which languages account for almost all our future teachers, arrive at the university with sufficient background to be placed in an advanced language course, usually a course in textual interpretation and composition. Future teachers of Spanish and French therefore derive their models of introductory-level language teaching not from Spanish and French courses taken at the university but from their experience in high school, from their experience of starting another foreign language in college, and from their courses, observation, and student teaching at the School of Education.

The future teachers' development of language skills at the university takes place in courses where the language is used more as vehicle than as object and where practice and modeling take place in conversations, lectures, reading, writing analytical compositions, and occasionally performing in a play. Since in Spanish, in French, and for the most part in German all aspects of literature, culture, and grammar are taught in the language—from syllabi to instructors' comments on student compositions—the experience is a form of immersion.

As majors, future teachers take courses usually taught in small classes of fifteen to thirty by senior faculty members who also teach in the MA and PhD courses of the departments.[3] Of the 120 credit hours required for the BA, the standard major in most language departments consists of thirty credit hours (essentially ten courses) beyond the courses that satisfy the college foreign language requirement.[4] Many language majors take a second major in a field such as economics, government and foreign relations, or English. Twelve hours of the major can be taken in an approved program of study abroad. The variety of courses offered that count toward the major is quite broad and depends on the department; courses range from phonetics, grammar review, and various levels of composition to literary studies organized historically, generically, and thematically to cultural history courses taught in the language. Undergraduates with sufficiently high grades in advanced undergraduate courses can take graduate-level courses, usually in the Distinguished Majors Program.[5] Assessment is typically done from out-of-class compositions, from written examinations based on readings, from oral examinations based on course content, from oral presentations in class based on textual analysis, or from the student's synthesis of individual research on a topic.

Concurrently with courses in Spanish and French, future teachers pursue their general education and begin courses in education studies: four semester hours in their second year at the university, eight in their third year, eleven in their fourth year, and twenty-two in their fifth year.[6] The students' study of education includes field experience in public schools, which in the first or second semester of their sophomore year begins with observation and shadowing. It progresses to tutoring during the third year; to working closely with a cooperating teacher, to unit planning, and to brief teaching experience in the fourth year; and to fifteen weeks of supervised teaching in a public school during the first semester of the fifth year.

The BA-MT program thus consists of a minimum of 150 hours; a minimum of 108 hours in the College of Arts and Sciences (of which 30 hours have been in the foreign language department or are approved transfer credits) and between 43 and 48 hours in the School of Education.

Despite our general satisfaction with this model, in which the students were using the language as a vehicle for literary and cultural study as they pursued the study of education, we knew that we needed to learn how practicing teachers of foreign languages in Virginia thought teachers should be prepared for the profession. There were two high school teachers on our team, and one of them was a graduate of our five-year program, so we had the benefit of their observations about their own and their colleagues' experiences. We also had the results of an extensive study of preparation for the teaching of Spanish. Finally, we did a survey of graduates of the program and currently practicing foreign language teachers in Virginia; from the graduates we received eight replies, from the teachers, seven.

The document "What Should Spanish Teachers Know?" grew out of the interaction of university faculty members and secondary school Spanish teachers in the context of the Center for the Liberal Arts. The center was founded in 1984, with the charge of studying teachers' needs and developing outreach programs to meet those needs. In the following decade, a rich variety of discussions, courses, institutes, workshops, and lecture series were attended by a large percentage of Spanish teachers in Virginia. For insight into what the university could do to help future teachers of Spanish, a workshop was held in 1989 at which fifteen Spanish teachers from different schools and with different years of teaching experience (from two to thirty-three) focused on the following questions:

How were you trained to teach Spanish?
How do you wish you had been trained?
What preparatory experiences are essential for teaching?
What preparatory courses and readings are essential for teaching?
Should study abroad be a mandatory part of training?
What do you now know that you wish you had known when you first entered the classroom?

We concentrated on the content of the Spanish curriculum, that is, on the what of teaching (those areas of language, literature, and culture that are the core of the discipline) rather than on the how of teaching, although the techniques of teaching played an important role in our deliberations.

The initial product of the workshop was a statement that presented an ideal Spanish major for university students being prepared to teach Spanish. To that statement was appended a list of suggested courses and a core list of literary, linguistic, and cultural items that all teachers might profitably know.

The next step took place between October 1989 and August 1991. The report, tentatively entitled "Preparation and Training for Teachers of Spanish," was prepared and distributed to Spanish teachers and selected college faculty members throughout Virginia. These people were asked to read it carefully, reflect on their experiences and knowledge, reflect on the implications of the statement and lists, and make their views known to the Center for the Liberal Arts. Enclosed with the report was a return postcard that enabled teachers to acknowledge receipt and to offer any short comments they might have; longer evaluations arrived in narratives or in the form of comments attached to the report.

To interpret and evaluate the information received from this survey, five Spanish teachers, who were the most experienced and who had been active in the center for years, met for a day in 1991 to revise the preliminary report. Their final recommendations appeared as the center document "What Should Spanish Teachers Know?"

The present survey of program graduates and practicing teachers showed remarkable convergence on the importance of practice using the language (speaking and writing especially) in courses and in a society where the language is commonly spoken. There was also a call for more attention to literary texts that could be used in the secondary school classroom. Former students complained about the difficulty of reconciling their need to study abroad with the combined course and teaching-practice requirements of the BA-MT program.

These two surveys of the views of foreign language teachers and our own observations of the functioning of the program over the years led us to a sense that the overall approach was valid but that there was at least one important weakness in our practice. The mastery of the active language skills of speaking and writing was generally left to the students' initiative. That is, faculty members, in evaluating and grading, tended to consider brilliant insights into the nineteenth-century realist novel or contemporary cinema more important than a student's misplaced adjectives in an essay or faulty pronunciation during class discussion. Such an approach is entirely defensible, considering the university's primary educational mission of creating thoughtful and culturally informed citizens, and many students do take advanced courses in foreign languages to fulfill an area requirement under the general education requirements. But the future teacher of a foreign language needs to have mastery of the language in addition to cultural knowledge. At this point it was clear to us that we needed to change our approach to educating future teachers by strengthening the language component of their training.

We found this conclusion paradoxical, for two reasons. First, we had prided ourselves on not distinguishing future teachers from other undergraduates. It had seemed to us that a university with ambitious goals of general education should provide, in an egalitarian way, the same basic education to a future high school teacher as to a future politician, physician, or foreign service officer. In the context of United States society, where all too often teachers are relegated to an economic and political underclass, early separation of students who wanted to be teachers from students planning other career paths seemed to imply and perhaps to create an inferior status. Second, we found our resistance to treating future teachers differently in the College of Arts and Sciences surprising in view of the fact that we already provided them with a fifth year of additional study.

By not distinguishing future teachers from our other majors, we concluded, we were placing too great a burden on the future teachers, expecting them to know in advance which among the many aspects of language, literature, and culture available for study would be most useful to them when they started teaching in a high school or middle school. We were expecting them to perfect their mastery of the spoken language and of the finer points of grammar on their own while enjoying the great novels and plays of the tradition. We realized that the first step we had to take was identify the future teachers among our majors and identify for them the courses most likely to equip them for their careers. We needed to fine-tune the five-year program by creating a better fit between the highly structured and sequential requirements of the School of Education and the rather unstructured language majors, in which the students chose quite freely among a broad range of electives.

One thing on which we emphatically and unanimously agreed as a team was that we wanted to preserve the basic structure and values of the five-year program. We did not want to create a separate track for future teachers of foreign languages within the language major.

The approach to teacher education outlined above will strike many as being traditional in its values, for at least three reasons. First, it places a great emphasis not only on reading but also on literature. Second, the aesthetic dimension of culture is stressed. Third, our program is oriented toward the study of languages, literatures, and cultures in an international context, with relatively little attention paid to non-English-speaking populations in the United States. While we recognize that in effect there are today two major national languages of the United States, English and Spanish, as departments of modern languages and classics we perceive our mission—as it was aptly described by a member of another MLA team at a meeting in Houston—as being outward in orientation. We respect the choice of other universities to take an inward approach, but the University of Virginia is, by tradition and by the interests of its students and faculty members, international in orientation.

The aspect of our program that may be most controversial but that our committee's discussions lead us to confirm is the extensive study of literature and culture we expect of future high school teachers. In the area of content, we hope to form teachers whose knowledge and confidence will make them enthusiastic proponents of standards as an inspiring horizon. We hope to form teachers who are able to lead students toward the long-range cultural, community, and connectedness options that are usually invisible to all but the most privileged beginning students of foreign languages. We hope to educate teachers whose personal engagement in the second (foreign) culture will be readily apparent to their students from the first months of elementary or high school study.

Our concern is deeply practical. In the hectic, demanding day-to-day life of high school teachers, the breadth and competence—even the comfort level—of the beginning teacher translates into subtle but significant differences in a curriculum. A teacher of Spanish who has trouble explaining to students how Spanish varies from one country to another or from one community to another may translate that discomfort into a narrowing of classroom options. A teacher of French who has no knowledge of African and Caribbean French culture may miss valuable opportunities to engage students who are not oriented toward an exclusively European tradition. A teacher of German who excels in conversation but who is diffident about reading and discussing a short story may leave students with the idea that English and not German is the language of literature. As university teachers we can see the long-term effects of the values, attitudes, and abilities of middle school and high school teachers.

In addition to the curricular options that students have experienced before enrolling in the university, there is clearly a kind of metacurriculum to which they are sensitive. By *metacurriculum* we mean the usually tacit messages that are given along with any curricular item. Such a message may be as basic as the tone in which a grammatical concept is presented: a student notices when the French *passé simple* is treated as "something that I have to teach you but that you don't really have to know," and that student may be amazed later to find that this tense is necessary for reading the newspaper. More devastating are the metacurricular messages that make whole lines of future inquiry seem ominous or beyond reach, for instance, the idea that dialogue in Italian films or television is far too rapid to understand or that German literature is a complex and obscure matter that most normal people might as well ignore. Negative attitudes like these, no doubt derived from teachers' own experiences of prior study in a university or during a program abroad, will reappear later when students decide not to pursue their language study beyond a certain point for fear of encountering nearly impossible language tasks. But the metacurriculum need not be negative; we know that our most motivated students come to the university year after year eager for the horizon of literary and cultural learning that is ahead of them. Their attitudes are positive, because their teachers were comfortable, competent, and cultured. In forming future teachers for K–12 education, we have to remember that teachers are, for their students, not only the first representatives of the new language and the community that speaks and writes that language; teachers are also representatives of postsecondary education in general and very frequently give students a positive or a negative view of the world of learning that will follow the student's immediate environment.

Holding to the view that teachers of foreign languages should be competent far beyond the minimal requirements set for high school students and that this competency should be cultural in the broadest sense, we have proposed a revision of the university's curriculum to make sure that future teachers take an adequate range and depth of courses in language, literature, and culture. By *culture,* we mean both practical, behavioral culture and aesthetic culture. By *language,* we mean all four skills and the necessary understanding of linguistic conventions and constraints. At the University of Virginia, for French and Spanish and for most of the German curriculum, practice of the language is integrated into the study of culture and not limited to courses designated as language courses. Still, vigilant advising will be necessary to make sure that our students take full advantage of small discussion sections and courses that stress composition and revision.

We realize that the teaching of literature and culture, throughout American universities, has often become narrowly specialized and deliberately hermetic. If we expect future high school teachers to benefit from our teaching in these fields, we must try to encourage rather than discourage student interest in the study of literature and culture and we must make sure that students have an overview of the discipline before they take highly specialized courses. A commitment to the future of the teaching of literature requires us to rethink our teaching practices at the college level, to create some new courses, and to advise future teachers very carefully about their choice of courses in literature and culture.

It might be appropriate at this juncture to ask ourselves what we mean by *literature*. So many times, teachers view literature with nervous, skeptical eyes. We at the universities have so often forced our students to approach literature in awe, that is, to genuflect before the altar of Great Books. We demand that our students love and respect literature. We pontificate about it, deconstruct it, and sometimes teach students—unwittingly, of course—to fear it. Our brilliant classroom readings provoke various responses, from "Oh, wow!" to "Oh, what?" to "Oh, brother!" But perhaps we in higher education need to accept more responsibility, to become more flexible ourselves in our approach to the teaching of literature.

If literature is the Great Books curriculum, it is also a reflection of life. By that we mean it is something more than reportage. We respect realia and authentic materials, but literature is drama, emotions, and ideas expressed in a language carefully constructed and textured to reveal them. Language becomes, through the best literary expression, not only a reflection of the world as it is and as it was but also an open horizon for the imagination. Literature is plays, stories, verse, tales, and the lyrics of songs. It is the use of beautiful language—and also sometimes of ugly language—to express powerfully a view of the world. It is the potential of language at its fullest. Literature of the imagination is universal, and it must not be abandoned to theoretical trends, empty pieties, or a search for authenticity.

We should also say a word or two about culture in our foreign language departments. All undergraduates, and especially future teachers, should take advantage of the resources of the entire university to deepen their grasp of the subjects they care about. Future teachers of any language should therefore take courses in history, anthropology, classics, New World studies, sociology, and art history to help them understand the current and past realities of the nations and communities in which the language is used. We also advocate the study of the culture *in* the foreign language. The link between a culture's perspective and its language is, as the proposed national standards argue, not apparent from outside the language (Natl. Standards in Foreign Lang. Educ. Project). This is why we offer courses in Latin American society and culture taught in Spanish and courses in French African film taught in French. Even if future high school teachers of German will never teach a course on German history per se, they will repeatedly have to field questions about that history and its impact on Germany today and about the use of the idea of the German language to shape the idea of a German nation. Without sufficient cultural background, even a television newscast from Germany becomes a daunting teaching and learning experience. One recent graduate of our program identified as important "any course which will outline the culture of the language studied. It is very important to have most if not all of these courses taught in the target language." Many recent graduates have specifically urged the university to incorporate into the program courses in the emerging electronic realm of culture (television, the Internet, etc.).

No matter how complete our curricular offerings on campus, those offerings cannot replace the experience of living and studying or working in the environment of the second language and culture. Even native speakers of a language can benefit from the experience of study abroad to broaden their knowledge of the linguistic variety, the sociolinguistic differences, and the cultural resources of their language. Many of our students study abroad and transfer credits toward their major. For future teachers this experience seems essential to us, and we have decided to make work or study abroad a requirement for students graduating with a BA-MT in 2002 and thereafter. This requirement presents a scheduling challenge as well as a financial challenge. The courses in education, like most professional and preprofessional programs, are highly structured and tightly sequenced, so that summer study abroad is often the most feasible option, though not the most desirable culturally.[7] We are beginning the necessary work on funding to ensure that students with real financial need will be able to fulfill this requirement, but we also feel that students themselves should be aware of the need to study abroad and should build this requirement into their study plans. Its necessity has been brought home to us by practicing teachers. In their response to our questionnaire, foreign study was repeatedly cited as the decisive factor in their achievement of linguistic proficiency. As one former student put it, "As a result of studying abroad, yes, I feel proficient; however, if I had not chosen to do so, I don't think I would feel as comfortable."

We plan, then, to maintain our current practice but with three new requirements for students in the BA-MT program, above and beyond the requirements for other students pursuing a language major: study abroad, proof of language proficiency, and two additional graduate-level courses in the foreign language. Other changes, of the fine-tuning sort, apply to the faculty members rather than to the students. We will try to attract more students to the program, to provide within the language departments specific advising for five-year students, to identify courses we consider especially useful to them, and to involve them along with veteran teachers in the activities of the Center for the Liberal Arts, where considerations of content and teaching practice can meet. Finally, we pledge ourselves as faculty members and advisers in both the School of Education and the College of Arts and Sciences to meet once a year to make sure that we are aware of the program as a whole and not only in its two parts.

We realize that we have far to go if we are to create a course of study leading toward the development of language teachers who are fully equipped to meet the enormous and frequently changing demands of their chosen profession. The acquisition of proficient language skills, literary and cultural knowledge, and the methodology of teaching to transmit such knowledge to young people is hardly something that can be achieved in four years. Still, if the horizon of expectation is to remain open and broad, we must strive and experiment—and even fail—if we hope to prepare teachers for the coming millennium.[8]

Postscript

Since the foreign language departments finished their combined report two years ago, significant changes have taken place in the area of teacher preparation in foreign languages at the University of Virginia. The MLA project has provided us with the challenge to address our problems and the opportunity to resolve them. We have moved ahead.

At the most basic level, we have not only begun to talk productively with our counterparts in the Curry School of Education, we have also identified the students who are currently in the BA-MT program—students who used to be (in hindsight it seems hard to believe) nearly invisible to us. In addition, we have redefined our course offerings, tightened up our advising practices, worked in closer collaboration with the other departments involved in teacher preparation, and accepted our responsibility to train the students appropriately in the content areas. We share more information with one another, asking and answering questions that deal with the mechanics of teacher preparation.

What are we doing to sustain this MLA initiative? We have committed ourselves to instituting the recommendations in our report, that is, to revisit our course offerings with teacher preparation in mind, to provide study-abroad opportunities to all BA-MT students, to advise them thoroughly at every level of their five-year career, and to institute both a diagnostic examination and an exit proficiency examination for all prospective teachers.

Alicia Belozerco, *Department of Teacher Education, University of Virginia*
Julian W. Connolly, *Department of Slavic Languages and Literatures, University of Virginia*
David T. Gies, *Department of Spanish, Italian, and Portuguese, University of Virginia*
Janette Hudson, *Department of Germanic Languages and Literatures, University of Virginia*
Michelle M. Katstra, *Charlottesville High School*
John D. Lyons, *Department of French Language and Literature, University of Virginia*
John F. Miller, *Department of Classics, University of Virginia*
Greta Morine-Dershimer, *Department of Teacher Education, University of Virginia*
Isolina Nunez, *Western Albemarle High School*

Notes

[1]The College of Arts and Sciences requires four semesters of a foreign language, ancient or modern, or passage of the SAT II (acceptable scores range from 560 in Modern Hebrew to 660 in French; 650 is the acceptable score in most languages for fulfillment of the requirement). The study of a foreign language, though recommended, is not required for degrees in any of the other schools of the university.

[2]The five language departments represented were Spanish, Italian, and Portuguese; French; Slavic; German; and Classics. The department of Asian and Middle Eastern Languages, which does not currently offer a major, was not represented.

[3]There are 19 full-time faculty members in Spanish, Italian, and Portuguese; 16 in French; 12 in German; 7 in Slavic; and 7 in classics.

[4]In other words, in the rare instance when a student begins at the university with no prior experience of the language, she or he would take fourteen one-semester courses (forty-four credit hours) to complete a major in French or Spanish.

[5]The requirements of a distinguished major vary from department to department but usually require one or two courses beyond the thirty hours and a thesis written in the target language.

[6]The general education requirements for BA-MT students include, besides four semesters of a foreign language, the following minimum: two semesters of composition in English, two semesters of a social science other than history, one semester of historical studies, four semesters of mathematics and science, and a semester of non-Western perspectives. These are generally three-credit-hour courses.

[7]Foreign study brings out the contrast between the highly structured professional curriculum in the School of Education and the very flexible curriculum in the College of Arts and Sciences. Future teachers would benefit from a moderately increased flexibility in the requirements of the School of Education (e.g., the chance to transfer some education credit from study or fieldwork abroad) and from a moderate increase in structure in the College of Arts and Sciences (e.g., constraints in course selection for future teachers of languages).

[8]The adjustments that we decided to propose and that were subsequently adopted by the various departments of languages and by the School of Education are these:

1. Greater visibility and greater efforts to attract qualified participants. In the university catalog (the *Record*) and other publications, each participating department of languages and literatures will include a description of the teacher-preparation program as an option for qualified majors.
2. Advising. There will be one or more faculty members in each department designated as advisers to students preparing for a teaching career. All students declaring an interest in teaching and/or applying to the five-year BA-MT program will be assigned to one of these advisers.
3. Course selection. Certain courses in each department will be required of (or strongly recommended to) students in the BA-MT program. Simply completing a standard major will not suffice as the language (content-area) component of this joint degree.
4. Proficiency. Each department will administer a proficiency examination in speaking and writing. Students will have to attain the level specified by the department before receiving the MT and licensure. Although this evaluation is specifically a requirement of the Curry School for the MT degree that it grants, the school has asked the language departments to conduct the evaluation on its behalf. The proficiency evaluation will take place in three stages. First, at the end of the fourth semester of undergraduate study, students will discuss their plans for achieving the required language proficiency level with the adviser in the language department. This discussion may include an informal written exercise and an interview in the foreign language, and students will at that time review the scheduling of the upcoming diagnostic proficiency test. This conversation will be an opportunity for the students and adviser to discuss the students' plans for study abroad. Second, in the fifth semester of undergraduate study, students will take a formal language proficiency test for diagnostic purposes. The modalities of testing will be determined by the relevant department after consultation with the faculty members at the Curry School. In any event, the test used for both diagnostic and summative purposes will make use of resources outside the department

to realize maximum objectivity in the description of the students' speaking and writing ability. In Spanish, the speaking and writing portions of the ETS Spanish Proficiency Test will be used. In French, the simulated oral proficiency interview from the Center for Applied Linguistics will be used, and the Department of French will devise a writing proficiency examination; students will be responsible for the fee, currently $15. If students do not demonstrate proficiency in speaking at the Intermediate High level and in writing at the Intermediate Mid level, they will be counseled against pursuing the five-year BA-MT degree. Third, by the first semester of the final (fifth) year of studies, students will again take the formal proficiency test in speaking and writing administered according to the arrangements made by the relevant language department.

5. Practical experience of language. Each student in the BA-MT program will be required to spend a minimum of six weeks working or studying in a country (or region) in which the foreign language is spoken. The teacher education adviser in the foreign language department must approve the student's linguistic and cultural immersion project. The university will attempt to make available special financial aid for members of the BA-MT program for this purpose.
6. Communication and coordination between the School of Education and the College of Arts and Sciences. Once a year there will be a meeting between the foreign language education faculty member(s) of the Curry School and the teacher education advisers of the foreign language departments.
7. Approaches to teaching literature, culture, film. The departments of foreign languages will institute either separate or common workshops or courses on approaches to teaching the culture, literature, and film of the specific linguistic communities.
8. Advanced study of language. For participants in the joint BA-MT program, the total number of credit hours in the foreign language, literature, and culture has been increased from a standard 30-hour major to a 36-hour program (a 30-hour major and two graduate-level courses in the foreign language and literature department). Although students may perceive the two additional courses as a simple extension of their studies in the college, the six additional graduate hours are a requirement for the MT from the Curry School.

WORKS CITED

National Standards in Foreign Language Education Project. *Standards for Foreign Language Learning: Preparing for the Twenty-First Century.* Lawrence: Allen, 1996.

"What Should Spanish Teachers Know?" Spanish Project of the Center for the Liberal Arts. Oct. 1988. <http://www.virginia.edu/~libarts/spantea.htm>.

II

Assessment Issues

EDWARD M. WHITE AND VOLNEY S. WHITE

Assessment: A Blessing or Bane for Teachers of English?

We might as well face it: every member of an English department needs to know something about assessment these days. In the first instance, we spend an inordinate amount of time affixing grades to student work; we want to be as constructive and fair as possible in that part of our work, and, not quite incidentally, we want to be able to justify those grades in an increasingly litigious age. During the nine years one of us was chair of a good and responsible English department, every single member of that department needed to deal with a more or less formal grade appeal. One student in particular remains in my mind. She claimed that the paper her professor had given a grade of D was really worth an A. How did she know? She presented the all-purpose paper in its several almost identical forms, used already for three other classes, with various instructor comments inscribed at the end: two As and one B.

Grim laughter there, of course. But let's not overlook the underlying issue: our evaluation of student work expresses our values. If we cannot clearly maintain and articulate those values, our professionalism is put in question. It was hard to convince that student that her grades related to any set of criteria at all besides the intuition of the individual teachers. Student complaints about grading may never go away, whatever we do, but we need to work toward some consistency in grading for our own sake as well as for the students'. We are accustomed to giving much thought to the ways we respond to and evaluate literature, but few of us are used to doing the same for the student texts we read and comment on. Often we learn this part of the job on the job, without training or theory to inform our practice.

Assessment includes grading of student work but encompasses much more. State legislatures, boards of regents and trustees, and administrators of all kinds are now asking for assessments of teachers and department activities as a matter of routine. These requests cannot be ignored, for serious financial, personnel, and program consequences follow them. Indeed, even if we have trouble respecting the way these assessment requests are often phrased, we must admit that these bodies have the right, even the duty, to ask if the resources they are spending on us (for our usually inadequate budgets) are yielding effective results. We all need to know enough about assessment to judge the importance and the meaning of these demands. And we need to know how to meet them in ways that are responsible and appropriate.

A further assessment responsibility that college and university English departments cannot ignore is to a very important group of undergraduates in our English classes: the next generation of schoolteachers. They will be faced with all the problems we have been outlining here: to make demonstrably fair and responsible evaluations of student work, to handle the large-scale student assessment programs that are now common measures of effective teaching and learning, and to demonstrate the value of the English programs they represent. Even more difficult is the challenge teachers face because of state and community demands for tests that teachers do not value or consider appropriate. In most cases, the next generation of schoolteachers will face such assessment problems under much less friendly conditions than those their professors are now experiencing in colleges and universities. We must help these teachers meet not only the same issues that English programs and faculties in higher education now confront but also the issues that are most pressing in secondary and elementary school. The quality and level of support that English receives in the future will depend to a considerable extent on the ability of all English teachers at all levels to understand the uses of assessment and to help the students in our classes do the same.

This essay provides the kind of information that every college and university English department member needs to know about assessment, and it suggests appropriate ways of using that information in the course of teaching. Although very few English faculty members have had course work in assessment and although no one would seriously suggest that books in the field of assessment can serve as pleasure reading, most college teachers have picked up a great deal of information about assessment in the natural course of events. To that extent, this essay should remind them of what they know and help them organize it. But there is also much that is new in assessment, and we hope to clarify some of these concepts as well. Finally, assessment has spread throughout education in so many and so varied ways that it is useful for teachers to gain control over the names and functions of the key players and the major concepts.

Essay Testing

The past twenty-five years have seen the development of essay testing to the point that it can be used for even as highly sensitive a purpose as admission to medical school (White, *Teaching* 270–97). A large and increasing shelf of books and journals testify to the scholarly interest in essay testing, both from those in composition and rhetoric and from those in assessment. Full-length studies have been published on the devising of writing assignments for assessment purposes (Ruth and Murphy) and on holistic scoring of writing (Williamson and Huot). The high-quality journal *Assessing Writing* began publication in 1994, and national attention was focused on the subject when the national-goals panel placed improvement in the communication skills of college graduates as goal 6 in its report to outgoing President George Bush. (For full discussion of the panel, its recommendations, and its implications, see *JGE: The Journal of General Education* 42.1 and 42.2 [1993].)

Two aspects of essay testing that affect all teachers demand particular attention: the creation of the essay test and the scoring of the completed test. Many of our students who will be English teachers will be involved in one or the other of these tasks for testing agencies (such as the College Board's Advanced Placement Program), statewide or district-wide proficiency programs, or school projects with other teachers. The standard practice among professional testers for developing essay questions follows a series of steps that classroom teachers at any level can adapt to their own purposes.

ESSAY TEST DEVELOPMENT PROCESS

1. A test development committee representing appropriate constituencies is appointed.
2. That committee develops precise test criteria. For instance, a placement test might list such matters as sentence sense, paragraph development, a certain level of reading ability. An equivalency test for

college credit might include understanding of metaphor, the ability to use quotations as evidence, and the ability to deal with irony.

3. The committee makes decisions about the kinds of questions that will give students the opportunity to demonstrate their ability to meet the test criteria.
4. The committee devises or solicits questions that meet the pattern and criteria decided on. At least five times the number of questions to be used need to be developed.
5. The committee evaluates the proposed questions, choosing the best ones for pretesting.
6. At least three times the number of questions needed are pretested.
7. The pretests are evaluated. The committee looks for questions that are *clear,* so students will not waste time trying to figure out what is called for but will be able to get right to work; *valid,* so good students will receive high scores and weak students low scores and so there will be a good range of scores, without too large a concentration in the middle; *reliable,* so the scoring of pretest papers will show considerable agreement by readers and so a scoring guide can be readily constructed to describe score differences; and *interesting,* so students will write with some genuine involvement and so the scorers will not go mad with boredom (and hence become inaccurate) (White, *Teaching* 61).
8. The best pretested questions are selected for revision and possible further pretesting.
9. The test is approved and printed, with directions to students for writing and directions to the scoring team on the criteria for scoring.
10. The committee produces an information booklet for students based on the test. The booklet contains a sample question, sample papers at different score levels, a scoring guide, and descriptions of the ways in which the sample papers did and did not meet the criteria as set out in the scoring guide.

ESSAY TEST SCORING

In order to gain test reliability, which yields meaningful ranking of papers, most essay-testing programs bring readers of the test together in one place, where they work cooperatively under the same set of scoring guidelines. The readers agree to agree on the characteristics of strong and weak papers, and the scoring guide must be applied fairly to every paper. Periodically, duplicated sample papers are distributed for scoring and discussion, as part of the effort to keep standards the same from reader to reader.

There is some controversy in the field about whether scoring essay tests consistently, which leads to test reliability, is an absolute good, since some disagreement about the value of a piece of writing is part of normal experience. Consistency, which strives to come up with the same score for a student paper no matter what reader rates it, values group consensus highly and offends those who value the uniqueness of their perception above that of a group. But without scoring consistency it is hard to argue that a test is fair to the students taking it.

Most large testing programs score papers *holistically*—that is, according to a judgment of overall value—as opposed to *analytically,* according to judgments about a series of subskills that are then added together. Analytic scoring is customary for teachers working with individual students, since that kind of assessment offers useful information about the writing to the students. Holistic scoring offers only an accurate comparative ranking of the papers taken as a whole, according to the scoring guide. But in large-scale testing, accurate and fair ranking of papers is usually just what is wanted.

Holistic scoring of a large number of papers (some scorings will deliver up to half a million test scores) has customarily taken place at a controlled essay reading, with a large number of readers working as a unit, producing scores at an average rate of twenty-five per reader per hour, with trained and experienced chief readers and table leaders working to achieve a remarkable rate of consistency—sometimes close to ninety-eight percent agreement. But as we enter the new millennium, we are starting to see these large essay readings replaced by new technologies. Students are being asked now to complete their essays, as well as their multiple choice tests, at computer keyboards, and the assessment of student writing also is starting to take place on computer screens. We can expect that this development will increase efficiency, and we can hope that it will decrease cost; whether it will also yield reliable and valid scores and meaningful information remains to be seen.

Assessment in the Classroom

Much of what has been learned about large-scale assessment in the field of English has been working its way back into the classroom, as English teachers return from essay- or portfolio-scoring sessions and review their classroom procedures. In many cases, the casual writing assignments and inconsistent grading typical of classroom teaching begin to look rather unprofessional beside the careful test development and controlled scoring of large-scale tests. This perception has led some English teachers to adopt new ways of assigning and assessing student work in their classes. Of course, there are substantial differences between what is appropriate for external assessments and the much wider range of innovative classroom practice. Nonetheless, when we look at what we do in class through the lens of large-scale assessments, we can see many ways to improve how we devise and respond to student work. While that devising and responding do not encompass everything of importance in English teaching, they do represent a large part of our interaction with the students in our classes. The prospective teachers in our classes will in turn be modeling, on the way we conduct our classes, both the assignments they give to their students and how they respond to those student assignments.

DEVISING WRITING ASSIGNMENTS

We have learned from large-scale tests just how complicated and difficult it is to devise essay questions on which students will demonstrate what they have learned and how well they can write. The many stages of essay test development described above serve, in part, to winnow out the ambiguous, misleading, and confusing questions that our students sometimes encounter under the time pressure of examinations. These same students will tell us that many classroom assignments are similarly difficult to understand; the most frequently uttered sentence in writing tutorial centers is the complaint "I don't know what the teacher wants." The complaint is not surprising. Few English teachers have thought much about better ways to devise the assignments they give to their students, and all too many English teachers are not particularly clear in their own minds about what they are asking for.

Part of the problem with devising a writing assignment has to do with the definition of purpose: Just what is it that the assignment is supposed to teach, to accomplish for the students? Some assignments will be purposely open, making the choice of topic part of the assignment. Other assignments will have specific goals, such as to demonstrate understanding of a poem or a scene, and hence will be much more focused for the students. When the students are aware of the purpose of the assignment and, not incidentally, aware of the criteria by which the teacher will evaluate their work, they will be able to proceed. But when the purpose is not clear or when the evaluation criteria are murky or mysterious, students have a hard time coming up with writing that satisfies the assignment, the teacher, and themselves. The assessment demand for clarity in testing translates into a demand for classroom assignments that, consistent with complex class goals and settings, should also be clear to students. Sometimes classroom teachers, just like struggling test-development committee members, elicit bad writing from students because, unintentionally, that is exactly what they are asking for.

Erika Lindemann proposes a series of questions for faculty members to ask themselves about their writing assignments, a heuristic that serves to bring the insights from assessment into the thinking of teachers asking for student work. The writing of writing assignments should not be a casual matter; it is, after all, a distinct and difficult mode of writing itself, one with its own demands for clarity, audience awareness, and the need for revision. The following version of that heuristic (adapted from Lindemann 196) exemplifies the kind of thinking that ought to go into the making of assignments that can support constructive English teaching and can serve as a model for prospective teachers:

Task Definition, Meaning, and Sequencing. What do I want the students to do? Is it worth doing? Why? Is it interesting and appropriate? What will it teach the students, specifically? How does it fit my objectives at this point in the course? What can students do before they undertake the assignment, and where do I expect them to be after they complete it? What will the assignment tell me? What is being assessed? Does the task have meaning outside as well as inside the class setting? Have I given enough class time to discussion of these goals?

Writing Processes. How do I want the students to do the assignment? Are they working alone or together? In what ways will they practice prewriting, writing, revising? Have I given enough information about what I want so students can make effective choices about subject, purpose, form, mode, and tone? Have I given enough information about required length and about the use of sources? Have I prepared and distributed a written assignment with clear directions? Are good examples appropriate? Have I given enough class time to discussion of these procedures?

Audience. For whom are the students writing? Who is the audience? If the audience is the teacher, do the students really know who the teacher is and what they can assume the teacher knows? Are there ways and reasons to expand the audience beyond the teacher? Have I given enough class time to discussion of audience?

Schedule. When will the students do the assignment? How does the assignment relate to what comes before and after it in the course? Is the assignment sequenced to give enough time for prewriting, writing, revision, and editing? How much time in and outside class will the students need? To what extent will I guide and grade their work? What deadlines (and penalties) do I want to set for collecting papers, and what should I collect at various stages of the project? Have I given enough class time to discussion of the schedule?

Assessment. What will I do with the assignment? How will I evaluate the work? What constitutes a successful response to the assignment? Will other students have a say in evaluating the paper? Will the writer of the paper have a say? Does the grading system encourage revision? Have I attempted to write the paper myself? If I did, what problems did I encounter? How can the assignment be clarified or otherwise improved? Did I discuss evaluation criteria with the students before they began work, and will I discuss it again as the due date approaches? (White, *Assigning* 6–7)

RESPONDING TO WRITING: COMMENTING AND GRADING

Just as assessment concepts can help English faculty members create more-effective classroom writing assignments for their students, these concepts can also be valuable in the time-consuming and essential work of commenting on and grading the work students hand in.

The limitations of holistic scoring, which produces only a ranking of test papers or portfolios according to a scoring guide, have led to new thinking about the issue of responding to student work. In particular, the opportunity to separate responding from grading has opened new possibilities for student-teacher interaction during the production of student writing. Most English teachers are uneasy with the role of evaluator of student work, though it is a necessary part of the job; now to that limited function they have added the more desirable and creative role of coach, helping students produce writing through a series of drafts. Teachers who have taken on both roles tend to find it more satisfying to help students turn out their best work over a period of time than merely to write a grade and comment on a single draft, often a first draft produced the night before it is due. Four recent books on responding to writing show the vitality of the coaching approach to writing assignments (Anson; Freedman; Lawson, Ryan, and Winterowd; Straub and Lunsford).

But the grading always awaits us, and we should expect that new concepts of assessment will help us in the task. We indeed find that English teachers who have participated in large-scale assessments adapt some of the procedures from those assessments to classroom use. This adaptation often occurs in three stages, all focused on the use of written scoring guides that are now routine in large-scale assessment programs.

The first stage occurs when an English teacher returns from a holistic scoring session with a keen awareness of ways to achieve consistent assessment of student writing, in part from the use of a clear scoring guide. Since scoring reliability is a matter of simple fairness, the teacher is likely to draw up a similar guide for the grading of class papers. When the criteria for scoring are written out and at hand, the grading goes much more smoothly, and student complaints about grades can be resolved by pointing out the criteria that were applied consistently to all papers in the class (for sample scoring guides, see White, *Teaching* 298–99 and *Assigning* 45–98).

This concentration on a scoring guide for the assignment leads quickly to a second stage. Once the criteria for grading have become clear enough to the teacher to be set down in writing, why should the teacher not share them with the students when handing back the papers? For that matter, why should the criteria not be shared early in the writing process, so students can know from the outset the standards for judgment to which they will be subject? Indeed, if students are involved in the creation of the scoring guide, they will see the standards as partly of their own devising. Teachers who use scoring guides in this way spend more time working constructively with students as students write their papers, since the standards for performance are clear and public and the students are more ready to seek help in meeting them.

The third stage opens new possibilities for the use of student and teacher time. Since the standards for judgment set out in the scoring guide are both clear and public, and since they have at least in part been developed by the class, the teacher can now ask the class members to respond to and even grade the papers written by their peers. The students now have both a vocabulary and a scale (say, from a high 6 to a low 1, more and more the standard numerical scale for holistic scoring) to use in discussing and evaluating the writing they examine, so they need no longer deliver only the vague and unhelpful comments common to unstructured peer groups. Instead, they can (and in fact do) hold the other students' essays to the standards set out in the scoring guide. Moreover, by learning how to read and evaluate the papers written by other students, they learn how to read and evaluate their own.

This procedure has the magical value of increasing student learning at the same time that it decreases the teacher's paper load. And it gives prospective teachers in class invaluable experience in assessing writing consistently, according to clear and high public standards—crucial training for every English teacher. Although few teachers will want to use peer grading for final drafts or for crucial decisions on course grades, many students write better drafts for peer groups than for the teacher and gain more from a peer group's critique (when it is related to a scoring guide) than from the teacher's comments.

The lessons in reliability developed at large-scale scoring sessions can help us teach more effectively and train the next generation of teachers by supporting simple fairness in grading, by restoring credibility to grades when the criteria are made clear and public, and by allowing students to internalize standards for their peers and themselves. Grading is not likely to become a pleasant activity, no matter what we do, but we can use what we have learned from large-scale assessments to exercise our professional responsibilities for class assessment in new and creative ways.

PORTFOLIO ASSESSMENT

A portfolio is a collection of materials accompanied by the writer's reflective essay on their meaning and value. In recent years, this collecting of material, which was adopted from the fine arts and which uses techniques developed by essay testing, has come to represent for English teachers a new and flexible way to assess student learning. Portfolio assessment can be structured in many ways. Portfolios are being used at the University of Arizona for first-year placement; at Miami University, Oxford, for equivalency assessment; at New Mexico State University, Las Cruces, and at Washington State University, Pullman, for a rising junior assessment; and at California State University, San Bernardino, for outcomes assessment of the English major for graduating seniors. In all cases, students collect existing materials and arrange them for assessment according to the specifications of the particular institution and of the particular purpose. Invariably, students find such assessment less painful and more creative than traditional assessment modes. Much experimentation is proceeding as faculty members attempt to reduce the substantial cost in time and money necessary to conduct a portfolio assessment; additional experimentation will be needed to increase scoring reliability of portfolios to the point that they can produce consistent and useful information for assessment (Belanoff and Dickson; Black, Daiker, Sommers, and Stygall; White, Lutz, and Kamusikiri; Yancey).

MULTIPLE CHOICE TESTING

Most English teachers dislike multiple choice tests, in large part because such tests seem in their very form to argue against the kind of learning that the humanities encourage. But we must recognize that multiple choice testing is an essential part of the American educational scene, that most of our colleagues in other disciplines use and value them, and that schoolteachers must deal with them regularly. So we need to clarify for ourselves and for those of our students preparing for teaching just what multiple choice tests can and cannot do for teachers and students.

To begin with, we should grant that multiple choice testing may be appropriate for certain kinds of assessments. An introductory literature class having hundreds of students may routinely use this format; a well-constructed multiple choice test for that class can examine students' knowledge of certain kinds of facts, language use, and other matters. Indeed, clever multiple choice test items can yield a great deal of information about the breadth and depth of student knowledge, and not only for a large class or for inert facts. Supporters of multiple choice tests will argue that such tests are indirect measures of writing and reading and that indirect measurement is often perfectly valid and appropriate. English departments at institutions using the Scholastic Assessment Tests for admission of first-year students and the Graduate Record Examinations for admission of graduate students rely more heavily on these test scores than they are perhaps willing to admit. Many teachers in fields such as the hard sciences, mathematics, or psychology are strong defenders of multiple choice testing, and we should acknowledge the logic of their position. Furthermore, we must recognize that overwhelming student loads are common for English teachers in the secondary schools—typically 150 students every day—and that teachers with so many students usually do not have the time to assess much writing. Sometimes, under difficult working conditions a computer-scored test is the only way to survive.

Yet the distaste for multiple choice testing on the part of English faculty members is not a matter of whim or blind humanistic distrust of machines. Traditionally and logically, an indirect measure is preferable to a direct measure only when the indirect shows clear advantages over the direct. Until recently, advocates of indirect (usually multiple choice) measures could point to the high cost and low reliability of scoring actual writing as compared to the low cost and high efficiency of multiple choice answer sheets. With the development of accurate and reliable methods of grading student essay tests, the argument has shifted: the high development costs of multiple choice testing, the need for constant revision of multiple choice tests under truth-in-testing laws, the lower validity of such tests, and the damage to curriculum such tests cause by devaluing actual writing and reading—all call for justification of multiple choice measurement in the field of English. The traditional argument that multiple choice testing is similar to but less costly than direct measurement is no longer self-evident. Prospective teachers should become aware of this shift so they can offer reasonable and cost-effective alternatives, when appropriate, to the multiple choice tests they will encounter in their schools.

The most profound objection that English teachers have to multiple choice tests of writing and reading is that such tests examine a world entirely different from the one in which real writing and reading exist. When we enter a multiple choice test, we must accept a worldview in which questions, however complicated, have one and only one correct answer, which is to be selected from given options—a situation unlike anyone's experience outside the testing room. When we write, we inhabit a quite different world, one in which we must select from many options, options that we have ourselves generated, and in which most answers are at best only partially true. However simple the writing task, we must select appropriate vocabulary, frame sentences, connect ideas, and express our views. As writers, we know that life is complex and that simple answers are usually wrong. Again, when we read literature, we interact with a rich text that offers a wealth of possible meanings, most of which are in part a function of who we are. Reading, as all poststructural theories maintain, is a complex meaning-making activity that varies from reader to reader. But if we are good test takers, we must sink those perceptions of the nature of reading and writing, along with all the other ambiguities and problems of life, and focus on the only question that matters in the multiple choice world: What answer will the test maker accept as correct?

We should not go along with the misleading terminology that calls such tests objective. The test scoring, now almost invariably done by computer, is certainly consistent, and every test answer sheet is treated the same by the machine. But the decisions about how to test, what to test, what items to use, what is to be considered correct and what wrong, and what the results mean are anything but objective. We should not accept a term that appears to be descriptive but in fact renders a misleading judgment of the nature of multiple choice testing. Such tests are not created by the machines that score them.

When we English teachers object to multiple choice tests of reading and writing, then, we are not only protesting the validity of such tests. We are also uncomfortable with the world of those tests, which seems quite contrary to the world of writing and reading that we prefer to inhabit. Yet we must admit that we also inhabit a world in which these tests and the scores they deliver are routinely used to measure student, teacher, and school success; we ourselves use them when we need to, and prospective teachers will be using them frequently. We thus have an obligation to our students to help them inhabit both worlds successfully.

Large-Scale Assessments

The most surprising and encouraging development in large-scale assessments over the last decade has been the addition of writing to the familiar multiple choice formats most of us remember from our own applications to college or graduate school. The higher the level of the test, the more likely it is to contain an essay portion. Thus, the Medical College Admission Test (MCAT), Graduate Management Admission Test for business school (GMAT), the Law School Admission Test (LSAT), and the Graduate Record Examination for doctoral programs (GRE) all now contain written portions as well as the usual multiple choice sections. Similarly, written responses are usually required at many universities on the increasingly frequent rising junior test or on the graduation-requirement test for the bachelor's degree, and they are likely to appear also on the placement or equivalency tests that entering college students often take. The primary and secondary schools have not held back in this pell-mell rush to assessment, though they are rather less likely to ask students to write. Some school systems begin assessing even in the first grade, to assure themselves that children aspiring to move to the second grade will be truly worthy. A typical student these days is likely to encounter, no later than the fourth grade, proficiency tests developed not by his or her teacher—or, indeed, by any teacher—but by commercial testing firms. After the fourth grade, large-scale assessments have become a normal part of school life. And more and more of these tests require the test taker to do some actual writing.

HIGH SCHOOL PROFICIENCY TESTS

Among the most important of these school assessments are the minimum proficiency tests required for high school graduation in many states. College professors should understand that these tests have little relation to college-level skills or requirements. It seems a paradox that the high school graduation-proficiency tests are often administered to first-year students rather than to seniors, but there are two reasons for this: (1) the level of passing performance is set at such low levels in reading, writing, and arithmetic that most good students can in fact pass them at age fourteen or so; (2) those who cannot perform even at those levels are so numerous that special classes and tutorials need to be set up, as early as possible, to help students eventually qualify for a high school diploma.

These high school proficiency tests are often selected by local school districts—in California, they must be so selected—but in many cases they turn out to be commercially produced and nationally normed. Far too often, schoolteachers have no say at all about the tests that are selected by district school administrators in the name of efficiency, cost containment, and easy comparison with other school districts. Sometimes teachers will protest that the national multiple choice tests, despite their fancy names—such as the Comprehensive Test of Basic Skills (the CTBS, created and promoted by McGraw-Hill) or the Stanford Achievement Tests, Ninth Edition (colloquially called the Stanford Nine, though it is produced and marketed by Harcourt Brace)—ignore the backgrounds of their students or trivialize the substance of reading and writing. Such protests normally fall on deaf ears. Where the teachers have been able to exert a little influence, English proficiency tests may include some reading of literature and even a bit of writing by the students, which is scored holistically by local teachers. Where English teachers are well organized, the proficiency tests are more likely to reflect the reading and writing done in class.

Schoolteachers need to be aware that more options than multiple choice tests exist for assessment and that assessment tests should be devised that are appropriate both for the students and for what the students have learned. In too many school districts, the procedure is backward: the teachers must wait to see what the test demands and then hurry to teach accordingly, however poorly the test may fit the students or what the teachers know about learning to read and write. But many other school districts have come to value teacher advice on assessment, if the advice is well informed. We should encourage prospective teachers to seek membership on advisory boards for school districts and be active members of teacher professional organizations that will lobby for good testing practice. At the same time, all teachers should understand that control over tests is a highly political locus for power that school administrators and school boards are often unwilling to share with teachers. So teachers may have to live with tests that ignore important features of their curriculum.

Some of our students will wind up in districts that use assessment in ways that undermine teaching instead of supporting it. For example, a teacher might be aware of the value of revision for improvement of writing and ask students to revise and edit their work as an integral part of writing instruction. Such a teacher may also ask students to write about the literature they read, as a way to help them understand it. Then the school assessment will give a multiple choice test on niceties of grammar and punctuation, publishing the results as a measure of the quality of instruction. The students — as well as their parents and, indeed, the community — will wonder why the teacher wasted the students' time with all that reading and writing instruction when what really matters — that is to say, what is really tested — is the ability to edit the prose given on the test. Furthermore, it is unlikely that students will take seriously and hence perform well on tests that do not examine what they have been taught. Meanwhile, the reports of test scores, particularly nationally normed tests of mechanics and usage, are usually widely publicized as indicators of the quality of teaching and learning in the schools. The reports become material for local political campaigns and affect real estate values in the school district.

Many teachers have learned how to teach to tests they do not value or consider appropriate while at the same time they help their students reach goals that they do value. Teachers must teach to the tests that their students will need to take. There is no point in arguing that this should not be the case; it is the case. The best situation, of course, is to have tests that are worth teaching to. But the harsh reality is that inappropriate tests are likely to be on the scene for a long time and that both teachers and students will be judged by them. The best advice a teacher can offer students is to remind them, as the occasion warrants, of what these tests demand. This strategy is not unfamiliar to the college situation. We remember the strictly formalist Shakespeare professor who, formalism notwithstanding, points out Renaissance motifs in *The Tempest,* mentioning casually that we might remember that for the Graduate Record Examination. Our fiercely New Critical professors in the 1950s helped us understand (in passing, as it were) a historical perspective they did not share, since they knew that was still (and still is) an important part of the test. If teachers know about the tests their students must pass, they can help them in similar ways to prepare, without doing great violence to their own sense of what is important in class.

The prospective teachers in our classes should understand this situation, so they will not be surprised at the paradoxes many of them encounter as they begin their teaching careers and so they can be active agents for change in their schools. Teachers need not sit by passively when their students are given inappropriate and invalid tests, tests whose results will be used as evidence that the school is inadequate. (Of course, some schools are inadequate by any measure, but every school has serious and creative teachers.) We can suggest to our students that when they are teachers, they will need to work with their colleagues to develop pressure for assessment programs that support rather than undermine a reading-and-writing curriculum. Meanwhile, teachers will need to help their students handle tests that pose challenges different from those the teachers might like, and help them preferably with a sense of humor and the awareness that some things just have to be put up with.

ASSESSMENT OF ENTERING COLLEGE STUDENTS

Large numbers of entering college students, sometimes half or more in some selective public universities, wind up in remedial or developmental courses for their first year in college, a disappointing result for them, their teachers, and the public whose taxes more or less support such programs. A member of the California legislature, announcing his opposition to state funding for remedial work, complained, "Why should we pay for this twice?" With remediation a high-profile issue in many states, one needs to be aware of what college placement, proficiency, and equivalency tests can and cannot do. Part of the problem is that college faculty members often do not know the assessments their institutions use and so cannot help schoolteachers prepare students for them.

A student who has passed high school proficiency exams is not necessarily ready for college or for college entry-level tests. Many if not most college-bound students will have passed their proficiencies by the tenth grade and will be reading and writing at a higher level. Their concern is with the battery of tests they face for college. Three kinds of large-scale tests await the high school seniors preparing for college: college aptitude tests, college course equivalency exams, and college placement tests. Although these tests are often confused with one another and sometimes treated as if they were interchangeable, each has specific purposes and designs.

College Aptitude Tests. Two commercial tests dominate the field: the Scholastic Assessment Test (SAT), formerly the Scholastic Aptitude Test, administered by the Educational Testing Service (ETS) for the College Board, and the American College Testing program (ACT). These are both multiple choice tests (although ETS is experimenting with some short writing passages on the SAT) designed to give admissions offices information about probable college success. Both tests measure the likelihood of a student's returning to college after completing the first year; naturally enough, they therefore both correlate highly with parental income. These tests are frequently misused by administrative and governmental figures, who seek to convince their audiences that the scores delivered by the tests mean more than they actually do. For example, the former education secretary William Bennett liked to compare one state's average score with another's and to call the SAT a "report card for the nation's schools," even though the percentage of high school graduates taking the test varies dramatically from state to state. Neither the SAT nor the ACT pretends to measure reading or writing ability, although at the very high and very low ends of the proficiency range they probably do, and so they should not be used as placement or equivalency tests. Since these tests claim to measure overall ability, they assert that short-term study will not improve scores on them (though the expensive commercial test-preparation outfits dispute this). Extensive reading and writing over a period of years still seem to be the best preparation for success on these tests.

First-Year English Equivalency Tests. First-year English equivalency tests are intended to award college credit for one or more college English courses by examination. That is, the tests seek to measure students' abilities to accomplish the overall goals of any first-year English course, and many colleges treat passing scores on the tests—passing scores are always determined by the receiving institution—the way colleges treat transfer credit. The argument for such credit is based on the assumption that some students can learn outside class what most students learn by taking a course. If students have learned independently what a course seeks to teach and can show on a test that they both know and can do what is taught, they should receive credit for what they have learned without having to sit through the course.

While it is hard to dispute this idea in theory, many English faculty members are decidedly uncomfortable about students' gaining credit for work without taking a class. This discomfort is most pronounced with regard to the composition course, since that course, among other things, inducts students into the discourse community of college writers. While entering students may indeed learn on their own certain skills taught in college writing courses, such as the proper use of sources, complex organizational patterns, and sophisticated reading ability, it is not likely that even very talented students will understand in high school or on their own how to write for the audiences that they will be facing throughout their college years and beyond. Furthermore, there is a consistent undercurrent of suspicion among English faculty members that the equivalency tests themselves are less than valid, that is, that they do not in fact measure student learning as well as a course grade does.

It is important to note that equivalency exams are entirely distinct from the aptitude tests discussed above as well as from the placement tests that are discussed next. Whereas aptitude tests seek to measure, by looking at general abilities, the likelihood that students will be successful in college, equivalency tests seek to measure whether students have learned a particular curriculum at a level that is generally assumed to be acceptable nationally. Therefore, even if the exam designed to give credit for a course you teach does not measure exactly the reading and writing done in your course, it is designed to come close enough that you accept its vision of your curriculum in the same way you would accept the judgment of a colleague from another institution. A high score on the equivalency test is intended to mean the same thing as a high grade in your course, in the course of the instructor down the hall, or in the course of a professor at the nearest state university.

Although these assumptions tend to make faculty members uneasy, equivalency exams have established a firm foothold at almost all colleges and universities. Students seem to know much more about the tests than do college faculty members or high school teachers, few of whom have ever seen one. College policies on these tests are stated in every college catalog, and these policies are usually carried out by the admissions office or by the records office without much publicity or communication with faculty members. As long as relatively few students take advantage of equivalency exams to gain credits toward graduation and as long as the machinery works efficiently and quietly, faculty members generally seem content to ignore the situation.

The most prominent equivalency program in the United States is the Advanced Placement Program (AP) administered for the College Board by ETS. This program involves much more than the AP tests, which come in the spring as a culmination of a high school instructional program. Most high schools with access to extra resources and well-trained teachers will offer AP classes in a wide variety of subjects to their college-bound juniors and seniors. Both the teachers and the students in these courses are in a special situation: relatively small classes of the best students. ETS offers curriculum advice, teaching materials, and other kinds of support. As a result, some AP courses are splendid environments for learning, and some students will claim that the best college course they ever took was an AP class in high school. And studies by ETS tend to show that students who receive college units through AP tests do not generally abbreviate their college years; rather, they take more advanced courses than they otherwise would.

But there is a dark side to advanced placement. Many inner-city schools cannot afford to offer such classes. The idea of a special class for a privileged group of students seems undemocratic to some and divisive to others. Then, too, some AP classes have an extremely narrow curriculum, spending almost all their time preparing students to take the AP tests and thus restricting writing to impromptu test responses and defining the reading of literature as essentially grist for testing. The two AP tests in English, one focusing on literature and the other on composition, seem not to reflect many current notions of either field. Both their reliability (i.e., fairness and consistency) and validity have been called into question (Mahala and Vivion). The tests include three separate essay questions, graded holistically by a battalion of readers each spring, and an elaborate multiple choice portion. The test scores are reported on a compressed scale from 5 (high) to 1 (low), and the College Board recommends that scores of 3, 4, and 5 — scores attained by a large majority of those taking the tests — are deserving of credit.

Students seeking credit by examination without access to AP classes or tests have yet another ETS–College Board equivalency testing program they can attempt: the College-Level Examination Program (CLEP). Originating in the armed forces educational programs during World War II, CLEP became a kind of poor person's AP during the postwar period. In recent years, the College Board has sought to upgrade the multiple choice tests that CLEP administers to students, who then may claim either general education credits (by passing the general exams) or subject-matter credit (through the subject exams). The arguments and objections to AP apply also to CLEP, though the optional written portions of the subject exams and the absence of writing on the general exams makes CLEP even more suspect than AP to most English faculty members. More troubling still, we can look forward to a future in which aggressive and enterprising private for-profit educational firms, such as the Sylvan Learning Systems, will be moving into the lucrative credit-by-examination market.

Finally, most colleges and universities offer their students faculty-devised equivalency examinations, often called campus challenge exams, as an option to taking and passing many courses. Mentioned — or, rather, buried — in obscure corners of the college catalog, these opportunities are generally ignored in practice. Only unusually persistent students, willing to risk the ire of challenged faculty members, are likely to press their case, and very few indeed actually manage to receive credit through this rocky route.

College Placement Tests. Whereas the college equivalency tests seek to discover if students have mastered on their own the curriculum of a college course of study, the placement tests seek to determine if students are ready to begin that course of study. For this reason, the same test should not be used for both purposes. It would be cruel to give an equivalency test to students about to enter the course, since almost all of them would fail the test. By the same token, even a very high score on a placement test, which shows that a student is ready to embark on a particular course of study, does not indicate the student's mastery of material yet to be studied. This important distinction is sometimes blurred on English tests given to entering college students: those scoring at a high level may be exempted from first-year English, while those scoring at low levels may be placed in remedial or developmental courses. The unfortunate conclusion to be drawn from this confusion of assessment policies is that such a first-year English class has no clear goals or course of study, since readiness to take the course is not distinguished from successful completion of the course.

A substantial debate about the effectiveness and appropriateness of college English placement tests has been going on for some time. The traditional view is that a first-year composition course should assume student ability to read straightforward prose with comprehension and to write complete sentences and developed paragraphs in academic prose with an adequate vocabulary. The course would then go on to teach such matters as the sophisticated use of sources for research, the ability to analyze more complex reading, including some literature, and ways of developing and demonstrating arguments through a variety of patterns and for a variety of collegiate or professional audiences. The first-year course is normally required of all students, since these matters are crucial for success in college. A placement test is essential for such a vision of the first-year course, because students who are not prepared to take the course will either fail it, if it proceeds as planned, or reduce the quality of the course, if the teacher substitutes such matters as sentence construction and reading comprehension for the more substantial work of the curriculum. Thus a placement test protects the quality of the course by admitting only those with the background to succeed in it; the test also protects from failure the students with weak preparation, by identifying them and placing them in remedial or developmental courses to upgrade their abilities.

A wholly different vision of the course and the placement test argues against this traditional pattern. Some composition scholars calling themselves new abolitionists point out that such a placement test depends on both a first-year composition course and a remedial-developmental program that are well conceived, well staffed, and well supported. But few colleges and universities have that kind of course and program. To the contrary, the argument goes, the first-year required course forces unwilling students to study an uncertain curriculum with inexperienced and reluctant teachers, who are in front of the class largely as a way of paying their way through graduate school. The exploitation of the teachers—low-paid and poorly trained teaching assistants, in many instances—matches the neglect of the students, who learn little under these conditions. Even worse, the new abolitionists maintain, the placement test identifies a group of instant failures, a process of negative labeling that is confirmed by the halfhearted teaching from unwilling and even worse paid recruits cursed with remediating such students, who, as predicted, usually drop out of college. Thus the placement test, along with what these critics call "the universal requirement," should be abandoned, and an elective English course should take its place, one aimed at helping students express themselves and explore the possibilities of imaginative discovery through writing and reading.

This debate has gone on for over a hundred years (see Connors) and will not be easily settled. The clear conflict between the two visions of college composition does point out that an English placement test has meaning only in relation to the program into which it places students. Test scores produced by national or statewide placement tests may or may not have a connection to the program on your campus, and for that reason the most effective placement tests are local. Many administrators and some faculty members believe that someone can come up with an objective and generally applicable definition of remedial writing. They imagine remedial writing to be like a skill taught in high school, a skill that therefore ought not to be considered college-level. Using the same reasoning, some mathematicians argue that all college math below calculus should be considered remedial. But American education is not structured sequentially, particularly not in its two foundation disciplines, English and mathematics. In both these fields, the work done by and expected of the best high school seniors is at a higher level than most first-year college courses.

The fact is that there is no single, context-free definition of remedial English. Every institution needs to develop an operational definition of the term, on the basis of what actually happens in the first-year college course. A remedial student is one who lacks whatever is expected of those entering the regular program — not, we need to remind ourselves, of those completing the program. If the first-year course is coherent and consistent and has goals that are agreed on and implemented, then those teaching it can decide on what a student must know to succeed, and a placement test can determine who should and who should not enter the class. If a remedial-developmental program is in place, with sufficient tutorial support and a professional faculty, students who do not pass the placement test will be grateful for the chance to develop their abilities to the point that they can succeed in the regular program. But where this kind of curricular and professional support is lacking, where the articulation between the remedial-developmental program and the regular program is unclear or haphazard, then the placement test probably does more harm than good.

Assessment and curriculum go hand in hand on this issue; either they work smoothly together to help students succeed in a clearly defined sequence, or they express the confusion and neglect of the first-year writing program that are still typical of many United States universities. We can expect the situation to improve under the pressure of the PhD programs in rhetoric and composition now in place at over seventy universities, with more such programs appearing every year. The graduate students in them either are or will be working inside our writing programs: they may tutor students on the side or more formally in a writing center, they may work as interns with faculty members as part of their own education, or they may even be responsible for classes as teaching assistants. They notice quickly when our first-year writing programs lack theoretical or pedagogical strength and consistency and when assessments for students are not well related to the courses into which students are placed. Placement testing becomes the focus of many of these concerns, just as it can be the focus for developing a coherent and well-conceived program, precisely because it cannot be relegated to national testing outfits or outside groups.

Meanwhile, another dimension of placement testing takes place in secondary schools, where some students are allowed to enroll in gifted and talented education (GATE) programs if they score high enough on school proficiency tests — almost always multiple choice tests. Admission into AP classes is also controlled largely or entirely by test scores, even though the tests may have little to do with the abilities needed for success in those classes. College English faculty members need to be aware of the many problems and issues surrounding placement tests and help their students develop a healthy skepticism about placement tests.

ASSESSMENT OF CONTINUING COLLEGE STUDENTS

The extension of writing proficiency testing to the mid-career university level is a relatively new phenomenon on the American educational scene. Subject-matter comprehensive examinations are, of course, both traditional and common at the graduate and undergraduate levels, and placement testing has been common since Harvard began examining entering students in 1874. But only within the last thirty years has a special writing proficiency certification begun to be added to course requirements for the college degree — no doubt as a reflection of general discomfort with university educational standards. Sometimes these certifications take place as an added exit examination for first-year composition courses; sometimes they occur at the point of entry to upper-division standing (rising junior exams); and sometimes they are graduation or degree requirements, to be completed after achievement of upper-division standing or even graduate status. For example, every applicant for a degree from any campus of California State University must present evidence that he or she has met the *upper-division* writing requirement of that campus.

To those outside the university community, it might seem odd that the bachelor's degree should need the support of additional certification in reading and writing skills. If a college degree does not in itself certify a high level of literacy, one might well wonder if it means anything at all. Nonetheless, in recent years the general public has lost much of its faith in the ability of college faculty to maintain reasonable academic standards. The institution of these examinations, often under political pressure from legislatures or regents, is a clear sign that we have much work to do to regain the trust of our wider constituency. Such solid members of the national university community as the City University of New York, the California State University, and the Georgia State University systems have felt it necessary to protect the quality of their degrees by a writing certification requirement. For various reasons — a high proportion of community college transfer students; increasing student-faculty ratios, which serve to diminish the amount of writing assigned in all classes; widening diversity in the student body — these institutions and many others essentially assert by this requirement that a student may complete all course requirements for the bachelor's degree and still be unable to read and write at an acceptable level. Thus it is no surprise that outside communities, including political bodies, have also demanded certification examinations in addition to the traditional course requirements for a degree. Faculties are sensitive about this level of distrust, but we could also see the demand for writing certification in the context of certifications required of many professions: law students must pass the bar exams as well as their course work, and medical students have board exams to deal with after their residencies.

The means of assessing college writing performance are based in either certain advanced course requirements or mandated tests—occasionally in both. A course has the advantage of including instruction as well as assessing, but there is always the danger that a course will be replaced by a test in times of tight budgets.

Course-Based Assessment. The most popular way to ensure that college graduates will write well enough for the institution is also the most difficult to implement successfully: the writing-intensive course. The course appears to be the ideal solution: each academic major offers a writing course in the major and certifies its own students. Unfortunately, in most cases, these programs begin with great enthusiasm but shortly tail off into routine departmental courses. Unless there is strong central oversight, the more narrow interests of a department lead to less and less writing and more and more professional specialization; small seminars give way to larger and larger enrollments; faculty development programs and support from writing centers tend to diminish as time goes by. Worse, such programs sometimes lead to less writing across the curriculum, since students come to expect to write only in the writing-intensive courses. Thus the college or university begins to resemble the high school, where almost the only department to require writing is the English department. It is ironic that a graduation requirement designed to enforce the importance of writing for all learning often turns out to signify that writing occurs only in designated writing courses.

Less ambitious course requirements seem to be more effective for assessing student writing ability. Some institutions ask the English department to give required writing courses to upper-division students in all majors, but most English departments will avoid such a task if at all possible. Staffing a first-year composition course is difficult enough for most English departments; another required writing course with many sections to be staffed is a department chair's nightmare. Besides, most English departments are unwilling to be the sole custodian of a university's literacy obligations. Other institutions base the course requirement in the general education area and ask groupings of disciplines (e.g., the natural sciences) to offer required upper-division writing courses as part of the general education requirements. This route seems the most successful yet to evolve. It is generally more effective to assess continuing-student writing by a course than by a test, since a course not only judges performance but also helps students reach appropriate standards.

Test-Based Assessment. Assessment by means of a course has many advantages for students, who thus receive instruction; for the faculty, who thus are in a position to help students achieve the needed level of writing ability; and for the institution, which thus can provide instruction as well as assessment. But many institutions find that upper-division writing courses are expensive, trouble, and inefficient. These institutions resort to tests to satisfy the felt need to assess the writing of students applying for graduation. In most cases, the test consists of a writing task of some sort devised by the local faculty, often in combination with a commercial multiple choice test. The passing level is sometimes set very low, particularly at institutions where the only writing that students do is in their English classes, since the institution has an obligation to provide some kind of instruction to those who do not pass. Therefore, in another ironic twist, the institution relying on a test to assess students winds up with an instructional program, but instead of a bona fide writing course it now must offer a peculiar, misbegotten college class: the *upper-division* remedial writing course.

The general institutional problem illustrated by these assessments of continuing students is simple: an assessment, particularly when it is only a test, has limited value of providing information about student performance and hence has limited value for improving educational quality. Some administrators and politicians believe that assessment has a kind of talismanic power for improving education, that an assessment will inevitably lead to higher performance. Some cynics have parodied this argument by saying that, by this logic, an effective and efficient way to improve the nation's health would be for the federal government to distribute fever thermometers to every household. Indeed, no assessment can by itself change standards or improve curriculum, though the information it provides may suggest possible changes.

ASSESSMENT OF PROSPECTIVE TEACHERS

Many of the prospective teachers in our college classes will face another curious proficiency assessment before they enter a teacher-training program or, in some cases, complete their certification as teachers: basic-skills tests. These tests derive from the same abiding suspicion we have mentioned, that the college degree is no sure indication of clear competence in reading, writing, and arithmetic. The prospect of teachers without elementary skills stirs political forces into action, though not to the point of raising teacher salaries, status, or working conditions so that highly qualified students will find the field more attractive. Instead we find an additional assessment asked to solve the problem. In California and Oregon, for instance, the college graduates enrolling in or completing their professional training as teachers must also pass the California Basic Educational Skills Tests (CBEST), an elementary examination of reading, mathematics, and writing generally requiring abilities expected of early high school *students.* Astonishingly, significant percentages of those who take the test do not pass one or more of its sections, even on repeated retakes. One lawsuit in California, claiming that the standards were too high for certain racial groups, has been dismissed by the courts. Similar tests exist in other states, such as Texas; and at the national level we have the Praxis Series administered by the ubiquitous ETS.

The assessment of reading and writing has something in common with the monster Orillo in Matteo Boiardo's romance, *Orlando Innamorato.* When the hero's sword lopped off any part of the monster, the member immediately rejoined the body, and the monster was as formidable as ever. Only by a heroic feat of dexterity could the monster be vanquished: the hero slashed off the monster's arms and immediately flung them into the river. But assessment is a challenge more formidable than Orillo, as any English department chair knows who has confronted the assessment monster at legislative or trustee hearings. Neither fire nor water, neither scorn nor common sense will suffice to defeat its power, however we may hack away at it. We must devour the monster piece by piece. By making it a part of us, we can make it serve our purposes and the purposes of those who follow us. Mythology warns that in the process we may become partly monstrous ourselves, but that is a danger we must meet or even welcome. The teaching of English at all levels is a job for monsters, as our students keep telling us, and we need all the help we can get.

WORKS CITED

Anson, Chris M., ed. *Writing and Response: Theory, Practice, and Research.* Urbana: NCTE, 1989.

Belanoff, Patricia, and Marcia Dickson, eds. *Portfolios: Process and Product.* Portsmouth: Boynton-Heinemann, 1991.

Black, Laurel, Donald A. Daiker, Jeff Sommers, and Gail Stygall, eds. *New Directions in Portfolio Assessment: Reflective Practice, Critical Theory, and Large-Scale Scoring.* Portsmouth: Boynton-Heinemann, 1994.

Boiardo, Matteo M. *Orlando Innamorato.* Introd. and trans. Charles S. Ross. New York: Oxford UP, 1995.

Connors, Robert J. "The Abolition Debate in Composition: A Short History." *Composition in the Twenty-First Century: Crisis and Change.* Ed. Lynn Z. Bloom, Donald A. Daiker, and Edward M. White. Carbondale: Southern Illinois UP, 1996. 47–63.

Freedman, Sarah W. *Response to Student Writing.* Urbana: NCTE, 1987.

Lawson, R. L., S. Ryan, and Ross Winterowd, eds. *Encountering Student Texts: Interpretive Issues in Reading Student Writing.* Urbana: NCTE, 1989.

Lindemann, Erika. *A Rhetoric for Writing Teachers.* New York: Oxford UP, 1987.

Mahala, Daniel, and Michael Vivion. "The Role of AP and the Composition Program." *WPA: Writing Program Administration* 17.1–2 (1993): 43–57.

Ruth, Leo, and Sandra Murphy. *Designing Writing Tasks for the Assessment of Writing.* Norwood: Ablex, 1988.

Straub, Richard, and Ronald F. Lunsford. *Twelve Readers Reading: Responding to Student Writing.* Cresskill: Hampton, 1995.

White, Edward M. *Assigning, Responding, Evaluating: A Writing Teacher's Guide.* 3rd ed. New York: St. Martin's, 1995.

———. *Teaching and Assessing Writing: Recent Advances in Understanding, Evaluating, and Improving Student Performance.* Rev. and expanded ed. San Francisco: Jossey-Bass, 1994.

White, Edward M., William D. Lutz, and Sandra Kamusikiri, eds. *Assessment of Writing: Politics, Policies, Practices.* Research and Scholarship in Composition 4. New York: MLA, 1996.

Williamson, Michael M., and Brian A. Huot, eds. *Validating Holistic Scoring for Writing Assessment: Theoretical and Empirical Foundations.* Cresskill: Hampton, 1993.

Yancey, Kathleen B., ed. *Portfolios in the Writing Classroom: An Introduction.* Urbana: NCTE, 1992.

JUDITH E. LISKIN-GASPARRO

Issues for Foreign Language Departments and Prospective Teachers

The early 1980s marked the beginning of what has come to be known as the proficiency movement, with a series of oral proficiency interview (OPI) tester–training workshops intended for college faculty members and funded through grants from the United States Department of Education. College faculty members applied to attend workshops held in their region and, as was the policy at that time, the workshop organizers gave first priority to applicants whose oral proficiency was at the Superior level,[1] since those applicants could conduct interviews over the whole range of the ACTFL scale. The screening device was a taped speech sample that workshop hopefuls submitted along with their other application materials. An applicant to one of these early workshops, a well-established professor of French at a branch campus of a state university, appended a note to his taped speech sample. The note foreshadowed what over a decade later became a national-level concern about the subject-matter competence of language teachers, especially their linguistic proficiency: "I have taught French in high schools and colleges—all levels of language plus literature. I lead groups to France, and I am in good standing in my department and at my university. And yet this is the first time in my twenty-nine-year career as a French teacher that anyone has asked me to demonstrate that I can actually speak the language."

In a futuristic look at foreign language teacher education, Genelle Morain underscored the need for linguistically proficient teachers by putting high-level language skills at the top of her list of features of the language teacher of the twenty-first century. Without it, she said, our efforts in the classroom are doomed to disaster or, at best, mediocrity: "The sine qua non of a good foreign language teacher is the ability to communicate with ease in the foreign language. Lacking this skill, confidence crumbles and disaster slips into the classroom in assorted guises" (101).

Faculty members in departments of languages and literatures are in the best position to ensure that new teachers arrive at their first classrooms with not only a level of oral skill that will enable them to "communicate with ease" in the target language but also with knowledge in the areas of culture and civilization and language analysis (ACTFL, "Provisional Program Guidelines"). Education programs work with preprofessional teachers to transform their content knowledge into pedagogical knowledge for teaching, but it is through their major in language departments that these students acquire the necessary raw material, both the specialized content knowledge and the linguistic tools.

At the same time, language departments and teacher-preparation programs are both constructed and constrained by wider educational and social forces. That the linguistic proficiency of beginning teachers is a major topic of concern in foreign language professional circles is related to such realities as the limited place of foreign languages in K–12 curricula and the marginalized status generally of speakers of languages other than English in the United States. It is one of the great ironies of the late twentieth century that initiatives to improve the linguistic proficiency of beginning foreign language teachers exist side-by-side in state legislatures with language policy measures that discourage the development and maintenance of bilingualism.

This essay examines the roles that assessment does or could play in the preparation of future foreign language teachers. The first section situates the language proficiency and content-area knowledge of beginning teachers within the larger educational and legal context. The second section discusses the transition from high school to college, focusing particularly on how assessment might serve as common ground on which foreign language instructors at both institutional levels can talk about establishing a firm foundation for linguistic knowledge and proficiency. The final sections deal with the roles for assessment within the foreign language major.

Language Proficiency and Professional Certification

ISSUES AND PROBLEMS

Two surveys of foreign language teachers in the 1980s give support to current concerns about the oral proficiency levels of beginning teachers.

Henry Brickell and Regina Paul found in 1981 that only fifty percent of the teachers in their sample had studied abroad and that most had followed a traditional literature curriculum in college. In a 1989 survey of teacher preparation programs almost a decade later, Leslie Schrier found that more than half of the five hundred responding institutions continued to offer only a literature-oriented major. The resulting profile of the typical language teacher, confirmed by W. C. Wolf and Kathleen Riordan's findings in a 1991 survey of members of state-level foreign language associations, is a person whose undergraduate focus on reading and writing about literature and limited study-abroad experience do not constitute a good match with the content and format of the interactive, communicative language classroom that is the goal of current K–12 language instruction.

Reformers in teacher education have urged that beginning teachers in all fields receive stronger preparation. In 1986, the first report of the Holmes Group (*Tomorrow's Teachers*) recommended education for teachers that is "intellectually more solid" as well as "standards of entry into the profession—examinations and education requirements—that are professionally relevant and intellectually defensible" (4). The Interstate New Teacher Assessment and Support Consortium (INTASC), formed in 1987, seeks to enhance collaboration among states in reforming teacher education and setting standards and procedures for assessment for licensure (Heining-Boynton). Various other reform efforts at the national level have the same goals—stronger subject-matter preparation combined with assessments to make both the teacher education programs and the students in them accountable for the skill and knowledge levels of beginning teachers.

KNOWLEDGE AND SKILLS: WHAT TO ASSESS

The history of educational assessment in the United States provides ample evidence that the general public, legislators and other policy makers included, have repeatedly viewed assessment as an appropriate response to real or perceived deficiencies in the educational system (Madaus, "Influence"; Madaus and Kellaghan). Invariably, assessment efforts are invested in those areas that are most amenable to large-scale measurement. In foreign language education, we seem to have struck an unspoken agreement that the acquisition of content knowledge is the province of the language and literature departments and will not be subjected to external assessment but that the attainment of a level of oral proficiency deemed sufficient for foreign language teaching is an area open for public discussion and externally mandated assessment.

The reasons for this unspoken agreement are largely historical and discipline-specific. Thanks to the recommendation twenty years ago of Jimmy Carter's President's Commission on Foreign Language and International Studies that the foreign language profession establish "language proficiency achievement goals for the end of each year of study at all levels, with special attention to speaking proficiency" (*Strength* 38), Congress made considerable resources available for the creation and dissemination of *ACTFL Proficiency Guidelines* and for the training of teachers in assessment, curriculum development, and teaching approaches that would be consonant with the guidelines. Janet Swaffar, Kathryn Arens, and Heidi Byrnes view the resulting changes in language instruction revolutionary enough to term them a paradigm shift. In the proficiency instructional model that emerged in the 1980s, the focus shifted away from linguistic accuracy as an independent goal and toward "communicatively effective classrooms" in which student language production "depends as much on [. . .] cognition and communicative interaction as it does on language competence" (9). This emphasis on oral communication, coupled perhaps with such trends as a decline of interest in canonical literature and the tendency to view undergraduate education through an increasingly vocational lens, has led to the privileging of oral skills and practical applications of language study.

Concomitant with the making of oral proficiency the principal goal of language instruction has been the absence of a tradition in the humanities to specify and quantify the outcomes of study. As departments have opted for genre- and theory-based courses in lieu of surveys of canonical literature (Bretz and Persin; Cipolla) and have expanded the notion of the traditional literature major to include cultural studies and other sorts of interdisciplinary work (James, "Bypassing"), the core of knowledge that might serve as the basis for outcomes assessment becomes even harder to define.

Thus, although reform efforts in education include calls for stronger subject-matter preparation for new teachers and count on assessment to serve as an agent of change, the reality in the foreign language field is that we have experience and expertise in the assessment of oral proficiency, which is considered the skill area of primary importance for K–12 teachers, but neither experience nor expertise in the assessment of literary interpretation skill and of cultural knowledge and understanding. When we take into account that most high school foreign language instruction takes place at the first- and second-year levels (ACTFL, "Foreign Language Enrollments"), levels at which students' language skills are still quite minimal, the argument in favor of assessing preservice teachers' oral proficiency exclusively becomes even stronger.

What level of oral skill should be asked of beginning teachers? According to the *ACTFL Proficiency Guidelines,* a rating of Advanced is the minimum level needed to communicate with ease over a range of topics and conversational settings. Proficiency at the Advanced level means being able to produce paragraph-length discourse; narrate and describe in past, present, and future time; and make oneself understood to native speakers (Buck, Byrnes, and Thompson). Speakers at the Advanced level can tell stories, speak relatively accurately, and find alternative communicative paths when they come up against linguistic difficulties. As teachers, they are able to teach entirely in the target language. In a word, they are what the layperson would term fluent.

While Advanced-level proficiency is clearly the professionally appropriate standard to set for beginning teachers, it is a distinctly difficult standard to meet. A study conducted at Middlebury College to examine gains in oral proficiency levels in two different instructional contexts found that no students of Spanish in the undergraduate college became Advanced-level speakers over the course of an academic year (Liskin-Gasparro, Wunnava, and Henry). This finding is particularly significant for two reasons: (1) the oral proficiency ratings in this study are highly reliable, since the oral proficiency interviews (OPIs) were conducted and rated by certified testers, with discrepancies resolved by a third, independent rating;[2] and (2) belonging to a selective institution that has a reputation for excellence in languages, Middlebury students tend to be very motivated and able language learners. The only Advanced-level speakers in the undergraduate population were seniors who had previously spent a semester or a year on a study-abroad program. The other half of the Middlebury College study dealt with proficiency gains among students in the college's Spanish School, where students engage in intensive language and content-matter study in a full-immersion summer session. The principal finding was that about half the students who started the program as Intermediate High speakers had attained the rating of Advanced six weeks later.

The implication of this study is clear: Without a significant linguistic immersion experience, it is a rare language major who will graduate from college with an oral proficiency rating of Advanced. The importance of study abroad in the context of foreign language education programs cannot be overestimated, since if beginning teachers do not have at least one semester of study abroad, preferably when their proficiency is already Intermediate Mid or Intermediate High, they will step into their first classrooms without the linguistic tools they need to communicate easily and comfortably in the target language.

Practical and economic considerations make a study-abroad requirement for foreign language majors problematic at best and perhaps illegal at worst. Students choose not to study abroad for a variety of reasons: they may lack self-confidence or be unwilling to leave family and friends; their parents may be resistant to the idea; or the students may not be motivated to do the necessary legwork and planning to save money or seek out financial aid. An externally mandated assessment could push reluctant or unaware students to take responsibility for the development of their language skills.

ROLE FOR ASSESSMENT IN CERTIFYING THE COMPETENCE OF BEGINNING LANGUAGE TEACHERS

Several foreign language associations have been working for close to a decade to develop guidelines for the professional preparation of teachers. While there are some differences among these guideline documents, all favor Advanced as a baseline level of proficiency for beginning teachers (Nerenz). As early as 1989, the American Association of Teachers of French (AATF) proposed a two-tiered professional credentialing system, Basic and Superior. Candidates who demonstrated proficiency in speaking and writing at the Advanced level and proficiency in listening and reading at Advanced High would qualify for Basic competence, while proficiency ratings of Superior in all four skills would qualify an individual for a certificate of Superior competence (Nerenz; see AATF Commission). More recently, the National Board for Professional Teaching Standards named a Foreign Language Credential Committee to develop and refine standards for the recognition of teachers who have attained a high level of professional accomplishment (ACTFL, "National Board").

ACTFL's reform efforts directed at entry-level teachers began in 1988 with the publication of its "Provisional Program Guidelines for Foreign Language Teacher Education." The AATF and the other major language-specific organizations (the American Association of Teachers of German [AATG; Schulz et al.] and the American Association of Teachers of Spanish and Portuguese [AATSP]) followed shortly afterward with their own guidelines. Interestingly enough, the three language-specific associations have followed different paths in developing their standards. The AATF, as mentioned above, advocated two levels of professional credentials and also divided content knowledge into two distinct sections, literature and culture. The AATG, which modeled its standards on the generic ones produced by the National Board for Professional Teaching Standards, was much less specific in describing the content knowledge expected of teachers (Lafayette). Following the ACTFL model, the AATSP designed its document as a set of program guidelines for teacher education programs (AATSP) rather than as standards for entry-level teachers.

Currently, the National Standards Collaborative Project, made up of representatives of these organizations, is engaged in the process of writing standards for beginning teachers. It should come as no surprise that, with the exception of spoken language proficiency, assessment measures do not exist for any of the subject-matter areas under discussion or for the competencies described in already existing documents. An examination of the reports of a few thoroughgoing curriculum reform and assessment reform projects undertaken by language departments indicates that such efforts show considerable promise at the local level. Two of these projects (Henning; Lewis), developed under the auspices of a grant to the State University of New York by the Fund for the Improvement of Postsecondary Education, devised assessment programs for their institutions' foreign language majors. Sylvie Debevec Henning reported on the part of the project that articulated a sequence of four levels of literary interpretation. Catherine Porter Lewis reported on the development of culture guidelines, which were divided into two categories, culture-behavior and civilization-knowledge, each of which was further broken down into content and skills. The working group then developed descriptors for four levels of proficiency for each of these four subcategories, along with assessment instruments. The assessment system was multifaceted, including interviews, roleplays, cultural vignettes with a choice of follow-up behaviors or solutions, self-assessments, and a grid completion. Dorothy James and her colleagues in German at Hunter College, the architects of perhaps the best-known curriculum-reform initiative in a postsecondary foreign language department, described a program to integrate language skills development in German literature classes and to individualize instruction according to students' skill level ("Reshaping").

The intuitive appeal of these projects, most particularly in their potential to effect a significant shift in departmental thinking from viewing the language major as a series of courses to be taken or credits to be earned (Lafayette 150), confronts almost immediately the many practical obstacles associated with designing and managing a complex assessment system. The more specific and factual the content-area standards are, the more straightforward the assessment can be; but performance-based and integrative standards require open-ended assessments, which are difficult to administer and score.

Commercially produced tests have the advantage of transferring the tasks of test development, administration, and scoring to the testing company, but they also reduce the role that foreign language associations can play in making decisions about test content and design. The few standardized foreign language assessment initiatives aimed at content-matter competence have had, in fact, a lukewarm reception. The Educational Testing Service's new NTE Praxis Series, Professional Assessments for Beginning Teachers, samples knowledge areas broadly in one or more tests in five languages and in addition offers a separate examination in foreign language pedagogy. The assessment batteries in French and Spanish include five tests: two multiple choice tests that cover listening, reading, and structure and also give some attention to language analysis and cultural knowledge; an essay test in the target language on linguistic, literary, and cultural analysis; a production test in speaking and writing; and a language-specific pedagogy test comprised of three essays. Despite the array of choices, currently only eighteen states and the District of Columbia require a NTE Praxis Series test in a foreign language. Most of these states require one of the general language and knowledge tests and, if the states have a second one, it is the production test in French and Spanish. In other words, states are opting for language skills assessment for entry-level teachers.

The state of Michigan chose to undertake its own test-development program. According to Anne Nerenz, the foreign language test battery developed by National Evaluation Systems for the Michigan Teacher Competency Testing Program has not lived up to expectations. The Michigan Foreign Language Association has criticized the test battery's narrow scope (it has no listening comprehension, writing, or speaking components) and the "variability in emphasis and content coverage among the tests of French, German, and Spanish" (194).

Despite efforts of the professional associations and a few local projects to expand the notion of professional competence for entry-level foreign language teachers, it appears from their selecting instruments in the NTE Praxis Series battery that state-level educational policy makers interpret this competence as language proficiency, along with knowledge about the structure of the language. Although leaders in the profession advocate holding entry-level teachers accountable for the content in their language majors as well as for linguistic skills and linguistic knowledge, so far there is consensus only on the linguistic aspect.

ISSUES IN THE LANGUAGE PROFICIENCY ASSESSMENT OF BEGINNING TEACHERS

Given the complexity of defining and describing performance standards and designing evaluation instruments, the foreign language profession should count itself fortunate to have in place the ACTFL proficiency guidelines and the oral proficiency interview, as well as several versions of the tape-mediated simulated oral proficiency interview (SOPI), for the assessment of the oral proficiency of beginning teachers. But even this evaluation procedure is subject to numerous constraints. The section that follows discusses some legal issues that have arisen in teacher-certification testing. Then the case of oral proficiency testing for foreign language and bilingual teachers in the state of Texas, perhaps the most well-established testing program in our field, is presented.

Legal Issues. Certification tests for teachers have been challenged on two grounds: the due process clause of the Fourteenth Amendment to the United States Constitution and Title 7 of the Civil Rights Act of 1964 (Madaus, "Legal and Professional Issues"). The due process clause turns on issues of whether a government action is fundamentally fair or not. In teacher-certification testing, a key issue is that of instructional validity, that is, whether there is a good match between the content of the test and the content of the curriculum of teacher education programs. The plaintiffs in *Allen v. Alabama State Board of Education* (1985) successfully argued, as a due process issue, that "successful completion of a state-approved teacher training program creates [the] understanding that one will receive a teaching certificate."

Title 7 of the Civil Rights Act of 1964 mandated nondiscrimination in employment by reason of race, sex, or national origin. In addition, it created the Equal Employment Opportunity Commission as an enforcement agency. Once a plaintiff has proven that the state is an employer (and not just a teacher-licensing board, as states have tried to show), then the plaintiff must prove that the tests have "substantial adverse racial impact" (Madaus 217); this is said to occur when the passing rate on the competency test of a race, gender, or ethnic group is less than eighty percent of the passing rate of the highest-scoring group.

According to George Madaus, "the most important feature of any test is the accuracy of the inferences or decisions made from the score" (210). In teacher-certification testing, the question that must be asked is whether a passing score on the test predicts adequate performance of a teacher's duties. A test will withstand a court challenge if the defendants, usually the state board of education and test contractors, can demonstrate that the test has curricular validity or content validity. These two paths to test validation are both based in job-relatedness. The curricular-validity approach involves comparing test items to the content of the teacher education curriculum, to make sure that students were taught the material reflected in the test items. The content-validity approach, which is more commonly used, entails demonstrating that the content of the test is representative of the content of the job. To ensure content validity, test contractors engage in a multistage process of job analysis; development of a list of work behaviors; modification of the list on the basis of the judgment of experts; drafting, reviewing, and revising items; content-validity checks, and so on. The goal is to develop a test that accurately predicts job performance.

The Case of Texas. The complex legal history of teacher-certification testing constitutes strong evidence of how difficult it is to mount and maintain a testing program that accurately represents the tasks teachers must perform; that corresponds to the content of teacher-preparation programs; and that does not affect adversely members of any gender, racial, or ethnic group. The state of Texas has developed the most ambitious foreign language teacher-certification test of oral proficiency to date, so exploring its history, current status, and plans for the future should be instructive.

Texas has been testing the language skills of bilingual and foreign language teacher candidates since 1987. In 1987, listening and reading skills were assessed with a written test. The ACTFL Texas Project (Hiple and Manley), initiated in 1983 as a collaborative effort by ACTFL, the Texas Education Agency, and the Texas Foreign Language Association, led to the development of the Texas Oral Proficiency Test (TOPT), first administered operationally in 1991. The TOPT, developed by the Center for Applied Linguistics and now managed by National Evaluation Systems, is a simulated oral proficiency test: candidates respond on their individual cassette tapes to prompts from a master tape, which they also view in their test booklets. The test-development process, recorded in detail by Charles Stansfield and Dorry Kenyon, included a job analysis; the development, field testing, and scoring of a trial form; the development of a final form; and three separate studies to set the standard for the passing score. The

Passing Rates for the Texas Oral Proficiency Test by Ethnicity, 1995–96

	TOTAL		HISPANIC		AFRICAN AMERICAN		OTHER	
	NUMBER TAKEN	NUMBER PASSED	NUMBER TAKEN	NUMBER PASSED	NUMBER TAKEN	NUMBER PASSED	NUMBER TAKEN	NUMBER PASSED
Language								
French	56	28 (50%)	6	2 (33%)	0	0	50	26 (52%)
Spanish	369	254 (69%)	235	208 (89%)	5	0	129	46 (36%)

(Data were supplied by Pamela Tackett, Director of Assessment, State Board for Educator Certification, Texas.)

test consists of fifteen prompts: five picture descriptions, five topics, and five situations. Although the prompts are independent of one another, all are set in an educational context.

In 1997, almost six years since the TOPT became operational, 215 tests had been administered in French and 2,670 in Spanish. The Spanish TOPT serves both candidates for secondary foreign language certification and those who seek certification in elementary education with a bilingual endorsement. For 1995–96, the most recent academic year for which figures were available at the time of this writing, the overall passing rate was 50% for French and 69% for Spanish (see table above).

The ethnic categories in the table are self-reported. As one might expect, the passing rate for Spanish TOPT candidates who reported themselves as Hispanic was considerably higher than for those who reported themselves as other (*other* meaning non-Hispanic and non–African American—89% and 36%, respectively). The Hispanic group was more numerous as well—56% of the total, compared to the "other" group, which accounted for 40% of the total. Ethnic diversity within the French test-taking group has been very small throughout the history of the TOPT; although perhaps worrisome for other reasons, this lack of diversity in French teacher candidates makes analysis of the French data relatively straightforward.

The low passing rates for Spanish test takers is indeed a cause for concern, particularly when one notes that in 1995–96, the TOPT's fifth year of operation, only 36% of the non-Hispanic test takers got a passing score of Advanced. This same concern for teacher-certification test performance in all fields motivated the Texas legislature to establish the Accountability System for Educator Preparation (ASEP) programs and to direct the State Board for Educator Certification to establish standards to "govern the continuing accountability of all educator preparation programs" (Texas,

State Board). These standards, which went into effect in September 1998, entail using as indicators of the quality of teacher preparation programs both the results of certification examinations and a performance-appraisal measure for beginning teachers. Programs are expected to produce a first-time pass rate of at least 70% and a cumulative pass rate (i.e., the pass rate for students who attempt a competency test more than once within a two-year period) of at least 80%. As outlined by statute, the status of teacher education programs whose graduates fail to meet these minimums for three consecutive years will be in jeopardy.

Given the severe consequences for teacher preparation programs whose students fall short of the state-mandated standard, the TOPT is taking on an even more powerful role than it currently enjoys. Until now, those affected by an institution's low passing score have been individual students, many of whom most likely find themselves in the uncomfortable situation of having satisfied all their institution's requirements for graduation as a language major and an educator, only to find that their accomplishments do not translate into a score of Advanced on the state-mandated oral proficiency test. But with the legislation cited above, the postsecondary institutions that prepare foreign language and bilingual teachers are also affected.

The power of assessment, particularly "high-stakes" assessment (Madaus, "Distortion"), to drive instruction is both a blessing and a curse. As an arm of public policy, a test, particularly a good test like the TOPT—carefully designed and validated to correspond to the linguistic demands of language teaching as well as be consonant with standards set by national foreign language professional organizations—can force language departments to expand their curricula and update their pedagogical approaches as perhaps no amount of voluntary collaboration and the offering of professional development opportunities can do. But when "test results are directly linked to important rewards or sanctions for students, teachers, or institutions [. . .] the process corrupts the test's ability to serve as a valid indicator of the knowledge or skill it was originally intended to measure" (Madaus 29–30).

Should foreign language educators and policy makers in Texas be pleased or concerned about the potential effect of the TOPT on undergraduate foreign language education? Probably both. One danger is that language departments may "teach to the test" by increasing their focus on those skills that are measured by the TOPT and in the process excluding traditional areas of strength; the result would be a language major program that is virtually devoid of humanistic content. A second danger is that language departments and colleges of education, under fire from externally imposed mandates, may avoid collaboration, each choosing instead under the pressure of the situation to cast blame on the other for a low passing rate.

A positive effect of raising the stakes associated with the state-mandated test will consist of carefully conceived courses and programs that support student performance on the TOPT by integrating language skill development with other aspects of a future teacher's preparation. The University of Texas, Austin, for example, now offers a course in advanced Spanish conversation that is based on principles of discourse analysis: students analyze the rhetorical structure of various types of printed and oral texts and then construct their discourse on those models. They develop skills of rhetorical organization and practice impromptu oral performance, both of which will help them on the TOPT. A faculty member in the same department conducts an intensive three-week course in Mexico that she designed for Intermediate High speakers who are planning to take the TOPT (Foerster).

The upper-division Spanish offerings at the University of Texas, San Antonio, have undergone more extensive revision. The faculty added a required fifth-semester composition-and-conversation course between the language requirement sequence and upper-division courses in literature, civilization, and advanced language. Two conversation courses have also been added, one a junior-level course that sequences language tasks by proficiency level and the other a senior-level public-speaking course. The department has also created two courses in advanced writing and one in advanced reading. Requirements for the major have undergone some changes as well: students must take a minimum of nine semester hours of advanced language courses to complement their content courses in literature and civilization. The department has instituted an oral assessment that students take as juniors when they declare their intention to seek teaching certification. The results of the assessment are used solely for advising, not for entrance or exit.

Barbara González Pino has been gathering data on teacher education in Texas since 1994. In the first phase of the research, she asked language department faculty members to respond to a questionnaire about their teaching philosophy and pedagogical practices. In the second phase, she and her collaborators observed language classes at various levels in all the institutions in the state that had foreign language teacher-preparation programs. The researchers found that the communicative language teaching philosophies reported in the questionnaires did not correspond to observed classroom practices. The typical classroom they observed was teacher-centered: students had limited opportunities to speak and even fewer opportunities to produce the kind of extemporaneous, extended discourse that characterizes the TOPT. The researchers also found that some faculty members were allowing their students to take the TOPT as juniors, a practice that puts these students at a disadvantage compared to those who take the test for the first time after four to six additional courses in their language major.

The Accountability System for Educator Preparation in Texas, like the outcomes assessment projects discussed above, has the potential to push language departments in favorable directions. The challenge is successfully to walk the tightrope between accountability and a curricular and pedagogical response to the TOPT that shrinks rather than expands the educational experience of future foreign language teachers.

Articulation: Making the Transition from High School to College

ISSUES AND PROBLEMS

The passage from high school to college language study is a challenge for many students. They discover that they have crossed a "cultural border" (Hall) to a place whose activities, values, and customs are quite different from what they are used to. Perhaps the most salient difference for students is the role that foreign language study plays in the two institutions. Two years of high school foreign language study may be required for college-bound students (the most recent MLA survey reported that 20.7% of four-year institutions had a foreign language entrance requirement [Brod and Huber]) but otherwise a foreign language in secondary schools is a discipline on the margin, in the category of the arts, rather than a constituent of the curricular core, like English or social studies. This picture changes at the undergraduate level. In 1994–95, 68% of four-year colleges reported having a foreign language graduation requirement (Brod and Huber 42). In the majority of these institutions, foreign languages are not only part of the general education core, they are a significant part, since a three- or four-semester foreign language requirement often entails a multisemester commitment from students. National secondary school enrollment figures also tell a disturbing story: even though the percentage of high school students who study a foreign language (42% of total enrollments in fall 1994 were in foreign language classes) is at the highest level since 1928, close to half the students are in first- and second-year classes (ACTFL, "Foreign Language Enrollments"

303). The sobering implication of these figures for secondary-to-postsecondary school articulation is that the majority of undergraduates take their first college language course after a considerable lapse of time, building on a knowledge and skills base that was not strong to begin with.

Other disjunctures characterize the transition from high school to college, all of which are well known through anecdotal accounts. Course placements prescribed by test results or by equivalency formulas (*x* years of high school language study is equivalent to *y* semesters of college study) can be quite unreliable. In addition, students may purposely manipulate the system, starting at the beginning of the sequence either from insecurity about their skills or to protect their GPAs. Finally, first-year college students may be unaccustomed to the fast past of college language instruction, substantial and regular homework assignments, and instructor use of the target language. Data on these topics are sorely lacking; the limited and sometimes contradictory findings on instructor use of the target language in the classroom, one area that has been investigated (see Duff and Polio; Kalivoda and Morain; Polio and Duff; Rollmann), illustrate the need for greater research into all aspects of classroom culture at both secondary and postsecondary school levels.

ROLE FOR ASSESSMENT IN SECONDARY-TO-POSTSECONDARY ARTICULATION EFFORTS

Writers of several recent *ADFL Bulletin* articles have reported on articulation projects under way at state and regional levels (Birckbichler; Jackson and Masters-Wicks; Metcalf; Sandrock; Taylor; see Lange for a thorough overview). While each project has unique features, all have in common elements of communication, collaboration, and assessment. All are quite ambitious and far-reaching. The Minnesota project, for example, focuses on proficiency-based assessment instruments designed by a team whose members come from elementary school, high school, community college, a branch of the university system, the main campus of the university, and the Minnesota Department of Education. The hope of the group is that the assessment instruments and the standards on which they are based will become a "common vocabulary and a common metric" that will enable language teachers and policy makers at all levels in the state to set and work toward realistic goals for the transition from high school to college and from second-year to third-year college courses (Metcalf 52).

The Minnesota project and those in Ohio (Birckbichler), the Northeast (Jackson and Masters-Wicks), Wisconsin (Sandrock), and New York (Taylor) are large-scale, multiskill projects whose scope goes far beyond placement testing of incoming students. All but the New York articulation project are still in the developmental stages. It may be instructive to describe two smaller-scale efforts initiated by single universities, the University of Iowa and the University of Pennsylvania, which are now firmly established in the local administrative and instructional cultures. Both these projects grew from the desire to improve articulation from high school to college; encourage students to continue past the requirement into upper-division courses; and, at Penn, replace seat time with competency as the basis of the language requirement.

Articulation at the University of Iowa. As mentioned above, insecurities about skill levels, lack of familiarity with the style of instruction at the postsecondary institution, or fear of low grades may motivate students to move backward in language course level rather than forward when they make the transition from high school to college. These attitudes may be difficult to change without a system that provides students with the extra motivation, using both a carrot and a stick, to continue to progress in the instructional sequence. The University of Iowa's Foreign Language Incentive Program (FLIP) is such a program.

Instituted in 1991, FLIP was designed to encourage students to study a foreign language beyond the fourth-semester requirement course. It targets entering students who have had no previous college-level language instruction and who score at or above the fourth-semester level on the Foreign Language Placement Test.[3] Although students may exempt the graduation requirement through four years of high school language study alone, the carrot in the program is the possibility for them to receive FLIP credit—free, nongraded credit toward graduation—for language work done in high school that is equivalent to more than the one year of college language study that the University of Iowa expects of entering students. A student whose placement-test score indicates enrollment at the fourth-semester level or higher and who enrolls in a course at the recommended level and receives a grade of at least B− receives either four semester hours of FLIP credit (if the student enrolls in the fourth-semester course) or eight semester hours of FLIP credit (if the student enrolls in a third-year course) in addition to the graded credit for the course taken.

The stick in the program is a two-year foreign language entrance requirement, together with the stipulation that students who fulfill that requirement—two years of one language in high school—cannot take the first-semester course, no matter how low their placement-test score. First- and second-semester courses are reserved for those who began their study of a language at another postsecondary institution or who are beginning a language they did not study in high school. The French, German, and Spanish language program directors designed Elementary Review courses in their respective languages for students whose placement-test score indicate that they are not ready for a second-year course. Elementary Review, arguably the most demanding course in the requirement sequence, is an intensive, fast-paced first-year course that requires substantial, consistent effort by students. As information about FLIP has filtered into the high schools through both official and unofficial (student-to-younger-sibling) channels, the word has got out that taking four years of language in high school is a lesser evil than facing Elementary Review after a gap of two or three years.

The success of FLIP can be measured by the number of students who are FLIP-eligible—those who score at the fourth-semester level or higher on the placement test—and by the performance of students who choose to enroll in FLIP courses. The population in these courses consists largely of students who have taken one or more language classes at the University of Iowa. An additional measure of success, albeit indirect, is the number of students who take four years of language in high school. Although the chief motivation of these students may be to avoid language study in college altogether, pursuing an extended sequence may well open a door to higher-level language study that might be more difficult to open at a later time. A study that examined these questions for 1991–94, the first three years of the program, found quite encouraging results, notably an increase from 32% to 44% in the number of entering freshmen who had taken four years of high school language study. About two-thirds of the students with high-enough placement-test scores to make them eligible for FLIP had taken four years of language in high school. FLIP students' grades in fourth- and fifth-semester courses were equal to or slightly higher than the mean for those courses (Snetzler). The number of entering freshmen with four years of high school language study continues to increase (48% in fall 1996), as does the number of FLIP-eligible freshmen who enroll in a fifth-semester course.

Foreign Language Requirement at the University of Pennsylvania. The University of Pennsylvania's proficiency-based language requirement, operational for more than a decade, has served as the pacesetter for later assessment-based articulation projects. The impetus for the requirement was the discovery, not unique to Penn, that a language requirement based on time units does not result in students' reaching a usable level of proficiency when they complete the requirement sequence. The current requirement at Penn involves a complex system of proficiency assessments in combination with formal study (for details, see Freed). Successful completion of course work is a component of the language requirement, but students must take proficiency tests in the various skill areas as well. In fact, students can receive a grade in the fourth-semester course only if they receive a passing score on the proficiency assessment. The system has a compensatory feature: very strong performance in one area of the proficiency assessment can compensate for weak performance in another, as long as the student receives a passing composite score. For example, students who have considerable difficulty with oral expression but who read quite fluently for their level may still be able to pass.

One of the most valuable features of all articulation projects, Penn's included, is the increased involvement of departmental faculty members in the lower-division language program. Even senior colleagues who do not teach basic language courses participated in the Penn program during the planning stages, and some have been involved in the proficiency assessments as well. Certainly the graduate teaching assistants have received valuable professional training in proficiency assessment and proficiency-oriented teaching. Five years after the French section of the department of foreign languages had implemented the proficiency-based requirement, Barbara F. Freed reported that the requirement had "resulted in a more integrated sequence of courses and improved articulation between elementary and intermediate courses" (142).

At an ACTFL oral proficiency interview workshop in November 1996 hosted by Penn, at which I led one of the Spanish sections, I gathered some personal evidence of the continued heightened awareness of faculty members and students about language proficiency and assessment. All the interviewees on whom the workshop participants practiced their nascent interviewing and rating skills were Penn students, TAs, or instructors. When I talked briefly with the students to explain the process and what they could expect, I found that all were very much aware of what OPI testing was. In fact, they had volunteered for the workshop to get additional practice for the upcoming OPIs that they would take as part of the proficiency assessment. The TAs and instructors, who served as our interviewees for the upper levels of the ACTFL scale, were familiar with the scale, curious about their own proficiency ratings and the structure of their interviews, and knowledgeable about the relation between language tasks and proficiency levels. Surely these common understandings and expectations within a program lead to more effective language teaching and increased collaboration among instructors.

PLANNING FOR ARTICULATION

Placement Testing. What, then, is the role of assessment in articulation programs for the transition from secondary school to college? Most faculty members responsible for elementary and intermediate language instruction at the postsecondary level would agree that an up-to-date placement instrument is essential. Throughout the 1970s and 1980s, many departments used multiple choice reading, listening, and structure tests produced a decade earlier by Educational Testing Service or the MLA and made available for institutional use. More recent placement tests have the following features: content validity, that is, the content and range of skills measured correspond to the courses into which the test score places students; score ranges for each of the placement levels that were determined through a concurrent validation study conducted at the institution; and a format that enables quick testing and placement of large numbers of students. Issues of efficiency argue for some machine-scorable sections, while the demands of content validity argue for the inclusion of skills that multiple choice items cannot measure, such as speaking and writing. A placement test that incorporates an oral interview or a writing sample is very effective, particularly for small departments; larger departments may be able to administer these additional assessments only to a limited number of entering students, perhaps those with high scores. Departments might design these oral interviews more as inducements than screening devices, combining them with a brief orientation and a personal invitation to enroll in an upper-level course.

The process of establishing score ranges for each course by administering the test to one's own language students greatly increases the rate of appropriate placement of entering students. While not a modest undertaking, a concurrent validation study is not difficult to design (for models, see Appenzellar and Kelley; Arendt and Morgan; Wimmers and Morgan), yields valuable information, and can also serve as a teaching and learning tool for graduate students and teaching assistants. The statistical consulting center or measurement-and-evaluation service of the institution is usually available for technical support, and some ingenious networking might even locate a graduate student in the College of Education who would undertake a norming study as a master's thesis project.

Proficiency Tests for Elementary and Intermediate Students. The University of Iowa and University of Pennsylvania use placement tests as only one component of articulation programs that are intended to support and extend language study. These instruments measure knowledge and skills in small, unconnected bits of text. For that reason they are referred to as achievement tests. The more broadly based projects, such as those in New York State (Taylor) and New England (Jackson and Masters-Wicks), involve articulating learning standards in terms of proficiency. The assessments developed for those projects are more properly referred to as proficiency tests or performance tests, because they integrate knowledge and skills that students have acquired over a period of time. The Minnesota project, for example, administers tests to incoming university students that are intended not only to place students in appropriate courses but also to support and encourage the kind of language teaching, at both high school and college levels, that integrates knowledge and skills, works with authentic texts, and immerses students in the target language from the beginning of instruction.

Articulation: Making the Transition to Content Courses

As secondary-to-postsecondary articulation efforts succeed in creating longer, uninterrupted sequences of study for larger numbers of students, the pressure on colleges and universities to undertake similar projects between lower-division and upper-division courses will increase as well. Many students cross yet another "cultural border" when they leave elementary and intermediate instruction and turn to advanced courses, which assume a certain level of language skill and the ability to use the language as a tool for learning.

ISSUES AND PROBLEMS

We know from articulation and retention problems in upper-division courses in our own institutions that many students experience the kind of instructional culture shock described by Joan Kelly Hall. Indeed, some observers (Bernhardt; James, "Bypassing" and "Teaching") have attributed the decline of the traditional literature major in part to the lack of fit in upper-division literature courses between students' skills and faculty expectations. The reasons for the decline of enrollment in literature courses are complex, attributable to changes in students' goals for language study (Siskin, Knowles, and Davis); changes in the lower-division curriculum that have created in students the expectation and desire for continuing support for language skill development in their upper-division courses (Bernhardt); and a traditional and perhaps stereotypical intransigence on the part of literature faculty members, which is expressed as reluctance or even refusal to explore ways of integrating language skill work into their courses (James, "Bypassing"). Elizabeth Bernhardt echoes the concerns of many when she urges that our primary focus be on students rather than on texts, predicting that "if we are teaching texts, then we are continuing down the slippery slope toward putting ourselves out of business" (6).

The growing literature on the teaching of foreign language literature at the undergraduate level is a counterweight to the predictions of doom, but it has the flavor of preaching to the choir: the dissemination of this work has been confined largely to those journals and sections of journals read by language program directors, department chairs, and others interested primarily in language teaching. James's seminal work to integrate language skills development in German literature classes at Hunter College and to individualize instruction according to students' skill level ("Reshaping") has served as both a model and a reproach to other departments unwilling to take on the challenge (James, "Bypassing"). But the increasing German enrollments at Hunter College (James, personal communication), in direct contrast to the national trend, strongly suggest that undergraduates are eager to engage with literary texts when appropriate linguistic support is provided.

Much of the work on the teaching of literature involves making texts more accessible to students by adapting the approaches and activities used in language instruction. Diane Birckbichler and Judith Muyskens, for example, provide direction for eliciting students' personal feelings and reactions as keys to analysis of texts. Camille Vande Berg ("Conversation Activities" and "Managing Learner Anxiety") explains how to adapt to literature classes small-group work, roleplays, and other oral-activity formats commonly used in elementary- and intermediate-level language instruction. Mary Lee Bretz and Margaret Persin, James Davis, and others suggest ways to introduce notions of literary theory in undergraduate literature courses.

Another line of research has involved the application of reading strategies to literary texts, particularly in bridge courses designed as introductions to the study of literature and culture at the third-year level. Topics addressed have included issues of text readability and selection (Knutson; Schulz); use of thematic scenarios to set the stage for the themes and conflicts of a text (DiPietro); and incorporation of a sequence of activities to enhance students' understanding, from prereading and prewriting activities (Arcuri) to postreading discussion, improvisations, and synthesis (Haggstrom; Harper).

ROLE OF ASSESSMENT IN MAKING THE TRANSITION TO CONTENT COURSES

Needs Assessment. Vertical articulation efforts within a department's foreign language major imply a primarily diagnostic and developmental role for assessment. A department might begin an articulation project by conducting a needs assessment: surveying its majors and minors on their perceptions about what they were learning in each course; administering proficiency assessments in speaking and reading to a stratified sample of students (e.g., a sample that includes categories such as pre- and poststudy abroad, majors and minors, new majors and majors close to graduation); and examining selections of writing drawn from this sample. But the identification of problem areas is only the beginning of the reform process. When undertaken collaboratively, needs assessments have the potential to highlight areas of excellence that can serve as leavening for the process of change as well as to inspire focused discussions on priorities and strategies for improvement.

Curriculum Planning. The Hunter College model (James, "Reshaping") seeks to individualize instruction in literature courses according to students' skill levels. Such individualizing, with the goal of grouping students appropriately, entails informal assessment of their proficiency in reading, writing, or speaking, depending on the demands of the curriculum being planned. Tasks that involve organization and classification of literal elements of plot, character, and setting, for example, would be reserved for students whose oral proficiency level is at the Intermediate High or Advanced level. Interpretive tasks that require the ability to work with abstract concepts in the target language would be assigned to students with strong Advanced or Advanced High proficiency. Not only ongoing, informal assessment is implied here but also close communication among departmental faculty members, to be sure that students are working with tasks that are neither overly challenging nor too simple for their ability level.

Student Advising. Appropriate advising, especially in large departments in which faculty members may not know all their majors well, is another role for informal assessment of language skills — and assessment also of career interests. Students and their advisers could use the results to inform course selection, study-abroad plans, and longer-range decision making. Bringing students into the assessment process gives them the message that they are ultimately accountable for devising their career goals and shaping their educational program to support those goals.

The foregoing are examples of formative assessments, internal evaluations that serve as self-monitoring and consciousness-raising devices: they highlight strengths, reveal areas in need of further work, and start the process of collaborative planning and problem solving. Assuming that such efforts are successful, the next question is how to describe and assess what students have learned over the course of their major in a foreign language department.

The Foreign Language Major: Assessing the Outcomes

A number of studies across more than a decade (Cramer and Terrio; Hiple and Manley; Kaplan; Liskin-Gasparro, Wunnava, and Henry; Magnan) converge on the findings that the oral proficiency level of foreign language majors graduating from college falls between Intermediate High and Advanced High and that a significant immersion experience (semester or year abroad) is most predictive of proficiency at the Advanced level.[4] But we know virtually nothing about our graduating majors' knowledge of literature, culture and civilization, and linguistics. Intracourse assessments in the form of examinations, papers, and oral presentations do little to illuminate either students' retention of the material beyond the semester in which they are exposed to it or their ability to use the material they learn in one course as background information for another. As discussed earlier, humanities departments have no tradition of specifying or assessing the outcomes of instruction, and it is not uncommon for faculty members to view such endeavors as in some ways antithetical to their disciplines. However, current calls for outcomes assessment of the major program stem not only from issues of accountability for departments and programs but also from the recognition that the process of engaging in such assessment can foster the type of reflective and integrative thinking that is at the core of the major program.

ISSUES AND PROBLEMS

Consider a language department at a branch campus of a state university. Its majors may declare a major after some combination of language study in high school, community college, and the university (lower-division courses). Students have to fulfill some distribution requirements in the major courses—so many credits of literature, linguistics, civilization, and so on—and elect the rest of their courses from among departmental offerings. Close to 30% of the majors study abroad, either for a summer or a semester; ten years ago, less than 20% of the majors did. More than half plan to teach and will complement their language major with general and subject-specific education courses, along with a field-based teaching practicum and a capstone student teaching semester.

What guidance do these students have in selecting the courses that comprise the thirty-six credits of their language major? Most students have drifted into the department because they liked their Spanish or French classes. In most parts of the country, few students have had direct contact with the target cultures or speakers. Ironically, the larger the department, the more options students have for their major program but the less likely it is that faculty members will know their advisees well enough to help them structure a course of study consonant with their developing interests and talents. The result is that many students, afraid to leave the familiar environment of language skills courses, delay and avoid content courses; they end up having sampled only superficially and with trepidation the range of departmental offerings in linguistics and literary and cultural studies.

Even if a course of study is carefully planned with the help of an adviser, students themselves play an important role in making it fulfill its promise. The most carefully integrated series of courses can fall flat if students are not primed to construct connections and meanings. Coherence must be sought on several fronts: between courses within the major; between language skill development and content within individual courses; and, for preservice teachers, between the literature and culture they are learning in their language department courses and the principles of teaching and learning they are studying in their education classes. We should not be surprised that students who fail to see or forge connections among their intellectual endeavors become disaffected with their studies.

ROLE FOR ASSESSMENT IN THE FOREIGN LANGUAGE MAJOR

Outcomes-assessment projects, whose purpose is to evaluate the effectiveness of programs and the quality of student learning, are a natural antidote to the lack of coherence within and between courses and programs. These projects are major undertakings, usually initiated in response to an external mandate. However, outcomes-assessment initiatives can function as leavening in the process of increasing faculty collaboration as well as student engagement with the intellectual substance of the major program.

Outcomes-assessment projects for the general education core at the State University of New York, Fredonia (Courts and McInerney), and for the French and Spanish major programs at Bates College in Augusta, Maine (Liskin-Gasparro; Williamson), have used portfolios as the principal assessment tool. An academic portfolio, like its artistic analog, is a compendium of samples of the owner's work. It is usually contained in a large binder and is composed of two types of work: the documents, or artifacts, that the owner has compiled in response to guidelines established by a department for its students; and reflections that the owner writes to accompany each artifact. For example, if a department is interested in exploring the effects of study abroad on its majors, the portfolio guidelines might call for the inclusion of artifacts related to study abroad, such as portions of a journal kept by the student or samples of creative work (drawings, photography, poetry) completed while abroad. Portfolios might also include samples of oral texts produced at the beginning and end of the major, essays written for one or more courses, reports on extracurricular activities related to the major, or other topics that the department might identify. Teacher education programs assist their students in the preparation of pedagogical portfolios, since these are now a routine part of the job search.

In contrast to controlled-assessment models, in which students demonstrate knowledge and skill development on cue, solely for the purpose of the assessment, the portfolio approach has students return to work they have already produced—to compare it to other pieces they have done, to evaluate it, and to reflect on how all their work, individually and collectively, fits into their overall educational program. This process of ongoing reflection embedded in the creation of a portfolio is perhaps the portfolio's most significant feature. The typical portfolio formalizes the reflection by asking students to introduce each item they select with a short essay (often referred to as a one-pager) and to introduce the portfolio as a whole with an intellectual autobiography. For language majors who are also preservice teachers, the theme of most autobiographies would most likely be the unfolding of the student's commitment to a teaching career.

The portfolio teaches students, as perhaps no number of multidraft writing assignments can, that no piece of work is ever truly finished. In their introductory one-pagers, students often document their changing relation to the particular artifact and, in so doing, see their growth of knowledge and skill over time and in response to academic and experiential learning. Some programs ask students to work on the autobiographical essay over a period of time, so they can become aware of and reflect on changes in their self-perceptions.

Majors in small departments often know one another well, because they have followed the same sequence of courses. In larger departments, majors may spend two or three years in a department without interacting outside class with other majors or with departmental faculty members. In the portfolio program, students meet periodically with their advisers, both so the adviser can help the student stay on track and so the adviser and student can talk about the contents of the portfolio while it is in the formative stages. The Bates faculty hope that the portfolio will serve as a vehicle for a closer working relationship with their majors and for deeper insights into students' abilities and plans.

The Bates portfolio plan includes taped speech samples at different stages of the student's major, recorded on a single cassette. The benefit of such a tape, in terms of the reflexive purpose that underlies the portfolio, is that students can document their progress in fluency and pronunciation. If a more formal assessment is desired—if, say, faculty members want to describe students' speaking skills, using ACTFL proficiency levels, in letters of recommendation—the oral proficiency interview may be an option for smaller departments, assuming that a trained tester is available. An attractive option for departments that do not have the expertise or capacity to interview a large number of students is the simulated oral proficiency interview, which yields a rating on the ACTFL scale. It is easy to administer—a group of students can take it simultaneously in a language lab. The scoring procedures are relatively straightforward, and the Center for Applied Linguistics provides self-instructional materials, including speech samples, for institutional or individual use. (The appendix to this essay gives contact information for assessment instruments.)

The preparation of foreign language teachers in their content specialty is a complex matter. Some language departments may have designed their major programs without keeping the needs of the future teacher in mind. Others may not have adjusted their programs to the academic profile of today's language student, who enters college with a background perhaps stronger in oral communication but weaker in literacy skills and knowledge of structure. Future teachers may be called on to wear several hats as they complete their undergraduate studies: competent readers of and writers about literary and cultural texts for their departmental majors, confident users of pedagogical ideas and materials for their education specialty, and skilled speakers of the language for their potential employers.

The role of assessment in this process is no less complex. Assessment is a double-edged sword. As an internal tool, it can serve as a mechanism for reflection and curricular innovation. In the German program at Hunter College, assessment of students' oral skills revealed not only that there was a considerable range of ability but also that some students simply could not cope linguistically with the demands of typical texts and tasks in advanced courses. This discovery motivated the redesign of the curriculum and, in the process, the revitalization of the program (James, "Reshaping"). But when assessment is imposed externally, particularly if important decisions are based on the results, there is a real danger that it will be used as a mechanism of censure and control. As the case of Texas demonstrates, even a high-quality assessment tool like the Texas Oral Proficiency Test runs the risk of creating new problems while trying to solve existing ones. If the accountability procedures for teacher-preparation programs in Texas go into place as planned, departments and programs may be in the unpleasant position of having to undertake radical change as an emergency survival measure rather than being able to plan for instructional improvement carefully and thoughtfully.

Those who shape a curriculum should keep in mind some key points in the academic preparation of a foreign language major who also expects to be a teacher of that language. The first is the transition from high school to college. Students may already have made a career choice, or at least have seriously entertained the possibility, because of positive experiences in high school language classes. College language departments can capitalize on students' motivation and early success through a placement process that puts them in as advanced a course as they can reasonably handle and that rewards them, as in the University of Iowa Foreign Language Incentive Program, for their prior high school achievement. Individualized placement tests in smaller programs, such as an oral interview for the most advanced students, can initiate the kind of early advising and personal attention that may keep students' motivation high.

A second key point in the life of the future teacher is the transition from lower-division to upper-division courses. Some programs have designed special bridge courses intended to ease the change in focus from oral skills to the reading and interpreting of texts. As in the Hunter College German department, faculty members can easily overestimate students' abilities and, as a result, pitch their courses at a level that students cannot manage. Informal assessment of students' language skills can give valuable guidance to faculty members in the design of such bridge courses, including selection of texts, appropriate activities based on them, and the amount and types of language skills development work to include.

Finally, as students progress through their major courses, an ongoing assessment process, such as the portfolio projects described above, can help them make the material they study their own. Over time, with this process departments can also understand better how their major program engages students intellectually and can expand in areas that appear to be most fruitful.

The real value of assessment, as presented in this essay, is to motivate change and to serve our educational vision. The challenge for us is to initiate the process of change and to manage and direct it. As the examples presented here have shown, assessment created and imposed from without can all too easily escape from our control.

Notes

[1]Although ACTFL produced proficiency guidelines for all four language skills, only the speaking guidelines have had a major impact on foreign language instruction and teacher education. According to the 1986 version of the guidelines, Superior-level proficiency was encapsulated with the following brief description: "The Superior level is characterized by the speaker's ability to: participate effectively in most formal and informal conversations on practical, social, professional, and abstract topics; and support opinions and hypothesize using native-like discourse strategies" (ACTFL, *Guidelines*).

[2]The study was conducted with funding from the United States Department of Education, which provided the resources to ensure to a high degree the accuracy and reliability of the OPI ratings.

[3]The Foreign Language Placement Test was developed in French, German, and Spanish and normed on University of Iowa students in second-, third-, and fourth-semester language classes. Students who are not FLIP-eligible are placed in the appropriate course on the basis of their scores. See Wherritt, Cleary, and Druva-Rousch for details of the test development process.

[4]The researchers cited here have studied French and Spanish majors almost exclusively. Students of non-Western languages may graduate from college with lower oral proficiency levels.

WORKS CITED

American Association of Teachers of French Commission on Professional Standards. "The Teaching of French—A Syllabus of Competence." *AATF National Bulletin* 15 (1989): 3–35.

American Association of Teachers of Spanish and Portuguese. "AATSP Program Guidelines for the Education and Training of Teachers of Spanish and Portuguese." *Hispania* 73 (1990): 785–94.

American Council on the Teaching of Foreign Languages. *ACTFL Proficiency Guidelines.* Yonkers: ACTFL, 1986.

———. "Foreign Language Enrollments in Public Secondary Schools, Fall 1994: A Summary." *Foreign Language Annals* 29 (1996): 303–06.

———. "National Board for Professional Standards Names Foreign Language Credential Committee." *ACTFL Newsletter* 10.2 (1998): 15–16.

———. "Provisional Program Guidelines for Foreign Language Teacher Education." *Foreign Language Annals* 21 (1988): 71–82.

Appenzellar, Anne B., and Paul H. Kelley. "Validity Study of the University of Texas, Austin, Test for Credit in Chinese: Spring and Fall 1985 and Spring 1986." Internal report to the Measurement and Evaluation Center, University of Texas, Austin. Sept. 1990. ED333040.

Arcuri, Guy. "Pre-reading and Pre-writing Activities to Prepare and Motivate Foreign Language Students to Read Short Stories." *Hispania* 73 (1990): 262–66.

Arendt, Ulli, and Rick Morgan. "Comparing the Performance of High School and College Students on the Listening, Speaking, and Reading Sections of the Advanced Placement German Language Examination." *Unterrichtspraxis* 28 (1995): 40–45.

Bernhardt, Elizabeth B. "Teaching Literature or Teaching Students?" *ADFL Bulletin* 26.2 (1995): 5–6.

Birckbichler, Diane W. "Ohio's Collaborative Articulation and Assessment Project." *ADFL Bulletin* 26.3 (1995): 44–45.

Birckbichler, Diane W., and Judith A. Muyskens. "A Personalized Approach to the Teaching of Literature at the Elementary and Intermediate Levels of Instruction." *Foreign Language Annals* 13 (1980): 23–27.

Bretz, Mary Lee, and Margaret Persin. "The Application of Critical Theory to Literature at the Introductory Level: A Working Model for Teacher Preparation." *Modern Language Journal* 71 (1987): 165–70.

Brickell, Henry M., and Regina H. Paul. *Ready for the 1980s? A Look at Foreign Language Teachers and Teaching at the Start of the Decade.* New York: Policy Studies in Educ., 1981.

Brod, Richard, and Bettina J. Huber. "The MLA Survey of Foreign Language Entrance and Degree Requirements, 1994–95." *ADFL Bulletin* 28.1 (1997): 35–43.

Buck, Kathryn, Heidi Byrnes, and Irene Thompson, eds. *The ACTFL Oral Proficiency Interview Tester Training Manual.* Yonkers: ACTFL, 1989.

Cipolla, William F. "Teaching Literature through Theory: A New Model for the Undergraduate Major. *ADFL Bulletin* 18.3 (1991): 13–15.

Courts, Patrick L., and Kathleen H. McInerney. *Assessment in Higher Education: Politics, Policy, and Portfolios.* Westport: Praeger, 1993.

Cramer, H., and Susan Terrio. "Moving from Vocabulary Acquisition to Functional Proficiency: Techniques and Strategies." *French Review* 59 (1985): 198–209.

Davis, James N. "Reading Literature in Foreign Language: The Comprehension/Response Connection." *French Review* 65 (1992): 359–70.

DiPietro, Robert J. "The Scenario Principle in the Teaching of Italian Literature." *Italica* 64 (1987): 365–76.

Duff, Patricia A., and Charlene G. Polio. "How Much Foreign Language Is There in the Foreign Language Classroom?" *Modern Language Journal* 74 (1990): 154–66.

Foerster, Sharon. Personal communication. Nov. 1996.

Freed, Barbara F. "Preliminary Impressions of the Effects of a Proficiency-Based Language Requirement." *Foreign Language Annals* 20 (1987): 139–46.

González Pino, Barbara. Personal communication. 15 May 1997.

Haggstrom, Margaret A. "A Performative Approach to the Study of Theater: Bridging the Gap between Language and Literature Courses." *French Review* 66 (1992): 7–19.

Hall, Joan Kelly. "Articulation in Foreign Language Education: A Case of Crossing Cultural Borders." *ADFL Bulletin* 28.2 (1997): 26–30.

Harper, Sandra N. "Strategies for Teaching Literature at the Undergraduate Level." *Modern Language Journal* 72 (1988): 402–08.

Heining-Boynton, Audrey L. "Standards and Foreign Language Teacher Education: Developing New Professionals during a Time of Reform." *National Standards: A Catalyst for Reform.* ACTFL Foreign Lang. Educ. Ser. Ed. Robert C. Lafayette. Lincolnwood: Natl. Textbook, 1996. 39–55.

Henning, Sylvie Debevec. "Assessing Literary Interpretation Skills." *Foreign Language Annals* 25 (1992): 339–55.

Hiple, David, and Joan Manley. "Testing How Well Foreign Language Teachers Speak: A State Mandate." *Foreign Language Annals* 20 (1987): 147–53.

Jackson, Claire, and Karen Masters-Wicks. "Articulation and Achievement: The Challenge of the 1990s in Foreign Language Education." *ADFL Bulletin* 26.3 (1995): 46–51.

James, Dorothy. "Bypassing the Traditional Leadership: Who's Minding the Store?" *ADFL Bulletin* 28.3 (1997): 5–11.

———. Personal communication. 22 May 1997.

———. "Reshaping the 'College-Level' Curriculum: Problems and Possibilities." *Shaping the Future: Challenges and Opportunities.* Northeast Conf. Repts. Ed. Helen S. Lepke. Lincolnwood: Natl. Textbook, 1989. 79–100.

———. "Teaching Language and Literature: Equal Opportunity in the Inner-City University." *ADFL Bulletin* 28.1 (1996): 24–28.

Kalivoda, Theodore, and Genelle Morain. Unpublished manuscript. Dept. of Educ., U of Georgia, 1988–89.

Kaplan, Isabelle. "Oral Proficiency Testing and the Language Curriculum: Two Experiments in Curricular Design for Conversation Courses." *Foreign Language Annals* 17 (1984): 491–98.

Knutson, Elizabeth M. "Teaching Whole Texts: Literature and Foreign Language Reading Instruction." *French Review* 67 (1993): 12–26.

Lafayette, Robert C. "Subject-Matter Content: What Every Foreign Language Teacher Needs to Know." *Developing Language Teachers for a Changing World.* ACTFL Foreign Lang. Educ. Ser. Ed. Gail Guntermann. Lincolnwood: Natl. Textbook, 1993. 124–58.

Lange, Dale L. "Models of Articulation: Struggles and Successes." *ADFL Bulletin* 28.2 (1997): 31–42.

Lewis, Catherine Porter. "Assessing the Foreign Language Major at the State University of New York: An Interim Report." *ADFL Bulletin* 21.3 (1990): 35–39.

Liskin-Gasparro, Judith E. "Practical Approaches to Outcomes Assessment: The Undergraduate Major in Foreign Languages and Literatures." *ADFL Bulletin* 26.2 (1995): 21–27.

Liskin-Gasparro, Judith E., Phanindra Wunnava, and Kathryn Henry. *The Effect of Intensive-Immersive Conditions on the Acquisition and Development of Oral Proficiency in Spanish and*

Russian. Final report to the US Dept. of Educ. Middlebury: Middlebury Coll. Lang. Schools, 1991.

Madaus, George F. "The Distortion of Teaching and Testing: High-Stakes Teaching and Testing." *Peabody Journal of Education* 65.3 (1988): 29–46.

———. "The Influence of Testing on the Curriculum." *Critical Issues in Curriculum.* 87th Yearbook of the Natl. Soc. for the Study of Educ., Part 1. Chicago: U of Chicago P, 1988. 83–121.

———. "Legal and Professional Issues in Teacher-Certification Testing: A Psychometric Snark Hunt." *Assessment of Teaching: Purposes, Practices, and Implications for the Profession.* Buros-Nebraska Symposium on Measurement and Testing. Eds. James V. Mitchell, Jr., Steven L. Wise, and Barbara S. Plake. Hillsdale: Erlbaum, 1990. 209–59.

Madaus, George F., and Thomas Kellaghan. "Curriculum Evaluation and Assessment." *Handbook of Research on Curriculum.* Ed. Philip W. Jackson. New York: Macmillan, 1992. 119–54.

Magnan, Sally. "Assessing Speaking Proficiency in the Undergraduate Curriculum: Data from French." *Foreign Language Annals* 19 (1986): 429–38.

Metcalf, Michael F. "Articulating the Teaching of Foreign Languages: The Minnesota Project." *ADFL Bulletin* 26.3 (1995): 52–54.

Morain, Genelle. "A View from the Top of the Tree." *Canadian Modern Language Review* 50 (1993–94): 101–06.

Nerenz, Anne. "Becoming a Teacher in the Twenty-First Century." *Reflecting on Proficiency from the Classroom Perspective.* Northeast Conf. Repts. Ed. June K. Phillips. Lincolnwood: Natl. Textbook, 1993. 159–205.

Polio, Charlene G., and Patricia A. Duff. "Teachers' Language Use in University Foreign Language Classrooms: A Qualitative Analysis of English and Target Language Alternation." *Modern Language Journal* 78 (1994): 313–26.

Rollmann, M. "The Communicative Language Teaching 'Revolution' Tested: A Comparison of Two Classroom Studies, 1976 and 1993. *Foreign Language Annals* 27 (1994): 221–39.

Sandrock, Paul. "Competency-Based Admission: A Project of the University of Wisconsin System." *ADFL Bulletin* 26.3 (1995): 55–57.

Schrier, Leslie L. "A Survey of Foreign Language Teacher Preparation Patterns and Procedures in Small, Private Colleges and Universities in the United States." Diss. Ohio State U, 1989.

Schulz, Renate A. "Literature and Readability: Bridging the Gap in Foreign Language Reading." *Modern Language Journal* 65 (1981): 43–53.

Schulz, Renate, et al. "Professional Standards for Teachers of German: Recommendations of the AATG Task Force on Professional Standards." *Unterrichtspraxis* 26 (1993): 80–96.

Siskin, H. Jay, Mark A. Knowles, and Robert L. Davis. "Le Français Est Mort, Vive le Français: Rethinking the Function of French." *Patterns and Policies: The Changing Demographics of Foreign Language Instruction.* AAUSC Ser. on Issues in Lang. Program Direction. Ed. Judith E. Liskin-Gasparro. Boston: Heinle, 1996. 35–69.

Snetzler, Suzi. Foreign Language Incentive Program: "Evaluation of Program: Student Characteristics and Performance from Fall 1991 to Spring 1994." Internal report. Coll. of Liberal Arts, U of Iowa. Sept. 1994.

Stansfield, Charles W., and Dorry Mann Kenyon. *Development of the Texas Oral Proficiency Test (TOPT): Final Report.* Washington: Center for Applied Linguistics, 1991. ED332522.

Strength through Wisdom: A Critique of US Capability: A Report to the President from the President's Commission on Foreign Language and International Studies. Washington: GPO, 1979.

Swaffar, Janet, Kathryn Arens, and Heidi Byrnes. *Reading for Meaning: An Integrated Approach to Language Learning.* Englewood Cliffs: Prentice, 1991.

Taylor, Irmgard C. "The Ever-Elusive Seamless Transition: New Efforts by the State University of New York and the Schools in Articulating Language Programs." *ADFL Bulletin* 26.3 (1995): 58–62.

Texas. State Board for Educator Certification. "Development of the ASEP (Accountability System for Educator Preparation)." Internal document. State Board for Educator Certification, Austin. 16 May 1997.

Tomorrow's Teachers: A Report of the Holmes Group. East Lansing: Holmes Group, 1986.

Vande Berg, Camille Kennedy. "Conversation Activities Based on Literary Readings." *French Review* 63 (1990): 664–70.

———. "Managing Learner Anxiety in Literature Courses." *French Review* 67 (1993): 27–36.

Wherritt, Irene, T. Anne Cleary, and Cynthia Ann Druva-Rousch. "Development and Analysis of a Flexible Spanish Language Test for Placement and Outcomes Assessment." *Hispania* 73 (1990): 1124–29.

Williamson, Richard C. "Portfolio Assessment for College Language Majors: Can It Work?" Northeast Conf. on the Teaching of Foreign Langs. New York, 8 April 1994.

Wimmers, Eric, and Rick Morgan. "Comparing the Performance of High School and College Students on the Advanced Placement French Language Examination." *French Review* 63 (1990): 423–32.

Wolf, W. C., Jr., and Kathleen M. Riordan. "Foreign Language Teachers' Demographic Characteristics, In-Service Training Needs, and Attitudes toward Teaching." *Foreign Language Annals* 24 (1991): 471–78.

APPENDIX

Resource Information on Assessment Instruments

Computer Adaptive Placement Examinations (CAPE) Available in French, German, and Spanish from Brigham Young University. Contact: Jerry W. Larson, Humanities Research Center, 3060 JKHB, Brigham Young Univ., Provo, UT 84602; 801 378-6529; larson@jkhbhrc.byu.edu.

Praxis Series: Professional Assessments for Beginning Teachers Available from Educational Testing Service, Praxis Series, PO Box 6051, Princeton, NJ 08541-6051; 800 772-9476; fax: 609 530-0581; www.ets.org/prxsets.html.

Proficiency Tests in Listening and Reading Available from the Center for

Applied Linguistics (CAL) in Arabic, Chinese (Cantonese and Mandarin), Hindi, and Polish. Contact: Program Director, [language] Testing Program, Center for Applied Linguistics, 4646 40th St., NW, Washington, DC 20016-1859; 202 362-0700; fax 202 362-3740; www.cal.org.

Simulated Oral Proficiency Interview (SOPI) The Center for Applied Linguistics (CAL) has SOPIs available in the following languages: Arabic, Chinese (Cantonese and Mandarin), French, German, Hausa, Hebrew, Hindi, Indonesian, Japanese, Portuguese, and Spanish. See contact information for CAL above.

Spanish Proficiency Test Available from Educational Testing Service. Measures proficiency in all four skills up to the Advanced level. Contact: Shirley Springsteen, Educational Testing Service, International Testing and Training Programs, PO Box 6155, Princeton, NJ 08541-6155.

III

Unresolved Questions

REED WAY DASENBROCK

Changing Teacher Preparation for a Changing Student Body

Teachers are trained—whether consciously or unconsciously—with a certain vision of the classroom in which they will teach. It is therefore not irrelevant to the question of how we are to train our teachers for the next century that the faces in those classrooms are very different from the faces a generation ago. Over the past generation, the racial, cultural, and religious composition of America's student population has been changing rapidly, and every piece of information we have suggests that the pace of that change is not slowing down. The teachers we are training now will be teaching different students, and we need to ask how that difference should affect the way we train teachers of English and other languages.

To begin with the large picture, the United States as a country is becoming less white, less Protestant, and less composed of monolingual English speakers. Immigration into the United States obviously comes from all over the world, but the major vectors of change involve a growing increase of immigration from Latin America and from Asia. Those vectors affect different parts of the country unequally, but they affect the entire country and affect big states—California, Texas, Florida, New York—more than most small states. At the present time, there are only two so-called majority-minority states, states where the majority of the population is composed of nonwhite minorities: Hawai'i and New Mexico. They are small and historically atypical states, but they provide laboratories where we can study the nation's future. California is projected soon to be the next such state; at that point, the trend will be unmistakable.

Many schools are majority-minority already, because the age of the nonwhite and the immigrant populations is younger than the white population on the whole, and on average nonwhites, both immigrant and not, have more children. So this national trend is felt even more in the school system. There is a structural reason why it has been felt less by those of us in the university. If a wave of minority students is working its way through the school system, then it would seem to be only a matter of time before the colleges and universities face the same situation. But the pattern of access to education in the United States is very unequal; with one important exception, minorities in the United States are not graduating from high school, entering college, graduating from college, or going on to postgraduate study in anything like the numbers their presence in the population indicates they should. This phenomenon has been called the leaky pipeline: at every stage in the educational pipeline, minority students drop out of the system and do not continue to the next stage.[1] Given the close relation between success in education and socioeconomic status, a relation bound to tighten in the next century, the leaky pipeline has serious long-term consequences for the entire nation. The conspicuous exception is, of course, the Asian American community, which not only has done much better than the other minority communities but also has done much better than the majority community. This exception—whatever its implications and however imperfectly understood—has had a complex effect on the debates surrounding minority achievement in the schools. Most concretely, it has led to a terminological differentiation among minority populations. When the phrase "underrepresented minorities" is used, the reference is to African Americans, Hispanics, and Native Americans—those groups whose representation in the educational system lags behind their representation in the population.

A little-noticed by-product of underrepresentation of minorities in higher education is that most college faculty members are shielded from a full awareness of the dimensions of the problem. The disparity in this respect between the environment of the secondary schools and the universities is one more factor, and a growing factor, that adds to the disparity between their cultures. Every such disparity increases the difficulty new teachers face in moving from one culture to the other and the difficulty faced by anyone wishing to bridge the gap between the schools and the universities.

Some of the questions that now stare us in the face are: How do we in the universities prepare future teachers for the environment in which they will teach when the university environment is so very different? Do the methods that worked for Dick and Jane in the 1950s still work today?

If not, how do we retrain current teachers who face a student population they weren't trained to teach? Can teacher-training programs help improve minority access to higher education? Before we can begin to answer this last question, we have to answer some deeper questions: What factors are responsible for the underrepresentation of minorities in higher education? Whose fault is it—the colleges and universities, for creating environments in which minority students do not succeed, or the secondary schools, for not preparing these students well enough? Or is the underrepresentation largely the result of home environment and socialization, in which case neither secondary school nor university may be able to do much about it?

We should be able to see how these questions intersect with other ones, with large issues and large anxieties, about the graying and browning of America, about the ability of America to compete in the new information-rich economy, in which a skilled workforce is essential. I revise this essay just after California passed a resolution banning bilingual education. It isn't clear yet what effect the resolution will have in practice, but the heated public debate about educational policy on this issue—a debate that reflects the larger national debate about such connected issues as immigration, affirmative action, and bilingual education—makes the task of designing curricula for training teachers that much more difficult.

One of the things we tell our students is that when analyzing problems it helps to have good information. Facts may not solve all problems, but they help us address them. They also help dissolve fears. We should start from the end product. In their new workplace our students will need much more complex and demanding literacy skills than they ever needed before. If our students are to participate fully in the economy of the twentieth-first century, they will need to read complex information and they will need to do much more writing than their parents or grandparents did. Years ago, we heard people arguing that we were moving to a new age of computers in which reading and writing would somehow become less important, but for the most part what people do with their computers is what I am doing with mine now—writing and reading. Moreover, the computer revolution has made literacy in English even more essential all over the world, as is shown by the estimate that eighty percent of the Internet is in English.

Professors of languages and literature tend to find many other arguments for the value of what we do and teach more persuasive than this broadly instrumental one. We like to read and write, and so we think these activities intrinsically valuable. I am of course persuaded by this as much as the next literature professor. But Northrop Frye sensibly said long ago that most defenses of literature were "intelligible only to those well within the defenses" (10). We must develop arguments that convince external audiences—our students, our administrators, taxpayers, and other people who pay our salaries—arguments that are persuasive to them, and I think we need extrinsic arguments for external audiences. Arguments about workplace literacy are probably more useful here than the language of Kantian aesthetics. The other advantage of our use of arguments about real-world consequences and the instrumental value of education in English is that these arguments work well in both the school system and the world beyond academia: two of the three Rs belong in English, after all, as do grammar and rhetoric in the old trivium and quadrivium.

What place do foreign languages occupy in this? It turns out that in the new economy they too have gained in importance. If mastery of a foreign language was once associated with finishing schools, with cultural sophistication, with—as I heard it once defined—art-history majors from Vassar, the reasons for mastering a foreign language have changed in many of the same ways that the reasons for mastery of our own language have. English may well be the language of the world—or at least the world language—but it's not the only language that counts. While more Americans speak another language now than at any time since the borders were closed in 1924 (between 1980 and 1990, the figures rose from 23.1 million or 11% of the population to 31.8 million or 14% [United States 624]), it also happens that an ability to communicate in another language is an important passport to employment. The second world language is increasingly Spanish, not coincidentally the most common American language after English, spoken in 1989 by fifty-eight percent of all non-English language speakers (McArthur 80), and by far the most popular "foreign" language studied in United States high schools and colleges. But many of the various Asian languages spoken by new immigrants are also important modes of access to emerging Asian economies. So the new pragmatic arguments for English overlap powerfully with new pragmatic arguments for ability to communicate in other languages.

The consequences that flow from this have direct implications for the ecology of language use and education in the United States. The study of foreign languages has traditionally been linked with status and prestige: it was the "better" schools, in terms of class, that offered foreign languages; knowledge of other languages was seen to be an important part of the cultural capital of the privileged. In contrast, education in English was important for the production of new Americans: it was felt that we needed to beat the Italian or Polish or Norwegian or whatever out of the new immigrants, and English was central to the upward mobility of immigrant groups. Despite the current rhetoric from the right about a flood of immigrants challenging the coherence of American society and the current rhetoric from the left about the unprecedented multicultural situation in which we find ourselves, little has changed in this dynamic of assimilation and Americanization. The imperative of education in English remains as powerful as ever, and ability to communicate in English remains the sine qua non of social mobility. The children in the schools are in fact Americanizing more quickly than ever, perhaps less because of school programs than because of the power of television and other media. What is new in this situation is that Americanization does not correlate in any automatic way with success in school. (There is in fact some evidence that Americanization in cultural terms among Asian Americans negatively affects performance in school; that is, that the less assimilated students are, the better they do in school.) The children of immigrants may be learning English more quickly than in previous generations, but the question of whether they are learning the skills associated with English literacy remains open. To put this another way, there are different Englishes out there, and not all of them are compatible with — let alone essential to — academic success. The task of the English teacher in this context isn't completely clear.

The opportunities available for foreign language programs are much clearer than those available for English programs. To speak a language is never to be fully competent in it; otherwise, native speakers of English wouldn't need classes in English. The United States has a population that speaks virtually every language spoken on the globe, and this means that heritage learners are a national asset. Creative educational policy and teaching can take advantage of heritage learners to create a demand for foreign language education by those committed to cultural conservation. But this demand can also be sustained by, or can also lend support to, pragmatic arguments about the importance of internationalism and other languages in a shrinking world and global marketplace. (The kind of dialogue between English and foreign language departments represented by the MLA Teacher Education Project should help establish communicative competence in any language as a goal both groups can endorse.) The diversity of situations reported in this volume clearly shows that there can be no single national strategy here; we need a complex set of niche strategies, which might endorse Japanese in Hawai'i but French in Louisiana and Maine, Laotian in Long Beach but Vietnamese in Galveston. Spanish is an option everywhere, but a national push to make it the official second language of the school system seems to me a pragmatic and political mistake. It is also a mistake to argue that languages are important only as vehicles of cultural nostalgia for points of origin: the right is surely right to fear the Canadian mosaic as a recipe for cultural and language policy. We ought not promote Spanish or anything else as a substitute for full literacy in English, not least because our students want that full literacy in English as much as we should want it for them.

So the changing demographics of America's schools combine with the changing nature of the American and world economy to present a rich opportunity for foreign language teachers. The field will have to work to take advantage of that opportunity, for a number of reasons. Many of our future language teachers will come, or at least could come, from the heritage language population, but that is a population that is not in the pipeline to provide teachers in anything like the numbers we need. To meet the need, foreign language departments across the country must pay more attention to teacher training in just the ways the six programs in the MLA project have. An even more difficult task is to change the attitudes of foreign language departments toward what they teach. French programs have long been centers of Francophilia, which places Paris in the center of the intellectual universe, as Alice Kaplan relates with love and exasperation in her *French Lessons.* What reorientation is needed as Haitians become an important source of the demand for French courses and therefore a constituency departments need to serve? What can we do to connect to that community and show them that their knowledge of French is an important asset? The change involved here is fundamental, but it pales in comparison to other changes we will need to make to respond fully to the opportunities created by the changing linguistic heritage of Americans. One important shift involves a rethinking of what languages we are prepared to teach. Most foreign language departments, like English departments, retain their orientation toward the languages and cultures of Europe; the precedence of German or Russian, for example, over non-Western languages isn't argued as much as unconsciously assumed. Professors of any language with a colonial heritage and a postcolonial present (most Romance languages fall into this category) have a comparatively easy time broadening their field to incorporate the world, given the fact that Spanish, Portuguese, and even French have more speakers outside Europe than in Europe today. The relocation of cultural creativity in these languages outside Europe is broadening these fields for all of us. But the broadening may not necessarily broaden the mental horizon of the departments in which these foreign languages are taught: the center of

French, for example, may move from Proust to francophone literature with greater ease than the centrality of French among foreign languages can be challenged.

Part of the reason for this difficulty is the way we connect a program in a given language with tenure-track faculty members who teach that language. For most of us, a language program isn't viable unless we have a full-time faculty member with a PhD to teach in it, even though most tenure-track faculty members are no more interested in teaching French or Spanish 101 than English professors are interested in teaching freshman English. This reflexive commitment of our profession, invested in the importance of our training, unfortunately works to restrict the number of languages we teach and therefore limits our ability to take advantage of the opportunity created by an increasingly multilingual group of people interested in studying the languages of their heritage. There are two problems here: first, underrepresentation itself makes it difficult for us to find qualified, suitably credentialed teachers of lesser taught languages. The second problem is that hiring a full-time tenure-track faculty member in a given area requires evidence of a demand that is hard to demonstrate before the person is hired—particularly when the course is completely new. The two problems together are virtually insurmountable, which is why even where there is an intuition that the demand for a language exists, the threshold for beginning courses in a language is often prohibitively high.

On my campus—New Mexico State University, Las Cruces—survey after survey has shown that Native American students want the opportunity to study a Native American language and that they find the absence of such languages in our curriculum, even though we teach Portuguese and Japanese, insulting. (We have the fourth largest number of Native American students of any four-year college or university in the country.) The logical language to start with is Navajo, spoken by eighty percent of our Native American students. I believe that there is sufficient demand for Navajo to make a Navajo language program a success, and I agree with the Native American students that the lack of such a program is telling. But who would teach the course? Nowhere in the country can one earn a PhD in Navajo, and I know of no Navajos with a PhD in linguistics. Moreover, such a program would begin with a single section, from which we could build—but how could we hire a tenure-track instructor (if one were to be found) and afford to have only one course for the person to teach? Innovative solutions are needed, and since this is a project I am currently working to realize, let me say that I hope an innovative solution will be found.

As complex as the challenge the new demographics pose to foreign language instruction is, the situation grows more complex yet when we turn to my own field, English. One of the lessons driven home by recent work in theory is that education in literature has never been a purely disinterested affair, that it has always partially been about the production of citizens or, to use a somewhat different idiom, subjects. In the United States, there has historically been a significant divide in English studies between those who have a pragmatic bent aligned with the production of "good Americans" through teaching them English and those who have a less pragmatic and more aesthetic orientation toward teaching "the best that is thought and said," to use Matthew Arnold's phrase. (This divide reflects cultural and social differences not just between secondary schools and colleges but also between public and private education.) Many professors of English at the college and university level (though far fewer teachers of English in the secondary schools) have begun to question both aspects of this complex educational mission. Their questioning stands in a close relation to, and can in a sense be seen as a response to, the changing demographics. Tacitly operative in the landscape of English studies has been the acceptance of an anthropological notion of culture: no longer used in the honorific sense of high culture worth imitating and studying, culture is seen to be a phenomenon that structures people's everyday lives, not just in "high art." Accepting the notion that Western culture is the cultural practice of Europeans and white Americans and, more important, accepting the notion that it is fitting for all people to continue to have and be a member of the culture in which they were born, we have come to find very problematic the assumption that education in English should give students access to a common core of masterpieces. Among the many reasons for this shift in attitude is the composition of our classrooms: the argument runs that African American students, say, have a right to study works that express their culture and not that of other people's. The traditional orientation of academia toward Western culture has been seen as a crucial part of the deculturation of other groups, as part of a colonizing process that should be rejected. Related to this shift is a loss of confidence in a more basic kind of civilizing associated with English teachers long before Huck Finn and Tom Sawyer: the notion that it was the job of the English teacher at lower levels of the curriculum to produce students capable of good English. English in this view has indeed been a discipline in Michel Foucault's sense, producing good subjects capable of following the rules of grammar and producing discourse that is socially acceptable and that reflects the structure of the society. We have by and large lost confidence in this presumption as well, for essentially the same reason: faced with students from different cultures who are intellectually competent but speak English differently from the way we learned it, we no longer feel that it is our duty to beat the bad English out of them. The CCCC resolution of some years ago asserting "students' right to their own language" ("Students' Right") was an early expression of this. The dominant view has moved from a more Romantic and precritical notion of student individualism to a more Freirean notion of critiquing the professional discourse experts who change students into passive subjects as they teach them the language of the insider.

So no one could say that the field of English studies has ignored the emergence of new kinds of students in our classrooms. If anything, one could say that we have ignored the fact that some of our students haven't changed. The logical conclusion of the argument that each student has a right to his or her own culture should leave some room in the curriculum for the masterpieces of European literature, since this body of literature can be seen as the cultural expression of our Anglo students. If "proper English" isn't what everyone should speak but is the dialect of a certain group, then that dialect must be that group's authentic expression and have value for that group. These arguments are nonstarters in the present context, in just the way that, on campuses where all-black student groups receive approbation and financial support, white student groups are stigmatized as divisive and racist. It seems to me that despite the demographic shifts sketched above, our student body is likely to remain majority-majority for a long time, so those who accept the culture-of-one's-own way of thinking implicitly concede a continuing central role for European literature in the curriculum. There are issues here we simply haven't thought through carefully.

It would be a mistake, however, to present the contribution of the new demographics to curricular questions in English studies as purely negative. The most exciting development in literature in English over the past century has been the emergence of powerful writing worldwide: not just the literary language of England and the United States, English has been a vehicle for creative expression on every continent and from a wide range of countries. The most exciting development in English studies over the past decade or two has been the emergence of postcolonial studies, the study of the literature in English produced by former British and American colonies around the world. To a large extent, this development has been stimulated by the new demographics: with Indian or African students in our classes, we have felt the need to find something they can relate to; comparably, interest in literature written by ethnic minorities in the United States has been spurred by their growing presence in the classes we teach.

This broadening perspective represents an opportunity for English departments in much the same way that heritage languages represent an opportunity for foreign language departments. On my campus, I introduced a course in Chicano literature in the English department despite the historical attitude of the Chicano Studies Program, housed administratively in the Department of Languages and Linguistics, that Chicano literature was theirs and we shouldn't teach it. The introduction of the course was in direct response to Chicano students who felt that the English department's failure to teach Chicano literature showed gross insensitivity to their concerns. Enrollment in the very successful offerings of Chicano Literature that have followed remain overwhelmingly Chicano, just as a large percentage of the students in our Native American Literature course are Native American, particularly now that we have a tenure-track Native American faculty member to teach the course. Students convinced that what they want to study is "their literature" constitute a growing population, which the tactically astute English department will wish to attract to its courses.

But such an approach will only go so far. Just as the niches created by heritage language learners, however important, do not do away with the need to convince monolingual Americans that they too need to learn a foreign language precisely because their own language isn't the only one worth knowing, we need a rationale for literary study that will state the case for studying the literature of others. The canonical revolution of the last generation, which has been so fruitful in bringing new writers to our attention, has not succeeded in producing a theoretical rationale why these writers should retain that attention: we have shied away from calling them great or aesthetically powerful, convinced as we are that the language of aesthetic evaluation in the past has been a cover for the privileging of Eurocentric values. Saying that we should study them because they represent a certain group gives us a reason to study categories of work, not individual works; thus the individual work is subsumed and in a sense lost in the larger category. This approach can also be criticized as culturally condescending, elitist, and not responsive to the individual identity of the writer. More important, it doesn't give outsiders a reason to study a given literature, and we need such a reason in order to justify our reading any work not produced by our own culture, however we define that culture.

The canonical revolution is largely positive and has brought excitement to the field, but the theoretical buttressing for that revolution has been less successful. Over the past decade or so, we have made a real effort to think through the implication of the arrival of new students into our classrooms from the point of view of those students, taken one by one or, rather, group by group. What do Chicanos or African Americans or Native Americans bring to and want to take away from a literature course? We have not yet put those points of view in the context of the whole class and the whole curriculum: Beyond a course in Chicano literature, what else should the student interested in Chicano literature take, whether that student is Chicano or not? How does a class fully representative of the complexity of America's population read a set of works also representative of that complexity? We need to move beyond the particularity of specific populations reading works by and about themselves: we need to do this in order to include everyone in the room, and ourselves, productively in the classroom dynamic.

The situation in the composition classroom is comparable in many important respects to that of the literature classroom. The last generation has seen a pendulum swing away from the old, teacher-oriented pedagogy toward a new pedagogy aimed at empowering the student. Although this swing has been motivated—at least in part—by our growing awareness of ethnic and racial difference, there are ironies in the new pedagogy. First, the new students in our classrooms are there for the reason immigrants have always been in our classes: they want to learn "proper English" as a vehicle of professional and social mobility. If we deny them what they want because we don't think that they should want it, we are still playing the role of authoritarian teacher we are seeking to avoid. Moreover, if we deny them because we feel that full education in English will deculturate them, we are ignoring important facts about the ecology of English today. I do not believe that culture and education are a zero-sum game in which the gaining of competence in English must somehow produce an equal and corresponding loss of one's original identity and culture. Surely the phenomenon of English as a world language—taken for granted as an official language in Singapore and India, in South Africa and Nigeria—suggests that this is not an either-or choice. Wole Soyinka and Salman Rushdie, V. S. Naipaul and Anita Desai—these postcolonial writers speak our language and speak to us powerfully, but what they say expresses a position and identity different from ours. The Soweto uprising in the 1970s—the beginning of the end for apartheid—was sparked when education in English was denied the residents of Soweto: what warrant is there to assume that these students were wrong in seeing English as crucial to their liberation, not as a tool of oppression?

Most positive in the changes in English studies over the past generation has been an increasing internationalization driven by our growing awareness of literature in English beyond our borders. A valuable side-effect of this internationalization is the possibility that the divide between English and foreign language departments can be bridged: as we both concern ourselves with the cultures and literary expressions of the world, as we see that English is one more foreign language and that Spanish and other languages are perfectly good American languages, it may become more evident that we have concerns in common and that we can learn from each other. If we in English have grown uneasy with our role of producing citizens in the sense of good Americans, the traditional orientation of foreign languages toward communicative competence in and appreciation of a given language may be a useful model. Communicating well, in English or in any language, is a boon. Surely we want those who have come to this country speaking other languages to become full participants in American life and culture (above all, in order to be able to enrich that life and culture), but they cannot without a command of English. Just as surely, we want to foster a greater command of other languages by monolingual Americans, whatever their race and ethnicity.

I suggest that we subsume our goal of advancing communicative competence in an array of languages under a redefinition of the project of producing good citizens. Those made politically uncomfortable with the traditional project of producing good Americans, either because of what they see as its ethnocentricity or its cultural nationalism, still ought to appreciate the social role it assigns to English instruction. We can welcome the fact that English instruction has had a social role, even where we might question the specific role. The project need not be rejected as much as broadened: I'm just utopian enough to think that education in languages and literatures can play a central role in the production of good world citizens, and I believe that is how we should redefine our task. This redefined project would provide an overarching goal nearly all of us could identify with and to which all our different professional specializations could contribute.

What of teacher training? I have been talking all along about what we need to teach our future teachers. They should have a rich sense of the world in which they live, with its clash of identities, languages, values, and cultures. I know of no better way to get a feel for that richness (short of direct experiences) than by reading the literature that expresses it. Future teachers will learn more about the scene of instruction in multiracial and multicultural America by reading literature written in and about such contexts, specifically by reading postcolonial literature, than from anything else. Where they do not understand, they will experience what it is like not to understand; where they feel frustrated, they will experience the frustration of cross-cultural understanding firsthand. We need teachers who are able to understand the experience of learners: "the best that is thought and said" of our time—which I take to be the literature of the postcolonial world—will change attentive readers' imaginative apprehension of the world. If teachers are to create world citizens, they must be world citizens themselves. Teaching these teachers both places a burden on us and offers us an opportunity. The world is a complex place, and our teaching must model its complexity for the future teachers who are our students.

Note

[1]For information about and careful analysis of this trend, see Miller.

WORKS CITED

Frye, Northrop. *Anatomy of Criticism: Four Essays.* Princeton: Princeton UP, 1957.

Kaplan, Alice Yaeger. *French Lessons: A Memoir.* Chicago: U of Chicago P, 1993.

McArthur, Edith K. *Language Characteristics and Schooling in the United States: A Changing Picture.* United States Dept. of Educ. Office of Educ. Research and Improvement. Washington: GPO, 1993.

Miller, L. Scott. *An American Imperative: Accelerating Minority Educational Advancement.* New Haven: Yale UP, 1995.

"Students' Right to Their Own Language." *College Composition and Communication* 25 (1974): 1–32.

United States. Dept. of Commerce. Bureau of the Census. *1990 Census of Population and Housing.* Washington: GPO, 1992.

HAROLD H. KOLB, JR.

Connecting Universities and Schools: A Case Study

An indispensable function of education, at every level, is to provide sound training in the fundamental ways of thinking represented by history, science, mathematics, literature, language, art, and the other disciplines that evolved in the course of mankind's long quest for usable knowledge, cultural understanding, and intellectual power. To advance moral conduct, responsible citizenship, and social adjustment is, of course, a vital function of education. But, like the other agencies which contribute to these ends, the school must work within the context provided by its own characteristic activity. In other words, the particular contribution which the school can make is determined by, and related to, the primary fact that it is an agency of intellectual training.

Arthur Bestor, *The Restoration of Learning*

How We Began

The Center for the Liberal Arts began as an experiment. Given what appeared to be the decreasing effectiveness of American schooling and given the expertise of universities in precisely those fields of knowledge in which the schools seemed deficient, a group of concerned faculty members at the University of Virginia came together in 1984 to discuss the following questions:

Does the University of Virginia have a responsibility to other levels of education — a responsibility to help define what Americans need to know and to assist in improving the teaching of the academic disciplines throughout the Commonwealth of Virginia?

Could outstanding faculty members be recruited for the effort?

Should preservice and in-service teachers be seen as part of the constituency of the College and Graduate School of Arts and Sciences and not just of the School of Education?

Could professors and K-12 schoolteachers work together?

Our tentative answer to these questions was yes, and we set about to test it by going to the schools to talk — and, more important, to listen —

to teachers and administrators. From these conversations, we concluded that no one, and everyone, is to blame for problems in the schools. Schools of education have dealt themselves out of academic subjects by focusing too exclusively on the affective side of learning. Arts and sciences professors—charged with creating and disseminating society's knowledge—have not recognized their role in disseminating this knowledge, through K–12 teachers, to the forty-six million students who make up the country's largest, and ultimately most important, group of knowledge consumers. Superintendents and principals are too likely to have been trained as administrative managers rather than as intellectual leaders. Parents, often juggling two jobs, have sometimes worried more about child care than child education. A system has grown up in which the academic training of teachers, the learning of those people we have put in charge of teaching learning, has been neglected. It is certainly true that there are knowledgeable people who are not good teachers. But that truism has an even more important counterpart: there are no good teachers who are not knowledgeable. We must do a better job of empowering teachers, and empowerment must include intellectual empowerment as well as increased salaries, telephones, computer networks, and a greater share in school governance. A social studies teacher with whom we talked stated: "You seem to be suggesting that to do my job well I need to be something of a historian, not just a history teacher. That's a novel idea, and it was never brought up in any of my training. But I like the idea, and I think you are right. Can you help me?"

What We Did

Armed with these insights, we returned to the university to see what could be done. Many of the difficulties of school education were clearly beyond our reach, but helping to improve the teaching and the learning of the arts and sciences disciplines in the schools seemed not only a possibility but also a responsibility. Our first task was to approach the president, the board of visitors, the provost, and the deans, for our vision had implications for the entire university. This approach was welcomed, and it came at precisely the right moment in our history. With confidence born of its recent emergence as a major international research institution, the University of Virginia was prepared to enlarge its mission statement to include the schools. A survey of arts and sciences faculty members revealed that 214 professors were ready to help. Some of these faculty members had served on a committee that persuaded the administration to largely eliminate the degree of bachelor of science in education and to require that most teacher candidates enroll in regular arts and science majors. This change led to a five-year double-degree program (BA-MT) for teacher candidates, and the average SAT scores of students going into teaching climbed from 1000 to 1200.

The next step was to create a permanent structure, the Center for the Liberal Arts—to be funded by the university, the state, and public and private foundations—in order to create and administer programs for schoolteachers and to establish an ongoing relation between the university and the schools. When an English high school chair unveiled her cynicism about what she called "the two-year phenomenon—you are really interested in us until the grant runs out and then you disappear," we appointed her to a three-year term on our advisory council.

We soon discovered that each discipline taught in the schools needed separate study. Thus we designed a procedure for investigating the issues and problems related to a given subject, for determining what improvements should and could be made, and for setting about to achieve them. This procedure has three stages:

Research. At the beginning we interview teachers and administrators, send out questionnaires, study school curricula, sample texts, and make a preliminary assessment of the issues.

Analysis. After completing the research phase, we bring together a group of teachers, administrators, school board members, state and community officials, experts in the field, and citizens for a five-day workshop in Charlottesville. This group considers the issues generated in the first stage, sponsors additional research as needed, makes recommendations, and outlines a specific plan for implementing the recommendations.

Action. After the workshop, the center refines and implements the workshop plan, which typically includes new graduate courses for teachers, in-service workshops, fellowships, opportunities for study abroad, and other programs appropriate to each discipline.

This model—research, analysis, action—has three aspects that distinguish it from conventional committee meetings and reports. The first is that it provides for an extensive investigation of issues, using a format that is based on university research procedures. Additionally, it builds in the participation of diverse groups—participation that gives us better decisions as well as greater authority when we take those decisions into the public arena. And finally, it establishes a specific and feasible plan of action.

The first plan we devised was for American literature. With assistance from the National Endowment for the Humanities, we created two kinds of programs to help schoolteachers increase their knowledge of texts, authors, and issues in American and modern literature and in American studies. During the school year, when teachers find that their heavy workloads make authentic graduate course work difficult—"I can't teach five courses and read *Moby-Dick* for Monday evenings"—we offered lectures, discussions, and colloquia that were correlated to texts being used in Virginia classrooms. These meetings between faculty members and schoolteachers were received enthusiastically by the teachers. One teacher put it this way: "You have hit on an area that really counts—refreshing the classroom teacher with content-based lectures. Rather than educational technique lectures, we need more ideas and information about literature."

During the summer, we offered, in Charlottesville and at school sites, intensive graduate courses that allowed teachers to transcend school curricula and units; to experience the challenge and pleasure of reading, research, and thinking that ranges beyond textbooks; to become scholars. The teachers' responses to these rigorous programs were even more enthusiastic than those for the lecture series, moving from the metaphor of refreshment to that of nourishment. One participant sent us the following note after attending a three-week poetry institute:

> In the seven years that I have been teaching English on the high school level I have taken required courses in how to teach reading, how to teach handicapped students, community health, how to teach elementary math(!), how to avoid being prejudiced against minorities, and how teacher interaction can lead to student achievement. It should be apparent why a course in poetry with not a "how-to" in sight would be food for the soul for someone who decided to teach literature because of a love for it.

These semester and summer programs proved that our initial assessment was accurate. Teachers were indeed eager to learn, and their gratefulness for the opportunity helped recruit faculty members, who for their part enjoyed discussing literature and sharing their knowledge with committed adults.

Following this start, and using the research-analysis-action procedure that we had established, we gradually brought the other disciplines on line. By 1990, we had organized programs in all subject areas for teachers throughout the state. At that point, with administrative support from the

Virginia General Assembly; with program support from NEH, the National Science Foundation, the Exxon Foundation, and the Andrew W. Mellon Foundation; and with a number of partnerships established with other institutions, we set about to increase the number of faculty members involved, to expand our range of topics, and to touch the lives and minds of more teachers. These goals have been achieved: as of spring 1999 we have created, for 9,422 Virginia teachers, graduate courses, lecture series, in-service programs, fellowships, and overseas study programs involving 393 arts and sciences faculty members—241 from the University of Virginia and 152 from 56 other colleges and universities. Our experiment has proved more successful than we had hoped, and the Center for the Liberal Arts is now established as a distinctive and permanent part of the University of Virginia, one that, according to the National Endowment for the Humanities, is "almost unprecedented in its cooperative action between a leading university and a state school system" (Richard Ekman, qtd. in "University of Virginia Project").

Why It Worked

The success of the center is based on what William McDonough, the "Green Dean" of the University of Virginia's School of Architecture, would call sustainable design, in terms both of organizational structure and program configuration. The simple fact that the center is a permanent organization has had far-reaching implications, which were illustrated by a recent discussion I had with the director of a private foundation. He had sent questionnaires to the principal investigators of all the educational projects that his organization had funded in the last two decades, asking for comments on the continuing value of these projects. Only five percent replied, a disappointment that has since led the foundation to turn its emphasis away from colleges and universities. "We think these were good projects," said the foundation director, "but they seem to have bloomed and died. There hasn't been enough continuity, enough accretion, enough momentum to sustain and spread the ideas they embodied."

In the last decade and a half, the Center for the Liberal Arts has become a gradually deepening repository of information and expertise concerning school-university collaboration and faculty member–schoolteacher relationships. Our faculty project directors (we have one in each academic discipline) and instructors have come to regard schoolteachers not as students but as professional colleagues in a community of learners; they have determined how to help teachers both to satisfy their immediate classroom needs and to soar beyond them. Our permanent status has given us the opportunity to recruit the best faculty members and to build our activities into the university's reward system. School-university collaboration at the University of Virginia is no longer regarded as "a valuable form of service"—often the kiss of death in promotion and tenure meetings—but as a significant and challenging form of teaching and research. With the schools, our ongoing operation has allayed cynicism about short-lived interest and has given us the time to negotiate the triangulation required for successful programs—triangulation between the demands of the discipline, the expressed needs of schoolteachers and school systems, and the expertise and interests of faculty members. The many teachers who have taken our programs provide a reservoir of advice for creating new programs; and, increasingly, alumni of CLA programs are participating as workshop leaders and institute coinstructors.

The center's permanence gives school-university collaboration a local habitation and a name and puts us in a position to contribute to discussions on a wide range of educational issues. It is a place where the state board of education can come for assistance in defining graduation requirements, and our investigation helped persuade them to mandate, for the first time in the state, an arts requirement for all Virginia students. The center is where our Phi Beta Kappa chapter turned when it wished to demonstrate extramural citizenship, and that organization now endows an annual summer fellowship for teachers. The center's permanence keeps the flag of collaboration high, and it has led us to the point where schoolteachers in the state—regardless of where they took their degrees—are now regarded as an important constituency of the University of Virginia. The fact of permanence has also lowered costs for individual programs, for there is a large expense in starting up a single activity from scratch, and a lot of waste in shutting one down. And finally, permanence has allowed us to form ongoing ties to other units and organizations.

We began with partnerships—working with academic departments, the Graduate School of Arts and Sciences, the state Council of Higher Education, the Division of Continuing Education—because that seemed like a good way to get started; we soon found that it was a good way to continue. Partnerships bring additional expertise and experience to a project, expand the resource pool of funds and faculty members, provide uniquely appropriate locations for activities, and extend our reach. As we initiated projects in the various disciplines, we made common cause with a number of partners: the Folger Shakespeare Library, Valentine Museum, Monticello, Virginia Foundation for the Humanities, the University of

Virginia's Valencia program, the University of Bonn's Transatlantic Summer Academy, Wolf Trap Foundation for the Performing Arts, North Carolina Shakespeare Festival, American Academy in Rome, Centre International d'Etudes Françaises d'Angers, Virginia Commission for the Arts, English-Speaking Union, Piedmont Virginia Community College, History Teaching Alliance, and the Virginia components of the American Association of Teachers of German and the American Association of Teachers of Spanish and Portuguese.

In some cases we joined or created coalitions of partners. In order to assist teachers of dramatic arts, we designed a Virginia Institute for Theater Arts that linked the University of Virginia, Virginia Tech, and Virginia Commonwealth University drama departments with the Heritage Repertory Theater and brought together faculty members, professional actors, graduate students, undergraduates, schoolteachers, and high school students (who served as an acting company under the direction of the teachers, who were themselves under the direction of faculty members) from around the state. Partnerships, we have discovered, not only increase the activities we can make available to teachers; they also, like permanence, decrease costs.

Providing high-quality programs at a low cost to outside funders has been an ongoing goal of the center and one that is particularly useful in the current climate of restricted funding. This aspect of our work is not a matter of doing programs on the cheap, for we believe in recruiting our strongest faculty members and remunerating them appropriately, and we believe in providing schoolteachers with the kinds of treatment and opportunities associated with a distinguished university. Many teachers have had their commitment to learning and teaching subtly strengthened by a luncheon in the Dome Room of the Rotunda, a conversation with Isabel Allende or Mempo Giardinelli or Helmut Kohl, or an opportunity to work with original manuscripts in the Barrett Collection. The trick has been to create ongoing support, funding alliances, and resource-sharing partnerships—with university departments, the Virginia General Assembly, the Virginia Council of Higher Education, school divisions, and other institutions, such as museums. We have now reached the point where our administrative expenses are subsidized internally, instructional costs are largely built into the university's regular operation, and other expenses are shared by partners and funded by foundations. This efficiency gives us a large dollar-for-dollar impact and allows us to offer more programs and reach a greater number of teachers, far beyond the small group of outstanding teachers (often those least in need of further training) who normally win fellowships and institute residencies.

Program design for the center has been a matter of constant revision, as we have gradually sharpened our understanding of school-university collaboration. We believe we now know the ingredients of good programs for schoolteachers, which require, in the first place, our best faculty members—those who realize that schoolteachers are colleagues who are proficient in teaching children. Experts in their fields, these distinguished scholars enjoy the challenge and have the ability to bring their expertise out into the world. Our faculty members also need to be flexible, for schoolteachers vary widely in their knowledge, and school systems differ in their methods of bringing teachers together, furnishing us with audiences of experts in one location, generalists in another. Providing assistance to schoolteachers is, as our most successful faculty members understand, a challenging intellectual enterprise that often requires reshaping and even rethinking aspects of their disciplines—rethinking that has implications for colleges and universities as well as for the secondary schools. Our classicists have increasingly come to believe that Latin teachers, and undergraduate classics majors, need to be educated not just in language and literature but in the history, art, architecture, and religion of Greek and Roman civilization as well. The more our modern foreign language professors work with schoolteachers, the more both groups eschew the notion that language study is a matter of grammar in school and literature in college. Whether in the third grade or the thirteenth, learning a foreign language requires a blend of linguistic, literary, and cultural study. And the extraordinary demographic changes that have transformed American schools—a small elementary school two miles from the University of Virginia now enrolls students who are native speakers of twenty-three different languages—have provided a specific context that has helped our history and literature scholars realize how historical interpretations and literary canons are shaped in social and political as well as intellectual arenas. Our schools are the outer banks of social change, and they experience first the waves that wash up later on the shores of the university.

Successful programs for schoolteachers also require careful planning, which needs to start almost a year in advance in order to allow for consultation with prospective participants. Many rounds of revision are needed to precisely tune teacher needs and faculty expertise, to achieve the delicate balance necessary for our teacher-scholar audience. Schoolteachers are, understandably enough, pragmatists. With an eye on the next day's classes, they scoop up handouts and seek ideas that can be plowed quickly back into the classroom. Our best programs simultaneously meet this demand for relevance and resist it, helping teachers with their immediate concerns but also deepening their knowledge for the future, often in ways whose applications cannot be foreseen.

We have also found we need to plan well in advance so that teachers can fit summer seminars into the complex rhythms of state recertification, school curriculum changes, and personal plans and vacations. Adequate planning allows for building in the participation of distinguished guest lecturers, of museums and other appropriate institutions. And it provides time to put in place a funding package, often in cooperation with school administrators, that achieves the center's goal of paying all expenses for all teachers in all of our programs.

Finally, we have learned that the small details of logistics can make a large difference, such as texts supplied well in advance of a course, comfortable quarters arranged for study and discussion, and flexibility in allowing the schoolteachers to determine their own course projects and credit/noncredit options. These details are received with gratitude by teachers, who take them as signs, as one fellowship winner put it, "that we, and what we do, are respected and valued by the society whose children we teach."

Where We Are Headed

We passed our fifteenth anniversary in 1999 with a feeling of accomplishment and confidence, yet much of what we have learned has persuaded us how much more there is to be done. The reform movement in American education is still groping. The ambitious goals pronounced by the President's Education Summit in 1989, in Charlottesville, remain embarrassingly unrealized, except in rhetoric. There is a kind of curious anti-intellectualism that manifests itself in contemporary American schools. This trait can never entirely be reformed or restructured or wished away, for it has deep roots in American history and values. But anti-intellectualism can be resisted, and schools should be the first line of defense.

The Center for the Liberal Arts and analogous efforts need to have a more profound impact. Having learned to work with individual teachers, we now need to work with entire school faculties and with school divisions. Having developed a cadre of faculty members skilled in teaching teachers, we must now recruit whole university departments. Having worked successfully with individual texts and topics and courses, we now need to become involved with entire school curricula. And having assisted more than 9,000 Virginia schoolteachers, we need to reach out to their 63,000 colleagues who have not been involved in center programs. While we value our alliances with highly competent senior teachers from strong school divisions who quickly sign up for our programs, we need to work more extensively with less confident teachers, with more middle and elementary schools, with smaller and more remote school divisions. These, of course, are general goals. Here are some ways that we plan specifically to achieve them in the coming years:

1. Extend the impact of summer seminars and institutes.

Most schoolteachers leave summer courses with high levels of intellectual stimulation and future resolve. In order to reinforce that stimulation and to assist teachers in putting their resolve into practice, both in terms of individual learning and school improvement, we need to offer more follow-up workshops. Typically held on a Saturday during the fall or spring semester, the one-day workshop brings teachers together once again with their seminar instructor. The day begins with a morning session, during which the teachers discuss the ways their summer learning has been applied, share ideas with one another, and retroactively critique the summer program. Then, after a communal luncheon, the instructor (occasionally a team of instructors) presents new materials and ideas that build on the work done in the previous summer. We also find that inviting the participants to bring administrators and teacher colleagues to the workshop sessions assists both in the translation of ideas into curricula and in the recruitment of new teachers for later programs.

2. Invite teachers to attend workshops and courses in teams.

Most of our activities thus far have been aimed at, and achieved their success with, individual schoolteachers. Although there is a good deal of rhetoric in the education community about the multiplication factor—teachers are supposed to return from courses and workshops to conduct in-service programs and share their new knowledge with their colleagues—such dissemination seems to happen haphazardly and infrequently. But the multiplication factor can be energized, we have found, when two or three teachers from one school or school division attend a program together. They return to their home institutions with greater momentum, with the opportunity of continuing discussion with one another, and with the confidence of a group. Thus they are more likely to be able to effect changes in both formal settings—curriculum and textbook committees and in-service programs—and in informal exchanges with their colleagues.

Schoolteachers grouped by the discipline they teach tend to create a community of the intellect, to think of themselves not just as teachers but also as historians, literary critics, mathematicians, foreign language experts, scientists. And that attitude enables them to keep from being swallowed by organizational categories based on buildings, grade levels, and student abilities. A critical mass of teachers also has more influence with administrators—those persons who, in all but the most radically reformed schools, control the process by which texts are chosen, the curriculum is developed, and in-service programs are designed and supported. Arts and sciences faculty members have too long ignored school administrators, and we plan to invite curriculum coordinators, principals, and other administrators to a number of our activities for teachers.

3. Develop intensive relationships with entire school divisions.

In order to create systemic change, we need to work within the system, recruiting the encouragement and endorsement of superintendents and principals, designing programs in conjunction with both teachers and administrators, reaching large numbers of teachers at all levels. Such a strategy would link the power of universities—storehouses of the world's knowledge, centers for advanced research, agencies of dissemination—with the power of the schools to reach every American child in establishing the intellectual foundations for citizenship, vocations, and life.

What we need are ongoing networks of collegial relationships between schools and universities as institutions, and between schoolteachers and professors as coworkers. We need to make it possible for schoolteachers not simply to take a course but also to have frequent and easy access to the life of the university. We envisage, for example, ongoing colloquia at the university led by department chairs and senior scholars that update schoolteachers on issues and trends in the disciplines and keep them informed about developments in undergraduate and graduate studies. Reciprocally, we need to send faculty members out to the schools to discuss texts and ideas in specific disciplines and to participate as well in on-site conversations about adopting texts, instituting new curricula, creating interdisciplinary courses, and coordinating programs between colleges, high schools, and middle and elementary schools.

In our continuing quest to work more closely with school administrators and to make it easier for them to understand the various university resources available, the center is currently working with other University of Virginia organizations to design a Consortium for the Education of Teachers. This partnership, "whose purpose is to assist schools and teachers in keeping current in areas of knowledge and strategies of instruction" ("University of Virginia Consortium"), will include, among others, such units as Arts and Sciences, Curry School of Education, Center for Instructional Technologies, Jefferson Area Mathematics Teachers' Project, and Summer Foreign Language Institute. The consortium's charter, in its present draft version, reads as follows:

> The consortium arranges courses, programs, and fellowships for teachers in such fields as English language and literature, history and social studies, mathematics, science, foreign language, fine arts, special education, educational psychology, reading, linguistics, technology, and multicultural awareness. We are especially interested in designing, in cooperation with school administrators and teachers, comprehensive and ongoing in-service programs tailored to the specific needs of individual school divisions and groups of contiguous school divisions.

4. Assist teachers with the new technologies.

Technology in the schools is a much discussed but not always understood subject, and political sloganeering has not helped: "a computer in every classroom" is about as useful as a horse in every cavalry company. Just what is the state of computing in Virginia schools? What equipment is in place, and what are the levels of expertise among schoolteachers and students? In order to determine these facts before attempting to offer technological instruction to teachers, we conducted a state-wide survey in the winter of 1996–97. What we found, not surprisingly, was a huge variation in equipment and skills from school to school, a feeling among many teachers that they have missed the electronic boat, and an absence of programs that connect information technology to the academic disciplines, especially the humanities disciplines. Most schools are undersupplied with hardware, software, and Internet connections; most teachers are undersupported in their efforts to use the new information technologies.

We did find in our survey that school administrators are very interested in technology. That interest is appropriate, since finding, using, creating, and storing information is what education is all about and precisely what the computer and the Internet assist with so brilliantly. The current focus on technology in K–12 is timely, since schools seem to be lagging behind society and schoolteachers are lagging behind other professionals, sometimes even their students. State education officials are also focused on technology, but the problem with the state approach to computer literacy for schoolteachers is that it ignores the application of technology to the subjects actually taught. The "Technology Standards for Instructional Personnel," adopted by the State Board of Education in June 1996, treats computer literacy as a separate subject. These standards fail to mention a single field of study to which computers might be applied, and their general recommendations—"operate a computer system," "utilize software," "apply knowledge of terms"—are unanchored to any reference to specific hardware or software, search engine, or browser. More ominous is the provision in these standards that computer literacy might itself be substituted for "content" knowledge: "Course work in technology will satisfy the content requirement for licensure renewal for license holders who do not have a master's degree" ("Technology Standards" 2; item 1.4).

Teachers know better, and they are asking for ways to use technology to deepen their learning and improve their instruction in the disciplines they teach: "What is out there in my field?" "How do I find it?" "How good is it?" "How can I use it in my classroom?" These sensible questions deserve content-specific answers, and here the center is well positioned to provide a response. Advanced information technology is not a destination but a vehicle, not a "content area" but a tool for more efficient learning and teaching of language, literature, history, math, science, and art. Our faculty members are quickly becoming expert in the use of this ever-evolving tool, and the University of Virginia has emerged as a world leader in the application of information technology to humanities teaching and learning. Our Electronic Text Center is now receiving 131,000 hits (49,000 accesses) a day on its various electronic products.

5. Extend our outreach.

Dissemination of information to other institutions has always been an implicit part of the center's mission. Since the beginning, the center founders and participating faculty members have been interested not simply in a production line of programs but also in the philosophy of collaboration, in getting it right, in establishing (as our dean of faculty put it) a benchmark for school-university cooperation.

In 1987, this aspect of our mission became intensified, for, in rapid succession, the center was featured in an article in *Change* magazine and received awards from the State Council of Higher Education, the Virginia

Board of Education (for leadership in "the rejuvenation of elementary and secondary education"), and the National University Continuing Education Association (for "innovative and creative programming"). This new level of visibility led to requests for information from outside the state, and we began a series of consultations, sharing what we had learned, making our example available to others at meetings and conferences, making visits elsewhere and hosting visits to Charlottesville. We will continue such activities, and we propose now to make them an explicit and formal part of our mission, building them into our schedule and our budget. In addition, we will intensify our outreach effort by expanding our new Web site and serving as a mentor to other institutions.

The center's Web site (www.virginia.edu/~libarts) was designed to provide Virginia schoolteachers with current information about CLA programs and fellowships, and to allow them to register for programs electronically. It includes a calendar of events and detailed descriptions of our offerings. The site is organized to expand teachers' knowledge and to help them use technology effectively in their specific content areas. The classics section, for example, contains annotated lists of online classics resources and is divided into subsections for different types of classics instructors: elementary school mythology teachers, high school mythology teachers, social studies teachers, and Latin teachers. Teachers using the classics section are able to request information using the Ask a Professor feature, and their electronic questions are forwarded to appropriate professors. This feature, included with each discipline section, is a response to earlier requests from teachers for "a telephone hot line to the faculty." The discipline pages also provide a Make a Suggestion box, which connects the user to the center by e-mail. The Internet allows us to fine-tune our offerings as comments are received from teachers, and it allows teachers, no matter how geographically remote their school districts, to enter the communities of scholars that bind academic disciplines together. We anticipate that, as schoolteachers become more fluent electronically, their use of our Web site will increase exponentially.

In addition to offering content-specific guidance to schoolteachers throughout the year, the center's Web site offers opportunities, during our institutes and other programs, for teachers to evaluate the site and to contribute to it the fruits of their scholarship and the teaching materials they develop. Finally, the Web site provides a model of collaboration foranalogous endeavors elsewhere, allowing us to share program and organizational information with individuals and institutions attempting similar projects in other states.

Mentoring was new to the center in 1993, when we were asked to be a "mentor institution" by the Association of American Colleges in its project Strengthening Humanities Foundations for Teachers (Johnson). We soon discovered that mentoring was a powerful strategy for modeling and change. The long discussions and on-site visits with other institutions facilitated by this project created relationships that were both intensive and expansive, allowing, for example, the right people to be recruited by both partners and necessary changes to be made to ideas transplanted to new climates. The difference between a presentation and a mentorship, we discovered, was the difference between a lecture and a tutorial, or between an after-school discussion with teachers and a summer institute.

School-University Collaboration in the Twenty-First Century

We stand now on the threshold of a new phase. We have answered the questions with which we began: the University of Virginia does have a responsibility to assist in improving the learning and the teaching of the academic disciplines in the schools, our best faculty members have agreed to assist, the university now offers graduate courses in arts and sciences for in-service teachers, and professors and schoolteachers have joined together in fruitful partnerships. We have established a permanent structure for school-university cooperation, and we have learned how to deliver powerful and appropriate courses and programs for schoolteachers. Now we need to take the next step and, building on our experience, extend the impact of our activities from individuals to school divisions throughout the Commonwealth of Virginia and, by example, to other states.

Support for the work of the center has remained steady, even in difficult times. Many academic centers in Virginia higher education have been terminated, and others have sustained substantial cuts in state allocations. The Center for the Liberal Arts continues to be funded, and at the same time the support for our programs from school divisions has increased. Sixty-three percent of the superintendents now contribute to programs in which their teachers are enrolled for academic credit. With an administrative structure in place and supported, with faculty members experienced in working with schoolteachers already recruited, and with extensive contacts with teachers and school systems well established, the center is in an excellent position to move forward. With outside funding for program support—none is needed for start-up costs, space, computers, personnel, or the basic platform of administration provided by the state—we are prepared to make the transition from isolated improvements to systemic change on both sides of the educational equation. On the one hand, we hope to convince the schools that knowledge and scholarship are essential components of every teacher's continuing education, that mastery of the discipline is the sine qua non of good teaching. On the other hand, we wish to further our campaign to persuade colleges and universities that schoolteachers, and ultimately their students, are an essential part of the constituency of higher education.

WORKS CITED

Johnson, Joseph S., Jr. Letter to the author. 4 Feb. 1994.

"Technology Standards for Instructional Personnel, Authorized by the Board of Education for the Virginia Register of Regulations' Provisions of the Administrative Process Act." 27 June 1996.

"University of Virginia Consortium for the Education of Teachers." Draft document. Center for the Liberal Arts. 28 Feb. 1999.

"University of Virgiinia Project for Teachers Is Bold, Simple." *Richmond Times-Dispatch* 1 Jan. 1986:1.

APPENDIX

Representative Programs for Schoolteachers Offered by the Center for the Liberal Arts

Since 1983, more than 230 University of Virginia faculty members (along with faculty members from other institutions, as well as writers, artists, ambassadors, and museum personnel) have offered programs for some 9,000 Virginia schoolteachers. In the sampling of these activities given below, program type is indicated by the following key: (s) = seminars and residential institutes, (l-d) = lecture-discussion series, (w) = workshops, (s-a) = study-abroad fellowships, (sp) = special programs.

The Arts

American Art: Themes and Approaches (s)
Art History: Practice and Interpretation (s)
Tour to National Gallery of Art, Washington, DC (l-d)
Using Art in the English and Social Studies Classroom (l-d)
Visual Literacy for English and Social Studies Teachers (l-d)
Are the Arts Important? (w)
Coalition Conference on the Arts in Education (w)
Artist-in-Residence (sp)

Chemistry

The Chemical Web of Life on Planet Earth (satellite TV course; l-d)

Classics

Ancient Athens: Its Life, Literature, and Culture (s)
Ancient Literature and the Modern World (s)
Athenian and American Democracy: The Ideals and Realities (s)
Classical Archaeology: Rome and Roman Italy (s)
Classical Mythology in Literature, Art, and Film (s)
Selected Readings of Augustan Poets (s)
Seven Greek Tragedies in Translation (s)
The Augustan Age (l-d)
Classics for English Teachers (l-d)
Mythology and the Emergence of Greek Gods (l-d)
The Romans and Their World (l-d)
Understanding the Greeks and the Romans through Their Literature (l-d)
Preparation and Training for Teachers of Latin (w)
Teaching the Ancient World (w)
Homer's *Odyssey* (w)
Fellowships to study the ancient world in Greece or Italy at the American Academy in Rome, the American School of Classical Studies in Athens, and the Vergilian Society's Villa Vergiliana in Naples (s-a)

English

American Literature: 1912–1930 (s)
The American West: Fact, Symbol, Myth (s)
Contemporary American Poetry (s)
The Doom of Romance (s)
Faulkner (s)
Film Theory (s)
Forms and Practices of Fiction (s)
The Harlem Renaissance (s)
Hawthorne and Faulkner (s)
Major Works of Southern Literature (s)
Modern American Poetry (s)
Modernism and the Novel in the Twentieth Century (s)
Reading, Understanding, and Teaching Poetry (s)
Studies in Contemporary Fiction (s)
American and British Romanticism (l-d)
American Autobiography (l-d)
American Humor (l-d)
The Arthurian Tradition and Shakespeare (l-d)

Beowulf (l-d)
Brer Rabbit in the Elementary School Curriculum (l-d)
Canterbury Tales: Prologue (l-d)
Christopher Marlowe's *Dr. Faustus* (l-d)
Contemporary Southern Literature (l-d)
Daniel Boone as Man and Myth (l-d)
Eudora Welty's *The Golden Apples* (l-d)
Eudora Welty and Katherine Anne Porter (l-d)
Folklore and Fakelore (l-d)
Foundations of the Modern in Literature and Art (l-d)
The Great Gatsby (l-d)
Literary Foundations: Shakespeare, Homer, and the Bible (l-d)
Mark Twain, William Faulkner, and Gabriel García Márquez (l-d)
Puritan History and *The Scarlet Letter* (l-d)
Recasting the Canon (l-d)
Shakespeare: *Much Ado about Nothing, A Midsummer Night's Dream, Twelfth Night* (l-d)
Shakespearean Comedy, Romantic Poetry, and Contemporary Fiction (l-d)
Studies in Twentieth-Century African American Writers
Ten American Women Writers, from 1897 to 1987 (l-d)
Texts and Contexts of Early American Culture (l-d)
What Every High School Teacher Needs to Know about Literary Theory (l-d)
The Writing Process in Slow Motion (l-d)
World Literature and Culture (l-d)
American Literature: What Should Our Citizens Know? (w)
Designing American Studies Programs (w)
Fellowships to study English language and literature in the British Universities Summer Programs at the University of London; University of Oxford; and the University of Birmingham, Stratford-upon-Avon (s-a)

French

Contemporary French Language, Culture, and Literature (s)
France Today: What Every French Teacher Should Know (s)
The French Connection: From Classical France to Contemporary Africa (s)
The Meaning of Culture in the Study of French (s)
Teaching French 1, 2, and 3 (s)
Telling the Tale: Narrative and the Novel in France (s)
Advertisements: Reflections of Contemporary French Society and Culture (l-d)
Claude Beauclair (l-d)
French Literature and Journalism (l-d)
Teaching Effective Reading Strategies in French (l-d)
Teaching the History of French Civilization: Strategies and Suggestions (l-d)

Using Technology in the Language Classroom (l-d)
Aspects Sociaux et Culturels de Deux Mondes Francophones: Images et Textes, le Québec et la Suisse (w)
Civilization: France in the Sixties (w)
French 1, 2, and 3: Creating a Solid Base for Communication (w)
French Advanced Placement Workshop (w)
French-Speaking Cultures Today—in Multimedia (w)
Langues et Cultures du Monde Francophone (Afrique, Antilles, Maghreb) (w)
Le Cinéma Français: Langue, Littérature, Culture, Civilisation (w)
Les Français: Qui sont-ils? Où vont-ils? (w)
Raymond Jean (w)
Fellowships to study French language and culture at Centre International d'Études Française d'Angers, Centre Audio-Visuel de Langues Modernes (CAVILAM) at the University of Clermont-Ferrand in Vichy, and the Institut d'Études Françaises d'Avignon at the Centre Universitaire d'Avignon (s-a)

German

Attaining Proficiency in German (s)
Postwar Germany (s)
German Culture in Multimedia (w)
Innovations in Teaching German (w)
Oral Proficiency in German (w)
Secondary and Postsecondary German Instruction: The Articulation Issue (w)
The Study and Teaching of German in Virginia (w)
What German Teachers Should Know (w)
Fellowships to study current European affairs at the Bonn Transatlantic Summer Academy (s-a)

History

The Bill of Rights in American History (s)
Civil War Studies (s)
Creating Online Materials for Teaching United States History (s)
Establishing Democracy (s)
Exploration and Contact: The Atlantic Basin in the Sixteenth through Eighteenth Centuries (s)
History of Richmond (s)
New Approaches to American History (s)
African American History and Culture (l-d)
America's Changing Place in the Twentieth-Century World (l-d)
Contemporary Historical Studies: Issues and Authors (l-d)
Families and Schooling in Central Virginia (l-d)
Global Awareness: New Perspectives (l-d)
The History and Culture of the Islamic World (l-d)

Understanding Diversity: Issues and Ideas (l-d)
United States History, 1800–1980 (l-d)
The Bill of Rights in American History: Follow-Up Workshop (w)
First Freedoms: America and Religious Freedom (w)
History of Richmond: Follow-Up Workshop (w)

Humanities

Charlottesville Schools Colloquium: New Knowledge, New Formats (l-d)
Charlottesville Schools Colloquium: Teaching Writing: What Works, What Doesn't (l-d)
Fellowships to study current European affairs at the Bonn Transatlantic Summer Academy (s-a)
Fellowships to study the history and architecture of late imperial and modern China in the Weedon Asian Studies Program in Beijing (s-a)

Japanese

Japanese Pedagogy Workshop (w)

Linguistics

Between Two Cultures, between Two Languages (s, w)

Mathematics

Algebra for Elementary and Middle School Teachers (s)
Calculus Revisited (s)
Exploring Data and Chance for Elementary School Teachers (s)
Geometry for Elementary and Middle School Teachers (s)
Introduction to Contemporary Mathematics (s)
Mathematical Modeling (s)
The Mathematics of Manipulatives (s)
Physics Institute for Mathematics Teachers (s)
Probability and Statistics (s)
Discrete Mathematics and Algorithms (l-d)
The Emergence of Modern Mathematics (l-d)
Mathematics and Science (l-d)
Number Systems and Number Theory for Elementary and Middle School Teachers (l-d)
Virginia Mathematics Coalition: Regional Workshop (w)

Physics

High School Physics Teachers' Institute (s)
Physics Institute for Mathematics Teachers (s)
Physical Science: The Threshold of Scientific Literacy (satellite TV course; l-d)
Topics in Classical and Modern Physics (satellite TV course; l-d)
Physics Design Workshop (w)

Russian

Beyond the Curtain Lies a New Time of Troubles (w)

Spanish

El Caribe: Literature, Culture, and Politics of the Caribbean (s)
Latin America Today: History and Politics in Literature (s)
Latin American Literature: Comparative Perspectives (s)
Spain Today and toward the Year 2000 (s)
Spanish Film (s)
Teaching the Authors on the AP Spanish List (s)
Chile: Literature and Culture (l-d)
Reading and Writing in the Foreign Language Classroom (l-d)
Spain after Franco: Cultural Movements (l-d)
Spanish Language and Culture (l-d)
Spanish Oral Proficiency (l-d)
Argentina: Literature and Culture (w)
Everything You Wanted to Know about Spanish Linguistics but Didn't Know How to Ask (w)
Isabel Allende (w)
La España Actual (w)
La Lingüística en la Escuela Secundaria (w)
The Latin American Historical Novel: Tradition and Innovation (w)
Mexican Literature and Culture (w)
Oral Proficiency in Spanish: Theory and Practice (w)
Spanish Teaching in the High School: Where Does the University Fit In? (w)
Why Study Spanish? (w)
Hispanic Studies Program in Valencia, Spain (s-a)

Theater

Exploring Directing (s)
Folger Shakespeare Institute (s)
Hi Concept / Lo Tech (s)
Performing Culture: Masks, Myths, and Folktales (s)
Shakespeare: *Othello* (s)
Drama Symposium: *The Trojan Women* (w)
Drama Workshop for Teachers: Heritage Repertory Theatre (w)
North Carolina Shakespeare Festival (w, sp)
Shakespeare Live! Performance (w)

Women's Studies

Women in History, Literature, Science, and Art (w)
Gender and Race for Virginia School Professionals (w)

DEBORAH K. WOELFLEIN

Great Expectations, Hard Times

Each time we are lucky enough to get the energy of new teachers in our high school English department, I watch their evolution with interest and nostalgia. I think back to my first year teaching high school in northern New Hampshire, when the assistant principal had to stand in the back of my classroom to help me maintain order. Teaching is a wonderful vocation, but it takes a thorough, careful preparation of mind as well as of personality. Colleges and universities that contribute to this effort could benefit from information I have gleaned from interviewing candidates for positions; teaching courses for English education majors; working closely with interns, their mentors, and new teachers; and talking with a wide range of secondary school staff. Three concerns emerge: the shock of entering the real world of public schools, specific ways that postsecondary English departments can ease that transition, and weaknesses that new teachers often bring with them.

Let me describe for you the experiences of a fictional, typical beginning English teacher, Mr. Eager. When he interviews for his position, he mentions that he especially loves Shakespeare and drama. He displays his portfolio full of creative lesson plans, including a unit that will lead students to write and produce their own plays. His enthusiasm about young people, writing, and literature is contagious. The department head tells Mr. Eager that someday he *might* get to teach Shakespeare. He will start off teaching mainly average-ability students, though, with a couple of sections full of repeaters, kids who have failed the class and need to make it up. Thrilled to be offered a job, Mr. Eager believes that he can reach every child.

After spending the summer gathering materials and reading, picking up posters and thinking of displays he could use to start building up a community in each classroom, he begins his career. Unfortunately, being the newest department member, he finds that he will be traveling to five different classrooms and to the cafeteria for lunch duty. The supply-closet guardian tells him that he may have only two different colors of construction paper and only enough to cover two bulletin boards. One teacher is thrilled with Mr. Eager's posters, as her boards have been empty for years. Another offers Mr. Eager a corner of a table and one wall. A third one warns him that she'll be checking the room every day to see which of his students are writing on her desks. She tells him not to open the curtains ever, as they might not close again. He gets used to pushing two different carts through the halls, one loaded for morning and the other loaded for afternoon. He only occasionally confuses the two carts or loses an essay.

He comes to department meetings armed with bibliographies of multicultural and women's studies titles, ready to add zest and variety to what he views as a traditional curriculum. Within a month, he's feeling discouraged, because it seems that his department head and other colleagues shoot down every title: "Too controversial for our conservative school board," "Too current to be included yet," or, most practically, "It takes two years to add a new book to the curriculum." The part that gets him down the most is the paperwork: attendance updates, demerit forms, progress reports, office referrals, day sheets, IEPs (individual education plans), ISA (in-school adjustment) work requests, 504 plans (for extended absence), Step I professional growth objectives—all in triplicate, all intimidating, all important. They take time away from his teaching.

Mr. Eager keeps his chin up, remembering his dream to be the first to expose his students to some so-called classics that he loved in high school. *Gulliver's Travels*! What fun it will be for his students to meet the Yahoos and to write their own imaginary, satirical voyages! Within a week he's down again: the kids aren't reading the material. Or, if their claims not to understand it are true, he wonders what he can do to help them get through the diction and allusions. Moving on to *To Kill a Mockingbird* does not bring forth the lively discussion that he anticipated. The students complain about the number of pages he assigns, maybe twenty-five to thirty a night. They work from twenty to thirty hours a week, they say, or they have so many soccer games and practices that his assignments are unreasonable. He gets a voice-mail message from an irate parent, who asks if he has read her daughter's IEP. A couple comes on open-house night to make sure that Mr. Eager knows how busy their son is: their son takes all honors classes, has a tremendous amount of schoolwork, and is involved in many activities. They do not expect him to have to complete any assignments over winter vacation, which is family time. Mr. Eager wonders if things have really changed so much in the short time since his own high school days.

When Mr. Eager teaches *Romeo and Juliet,* he brings in a copy of the Franco Zefferelli production that he taped off-air. His students love it, comparing it to the Leonardo DiCaprio version, but his department head speaks to him about copyright laws and lets him know that she heard from a parent whose daughter mentioned a nude scene. Once again, Mr. Eager feels deflated.

One of the repeaters classes, a group of twenty-six students in which sixteen have IEPs, tells Mr. Eager that they never do homework: "No one else gives us work. If you do, we won't do it anyway." Mr. Eager calls their bluff and learns that, indeed, seventy percent of them do not complete reading assignments. When he tries to make connections from Holocaust readings to their personal lives, some perk up, but at least half try to keep their heads on their desks. He finds that neither the literature alone nor what he thinks to be great questions is enough to pull the kids into the work. Titles for this class are limited, and he discovers too late that other teachers of the same course have grabbed the more interesting books right away. He ends the year with five different preparations because of book-rotation problems.

I have painted a bleak picture, but nothing in that picture does not happen in every middle or high school across the country. These tribulations are normal consequences of the public school system; many of them are thought to be necessary to protect teachers and students and, of course, the taxpayers' pocketbooks. I can look at them with amusement, understanding how to get through them and seeing how trivial they are in comparison to my interactions with students. I can go home at night and, without feeling crushed, pull apart a lesson that fell flat. I know that I will have another chance to try it after some tinkering—if not next semester, maybe next year. When teachers first start, however, each of these hurdles looms large, especially if they are not prepared to face them. And I have not even mentioned classroom management or the amount of preparing and correcting that truly overwhelms new teachers as well as some veterans. I could write a separate essay on the importance of a strong work ethic and excellent time management skills for all new teachers.

College and university professors can help make the transition easier if they let their students know that when their students enter their own classrooms, they must accept the responsibility to maintain, pass on, and improve the values of a community. Although we each feel autonomous when we close the classroom door and face our students, every decision we make reaches outside those walls. New teachers probably have thought about the influence that they will have on their individual students. Indeed, most go into teaching hoping to make a difference in the world through the future adults that they will help shape. Although they will often feel that they are accomplishing nothing, they will sow invisible seeds that sprout in years to come. If they can stick it out, they will actually have an occasional student come back much later to say thanks.

New teachers who succeed arrive in a school building with a good balance among three important qualities: resourcefulness, respect, and confidence. There are ways that colleges and universities can help foster each quality.

We secondary school teachers notice that many graduates enter our schools with the feeling that curricula already in place are seriously flawed and should be de-emphasized in favor of newer titles and units. Some candidates for positions openly sneer when they review a reading list that contains several traditionally taught titles. They will sometimes ask if they really have to teach them. New department members bring fresh ideas, which we welcome, but an attitude of respect for what a school considers important will prompt department heads and administrators to listen to suggestions for change. Unfortunately, the way that most budgets work delays innovation. Like many other department chairs, I submit a detailed budget for the *following* school year when I return to school each September. My department members and I have to think ahead a whole year when we look for materials, and we must proceed cautiously because of the enormous expense and other factors involved in making major changes. Given the cost of anthologies and the fact that most courses enroll hundreds of students, each textbook decision has to last around ten years. Conservative elements in many communities prompt public schools to do detailed studies that address appropriateness and readability before ordering any new books. When people visit my particular school and look at our curriculum, they expect very traditional classrooms. Judging by the printing on the pages of our language arts guide, they are right, but visiting actual classes proves otherwise. In order to pilot new titles and freshen our reading lists, we sometimes Risograph our way around conventionality, often bringing in copies of poems or stories that are current and potentially controversial. We have just completed a total revision of our curriculum. It took two and a half years and the commitment of many teachers from first grade up through twelfth. We studied our state instructional frameworks, looked at test results, and built up a sequential series of clear objectives for several strands. Our school district has promised training to help veteran as well as new teachers learn how to implement brand-new goals. When we begin to update book lists, we know that our newer teachers will be our best resources.

New teachers should visit as many classes as they can, not only in their own departments but throughout the building. Teachers' lounges, where staff gather during their lunch or preparation periods, often become sources of negative energy where complaints build up and morale is pulled down; newer teachers should avoid them. Instead they should seek out teachers willing to collaborate, ones who will welcome their ideas and energy. My school has five freshmen teachers who meet every Friday afternoon to plan units and activities. Two of them are fairly new teachers, and the energy during those sessions is electric. A good chunk of what these five do is to reflect back on what worked and what fell short in the past week. They have already made contact and welcomed in our two new teachers for next year.

My own students groan about having to apply comma rules to their writing or having to go back and change passive voice to active. They yearn to write in fragments as, they love to point out, some of this year's most significant authors do. I explain that before they can break the rules and go off in various directions, they need to know what the rules are. They must understand conventions before they can perfect their own styles. So it is with newer teachers and curriculum. Before they reject what a school and community value, they should work with it. They will not enjoy every book or unit, and they can certainly look for replacements and improvements, but in most schools they must follow a procedure to replace and improve. This step can protect them from costly mistakes in more ways than one.

Teachers often have gaps in traditional areas, units that are essential to an understanding of subjects more complex and contemporary. One teacher might know very little about mythology, and another might be uncomfortable teaching poetic forms. What happens when new teachers have to teach a book or unit unfamiliar to them? Most who feel shaky about material avoid the task or rely on someone else's folders to get them through quickly. A fledgling teacher needs to be able to analyze a task, split it up into its parts, find the resources that will help, and get right to work on planning a unit without being intimidated. For example, if the curriculum specifies that students do a persuasive-speech unit, we care less that the teacher has been trained in that area than that the teacher knows how to get ready to teach it. We want the teacher to be able to take any book, essay, poem, play, or story apart, analyze its elements, find out what is important to emphasize, and design units that will help students achieve specific objectives. We want a teacher who can envision the end product of a writing or speaking assignment and then back up to plan the various activities and the rubrics that will get the students to that place. College and university professors could aid their students by modeling the process they follow to shape their own units. If they stop now and then to explain or, even better, to have their students discuss why certain materials or approaches were chosen, all would benefit, even nonteaching majors. Asking students to suggest alternative texts, sequences, or activities results in lively discussions. For the secondary school teacher, resourcefulness and confidence play off each other and actually influence classroom management. Good planning brings a sense of preparedness and focus, and that sense heads off most discipline problems.

Grammar is a weak area with most new teachers. I recently read through more than two hundred cover letters and résumés; more than a third had errors. An applicant for an English teaching job who sends off such important documents with even one mistake will find it very difficult to get hired. The last course that I took before my student teaching was Advanced Grammar and Composition. A whole semester of not using the verb *to be* was a challenge for which I have silently thanked Yvonne Ground many times over the years. Teaching candidates should also take a public-speaking course for the practice in enunciation and to gain confidence. The few who do get interviews for positions can ruin their chances in the first few moments if they do not speak well. Articulate, enthusiastic speakers have few discipline problems.

One young teacher that I spoke to criticized her education classes. She felt that her most valuable studies in college and graduate school were humanities and Shakespeare courses. She found that students respect most those teachers who know something and are able to relax in front of their students enough to be themselves. Kids sense when a teacher is shaky, and they go for the jugular. This young woman treats every student from the stance of one intelligent person talking to another intelligent person. It works, especially with at-risk students, who see her as a model and work hard to live up to her image of them.

Being well trained, having the resources to draw on a solid knowledge base, gives new teachers the confidence to jump into a new community and find their niche. When I interview candidates, I always search for some facet that will bring new character to our department. Each of our sixteen members has a slightly different specialty, which I enjoy nurturing and bringing out at department meetings, where people share successes, questions, and plans. Even our two newly hired members will feel valued this fall. One brings years of experience modifying units for special education students; another has a background in middle school philosophy and has worked with debate teams. English teaching majors should all try to have a focus that makes them unique, so that they can feel like contributing members in a department. Having something to contribute also brings confidence as others come to see you as a resource.

Back to Mr. Eager. He is feeling great now that it is June, because he has learned that another new teacher will be coming in the fall. Mr. Eager will have a room of his own next year. He knows how to play the book-grabbing game now. He snuck into the book closet late one afternoon and hid all the copies of *The Outsiders* in a place where only he can find them. He has survived the most grueling year of his life, and he has learned an important secret: the supply-closet guardian can be bribed with chocolate. He's looking forward to September. So is his assistant principal, who will not have to follow him around to five different classrooms.

SARAH MICHAELS

Stories in Contact: Teacher Research in the Academy

In her acceptance speech in Stockholm for the 1993 Nobel Prize in Literature, Toni Morrison argued for the power of divergent stories in contact. She made a case not for the power of narrative language per se but, rather, for narratives that come together and interpenetrate—as a way of making new meanings possible and charting new paths toward human contact and connection.

Interestingly, Morrison develops her point not by analytically explicating the transformative power of narratives but by instantiating it in the course of her speech. She tells a story—in two parts. She first introduces us to an old, wise black woman, completely blind but regarded in her rural community as having special powers to see and heal. The old woman is approached by some young teenagers from the city who want to show her up as the fool and fraud they believe her to be. The youths, knowing she's blind, demand that she tell them whether the bird one of them is holding is alive or dead. The old woman's response is soft but stern: "I don't know. I don't know whether the bird you are holding is dead or alive, but what I do know is that it is *in* your hands. It's in *your* hands" (11). The repetition is not for emphasis. The shift in stress (apparent in the oral version but not in the published written text) from "*in* your hands" to "in *your* hands" signals the children's responsibility for the bird—its life or death.

Morrison then develops from the old woman's reprimand an extended metaphorical passage, treating the bird as language: either alive (generating meaning) or dead (destroying or denying meaning).

> [I]f the bird in the hands of her visitors is dead, the custodians are responsible for the corpse. For [the old woman] a dead language is not only one no longer spoken or written, it is unyielding language content to admire its own paralysis. [. . .] Ruthless in its policing duties, it [. . .] actively thwarts the intellect, stalls conscience, suppresses human potential. Unreceptive to interrogation, it cannot form or tolerate new ideas, shape other thoughts, tell another story [. . .]. (13–14)

Morrison contrasts this dead language with "word-work": "Word-work is sublime [. . .] because it is generative; it makes meaning that secures our difference, our human difference" (22).

The story comes to a point of neat closure, where the old woman's words—extended by Morrison's metaphorical treatment—can be taken as profoundly wise and generative. When I first heard this speech, I fully expected the story to end there. It didn't; it continued on into what I now think of as part 2 (the children's story).

Returning to the cruel and misguided teenagers, Morrison gives them reason and sensibility, showing the inadequacies and limitations of the old woman's perspective. The woman's words, which seemed at first a good example of word-work—pithy and full of potential for teaching and transforming the youths—are now shown to have been a way of ignoring and closing down meaning, completely shutting the teenagers out of the old woman's story. It turns out that the kids had no bird in their hands. Refusing to be silenced or put in their place by the old woman, they respond:

> Your answer is artful, but its artfulness embarrasses us and ought to embarrass you. Your answer is indecent in its self-congratulation. [. . .] Why didn't you reach out, touch us with your soft fingers, delay the sound bite, the lesson, until you knew who we were? [. . .] You trivialize us and trivialize the bird that is not in our hands. (25–26)

The children speak back. They demand that the old woman give them authentic language, the true and rich particularities of her own life stories, and in turn tell her a haunting story of their own, as an example of what they are looking for from her.

The old woman, once given access to *their* story, comes to know and trust them. The two parts of the story come together and interpenetrate. Everyone is changed in the process: the old woman and her young interlocutors (and, of course, the listeners to Morrison's speech). The old woman's parting words are, "I trust you now. I trust you with the bird that is not in your hands because you have truly caught it. Look. How lovely it is, this thing we have done—together" (30).

Morrison's story is humbling, cautioning us about the limitations of one-sided monologues. In making my case for teacher research in the academy, I acknowledge that I don't know the world of English departments at all well. But let my words be taken as the first part of a multiparty dialogue, so that (in spite of this monologic format) we might eventually come to know and think with one another's experiences and concerns.

In that spirit, I locate myself and my work. I am a sociolinguist by training and for the past ten years have been working closely with public school teachers from the Boston and Worcester areas who are experimenting with the tools of ethnographic observation and discourse analysis—looking closely at the talk and texts in their classrooms. Although using a varied set of tools that originated in the academy (drawing on colleagues in and research techniques from anthropology and sociolinguistics), the teachers from the start used these tools to ask and answer their own questions.

I have worked primarily with elementary school teachers from urban public schools and also, more recently, with middle and high school teachers of mathematics and science. The concerns of these teachers are quite different from those of teachers of language arts or English literature. But I hope that Morrison's faith in stories in contact—as a route toward transformative word-work—will make the readers of this essay willing and active coconstructors of connections between my work and their worlds.

What are the implications of my work with inner city elementary and secondary public school teachers for professors of English? First and foremost, I think about teaching, at any level, the way Morrison thinks about the old woman and the teenagers—as fundamentally about worlds and stories in contact. And these worlds are made and remade through language.

Our classrooms, whether containing a second-grade science lesson or graduate seminar, are discourse spaces. These spaces instantiate a set of social and intellectual practices, a constellation of ways of speaking, acting, valuing, being in one's body. The literacy theorist James Paul Gee refers to this constellation of norms and practices as discourse with a capital *D* (*Social Linguistics* and "Vygotsky"). The nature of the Discourse space—what kind of talk occurs, who gets to talk and how much, how talk and text are shaped and evaluated, how participants are arranged and positioned as knowers, and how the making of meaning extends beyond language—

critically influences what kinds of intellectual moves are practiced, what gets learned, and what identities are taken up and tried on by participants. Gee's notion of Discourse resonates with and draws on the work of Michel Foucault (*Archaeology* and *Order*), Ludwig Wittgenstein's notions of "language games" and "forms of life," Mikhail Bakhtin's and Valentin Voloshinov's notions of "social languages" and "speech genres," Pierre Bourdieu's notions of "habitus" and "a feel for the game," and the extension of all these ideas by many other theorists of mind in sociocultural context (Halliday; Wertsch; Lemke; Bernstein; Hymes; among others).

The kind of forms of life or language games we create through talk and text in our classrooms determines the kind of communities of practice we engender and whether students come to be talked into, or inducted into, or apprenticed into our worlds. As Morrison says (quite bluntly), the bird can be alive or dead. At the college or university level, while we like to think about our work as forms of intellectual apprenticeship, we are not (at least many of us are not) oriented toward looking closely—as an ethnographer or discourse analyst might—at the discourse practices we orchestrate. Oddly enough, this is something that the elementary school teachers I have known and worked closely with are willing to do and do brilliantly, and these teachers contributed to a growing body of practitioner-initiated research. Much of the work of these teachers in the Boston-Worcester area has been presented at national conferences and published in prestigious educational journals (Phillips; Ballenger, "Because") as well as in book form (Gallas, *Languages, Sometimes,* and *Talking;* Reddy, Jacobs, McCrohon, and Herrenkohl; Ballenger, *Teaching*). Through this work, these teachers (in their hybrid identities as teacher-researchers) are gaining increasing visibility and credibility in the larger educational research and policy debates of our time.[1]

The focus of this particular brand of teacher research is on literacies as talk, emphasizing the kind of talk and text, the ways with words, that are engendered in the classroom. Teacher-researchers audio- and videotape their classrooms, with emphasis on talk that is orchestrated by the teacher. They typically look at what roles they play and what expectations for talk (often implicit and subtle) they hold, as well as at the ways with words their students bring from their home communities. They tend to focus particularly on those students whom they find it hard to connect with, hard to coconstruct meaning with, and it often turns out that these are students who are not terribly good at school-based language games.

This kind of teacher research often draws attention to the ways that teachers miss or misjudge their students' understandings, just as the old, wise woman misjudged the teenagers in the first part of Morrison's story. The use of audio- and videotape recordings and transcripts has turned out to be a powerful mechanism for making the complexities of classroom life observable and transportable. This mechanism makes it possible to bring one's classroom "to the table" in discussion with interested colleagues, as a shared text and focus of inquiry. Taping, transcribing, and looking together at transcripts becomes a tool for slowing down one's interpretive processes and, often, for deriving new understandings of the strengths of one's students. Looking closely at tapes and transcripts helps teachers see the power of language to generate (or deny) meaning, sensibility, and human connection. It is a tool, in Morrison's words, for bringing stories into contact.

There are two aspects of this practice that bear more discussion: the emphasis on using raw data (in the form of audio- and videotape recordings or students' work) as opposed to anecdotes about what happened on a particular occasion or typically and the emphasis on collegial review of one's data.

By raw data I mean not already interpreted accounts or anecdotes of what works and what doesn't but the rich, unedited, messy talk of real classrooms, with all the false starts, interruptions, and missed opportunities. People bring transcripts full of hard-to-interpret or even incoherent remarks, produced on the fly, that turn out—once they are revisited—to be not nearly so off the wall as was first thought. Rehearing what was said (via the laborious process of transcribing a tape) and reseeing talk in a transcript has become a way, as in Morrison's story, to give reason to one's students. It's a way to give them more time and space to be heard, and allows teachers to step back and assess their role and responsibility in creating the discourse space. In practice, use of raw language data often ultimately leads to increased trust and connection between teacher and students, allowing them (as Morrison's old woman and teenagers) to build new meaning together.

That teacher-researchers come together as colleagues to do this work allows multiple perspectives to be brought to bear on the data—though the data are still one's own. The teacher has far more insider knowledge of the situation and the students and hence has the right to claim knowledge about what's happening and what it means. But the collaborative process, in my experience, turns out to be far more transformative than reflection in isolation. The group pushes teachers further in making the familiar strange, rethinking what's possible, and coming to value more of their students as having powerful minds and cogent arguments, not always, perhaps, fully explicated or expressed in the ways that were expected.

How does this transformation happen, especially among professionals who often don't collaborate well? The process of bringing transcripts to the table with colleagues creates a space that rarely exists in the context of faculty meetings, faculty dining rooms, or even workshops on teaching. It often allows one to see one's world in concert with the experiences, vantage points, interests, and tools of others while remaining in command of the data and the ultimate interpretations that result. It allows the teacher-researcher to take from the collective resources of the community all and only what seems helpful and reasonable.

In the game of bringing one's classroom to the table with colleagues, the others looking at the data are positioned as allies, not outside critics or, typical in our scholarly work, blind reviewers. That they too bring their data to the table builds a reciprocity that induces trust and a willingness to expose problems instead of merely touting successes. In my experience with elementary school teachers, this kind of discourse space can build bridges across grade levels, disciplines, even institutional boundaries; it creates an environment where people explore problematic aspects of practice that they would not ordinarily air publicly.[2] I have seen elementary school teachers work as valued coresearchers with senior academics and, just as remarkable, high school physics teachers working side by side with elementary special education teachers. In several places, this kind of work has been sustained (with no outside funding) over many years, simply because it turns out to be so intellectually rewarding and productive. One Clark University English professor claims it made him radically rethink his teaching—for the first time in his career. A math professor (who began this work as a content adviser to schoolteachers) began videotaping his classes and claims he now hears things in students he never heard before. This work seems to create a space where divergent worlds come together, intermingle, and create the possibility for teachers to reach new understandings—not only of the data but also of one another and their students.

How do these teacher-researchers analyze classroom practice? What do they look for? Typically, the work proceeds with participants bringing audio- and videotapes and field notes to the table, with primacy given to transcripts of talk and examples of students' writing (a kind of self-collecting data). Of course it's important to recognize that transcripts don't in and of themselves speak. Seeing what's in a transcript requires a metalanguage and set of analytic tools, tools that enable one to see patterns, significance. A transcript inevitably leaves out a lot of information (nonverbal, intonational information, but also information with respect to a student's classroom status, ethnicity, etc.). Bringing a piece of student work to the table strips it of all the social interactions that surrounded the text and shaped it—the assignment, class discussion, collaborative work, and so on (Michaels). The seemingly precise tools for analyzing talk and text, counting and coding, can just as easily blind people to some of the patterns. Looking at words per turn, for example, can be very misleading as an indicator of quality of talk. There is no simple set of tools or approaches for determining what a key situation is, how representative of others it is, how many instances of it need to be collected, and what units of analysis are appropriate. These are long-standing, vexing problems, for teachers as well as for experienced classroom discourse analysts and experienced scholars of literary texts.[3]

Although there is no one right way to approach analyzing classroom talk and text, there are some obvious places to begin. I suggest below a few ideas that grow out of my current work with public school teachers. Again, a bit of context is important. In this work, we are all very much caught up with the fits and starts of education reform in Massachusetts, new curriculum frameworks, and new high-stakes state tests. Reform documents in content domains such as mathematics, science, and language arts uniformly call for sense making, discussion, more talk, more authentic investigation, less lecturing, more problem posing rather than algorithmic problem solving (Amer. Assn. for the Advancement of Science; Natl. Council of Teachers of Mathematics). But just more group discussion, particularly if it's unfocused or unguided, is not going to help us, particularly with kids who don't come from academically oriented, upper-middle-class homes. The goal is to figure out what kinds of talk, what kinds of discussion formats, and what kinds of problems to be discussed make for powerful learning in classrooms.

One direction this work is taking at the elementary school level is an effort to develop principles and indicators of academically productive talk. Lauren Resnick, a cognitive scientist and leading theorist and activist in large-scale school reform, is trying to formalize ways of looking for and promoting what she calls accountable talk. (Resnick is director of the Learning Research and Development Center at the University of Pittsburgh, Pittsburgh, which collaborates with many large urban districts around the country, and codirector of the national New Standards Project.)

By *accountable talk*, Resnick and her colleagues (Resnick and

Nelson–Le Gall) mean the talk we believe exemplifies the social and intellectual practices of a given domain, the enculturating forums and forms of talk that, in their terms, socialize intelligence (15). It is the talk we want to hold students accountable for producing and teachers accountable for encouraging and guiding. Resnick and her colleagues are attempting to come up with public standards for students, so students will know what the rules of the game are (particularly those students who have not been deeply enculturated at home into academic ways with words). At the same time, they want teachers to have a clear enough sense of the indicators of this talk so teachers can examine their own and colleagues' classroom discussions for evidence of these valued practices in action. As a first approximation, Resnick and her colleagues have identified three different levels of accountability. The talk must be:

accountable to the classroom community: students must attend to, build on, or relate what they say to what others say and make it clear, in their talk, that they are addressing the topic at hand

accountable to knowledge in the domain: students must provide compelling, explicated evidence[4]

accountable to standards of reasoning: students must use language in academically valued ways to build a compelling argument, analysis, explanation, or theory

Can this notion of accountable talk be useful for us at the college and university level? For it to be, we would need a metalanguage to talk about the kinds of talk we value; the nature of the moves and the intellectual practices they instantiate; the interactional patterns, turn taking and so on, required for equitable participation and practice. I don't have a metalanguage and categories to propose here, but I have a sense of places to begin, if professors were to bring a transcript of a class session to the table. At the simplest level, participation should be discussed—that is, who talks, how much, and what kinds of contributions are elicited and offered.

A transcript of ten or fifteen minutes of a representative sample of class talk would allow one to ask and answer a number of questions:

Who does the talking, the professor or the students?

Who gets a turn and how?

What is the sequence of turns and patterning of turn sequences? For example, is it teacher-student-teacher-student? Or teacher-student-student-student-teacher?

Who controls evaluation of talk and what form (explicit, implicit) does the evaluation take?

The amount, sequencing, and quality of talk of course have to be interpreted in the light of the purpose of the speech activity (or language game). That is, notions of productive or good (coherent, elegant, compelling, appropriate, enculturating) talk make sense only with respect to the kind of language game that is being played.

Participation frameworks, a construct developed originally by Erving Goffman and extended by Marjorie Harness Goodwin, might be useful in characterizing and theorizing the culture of talk and the forms of life (Discourse) and the forms of talk (discourse) in any given classroom. In Goffman's formulation, "When a word is spoken, all those who happen to be in perceptual range of the event will have some sort of participation status relative to it" (3). For Goffman, the participation framework is the amalgam of all members' participation statuses relative to the current utterance. Goodwin operationalizes and expands this notion, systematically showing how language is used to create social organization through the moment-to-moment creation of participation frameworks. Her work painstakingly demonstrates how linguistic expressions open up roles and stances with respect to the content expressed in the utterance.

Returning to the data that a teacher-researcher might examine: if the language game represented in the transcript is a lecture, there will be little back-and-forth between teacher and student or among students. (Still, some lectures are dead and some are alive.) If the language game is a group discussion with the purpose of checking to see whether the students have read the assigned materials, we will expect the tripartite pattern of teacher initiation (question), student response (answer), and teacher evaluation, which is often referred to as the IRE sequence (IRE is an acronym for *initiation, response, evaluation*). If the game is one of looking at a physics demo (with a counterintuitive outcome, so that none of the students know the answer in advance) and the students are asked to predict what will happen and justify their prediction, the teacher does not evaluate as right or wrong each student's contribution. A more likely pattern is some kind of revoicing sequence, where the teacher responds to a student's contribution with "So you're saying you think X will happen because Y?" or "So your position is in direct opposition to Suzy's, if I understand you correctly?" The student can then agree or disagree with the teacher's phrasing or say more. Notice that the IRE sequence is subtly but powerfully different from the revoicing sequence in terms of the intellectual roles and positionings of students and teachers. In the IRE, the students are positioned as learners and tested by the expert knower, the teacher, who sits in a position of authoritative judgment and evaluation. In the revoicing sequence, the students are positioned as theorizers and thinkers within a group of thinkers, and the purpose of the game is to develop a sayable theory, not to get the right answer. Here the teacher is positioned not as authoritative knower (the demo or experiment, once carried out and collectively interpreted, will tell the students the answer) but as intellectual ally who helps the students clarify and articulate better their theory for the group. Although both the IRE and revoicing sequences involve teacher questions and student answers, they create radically different participation structures and radically different environments for socializing intelligence (O'Connor and Michaels).

When characterizing and assessing accountable talk in a given transcript, we thus pay attention to questions of knowledge and authority, patterns of participation (asking about issues of equity and access to the practice), and the sequencing and internal structure of moves.

Developing a metalanguage for looking at talk in our classrooms serves two purposes at once. It allows us to reflect on our practices and improve them; it provides our students with a metalanguage and set of standards for participation, so they will have a sense of the rules of the game that we value and want to induct them into. Interestingly, developing an analytic focus on the norms for communication and participation is a research site where one's work as an English professor and one's efforts to prepare students to teach English and language arts in elementary or secondary schools might well come together very productively. Above and beyond developing in students content knowledge and analytic skills around a particular topic in, say, early American literature, one could (should) provide them with a set of tools that will equip them to reflect on the classroom conversations that *they* will go on to orchestrate as teachers. This is a far cry from a methods course. It's unrealistic to expect academics in English departments to prepare students for what and how to teach a given high school English class. The worlds of the academy and the typical American comprehensive high school are too far apart. But students can be prepared to think deeply about a classroom as a discourse space, by examining the university classroom as a discourse space. Professors can teach them (in large part by modeling this practice) how to question their own pedagogy, how to listen harder and give more reasons to students, how to critique the status quo, how to take risks and try new approaches—in other words, how to teach against the grain

(Cochran-Smith and Lytle). At the same time, to the extent that students would use these tools and strategies with other professional colleagues, professors would indirectly be preparing students to become more effective intellectual community builders and agents of change in their new institutional environments.

In the end, preparing students to be agents of change may be the most important legacy one leaves. High schools, as most of us know, are all too often structured in ways that prevent extended, thoughtful talk and the creation of coherent intellectual practices—among students and also among adult colleagues. We need more of our best and brightest students—those who want to connect with and develop the minds and hearts of young people—to go into teaching as a form of word-work. But if we do not prepare them to teach against the grain, to work as agents of change, they'll be beaten down by an educational system that is all too good at separating, stratifying, and finding deficits; at destroying meaning and destroying kids as meaning makers.

I end by harking back to Morrison's words about the power of working with language. Academics can apply that power in bringing their classrooms to the table with interested colleagues. By developing techniques and a metalanguage to slow down their interpretive processes, they model for students an intellectual practice and a set of generative tools for bringing stories into contact to promote new meanings and deeper understanding of divergent worlds. They demonstrate what it means to take care of that bird of language, ensuring that it lives and thrives in their own hands and engenders word-work in the hands of their students.

Notes

[1]Practitioner-initiated research is gaining increasing visibility nationally, with new journals and book series (e.g., Teachers College Press Practitioner Inquiry Series) and dedicated research-funding initiatives (e.g., the Spencer Foundation's initiative: Practitioner Initiated Research Mentoring and Communication). See Cochran-Smith and Lytle for a helpful typology, review, and presentation of teacher research.

[2]Vera John Steiner, a noted sociocultural psychologist researching the creativity that grows out of long-standing collaborations, believes that major paradigm shifts in one's thinking cannot happen without some kind of local or long-distance collegial community. In her view, breaking new ground in one's work requires a sustained discourse space in which multiple, divergent perspectives are allowed to enter, risks are taken, and new ideas and identities are tried out.

[3]One guide to discourse analysis in educational research can be found in Gee, Michaels, and O'Connor.

[4]The privileged or valued ways of reasoning or making an argument obviously

vary across disciplines and paradigms. What counts as compelling evidence in a class on Romantic poetry will differ from what counts as compelling evidence in a journalism class or a physics class on chaos.

WORKS CITED

American Association for the Advancement of Science. *Science for All Americans.* Amer. Assn. for the Advancement of Science Report of Goals in Science, Mathematics, and Technology. Project 2061. Washington: GPO, 1989.

Bakhtin, Mikhail M. *"Speech Genres" and Other Late Essays.* Trans. Vern W. McGee. Ed. Caryl Emerson and Michael Holquist. Austin: U of Texas P, 1986.

Ballenger, Cindy. "Because You Like It: The Language of Control." *Harvard Educational Review* 62 (1992): 199–208.

———. *Teaching Other People's Children: Literacy and Learning in a Bilingual Classroom.* New York: Teachers Coll., 1999.

Bernstein, Basil. *Pedagogy, Symbolic Control and Identity: Theory, Research, Critique.* London: Taylor, 1996.

Bourdieu, Pierre. *Language and Symbolic Power.* Cambridge: Harvard UP, 1991.

Cochran-Smith, Marilyn, and Susan Lytle. *Inside/Outside: Teacher Research and Knowledge.* New York: Teachers Coll., 1993.

Foucault, Michel (1969) *The Archaeology of Knowledge and the Discourse on Language.* Trans. A. M. Sheridan Smith. New York: Random, 1969.

———. *The Order of Things.* New York: Random, 1966.

Gallas, Karen. *The Languages of Learning: How Children Talk, Write, Dance, Draw, and Sing Their Understanding of the World.* New York: Teachers Coll., 1994.

———. *"Sometimes I Can Be Anything": Power, Gender, and Identity in a Primary Classroom.* New York: Teachers Coll., 1998.

———. *Talking Their Way into Science: Hearing Children's Questions and Theories, Responding with Curricula.* New York: Teachers Coll., 1995.

Gee, James Paul. *Social Linguistics and Literacies: Ideology in Discourses.* London: Falmer, 1990.

———. "Vygotsky and Current Debates in Education: Some Dilemmas as Afterthoughts." Hicks 269–82.

Gee, James Paul, Sarah Michaels, and Mary Catherine O'Connor. "Discourse Analysis." *The Handbook of Qualitative Research in Education.* Ed. M. Le Compte, Wendy Gillroy, and Judith Goetz. Orlando: Academic, 1992. 227–91.

Goffman, Erving. *Forms of Talk.* Philadelphia: U of Pennsylvania P, 1981.

Goodwin, Marjorie Harness. *He-Said-She-Said: Talk as Social Organization among Black Children.* Bloomington: Indiana UP, 1990.

Halliday, Michael. *Language as Social Semiotic: The Social Interpretation of Language and Meaning.* London: Arnold, 1978.

Hicks, Deborah, ed. *Discourse, Learning, and Schooling.* Cambridge: Cambridge UP, 1996.

Hymes, Dell. *Ethnography, Linguistics, Narrative Inequality: Toward an Understanding of Voice.* London: Taylor, 1996.

Lemke, Jay L. *Textual Politics: Discourse and Social Dynamics.* London: Taylor, 1995.

Michaels, Sarah. "Text and Context: A New Approach to the Study of Classroom Writing." *Discourse Processes* 10 (1987): 321–46.

Morrison, Toni. *The Nobel Lecture in Literature.* New York: Knopf, 1994.

National Council of Teachers of Mathematics. *Curriculum and Evaluation Standards for School Mathematics.* Reston: Natl. Council of Teachers of Mathematics, 1989.

O'Connor, Mary Catherine, and Sarah Michaels. "Shifting Participant Frameworks: Orchestrating Thinking Practices in Group Discussion." Hicks 63–103.

Phillips, Ann. "Hearing Children's Stories: A Report on the Brookline Teacher-Researcher Seminar." Penn Ethnography in Educational Research Forum, Philadelphia, PA. Feb. 1991.

Reddy, Maureen, Patty Jacobs, Caryn McCrohon, and Leslie Rupert Herrenkohl. *Creating Scientific Communities in the Elementary Classroom.* Portsmouth: Heinemann, 1998.

Resnick, Lauren, and Sharon Nelson–Le Gall. "Socializing Intelligence." *Piaget, Vygotsky and Beyond.* Ed. L. Smith, J. Dockrell, and P. Tomlinson. London: Routledge, forthcoming.

Steiner, Vera John. Personal communication to author.

Voloshinov, Valentin. *Marxism and the Philosophy of Language.* 1929. Trans. Ladislav Matejka and I. R. Titunik. Cambridge: Harvard UP, 1986.

Wertsch, James W. *Voices of the Mind: A Sociocultural Approach to Mediated Action.* Cambridge: Harvard UP, 1991.

Wittgenstein, Ludwig. *Philosophical Investigations.* Trans. G. E. M. Anscombe. Oxford: Blackwell, 1953.

BOB BROAD

Facing Our Professional Others: Border Crossing in Teacher Education

Tense and troubled borders crisscross the geography of teacher preparation in English. Consider the four disparate, often antagonistic, positions of those most directly involved in English education.

English studies professors are dedicated to the study of literature, language, and composition. They often view courses and innovations in education as distractions from the most important concern of future teachers of English: content. Many literature faculty members, for example, believe great texts merit a serious and sustained attention that leaves little time for studying noncanonical literature, film, television, and other popular media.

Like their colleagues in English studies, English education professors value the traditional content of the field, yet they tend to see command of a wider range of texts (e.g., young adult literature and nonprint media) and abilities (e.g., public speaking and composition) as crucial to the success of future English teachers in the secondary schools. They also typically place greater importance on the research and theory of pedagogy than their fellow English faculty members. Their approach to teaching English is disciplined and humanistic, rooted in the traditions of literature, linguistics, and rhetoric.

Education professors teach the science of planning and delivering units of instruction and evaluting successes and failures in teaching. Rooting their work in the social sciences, many of them doubt the rigor and value of the humanistic approaches dominant in English departments. Education faculty members also note with concern the absence from many English courses of research-based analyses of reading, writing, and learning.

Teachers of English in the secondary schools may view university faculty members in general as ignorant of and irrelevant to the contemporary conditions of schooling. First, literature faculty members in the universities have likely never tried teaching Milton, Melville, or Morrison to learning-disabled or gang-recruited teenagers. Progressive linguists need to take note of the political minefield through which advocates of Ebonics recently walked. The concerns of idealistic university faculty members often seem distant from the pressing constraints and demands of the secondary school English classroom. Second, learner-centered approaches to teaching reading and writing advocated by English education faculty members don't fit the demands of teaching in the schools. Certain texts are required reading, and only a particular kind of writing leads to success on the statewide writing exam. Giving students wide choices in what they read and write may work in the university, but it won't fly in the schools. Third, lesson plans as detailed and behaviorist as those required in a college of education are unnecessary and not worth the time demanded, for teachers face more pressing responsibilities. Besides, much of what education faculty members have advocated in the past has become outdated after a few years.

It is hard to say whether this cast of characters is performing a comedy or a tragedy. Those of us in any of the four positions sketched above might be amused by the misdirections and skirmishes resulting from our divergent viewpoints, or we might feel frustrated and alarmed. In either case, we are unlikely to believe that we can do much to change the script. Frankly, we are too busy fulfilling our day-to-day professional responsibilities in teaching, research, and service.

There is, however, a fifth group of actors in this drama. Student teachers enjoy neither the luxury of being able to ignore the four competing groups nor the power to bring them together. They are transients, bit players who must not only listen to our discordant chorus of voices but also distill from it ways to help their students appreciate and understand literature, master and explore language, recognize and wield rhetoric. If we four groups of leading players cannot muster the resolve to open the borders of English education for the good of the profession, perhaps we can be moved to do so by the plight of student teachers. They are the only party in English teacher preparation with whom all four of the other parties have regular contact. We know their faces, their struggles, their work; they metamorphose before our eyes from college students into prospective English teachers. So student teachers are not only the most aggrieved victims of our professional tensions and the key beneficiaries of the shift in professional relations for which I call in this essay; they are also the ethical focus of my proposal.

We are caught, I believe, in a culture of mutual dismissiveness and disregard. In *What is English?* Peter Elbow describes the situation this way: "I find arrogance and condescension to be the characteristic sins of our profession—qualities that lead people into not listening, not learning, not changing, and staying stuck in their positions"(59). To illustrate briefly the sins to which Elbow refers and to dramatize some of the attitudes that concern me, I offer two anecdotes.

Anecdote 1 might be entitled "Protesting a Test." At a professional conference, a university professor praised the "sophistication" of a new statewide reading test and lamented the storm of protest with which a group of secondary school English teachers had greeted the test "simply because its format was unfamiliar." He urged teachers to embrace the test and not to allow their fears of the unknown to lead them astray.

Later, in another setting, a high school teacher responded to the professor's comments. She explained that she and her colleagues resisted the test not because it was unfamiliar to them but because it lacked the two key features of authentic assessment: contextual validity and consequential validity. She and her colleagues were trying to foster literacy by requiring students to read, write, and perform creative and critical tasks with literary texts. The multiple-correct format of the new reading test was alien and largely irrelevant to the complex abilities these teachers wanted to promote. Furthermore, since every act of evaluation drives instruction, the test also threatened to undermine these teachers' best work by forcing them to focus on the rudiments of reading to the neglect of literary interpretation.

Anecdote 2 might be entitled "You're *All* like That!" During a visit to observe and evaluate a student teacher, a university supervisor sat on a bench in the high school lobby talking with the cooperating teacher, a seasoned instructor of secondary school English. This cooperating teacher was complaining bitterly about how arrogant, ignorant, and out of touch everyone at the university was regarding the realities of teaching English in public high schools. There was the usual mention of ivory towers as well as some other, less pastoral, images. In an attempt to acknowledge the views of the cooperating teacher, the university supervisor replied, "You're right, there *are* some faculty members like that at the university." In response, the cooperating teacher grabbed the univesrity supervisor by the arm and exclaimed "No! You're *all* like that, every one of you!"

What might have saved the university professor in the first anecdote and the high school teacher in the second from stumbling into ill-informed and destructive assumptions about their counterparts? The professor recognized that teachers objected to the reading test, but he assumed their objections were reactionary, based in ignorance of testing theory rather than in knowledge of both testing theory and the teachers' own instructional goals, as turned out to be the case. Had he discussed with the protesting teachers their concerns, and had he ventured into the schools to observe the high-level learning threatened by the test, the professor might have avoided making a condescending and unfair assumption regarding teachers' motives for resisting the test. He also might have learned something about authentic assessment.

The high school teacher in anecdote 2 similarly indulged in the habit of dismissiveness, only from the other side of the secondary school–university border. Had she made herself aware of the long history of work by faculty members on behalf of and in collaboration with teachers like herself, and had she inquired about the years of high school teaching experience from which most university supervisors benefit, she might have been slower to condemn all university academics for their arrogance and irrelevance. This teacher needed to learn more and condemn less.

Having illustrated some of the tensions and misunderstandings that mark teacher preparation in our field, I now turn to strategies for establishing dialogue and opening negotiations among the divided parties. From the two anecdotes related above—and from the many similar stories that any of us involved with teacher preparation could add—I believe we can discern several principles for improving our situation. I emphasize that all parties concerned with English education can and should think about ways to ameliorate the discord and alienation that mar relations among groups who should be strong allies. Generally, I characterize these actions as professional border crossing.

We should meet our counterparts face-to-face. The philosopher Emmanuel Levinas suggests that ethical relations depend foremost on seeing the other literally face-to-face. His ethical scheme presents a bracing and practicable challenge to our usual way of proceeding, in which those in different camps remain distant from us, invisible to us, and therefore relatively easy to caricature, dismiss, or disdain. Levinas's approach suggests that we must take the time and trouble to meet and talk in person with our counterparts across the hallway in the department, across the quad in the other college, or across town in the high school or the university.

We should travel into alien territory. While the first principle identifies the key condition of meeting, this second principle emphasizes the best location. One of the most promising themes in the programs described and envisioned in this volume is that of teacher educators embarking on friendly forays into one another's territories. If any action can help overcome the barriers built into our institutionalized relationships, it is leaving our familiar domains and venturing into those of others. There, we are more likely to notice important contingencies and contexts that help explain our colleagues' views and that may modify our own.

We should institutionalize and reward border crossing. Occasional face-to-face meetings and visits to one another's workplaces are good. Far better are regular, required, and rewarded meetings and visits. Educators work under tremendous pressures for meager rewards. When the pressure reaches its peak, what is neither required nor rewarded is neglected and even, in a way, forbidden or punished. If we value border crossing in English education, we must not only schedule it regularly but also make it necessary and beneficial to those who would participate in it.

Readers of this volume will have noticed numerous examples of border crossing in the actual and ideal teacher education programs described. Participants in the MLA Teacher Education Project have described collaborative teaching between university and secondary school colleagues; advisory boards that include institutional others; conferences in which members of the various parties in teacher education present their questions and findings side by side; and efforts to include a range of voices in the process of renewing a program, a department, or a school. More examples can be found in Ron Fortune's *School-College Collaborative Programs in English.* As Fortune observes, the most difficult element in sustaining collaboration seems to be the third of the border-crossing principles mentioned above: how to make regular and rewarding these efforts toward outreach. Perhaps readers of this volume will raise the issue with deans and provosts, who are in a position to support and reward border-crossing projects.

In their classic work of social philosophy, Muzafer Sherif and Carolyn Sherif suggested that the best way to overcome mutual prejudices is to have a small team of diverse individuals working together to solve a specific problem of immediate importance to everyone on the team. Following Sherif and Sherif, teacher educators could gather to solve a specific problem pressing on everyone in teacher education. Assessment of teaching candidates reverberates throughout the work of everyone involved in preparing future teachers, and might be one concrete example of a border-crossing project. Working groups could study assessment options, formulate recommendations, and work to see those recommendations implemented and refined. Not only would we likely gain better assessments; we would also gain better understanding and appreciation among group members.

Again and again, we discover systemic obstacles to the ideal of collaboration and mutual understanding. Reward systems neglect sustained collaboration across departments, colleges, and institutions. Educators face such intense demands on their time and energy that they feel little inclination or ability to reach out to colleagues. Perhaps most difficult of all, each party in English education is accustomed to being criticized and undervalued by the rest. As someone who works closely with English educators of all kinds—secondary school teachers, university faculty members of several kinds, and student teachers—I am distressed and discouraged by the "arrogance and condescension" that Elbow named as "the characteristic sins of our profession." But if we unravel prejudices along all these borders and weave a new fabric of professional alliance in English studies, this daunting culture and history can be altered.

In student teachers we see members of our profession who play a distinctive role and who therefore offer a unique possibility. As I noted earlier, no player on the scene of English education has more contact with all the other parties. In fact, student teachers complain that this is a particularly painful part of their experience. To take one common example: Tuesday morning, they observe an English teacher marching his ninth-graders through grammar worksheets; Wednesday afternoon, their professor in the Teaching of Writing course assigns Patrick Hartwell's "Grammar, Grammars, and the Teaching of Grammar" and proclaims that formal grammar instruction is not only useless but harmful to young students of writing.

If their mentors in universities and high schools seriously and permanently committed themselves to the border-crossing project I propose, a new possibility could open for student teachers. Instead of feeling caught in the cross fire among various theoretical or ideological camps, student teachers could use their position to keep all parties aware of the others. Caught between opponents in the grammar debate, they could ask their professors to confront the cultural and political pressures to teach formal grammar in the secondary schools. They could then return to that ninth-grade classroom to ask the teacher how filling out worksheets helps his students write better.

Just as shuttle diplomats cannot safely do their peacemaking during times of open warfare, we should not expect student teachers to take on this dramatic role until we—the professionals in universities, colleges, and secondary schools—lay down our barbs and begin a genuine conversation. Once the borders of English education are calm, I foresee a new and exhilarating role for student teachers in keeping communications among rivals open and honest and in maintaining the détente for which I have called. Not only would such student teachers be holding their university and secondary school mentors accountable to the shared professional standard of the border crosser; they themselves would be living that standard, in preparation for a career of collaboration, creative and critical engagement, and lifelong professional growth as an English educator.

Note

I wish to thank Tom Gerschick, George Rundblad, Julie Hile, Phyllis Franklin, Ron Fotune, and Lisa Thomas for their responses to drafts of this essay. For the strengths of the piece I am indebted to them; for its weaknesses I am solely responsible.

WORKS CITED

Elbow, Peter. *What Is English?* New York: MLA, 1990.

Fortune, Ron, ed. *School-College Collaborative Programs in English.* New York: MLA, 1986.

Hartwell, Patrick. "Grammar, Grammars, and the Teaching of Grammar." *College English* 47 (1985): 105–27.

Levinas, Emmanuel. *Difficult Freedom: Essays on Judaism.* Trans. Sean Hand. Baltimore: Johns Hopkins UP, 1990.

Sherif, Muzafer, and Carolyn Sherif. *An Outline of Social Psychology.* New York: Harper, 1956.

JAMES MARSHALL

Closely Reading Ourselves: Teaching English and the Education of Teachers

When we began the MLA Teacher Education Project, one of our first tasks was to describe and assess our English teacher preparation program in the light of recent discussions of educational reform and the quite visible changes in literary studies. How are we teaching teachers to be teachers, we were asked to ask, and are we doing it right? At the University of Iowa we started simply by cataloging the courses we required—so many of this kind of English course, so many of that kind of course in education—but we didn't get far before we realized that most of the courses required for a license to teach English were in fact taught in the English department. Those who would teach high school English were first English majors at the university, and the requirements for that major spelled out a fairly rigorous preparation in the discipline.

Now, it is not the custom to think of courses in English as courses in teacher preparation, except in an indirect, deep-background sort of way. We often think of teacher preparation as something that goes on someplace else—over in the Ed School perhaps—but not here, not in our classrooms. Our part in the process, as English faculty members, is to provide the knowledge, the content, the stuff that those preparing to teach will somehow package and deliver to a younger audience, with the help of faculty members in the Ed School. Such packaging is important work, valuable work, we might say, but not our work. Our work is different. Our work is about literature, not about methods of teaching.

But let me submit, as a kind of premise for what follows, that all teaching is about teaching—just as all writing is about writing—and that every class that enrolls prospective teachers is a class in teacher preparation. Jerome Bruner argues that by sitting in chairs we not only learn about chairs, we also learn about sitting (Bruner and Olson 1). By sitting in classrooms where literature is taught, we not only learn about literature, we also learn about teaching literature. And we learn it in pretty hard-wired ways. We have an extraordinarily long apprenticeship in our profession, because we are observing teachers from early childhood, studying their moves, puzzling over their folkways, considering how they think, and adjusting accordingly. By the time most prospective teachers graduate from college, they have spent at least sixteen years closely watching teachers teach, and the vast majority of those closely watched teachers were not consciously teaching courses in teacher preparation. How could any program that calls itself a program in teacher preparation undo such an apprenticeship? When students decide to become teachers, how could it overturn, unteach, everything that they have already learned about teaching? It is the indirect teaching about teaching, the unself-conscious training in teacher preparation that is powerful precisely because it is unnamed, because it remains largely invisible, almost natural. As the linguist James Paul Gee has argued, those discourses that we learn without fully knowing that we are learning them — that are learned in our lived-in environment while we think we are doing other things — are, like mother tongues, the discourses that we learn best. Teaching English is such a discourse, and we teach it everytime we teach English.

As part of our self-study, we thought we would look to the research to see what other studies had been done about the teaching of literature at the university, to see if there were models of inquiry that we might borrow from. But here we were stopped short. For the truth is that there are no published research studies about how the teaching of literature proceeds at the university, although there is a great deal of writing about this subject. We have reports like the one we ourselves were preparing, that is, reports on how departments of English organize their curriculum, how they evaluate their faculty, how much writing they assign, what periods or genres or authors or courses in theory are required. Such reports are legion — almost all of us have had to prepare them when our department is undergoing a review — and some prototypical, very early examples are provided in Gerald Graff and Michael Warner's documentary anthology of essays, *The Origins of Literary Studies in America,* published as a companion to Graff's *Professing Literature.* We also have histories, like those of Graff and Paul Lauter and David Shumway. We have arguments about what teaching ought to be, such as those constructed by Stanley Fish and

David Bleich and Robert Scholes and Jane Tompkins. We have more or less empirical reports of effective teaching strategies: the sometimes helpful "go thou and do likewise" genre of research on teaching. And we have memoirs, written from a student's or a faculty member's perspective—some angry and bitter, some warm and fuzzy—with an assortment of anecdotes and narratives that are tellable, according to the conventions of storytelling, precisely because they are not part of the normal run of events, precisely because they stand out from the dailiness of classroom life.

What we do not have are ethnographies of practice—studies not of the memorable, the special, the successful, the tellable but of our quotidian classroom patterns, our familiar routines, the conventions that we take for granted. We have no studies that place the ethnographer bodily in the classroom, taking field notes, interviewing faculty members and students, collecting artifacts, making tentative inferences, triangulating across data sources, submitting results to a scholarly press for review. Nothing. And this, we think, is surprising.

It is surprising, because the last quarter century has seen an enormous production of such ethnographies of teaching practice, studies of almost every educational venue one could name, from preschools in Harlem to community colleges in suburban San Francisco, from adult literacy programs to advanced placement high school classes, from ESL classrooms to private elementary schools, from junior high tutorials to writing projects for teachers. Almost any place where literacy is taught and learned has attracted serious ethnographic inquiry; scholars such as Shirley Heath, Anne Dyson, Bonnie Sunstein, Judith Langer, Susan Hynds, and Mike Rose have greatly enriched our understanding of how specific contexts shape the possibilities for reading and writing—in fact, shape what counts as reading and writing. Given this outpouring of research, one would have expected at least some interest in university classroom life. But except for studies of freshman composition, where the instructors are untenured adjuncts or graduate teaching assistants, there is little or nothing. Virtually all teachers working in the venues studied in the ethnographies—all the ESL and reading teachers, all the advanced placement teachers and university adjuncts—were themselves trained in universities, trained at least in part by people like us. And yet professors of English, teachers of literature, have never been studied as they have been. Why?

Perhaps you have already thought of an answer. But before I go further, let me describe briefly what we found in our small study of how one department teaches literature to its undergraduates. Unfortunately, it is not a full-blown ethnography or even close to one. It is a modest study, based on interviews and the analysis of classroom artifacts, mostly syllabi and writing assignments, and its findings will not, I'm certain, startle you. But I think the findings need to be considered, so English professors can ask if this is really what they want after all.

What we found when we talked to our colleagues, studied their syllabi and writing assignments, and asked them to think with us about what they did in their classrooms was the presence of what we came to call a normative, formalist script for the teaching of literature—a script so powerful, so taken for granted, so seldom questioned or even acknowledged, that, as one of our colleagues suggested, pointing it out is like reminding people that they tend to breathe fairly regularly.

The script goes like this:

Reading. In designing courses, faculty members tend to be highly specific in the texts they wanted students to read: not three poems by Emily Dickinson and two stories by Henry James, but this Dickinson poem for Tuesday and these James stories in this edition for next week. The net effect, of course, was to privilege the reading of particular texts in particular material forms. Moreover, most of the reading that faculty members required was literature as conventionally defined. It consisted of novels, stories, poems, plays, epics, and only sometimes nonfiction with literary credentials (autobiographies or essays).

Talking. In leading classroom discussion, faculty members told us that they wanted to be in control. As one of our colleagues said, "Obviously, I have an agenda. I mean, when I read a story I normally think, 'This is important, and this, and this,' so I certainly come in with my agenda. If I don't make it known to my students right away, it might come out in group discussion. But I selected these stories for certain purposes." Or, as another put it, "I try to think about the one main thing that must be said as far as I'm concerned in this class, and whether it is a question or just some passage we need to look at, I scope out a discussion around this main point. That seems really crucial to me." Faculty members, in other words, usually scripted classroom discussions ahead of time. Sometimes there were unlooked-for and much welcomed observations, questions, or insights that pulled those discussions one or even two levels deeper. But the norm—and the norm is what we were trying to describe—was to think of the discussion as anchored in a reading the teacher had already constructed, through a series of "main things" that had to be covered.

Writing. In assigning student writing, faculty members seemed to abide by a fairly sturdy set of assumptions; the writing itself was to abide by a fairly sturdy set of conventions. As one faculty member said, "I'm looking for old-fashioned arguments. I want to know that they can formulate an argument around a thesis." Or, as another suggested, "I grade them entirely on the basis of: Is there a thesis? Is there an argument? Am I going to be persuaded? I tell them this in advance." In fact, all the faculty members we interviewed told us that the argumentative essay, usually a close reading of a specific text with a thesis and with quotations as evidence, was a central and necessary part of their teaching. The argumentative essay was the primary vehicle through which students represented their understanding of what they read. More generally, it was a genre of writing, and a way of thinking, that faculty members felt students should master.

This repertoire of normative teaching practices — the close reading of selected texts in relative isolation from cultural contexts, the frequent reliance on teacher-directed large-group discussions, the privileging of thesis-driven, analytical essays — has been with us for at least fifty years now. It has remained stubbornly in place, even though the formalist assumptions that first nourished it have eroded and even though our scholarship has moved in entirely new directions. Why such hardy endurance? Here is where those unwritten ethnographies of practice might become relevant.

I would like to argue that our teaching has not changed much, because we don't talk about it much and, perhaps more telling, because we don't write about it much. Jack Goody and Ian Watt some thirty years ago, and Walter Ong a few years later, had much to say about the intellectual changes that are possible when a culture moves from primariliy oral to primarily written forms of discourse. One of those changes is that basic strategies of analysis and critique become possible. In embarrassingly simple terms, writing holds thinking still long enough so that we can think about it some more — discuss where it is weak, elaborate on it, revise it, discard it altogether. Such critique and evaluation, Goody, Watt, and Ong argue, are not usually possible in oral cultures, where the premium is on memory and preservation. I submit that teaching exists primarily in our profession in an oral culture. Teaching is what we talk about, in the halls, in our offices, but seldom write about. When we do write about it—in letters of recommendation, endorsements for teaching awards, tenure and promotion reviews—the language we use is normative, rather than analytical; it speaks of how well the teaching worked but not usually at length about how the teaching worked. We seldom take our teaching apart to see how and why it proceeds as it does, and that has worked to slow down or even stop its evolution. We need to more closely read ourselves.

One way to frame such a project might be to examine, on theoretical grounds, the consequences of privileging, even canonizing, one particular way of reading in our classrooms. Peter Rabinowitz makes such an effort in his essay "Against Close Reading." Arguing that a "commitment to close reading has become the *cantus firmus* in the multivoiced canon of contemporary criticism," Rabinowitz goes on to demonstrate how that commitment severely constrains not only how students read but what they read as well (230). We teach texts, he says, that lend themselves to the kinds of reading we privilege, while marginalizing those texts that don't. Or, to put it perhaps more brashly, we ignore the cues that authors have left about how their texts are to be read; we read them our way anyway. In this fashion, what is found in a text becomes not what is really there but what we expected to find or, rather, what our particular ways of reading made, almost inevitably, visible.

Against such a monopoly of reading practice, Rabinowitz proposes a more generous plurality of options. A receptivity to literary experience depends, he argues, not only on the care with which readers approach texts but also on the range of reading experiences they have already had and on the variety of interpretive strategies at their disposal. Four years of basic close reading in high school followed by several years of close reading in college literature classes does not usually provide for such variety. Instead, it encourages students to become skilled at one kind of interpretive strategy, the strategy that works best with particular kinds of canonical texts, and to ignore other kinds of reading practices and other kinds of texts. The net result, even for our better students—maybe, especially for our better students—is to narrow rather than enlarge the repertoire of reading practices students may need or desire when they leave our classrooms to become independent, self-governing readers.

Another way to frame a study of our teaching, therefore, is to examine the consequences of that teaching on the reading practices of those we have taught. Some statistics might be helpful. Carl Kaestle, in his comprehensive study of literacy in the United States, points out that the percentage of the population reporting that they read books regularly has remained fairly constant at about twenty to twenty-five (185). This statistic refers not only to the reading of literature, certainly not to good literature, however defined. It refers, rather, to the reading of any trade book with an ISBN number, and includes *The Celestine Prophesy, Hollywood Wives,* and *Thirty Days to Thinner Thighs* as major data entries. James Twitchell, meanwhile, in *Carnival Culture,* reports that three authors—Stephen King, Danielle Steele, and Tom Clancy—were responsible for fifty percent of all the fiction sold in the United States in the 1980s (72–73). And the publishers of Silhouette and Harlequin Romances point with pride to the fact that their products are responsible annually for about twenty percent of the book-length fiction sold in the United States. We don't have to do much calculation to realize that there is little or no correlation between the reading practices we teach in school and the reading practices in which most adults engage when they leave school. In fact, the numbers suggest that there is a smaller percentage of even once-a-year book buyers in the United States than there are college graduates and that frequent readers may more likely come from groups who did not complete college than from those who did.

Even college-educated readers of more "serious fiction" do not often seem to read as we have taught them. In his study of adult book-group discussions, for instance, Michael Smith found that participants were far more likely than students in classrooms to relate personal experiences, talk about important ethical issues, and share their emotional experience of reading. Participants felt free to offer tentative ideas and to disagree with one another, though in interviews they reported that they rarely did either of these things when they were students. And in her comprehensive study of the Book-of-the-Month Club, Janice Radway argues that one of the reasons the club found such a wide readership is that its editors self-consciously associated the club's selections "with a particular form of experience, a reading experience that was, above everything else, characterized by the pleasure it gave. The particular experience referred to again and again in reader's reports [. . .] was always bound to a certain extent with a feeling of immersion, a sense of boundaries dissolved" (114). The austere virtues of close reading and tightly argued analysis, however honored in the academy, are not likely to bring such pleasures. And it is such pleasure that readers seem to seek when they leave us. Assuming that they read at all.

As English faculty members, we needn't, of course, feel responsible for the reading habits of the American citizenry, and describing them as I have does not, I hope, represent a criticism of the habits themselves. But this general outline of reading practices outside the academy suggests that they have almost nothing to do with the reading practices we privilege inside the academy. In fact, the relation seems almost stubbornly inverse. College-educated adults generally ignore what we have taught them and read what and how they want. Or else they listened to what we had to say about reading but found it too labor-intensive, too slow and painful compared with other activities, and stopped reading altogether. To the extent that the second alternative is true, or even possible, I would say we have a problem.

It may be possible. For the last several years I have been offering a course on the teaching of literature in which students who are planning to become teachers are asked to read a good many novels—no fewer than thirty over the fourteen weeks—as well as write papers and think about instructional issues. Most of the books are intended for adolescent readers: they are short narratives, offering the minor pleasures of plot development, character growth, and clear resolution. They are books meant to be read by young people, to encourage the act of reading, to provide a version of the reading pleasure Radway describes. They will not, then, generally reward the slow, careful reading students employ in their other classes (unless they are read, perhaps, as part of some larger project in cultural studies). They mean pretty much what they say, and no amount of analysis will make them mean more than that.

This brute fact both puzzles and frustrates my students. Equipped as they are with well-sharpened close-reading skills (most are advanced undergraduate English majors), they want to use those skills with the books they read for me. But they can't, and so, for a while at least, they don't know what to say about those books. Some continue to read slowly (one told me that it took her years to learn how to do it, and now she doesn't know how not to do it), and therefore have trouble finishing the required minimum of thirty books. Some think that my insistence that they read fairly quickly, for plot mostly, is a kind of violation of professional ethics. But most, with encouragement, learn, or rather relearn, how to read *unprofessionally*—the way most readers read most of the time.

But more important than the way students read in the course, I think, is what they say about how they have come to be the readers they are. The first writing assignment invites them to draft a reading autobiography, a narrative that begins with their earliest memories of being read to and concludes with a description of the reader they have become. They start the project by listing all the books they can remember reading at various points in their lives, from Golden Books and paperback series (Nancy

Drew, The Baby-Sitters Club, Goosebumps); through science fiction (for the males, usually) and romance (for the females, sometimes, and sometimes with embarrassment); through the assigned but frequently unread classics of high school English classes; through the underground, racier, furtively communal reading they may have done as adolescents; and finally to the more challenging, more official reading covered in their university English classes. I've collected several hundred of these autobiographies now, and though the stories vary in their details, a fairly predictable plotline has emerged. Generally, the students report a wide, exuberant, almost promiscuous amount of reading from the ages of eight through twelve or thirteen, followed by a precipitous decline as they approach high school. From the age of fourteen or fifteen on, in most accounts, reading for school has replaced reading outside of school, and freely chosen reading for pleasure has pretty much disappeared. There is too much else to do, students say, and reading for school has made reading work.

The students in the class are teachers-to-be, and so how they read, and what and why they read, matter a good deal. What they are learning from us about reading matters a good deal as well. In one of the autobiographies, a student offered this meditation on a moment in one of her university literature classes. The professor was teaching a course on early-twentieth-century literature and culture and was leading a discussion of minstrel shows and blackface. My student wrote:

> In beginning the lecture on "black face," [the professor] said it was "a complex signifier, as we say." Who is *we*? Am I we? Are we the class? Or are we professors of my teacher's caliber? At the time I took *we* to be English scholars and found myself torn. I am a reader and critic of literature and have the degree to prove it. However, I am also a student, with only a BA, so maybe I am not we. I felt absolutely sure that the girls sitting next to me who had been discussing sorority gossip before class were not we. I wonder now if they do consider themselves to be we. I cannot picture them calling anything any kind of signifier. The point is, though, that by using the academic *we,* my teacher drew a line. There are people who use these literary terms and people who do not, and I am not sure that my teacher really invited us, as his intellectual charges, into the group. If language is power, then the powerful would seem to say *signifier* and those outside the loop would apparently say something else. After this lecture, I believe that most students in our class would say something else.

As this student and her peers approach the point of entering their own classrooms as teachers, what *we* will they be a part of, and into what *we* will they invite their students? Is it our *we* or some other? When we teach teachers — and we are always teaching teachers — we are also teaching those whom those teachers will teach. That is a lot of teaching, which is all the more reason why we need to know more about how and why we teach as we do.

WORKS CITED

Bruner, Jerome, and D. Olson. "Symbols and Texts as Tools of Intellect." *Interchange* 8 (1978): 1–15.

Gee, James Paul. *The Social Mind: Language, Ideology, and Social Practice.* New York: Bergin, 1992.

Goody, Jack, and Ian Watt. "The Consequences of Literacy." *Perspectives on Literacy.* Ed. E. Kintgen, B. Kroll, and M. Rose. Carbondale: Southern Illinois UP, 1968. 3–27.

Graff, Gerald. *Professing Literature: An Institutional History.* Chicago: U of Chicago P, 1987.

Graff, Gerald, and Michael Warner, eds. *The Origins of Literary Studies in America: A Documentary Anthology.* New York: Routledge, 1989.

Kaestle, Carl. *Literacy in the United States.* New Haven: Yale UP, 1991.

Ong, Walter J. *Orality and Literacy.* New York: Methuen, 1982.

Rabinowitz, Peter. "Against Close Reading." *Pedagogy in Politics: Theory and Critical Teaching.* Ed. M. Kecht. Champaign: U of Illinois P, 1992. 230–43.

Radway, Janice A. *A Feeling for Books: The Book-of-the-Month Club, Literary Taste, and Middle-Class Desire.* Chapel Hill: U of North Carolina P, 1987.

Scholes, Robert. *Textual Power: Literary Theory and the Teaching of English.* New Haven: Yale UP, 1985.

Schumway, David. *Creating American Civilization: A Geneaology of American Literature as an Academic Discipline.* Minneapolis: U of Minnesota P, 1994.

Smith, Michael. "Adult Book-Club Discussions: Toward an Understanding of the Culture of Practice." *The Language of Interpretation: Patterns of Discourse in Discussions of Literature.* Ed. James Marshall, Peter Smagorinsky, and Smith. Urbana: NCTE, 1995. 100–20.

Twitchell, James B. *Carnival Culture: The Trashing of Taste in America.* New York: Columbia UP, 1992.

DAVID A. FEIN

Challenges of Teaching Literature: Reflections on the MLA Teacher Education Project

The debate regarding the relative merits of language versus literature in the undergraduate language program is one that has raged (and I use the verb deliberately) for as long as this middle-aged professor can remember. Fiercely held convictions on both sides invest the debate with a particular vehemence and explosiveness that make this issue an especially divisive and dangerous one, guaranteed to set off fireworks in even the most harmonious and collegial group of university and secondary-level foreign language faculty members. I should state at the outset that I have no intention of rekindling this debate. I am more interested in searching for possible resolutions and categorically refuse to place myself squarely in one camp or the other. Nevertheless, the MLA Teacher Education Project, in which my department participated last year, has brought the issue sharply into focus for me and, I suspect, for many of my colleagues around the country who participated in the project. I approach the thorny issue with reluctance, afraid of pricking my fingers while trying to get a grasp on it. Yet our team and other teams have wrestled with it throughout the duration of the project.

Before proceeding, I should give a little of my background. A fairly typical product of the graduate training prevalent in the early 1970s, I received a heavy dose of literature courses as a graduate student. Practically every course I took was related to the study of French literature. Like most of my fellow graduate students, I paid a great deal of attention to literary theory and textual analysis, less attention to linguistics, and virtually none to pedagogical issues. We were expected to learn to teach through practice. We all experienced the usual problems of novice teachers, made the usual mistakes, felt the usual frustrations, and basically muddled through on our own, turning to one another for advice and support, having practically no guidance or supervision.

As a product of a mode of training heavily oriented toward literary theory, I naturally found myself engaged in literary scholarship as I attempted to establish a place for myself in the profession. Practically all my published work (including three books, with a fourth in press) relates to a rather narrow chronological period (a span of fifty years in the fifteenth century) and to one particular genre (lyric poetry). There is nothing unusual about this academic profile. In fact, it is one into which most of the colleagues of my generation could (with some slight modifications) comfortably fit.

I give this brief bit of autobiographical information to show that I am, both by training and by inclination, deeply immersed in the study of literature. Like most of the colleagues in my department, I have always enjoyed reading and reflecting on the meaning of what I read, discussing a text (whether orally or in writing), and, especially, challenging students to reflect on what they have read. This is, after all, what we are paid to do. Or so I thought for many years. An NEH-sponsored institute, forcing me into direct contact with high school French teachers, first brought me to the realization that the traditional literature course offered in our universities is of limited value to teachers (or those training to teach) at the secondary level. This realization was further reinforced by a follow-up survey that I distributed to all high school French teachers in the state of North Carolina (the survey was funded by the Research Council of the University of North Carolina, Greensboro). Virtually half the respondents felt that they had never been properly trained to teach French literature. Many said they encountered serious obstacles when attempting to teach literature, citing student resistance, the inherent difficulty of the exercise, inability to integrate the texts with the rest of the curriculum, and a lack of self-confidence. Sentiments ranged from frustration and apathy to outright hostility. It was evident that the question had touched a nerve.

There seems to be a widespread perception among secondary school teachers and among students preparing to enter the teaching profession that undergraduate language programs place a disproportionately heavy emphasis on literature. They feel that the time they spend in literature courses could be more profitably invested in the study of language and culture. Rather than view literature, language, and culture as interrelated areas, they tend to draw a sharp line between the first and the second two categories, feeling that courses in language and culture contribute far more to their preparation as teachers than do courses in literature. They generally perceive the teaching of literature as a passive and static process. It is clear that the lecture mode of instruction is still very much alive and well in many literature classes, and it is equally clear that many students find this mode of little use in preparation for their own teaching.

Some of the comments that follow are excerpted from the surveys we distributed to teacher education majors and secondary school teachers as part of our baseline study for the MLA Teacher Education Project; others are from the survey of high school French teachers that I conducted earlier. They may not always be expressed with elegance or concision, but the depth of their conviction and often the note of frustration is eloquent.

> "Literature is good, but should not be required. [. . .] The literature courses have done me little good." (teacher education major)
>
> "I think some of the literature courses are useful, but after a certain level, the only thing one ends up taking are literature courses, be it poetry, theater, et cetera." (teacher education major)
>
> "It seems that [literature] is all that is offered. [. . .] More culture is needed to have a real understanding of the underlying meaning/background in each novel, et cetera." (high school teacher)

The common complaint in these three comments is that major requirements tend to be overloaded with literature, at the expense of language and culture. Yet most undergraduate programs, or at least the ones our team studied, maintain a fairly reasonable balance among literature, language, and culture. This contradiction suggests that the problem lies not in the number of literature courses per se but in the way literature is approached in these courses. The third comment (offered by an experienced high school teacher) is especially revealing; its underlying assumption is that literature courses, by their very nature, cannot provide the cultural knowledge that secondary school teachers consider essential (with, it should be added, the blessing and encouragement of those of us who train them) to their preparation and their ability to fulfill the loftiest goals of their mission as language teachers.

Where did this artificial separation of literature and culture come from? Why do these teachers not view literature as a useful, valuable, even unparalleled source of cultural information? Could it be that we have somehow failed to communicate the message that the literary text is also a cultural artifact that, with proper manipulation, can yield precious insight into cultural differences? Why, in all the clamor for culturally relevant teaching, do we still hear so little about literature? We may believe that our literature courses adequately highlight the cultural issues buried in a given text, but the perception of our students should cause us to look a little more closely and critically at our approach to literature. Are we making a deliberate effort to explore the cultural resources of the works we teach, or are we (like our professors before us, and theirs before them) only interested in literature qua literature?

Taking a more positive approach than many, this high school teacher challenges us to expand our approach to literature:

> "If direction were made available to us as to strategies to teach grammar, culture, art, music, history through literature, I would love it."

The gentle rebuke that I read into this comment is that we are not exploiting the cultural totality and richness of the text as a resource for presenting culture, not approaching literature as a window into the distinctive cultural values of the period it represents. The rebuke reflects the interdisciplinary approaches so prevalent in contemporary critical theory. It urges us, as teachers of literature, to rise to the challenge. Unlike many of the other comments in the surveys, it is not hostile, showing a strong bias against literature. Rather, it reveals a refreshing spirit of open-mindedness, sincerity, and collegiality.

> "Not too useful in teaching high school. [. . .] [We need] less literature, more hands-on practice on how to effectively teach a foreign language." (high school teacher)

The assumption (and it is an assumption evidently grounded in personal experience) is that literature classes do not prepare students to teach the language. Literature and language courses in the mind of this person are strictly segregated from each other, neatly and conveniently compartmentalized in the curriculum. How did the natural connection between language and literature become severed? Why should literature courses not be useful in preparing our students "to effectively teach a foreign language"? What has gone wrong here? Did we somehow miss an opportunity to demonstrate to our students that literature is in fact an excellent resource for teaching language?

The overall impression created by the survey comments is that literature is in the process of disappearing completely from the high school curriculum:

> "I do not teach literature mainly because I believe it is inappropriate to try it at the high school level."

If literature is eliminated from most secondary-level programs, then it will obviously become increasingly difficult to make a case for the value of including a strong emphasis on literature in foreign language teacher education programs. With increased budgetary constraints, many high school teachers are in fact already struggling to keep their upper-level language programs alive. Desperately attempting to attract students, they will understandably reject anything that they believe discourages students from continuing to the advanced levels. Literature, (unfortunately for them, for us, and for their students) is often perceived as a turnoff.

Finally, survey comments reflect a perception that lies at the heart of the impetus that generated the MLA Teacher Education Project, namely, that we could be doing a better job of preparing teachers for the reality of classroom teaching. All three of the following comments come from experienced high school teachers:

> "I received a good [undergraduate] background in French literature, but no instruction on how to teach it in high school."
>
> "Although I was taught much literature in college, I was *not* taught how to incorporate it into a ridiculously demanding high school schedule."
>
> "I do not feel that I was at all prepared when I left [a certain university] to teach literature."

One senses frustration, irritation, possibly even disillusionment. There is probably little we can do to counter a genuinely antiliterary bias. In my own experience, however, I have found very few examples of such strong aversion to literature. Students drawn to the study of language, it seems to me, are intrigued by language in all its various forms, including literary manifestations. Indeed, when they are led (through skillful guidance) to approach a text as living language with all its attendant complexities, subtleties, and surprises rather than as simply words on a page (words that often have been lying on that dusty page for hundreds of years), they generally experience the same fascination that brought most of us into this profession in the first place. So I cannot accept the idea that there is some sort of inherent repugnance to the study of literature, a severe allergic sensitivity that, although hardly known in previous generations, has become inexplicably prevalent in today's students.

Early in the teacher education project, our team became aware that student and teacher concerns about training pertain more to presentation than to content. Not surprisingly, students and teachers much prefer dynamic, interactive, participatory courses over those in which they find themselves assuming an essentially passive role. We also discovered that students feel the lecture mode of instruction is more prominent in literature classes than in other types of courses. Negative comments about literature courses by and large relate not to the study of literature itself but to disappointing experiences in specific courses, experiences leading to unpleasant memories and unfortunate associations that may color the student's future attitude toward the teaching of literature.

We should begin to confront and accept some realities. Literature, by its nature, will challenge even the best prepared of students. Discussing in the target language such topics as imagery, style, symbolism, irony, and narrative technique requires a range of vocabulary and a linguistic facility that many students—most students—simply have not yet developed. Even to formulate a straightforward narration of a simple story often requires considerable effort on their part. When it comes to more-abstract elements of the text, they are in over their heads. This, of course, is where the lecturing begins. The professor's purpose is not so much to lecture as to draw the students' attention to certain important, and perhaps somewhat subtle, features that the professor considers essential to a proper understanding and appreciation of the text. I am not advocating that we totally abandon literary analysis or that we turn our literature classes into intellectually shallow exercises, limiting the discussion to who did what where and with whom. But after witnessing the sad status of literature courses in the eyes of our secondary school teachers and future teachers, I cannot shake the gut feeling that we are doing something wrong.

I would suggest that we continue to set our ultimate sights on the most interesting and most difficult aspects of the literature we teach—style, symbolism, irony, and so on—but that we also approach each text as an opportunity to integrate language and literature, allowing students to gradually build the vocabulary, the linguistic facility, and the self-confidence to discuss the text. If we expect our teacher education students to eventually bring literature into their own classrooms, and to do that with some degree of competence and enthusiasm, then it is essential that they, as students, have positive and active encounters with literature in the classroom. It is also essential that they be provided with a model for exploiting the literary text as a resource for teaching language and culture. We can do all this in our literature classes without abandoning the more traditional aspects of teaching literature. A few hypothetical examples will illustrate the kind of model I have in mind.

Professor A begins her class (a survey of French literature) with a brief quiz based on the assigned reading for the day. Immediately after the quiz, she distributes a short list of sentences taken from the papers she has just returned to the students. Each sentence contains at least one grammatical error, which students are asked to identify and correct. Next, they are divided into small groups and given one or two questions to discuss. These questions are taken from study questions that students were given at the end of the previous class to guide their reading of the text. Professor A circulates among the groups, pausing occasionally to answer questions or to pose questions of her own. Accustomed to the routine, the students are comfortable with the exercise and with her presence. When she feels that the topics have been adequately prepared, she opens the class discussion. Reasonably well acquainted with the text as a result of the study questions, the quiz, and the small-group discussion, the students have built enough self-confidence to venture deeper into their exploration of the reading. Their instructor skillfully leads them to discover elements of the text they were unaware of. Satisfied that the students have been given ample opportunity to develop and communicate their understanding of the reading, she now provides information that will permit them to situate and appreciate the text within a larger historical context. The students listen attentively, taking notes, and a few seek clarification on various points during the few minutes allotted for questions at the end of the class period. The text under discussion, by the way, was an essay by Montaigne, not by any means an easy author. And, yes, the entire class took place in French.

The issues associated with the teaching of literature are complex, and I certainly do not intend to offer this hypothetical classroom model as a solution to all the problems expressed in the student surveys and in many discussions generated by the MLA Teacher Education Project. There is growing interest in the teaching of language through literature throughout the college curriculum. Also, as teachers of language and literature, we must constantly challenge ourselves and our students to situate the subject area within an appropriate cultural context. We should reevaluate the efficacy of traditional approaches to the teaching of literature, searching for ways to engage more actively our students in the learning process.

As I hope I demonstrated in my illustration, I am not advocating the wholesale abandonment of the lecture mode. Indeed, when properly used, lecturing can provide students with an inspiring model of eloquent articulation and critical thinking. It has become one of serveral modes operating in the student-centered literature class. A more enlightened, a more integrated and collaborative (albeit less traditional) approach to the teaching of literature should result in more literature being read and discussed in more classrooms at every level of secondary and postsecondary study, and this broadly humanistic goal is one that all of us, regardless of our pedagogical inclination, should be able to embrace.

WORK CITED

Fein, David A. "Literature in the High School French Class." *French Review* 60 (1986): 191–95.

DORIS Y. KADISH

Teaching Literature in the Foreign Language Classroom: Where Have We Been and Where Do We Go Now?

Literature, I predict, will mean both less and more in the twenty-first century than it has in the past. In the minus column, the loss of literature's privileged status will continue; literature will remain only one rather than the only act in town. A multiplicity of diverse and sophisticated representations, both verbal and visual, surrounds us today. The printed page competes with movies, TV, music videos, computer games, CD-ROM materials, the Internet, and a host of other media sources. Most of us find aesthetic, psychological, or social satisfaction through diverse forms of culture, ranging from jazz, foreign films, and high literature to rap music, soap operas, and romance or mystery novels. Inasmuch as all these cultural products are part of people's lives, in every language, they need to be incorporated into our conceptualization of what future teachers of foreign languages will learn.

It would be wrong to conclude, however, that literature has lost its appeal simply by virtue of having to compete with other kinds of media. I'm afraid that many teachers today assume that students are not interested in literature and accordingly pay undue attention to the reported "I hate literature" phenomenon among students. More than actually hating literature, students dislike teaching approaches to literature that are unchallenging or that isolate literature from its rich social and historical context. In conducting exit interviews with the graduating language majors at the University of Georgia, I have found that with few exceptions students are as enthusiastic about classes and teachers that include challenging and contextualized treatments of literature as they are about other subjects, such as conversation, linguistics, or civilization. Clearly, it would be misguided to conclude that not teaching literature is the way to strengthen the preparation of future teachers. Such a move is unsound, both because it undermines the humanistic mission of an undergraduate education and because it weakens the linguistic and cultural preparation of students preparing for various careers, including precollege education.

I might add that assuming that literature has lost all appeal goes counter to some of the positive attitudes toward literature that have been emerging in recent times and that are evident in a variety of contemporary cultural developments. Consider the example of reading groups, whose growing popularity and increased sophistication Mary Cregan highlights in a recent article in *The Chronicle of Higher Education*. As she points out, more books are published today than ever before, and "Americans are spending more of their time reading than, say, surfing the Internet or even watching movies" (B4). Reading groups have become so popular that bookstores and book chains now provide postings of reading lists, make space available where members can meet, and even offer the services of store employees to lead groups; and, to meet this growing new market of readers, commercial presses publish reading guides not unlike materials used in literature classes (B5). To cite another example, we know that Victor Hugo has been all the rage for some time now with the millions of viewers of *Les Mis* throughout the world as well as the innumerable children and adults who have flocked to see the animated film version of *The Hunchback of Notre Dame*. These instances of an enormous popular enthusiasm for productions based on literary works of the past indicate that persons of all ages do want literature. In fact, people are often led to reading the text by seeing a performance: witness the new English translation of *Les misérables* that was featured recently in the windows of a prominent book chain. The pessimism about the fate of reading in contemporary society, expressed in works such as Sven Birkerts's *The Gutenberg Elegies* and by the academic world generally, is in one important sense unwarranted. Cregan suggests that if many literature professors have been slow to recognize the significance of reading groups, it is because they consider the kind of contemporary fiction often discussed in those groups as subliterary.

What we as teachers of literature need the most as we enter the twenty-first century is to find enriched and enriching ways of tapping into the intellectual interests of particular groups of readers and thereby meeting the many academic needs that literature can fill. Future teachers of foreign languages are one such group, with a special set of needs that we must work hard to address: the need to acquire the humanistic legacy that the university serves to transmit; the need to develop advanced linguistic and cultural competence in a foreign language; and the need to gain familiarity with and sensitivity to the broad range of social, ethnic, sexual, and racial identities that cohabit in the diverse societies of the modern world. The teaching of literature I have in mind can be designated as thick teaching, to echo Clifford Geertz's well-known "thick description" (7): a thorough, systematic analysis of the full range of heterogeneous patterns, symbols, and material details of a culture, including language. Recently, Kwame Anthony Appiah has drawn on Geertz's notion in articulating the related concept of thick translation, which I believe has broad relevance, beyond translation per se, for pedagogical practices in the foreign language classroom. As Françoise Massardier-Kenney explains, Appiah's project

> aims at creating in students a new appreciation of and respect for people of other times and cultures. [. . .] Appiah rightly points out that this type of translation is "academic" in the sense that it is associated with literary *teaching;* it is associated with the general objective of seeking to understand why people have spoken or written the way they have. The academic mode of translation does not treat the text as a thing made only to be bought and devoured but as a gendered linguistic, historical, commercial and political *event.* (61)

Some may look down on productions like *Les Mis* because they are commercial events. But that is not all they are. *Les Mis* was successful because it took a work of literature and made it into a complex "linguistic, historical, commercial, and political event"; and in so doing it created in its audience a sense of people in another time and place. Finding ways thus to make literature alive and meaningful, I would argue, is what needs to be happening in the foreign language classroom, now and in the future, as we face the challenge of teaching literature to increasingly diverse and technologically sophisticated groups of students.

In an attempt to tease out and piece together elements that could contribute to the thick teaching I propose as a goal for the future, I turn to surveying some of the stages through which approaches to literature have evolved over the past fifty years and what I see as the strengths and weaknesses of those approaches for preparing tomorrow's generation of teachers of literature. A convenient starting point is the French explication de texte, with its equivalents in other language areas, whereby selected passages are submitted to a close, detailed reading that at least linguistically corresponds to a thick teaching of literature. The strength of this approach is that it teaches students of literature to analyze works of poetry or prose and to discern in them a broad range of noteworthy phonological, syntactic, semantic, narrative, stylistic, rhetorical, historical, social, and other features. For students who are mastering a foreign language, such analysis is especially enriching; and its usefulness is not confined to persons possessing imperfect comprehension of language or literature. Even at the highest level of sophistication there is much to be learned by looking closely at a text: witness Roland Barthes's extended explication de texte in *S/Z,* in which he examines a short narrative work by Balzac line by line, thereby providing a wealth of theoretical, narratological, thematic, linguistic, artistic, and social insights. Admittedly, Barthes's work speaks a highly specialized, theoretical language that is out of reach of many readers. Even so, it sets a model of thick reading if not of thick teaching—a model of how linguistic and literary features of texts can lead to observations on subjects as diverse as nineteenth-century sculpture and painting, musical scores, male and female bodies, psychoanalysis, economics, class structure, and opera.

A number of reservations about explication de texte need to be mentioned, however. A very practical one is that students in American high schools do not typically learn literature through close readings of selected passages. A discrepancy may then exist between the ways students learn to approach literature in their English classes and the ways they learn to approach literature in their foreign language classes. Teachers often do not fully appreciate or acknowledge this discrepancy. Another pitfall concerns genre. Explication de texte works best when the text in question is a small-scale, complete, linguistically dense text such as a poem. Lengthy narrations, works containing a significant amount of dialogue, or works written in a lower register for a mass audience—the very kinds of works that often capture the interest of students most effectively—lend themselves far less well to close reading. It would be unfortunate if authors of anthologies or professors whose arsenal of literary approaches is confined to explication de texte were driven to select only texts that lend themselves well to that approach.

The most serious reservation that I have about explication de texte is its narrow focus. Generations of foreign language professionals have been trained through approaches that dwell far more exclusively on the intricate formal workings of texts than most undergraduate students and future secondary school teachers want to know. Despite its dazzling display of diverse social and historical elements, Barthes's *S/Z* never fully transcends the formalistic limitations of the explication de texte, his protest to the contrary notwithstanding (96). Such analysis perhaps had its raison d'être when professors were consistently or predominantly training the next generation of literature professors. But the exclusive use of this approach is not valid for students who are planning to teach in elementary and secondary schools or for those who intend other careers that call for a broader knowledge of literature in its cultural context. The challenge, then, is to enrich close reading with heavy doses of interesting, informative, intellectually challenging, and diverse information.

An example may help illustrate ways to transcend the limitation of the explication de texte. In a recent course that focused on Stendhal's *Le rouge et le noir,* I developed a form of thick teaching that I have called "contextualizing the canon" (Kadish), that is, combining canonical works with other, related, noncanonical or less canonical texts to provide an enhanced social and historical understanding of the past. Although Stendhal's novel is most appropriately used at an advanced undergraduate level because of its length and complexity, the combination of canonical and noncanonical material could be used with excerpts or shorter texts in lower-level literature courses. At a somewhat higher level, a similar approach has been proposed for a first-year graduate course in which the readings "include both canonical and marginalized texts and have a common central theme: adultery" (Murti 42). In my course, the focus was on the period surrounding 1830 in France and on the themes of literacy and oppression, a focus that invited consideration of key issues of class, race, and gender. One of the texts used to contextualize the canon was George Sand's *Indiana,* which has the merits of being contemporary with *Le rouge et le noir;* presenting a related but, in my opinion, a more woman-centered perspective; and raising important historical issues of race, slavery, and colonialism in nineteenth-century France. Another contemporary work is the text edited by Michel Foucault, *Moi, Pierre Rivière, ayant égorgé ma mère, ma soeur et mon frère . . .* (*I, Pierre Rivière, Having Slaughtered My Mother, My Sister, and My Brother . . .*). This text provides the first-person account that a peasant subject was required to write at the time of his arrest for the murder of his mother and two siblings and that was used by legal and medical authorities in judging his sanity for him to stand trial for that crime. A French film version of the story exists, which greatly enhances students' understanding of certain cultural and linguistic features of the period.

The inclusion of such noncanonical texts need not mean the exclusion of close reading. Indeed, in this course I continued to pay careful attention to the full range of such distinctive literary features of literary works as irony, symbolism, description, focalization, and the modalities of narrative voice. Observing those features required explication de texte on many occasions. But unlike my previous teaching of Stendhal's novel, those were not the only matters that were considered. The unit on literacy, for example, considered how literacy was an important issue not only for peasants and workers in the nineteenth century but for women and persons of color as well. Placing a subaltern text such as *Pierre Rivière* — that is, a text that gives voice to the oppressed, normally silenced classes — alongside *Le rouge et le noir* invited a host of observations regarding the class issues that play such a crucial role in Stendhal's novel. Students also gained insights into features of French society of the past, for example, how reading literacy differed significantly from writing literacy and how differences in literacy were based on geographical location or gender; for another example, material conditions in the lives of peasants such as property rights and marriage contracts. *Pierre Rivière* also has the advantage of having been published in an edition containing essays by Michel Foucault and other literary and historical theoreticians that open up this seemingly simple, popular story of a domestic crime to reflection on subjects like power, authorship, subalternity, madness, popular culture, and historiography. Whether one chooses to have students read the theoretical essay by Foucault in French or English depends on the level of the class; but in either case the essay could serve as an enriching adjunct to the reading assignment and the film, both of which would be in the target language, as a way to introduce undergraduate students to the existence and excitement of theoretical subjects.

This example of an integration of theory into literature courses leads back to my summary of approaches to teaching literature and to what I would designate as the theory phase that began in the 1960s and has continued in one form or another in many literature classes to the present time. On the positive side, I believe that theory propelled foreign language departments into the center of intellectual activity and created an atmosphere in which all literature classes, in English and in foreign languages, were infused with a new and healthy dose of reflection on what literature is and why we study it. Surely language students should be as much engaged in philosophical considerations about the meaning of literature as students majoring in English or comparative literature departments. Indeed, the theory phase often enabled language departments to have the kind of links with other disciplines that the national Standards recommend (Natl. Standards in Foreign Lang. Educ. Project) and that are fundamental to the humanistic mission of an undergraduate education.

Much as theory may have helped revitalize the teaching of literature in many foreign language classrooms, it has also had a negative side, when the subjects and materials selected were inappropriate for the student's level of understanding—of language, literature, or both. Peter Schofer brings out this problem in his essay "Theoretical Acrobatics," drawing our attention to the dangers of a potential gulf between the professor's theoretical interests and the reality of the undergraduate classroom (464). The problem is, of course, not unique to foreign language programs. If students have had little experience in reading novels, for example, they simply are not ready for highly complex theoretical considerations on narratology. The situation reaches the level of absurdity when students whose literary and linguistic background extends only a semester or two farther than the intermediate level are asked to discuss abstruse theoretical materials that require mastery of a specialized language not easily comprehensible even to native speakers. The purpose of assigned readings is to meet students at their level of competence in order to enhance and develop their linguistic, literary, and theoretical knowledge; it is not to give teachers the opportunity to pursue their own interests or research projects. At the very least, literature professors need to work hard to bridge the gap from language learning and exposure to advanced literary concepts. Schofer is right in criticizing the all too common situation in which "students are expected, with little preparation, to do advanced literary analysis and to make abstract, conceptual statements about literary texts" ("Literature" 325–26). In short, thick teaching never leaves language behind to dwell on ideas for their own sake.

Also, students' needs, backgrounds, and goals should not be excluded from the theoretical conversation found in departments of language, literature, and culture. While some students in foreign language departments enter with advanced placement or other forms of excellence at the secondary school level, other students who are admitted have less outstanding educational backgrounds. That is not to say that the less outstanding students should be spared exposure to literary theory; rather, the approach with them should be different. The needs of students who are planning on careers in secondary education also need to be considered. Let me provide an example. In a recent graduate course I taught, all teaching and class materials were in the target language and contained a heavy dose of theory; I gave the several secondary school teachers in the class the option of doing a pedagogical project instead of a final paper. One student chose to focus on the readings in narratology that had been used in the course, notably on the notion of focalization. Following up on my suggestion that she read Schofer's "Theoretical Acrobatics," the student was impressed with Schofer's idea of getting students of literature to be authors themselves as a way to improve language and literary skills; she used that idea effectively in her presentation. In the class in which she presented her pedagogical project, she began with an analysis of Renoir's painting *Le Moulin de la Galette,* where she asked the students to describe the scene as if they were one of the characters in the painting. They were asked, in other words, to adopt a visual and psychological perspective or point of view. After that exercise, she went on to explain the theory of focalization and to relate that theory to the previous activity of seeing things from a particular character's vantage point. Last, she distributed literary passages by Flaubert, a master of the narrative complexities of point of view, instructing the members of the class to answer questions such as Who sees?, Who speaks?, Who is addressed?, and so on. The result was a very lively and varied class that demonstrated how theory can be made both relevant and interesting in teaching a foreign language.

Next in my survey of approaches to teaching literature, and another source for key elements in the thick teaching I propose here, is gender studies and race studies. The increased visibility of gender studies since the 1970s has not abated. More recently, an emphasis on the topics of race, ethnic identity, slavery, and colonialism has gained a similarly strong foothold in literature classrooms; and I suspect that the emphasis on both gender and race will continue into the twenty-first century. I applaud these developments and am strongly committed to finding ways to introduce issues of gender and race into undergraduate courses at all levels. Today's students live in an increasingly complex and diverse society that requires a heightened consciousness of and sensitivity to issues of gender and race. Part of our mission as teachers is to provide skills in analyzing complex social phenomena, including ways to deal intelligently with the elements of gender bias, Eurocentrism, or racism that may arise in literary products from the past and present. Such analysis is a crucial component of the thick teaching of literature. As Naomi Schor has observed, teachers of literature need to reflect on a range of issues relating to gender that includes the choice of texts and literary genres, literary methods and theories, the specificity of women's practices of writing and reading, the silenced maternal voice, and the different voices of minority women. Schor admonishes teachers to make these issues part and parcel of foreign language teaching, which is often directed substantially if not predominantly at women students. For these students, being a woman need not be an extraneous or irrelevant factor. As Schor states, "today's students need no longer check their subjectivities at the door" (281). Many of these observations apply to race as well as to gender. It is essential that we take the time to provide appropriately diverse materials for foreign language students so that they do not reach the inaccurate and potentially insulting conclusion that only whites or males have produced or figured prominently in the literatures studied in our classes.

I do have a number of reservations about the application of gender studies and race studies to literature classes. I should note from the outset that the charge of putative political correctness, which some would argue has had a widespread and pernicious effect on the teaching and selection of materials in literature courses, is not one of the reservations. To my mind that charge has been based on isolated errors in judgment, mainly in exclusive or overly theoretical academic settings. My reservations actually go in the contrary direction: that there has been not too much but too little emphasis on gender and race. The newer approach of gender studies and race studies has not been sufficiently integrated into literature courses. Accordingly students fail to realize that those studies affect the center, not just the margins, of their academic activities. Sara Castro-Klarén points out, tellingly, that the SAT II in Spanish "mainly tests knowledge concerning Peninsular writers up to the end of the First World War" (43), a slate of writers in which women and minorities do not play a key role. Too often issues of gender and race are relegated to courses in composition and conversation, culture and civilization, women's studies, or certain specialized topics. The canon then remains intact, as does the definition of what constitutes really important literary subjects. In my exit interviews with graduating majors mentioned earlier, one of the questions I ask is whether in courses in our department students have been exposed to issues of diversity regarding race, gender, ethnicity, and social class. Rarely do the students say that they have not been exposed to those issues, which is encouraging. But they typically remember that exposure as having occurred in composition and conversation courses, which use textbooks or anthologies that make a concerted effort to include diverse materials, or in colonial and francophone literature classes. They report less often that those issues were raised in survey courses or literature courses focusing mainly on European authors or movements, although matters of gender and race typically affect most standard works and periods in literary history.

Related to the problem of gender and race issues being relegated to specialized courses is the problem of appropriate methods not being adopted. Gender studies and race studies entail more than just adding occasional works by women and minorities to the reading list; they also require that all works be approached in a way that takes into account the ongoing developments in the field. An images-of-women approach was popular and significant several decades ago, but it is no longer at the cutting edge of gender studies. Newer approaches tend to highlight issues such as different forms of agency exercised in subaltern history or diverse means of identity formation in minority groups. There is the further problem of grappling with the differences that may exist between our attitudes toward gender and race and those of the literature we are studying. Consider the example of francophone studies, which needs to deal with the fact that French and French Caribbean attitudes toward women's issues differ significantly from the American-style feminist ideas that many French teachers and scholars hold. It is precisely through a thick teaching of literature, which delves thoroughly and painstakingly into the workings of gender and race, that we can come to understand those differences. Taking our lead from cultural anthropologists, we need to refrain from thinking of either the target culture or our own in terms of lack or shortcomings and refrain from being either exclusively accepting or exclusively critical of the target culture's attitudes. Our role as foreign language teachers is to provide students with the opportunity both to understand and to analyze critically the literature of the countries they are studying.

On a practical level, one of the main challenges that foreign language teachers face in attempting to integrate issues of gender and race into literature courses is the difficulty of identifying and selecting texts. Regrettably, all too often teachers take the easy route, merely ordering the same books that they have used before or that their colleagues are ordering, books confined to male European writers. To supplement existing texts, one should be on the lookout for some of the wonderful new books that are being published and that can enrich and invigorate literature courses at all levels: if not necessarily as required reading for the students, at least as enrichment for the teacher. In a composition and conversation course, for example, a teacher might analyze the pictorial representation of a woman in the recent *Twelve Views of Manet's Bar,* which provides cutting-edge insights into the artistic treatment of a gendered subject (Collins). This analysis of Manet's painting can provoke stimulating and enlightening conversations about gender and French art. A similar use could be made of *The Fate of Carmen,* a probing analysis of the literary, musical, and filmic versions of *Carmen,* an opera that raises fascinating issues of both gender and race (Gould). The short novel, the film, and the libretto are all French-language materials that are easy to obtain and use as the basis for class discussion and outside assignments. With regard specifically to race,

I have worked in recent years in collaboration with other scholars to make available writings by women writers who dealt with issues of slavery and abolition (Kadish and Massardier-Kenney). There exists a growing body of other attempts along the same lines: for example, the recently published bilingual edition of the Cuban text *Autobiography of a Slave / Autobiografía de un esclavo* (Manzano). In addition to books, innumerable English and target language sites exist on the World Wide Web that provide access to texts, images, databases, current events, and other sources of information that can be used in conjunction with assigned works of literature to bring diversity and new life into the foreign language classroom. Distance learning, tapping into resources that exist at other institutions, is another avenue for enhancing diversity. In short, we no longer have to rely only on ordering published materials. The chief limitation here is our lack of ingenuity, energy, or creativity. Admittedly, there is also the limitation of inadequate funding in certain schools and thus limited access for students and teachers to existing cyberspace information. Informing oneself about the exciting new materials available through cyberspace and being able to articulate requests for funding with concrete examples of what students are missing out on may be one of the most effective ways to obtain additional funding.

The final stage in my historical survey is the cultural studies approach, which over the last decade has gained widespread acceptance in literature programs in both English and foreign languages. In principle, this approach corresponds the most closely to the thick teaching of literature. The overlap of the cultural studies approach with the preceding two approaches is considerable: indeed, many of the examples I have provided here fit as comfortably under a cultural studies rubric as within the boundaries of theory or of gender studies and race studies. The positive features of cultural studies and the reasons for its current popularity are numerous and noteworthy: it expands definitions of the literary canon and explores relations between high and low culture; it promotes a detailed, textured study of the past and present; it draws attention to minority groups and their cultural contributions; it problematizes issues of cultural and social elitism and hegemony; it foregrounds issues of identity formation in postcolonial societies. Like theory, cultural studies has produced heightened intellectual interest, philosophical depth, and interdisciplinarity in the teaching of literature, from which both students and professors have benefited. Cultural studies practitioners succeed in bridging the gap referred to earlier between traditional academic standards and popular cultural products such as *Les Mis* or the new film version of *The Hunchback of Notre*

Dame by deploying an arsenal of semiotic and ethnological tools in their analyses of a broad range of representations. One also needs to mention the appeal that cultural studies has, if perhaps in name only, for students, who routinely call for more culture in the foreign language curriculum.

The drawbacks of cultural studies for foreign language departments are perhaps as numerous as the advantages. One drawback, which was brought out in a report to the American Comparative Literature Association written in 1993 by Charles Bernheimer and others, is the monolinguism of cultural studies (Petrey 383). In the analyses cultural studies provides and in the texts it considers, the use of English is virtually exclusive. Cultural studies disregards linguistic difference in both its targeted audience and its subject matter. We need to remember that this approach arose in Great Britain in the 1960s at the Centre for Contemporary Cultural Studies at Birmingham and that it has focused much of its attention on issues of class and ethnicity in a British, exclusively anglophone context. The linguistic thickness that we need in teaching foreign languages simply was never an integral ingredient of cultural studies, as it has been in the explication de texte or other approaches applied in conjunction with the development of language skills. Another drawback of cultural studies echoes the drawback of theoretical studies: it is often far too theoretical and abstract for most undergraduate literature classes, especially in foreign language. Ironically, it is also far too theoretical in many cases to be read by the very subaltern subjects it studies. The useful ideas for teaching foreign languages in a cultural studies approach that have been proposed (e.g., Kramsch 189–204, 211–23) are not as widely known or applied as they deserve to be. Also, the everyday social practices that foreign language students want to learn about in courses in foreign language departments are really quite different from what is offered by cultural studies in the British mode. Indeed, cultural studies in its original sense has typically found its home in departments of communication in the United States, where studies of the media and related phenomena are central to the discipline (Grossberg 16). What ends up constituting cultural studies in foreign language departments often lacks definition and coherence; as Sandy Petrey states, "The recent anthologies offering overviews of cultural studies have two features in common: the dumbfounding heterogeneity of the topics they encompass and their resolute refusal to provide even a tentative statement of what Cultural Studies is" (384). A recent case in point is Jill Forbes and Michael Kelly's *French Cultural Studies: An Introduction.* While the introduction justifies the title in terms of the book's focus on issues of national identity and multiculturalism in the French-speaking world, in the book's essays cultural studies becomes an occasion to present diverse social and cultural topics from 1870 to the present time. Ultimately there is little difference between this material and the kind typically used in culture-and-civilization courses, though the subject matter of the book may be less hegemonic. The presentation of all material is in English, notwithstanding claims like the following: "If, as Lévi-Strauss suggested, a society's culture is the language in which it speaks to itself, then French society obviously speaks to itself in many voices" (Kelly 7). To the extent that those many voices are the ideas rather than the ideas embedded in the linguistic reality of the many groups that exist in French society, it remains to be seen whether cultural studies books of this sort will effectively further the goals of the undergraduate curriculum in foreign languages.

I have sketched out some theoretical parameters and some practical ideas for a thick teaching of literature aimed at meeting the special needs of the diverse population of students studying foreign languages, including secondary school education majors. Both theory and practice are essential ingredients to consider in the preparation of future teachers. On the theoretical side, literature teachers need to have courses that give them current, theoretically challenging approaches to literature, not just the old, tried-and-true analyses that often bore students and reinforce the "I hate literature" attitude. On the practical side, persons responsible for teaching literature and preparing secondary school teachers need to become more inventive, creative, and attuned to a generation of students who are not likely to enter academia as their profession. They also need to work diligently and practically to bridge the gap between lower-division language and upper-division literature courses. As Schofer reminds us, considerable work "needs to be done in introductory literature courses, where all too often little attention is paid to students' language needs" (Schofer, "Literature" 332). There is a world of exciting and effective ways of teaching that bridge that gap. One example from my personal experience in the past and from the activities of my Spanish colleagues currently is the use of literature in conjunction with theatrical performance as part of the foreign language and literature program. But many other ways to give new life and excitement to literature can be developed and have indeed been developed by Claire Kramsch, Sylvie Debevic Henning, and others (McCarthy 12–15). What is required is a balanced and pragmatic commitment to language and literature that focuses on students' needs. Making that commitment is the challenge to us as teachers of literature in foreign languages as we face the next century.

WORKS CITED

Appiah, Kwame Anthony. "Thick Translation." *Callaloo* 16 (1993): 808–19.

Barthes, Roland. *S/Z*. Paris: Seuil, 1970.

Birkerts, Sven. *The Gutenberg Elegies: The Fate of Reading in an Electronic Age*. Winchester: Faber, 1994.

Castro-Klarén, Sara. "The Paths Not Yet Taken." *ADFL Bulletin* 29.2 (1998): 42–45.

Collins, Bradford R., ed. *Twelve Views of Manet's Bar*. Princeton: Princeton UP, 1996.

Cregan, Mary. "Reading Groups Are Bridging Academic and Popular Culture." *Chronicle of Higher Education* 19 Dec. 1997: B4–B5.

Forbes, Jill, and Michael Kelly, eds. *French Cultural Studies: An Introduction*. Oxford: Oxford UP, 1996.

Foucault, Michel, ed. *Moi, Pierre Rivière, ayant égorgé ma mère, ma sœur et mon frère. . . .* Paris: Gallimard, 1973. *I, Pierre Rivière, Having Slaughtered My Mother, My Sister, and My Brother. . . .* Trans. Frank Jellinek. Lincoln: U of Nebraska P, 1982.

Geertz, Clifford. *The Interpretation of Culture*. New York: Basic, 1973.

Gould, Evelyn. *The Fate of Carmen*. Baltimore: Johns Hopkins UP, 1996.

Grossberg, Lawrence, et al. *Cultural Studies*. New York: Routledge, 1992.

Kadish, Doris Y. "Contextualizing the Canon: New Perspectives on *The Red and the Black*." *Approaches to Teaching Stendhal's* The Red and the Black. Ed. Dean de la Motte and Stirling Haig. New York: MLA, 1999. 112–20.

Kadish, Doris Y., and Françoise Massardier-Kenney. *Translating Slavery: Gender and Race in French Women's Writing, 1783–1823*. Kent: Kent State UP, 1994.

Kelly, Michael. "Introduction: French Cultural Identities." Forbes and Kelly 1–7.

Kramsch, Claire. *Context and Culture in Language Teaching*. Oxford: Oxford UP, 1993.

Manzano, Juan Francisco. *Autobiography of a Slave / Autobiografía de un esclavo*. Trans. Evelyn Picon Garfield. Detroit: Wayne State UP, 1996.

Massardier-Kenney, Françoise. "Towards a Redefinition of Feminist Translation Practice." *Translator* 4 (1997): 55–69.

McCarthy, John A. "W(h)ither Literature? Reaping the Fruit of Language Study before It's Too Late." *ADFL Bulletin* 29.2 (1998): 10–17.

Murti, Kamakshi. "Teaching Literature at the First-Year Graduate Level: The Quantum Leap from Language to Literature." *ADFL Bulletin* 25.1 (1993): 41–48.

National Standards in Foreign Language Education Project. *Standards for Foreign Language Learning: Preparing for the Twenty-First Century*. Lawrence: Allen, 1996.

Petrey, Sandy. "French Studies / Cultural Studies: Reciprocal Invigoration or Mutual Destruction?" *French Review* 68 (1995): 381–92.

Schofer, Peter. "Literature and Communicative Competence: A Springboard for the Development of Critical Thinking and Aesthetic Appreciation of Literature in the Land of Language." *Foreign Language Annals* 23.4 (1990): 325–34.

———. "Theoretical Acrobatics: The Student as Author and Teacher in Introductory Literature Courses." *French Review* 57 (1984): 463–74.

Schor, Naomi. "Feminist and Gender Studies." *Introduction to Scholarship in Modern Languages and Literatures*. 2nd ed. Ed. Joseph Gibaldi. New York: MLA, 1992. 262–87.

APPENDIX

Baseline Studies

The proposal the MLA submitted to the NEH calls for each of the participating departments in the MLA Teacher Education Project to prepare a baseline study of the courses and teaching practices that the department's prospective secondary school teachers encounter. Primary responsibility for gathering the information for this study rests with the team's chair, but we assume that all team members will be involved collaboratively in collecting and interpreting the findings and presenting them to department members and others. A study of courses and teaching practices in a single department does not readily lend itself to quantification. Therefore, team members face three challenges: (1) determining how to collect information from members of the department about the courses they teach; (2) making colleagues feel comfortable about the way the information will be used; and (3) determining what the collected information says about the effectiveness of the department's courses and teaching practices for prospective secondary school teachers. This last task is by far the most difficult and the most important that the team will undertake.

Each team must also decide how best to organize and present what it learns to the various groups that will use the information the team collects and interprets. You may want to have several versions of your study. The complete baseline study (including lists of courses, analyses of the features of these courses, lists of teaching practices, and the team's interpretations and conclusions) will provide team members with the information they need to determine what seem to be the department's strengths and weaknesses. An overview of the team's interpretations and conclusions, however, may be more useful to the department than detailed accounts of who does what in which courses.

Please note that the MLA has no position on any of the issues implicit in the questions that follow. Responsibility for decisions about teaching practices and the curriculum rightly rests with the faculty members in a department. The MLA staff members working on this project believe that there is no single approach to teaching or scholarship in the field that is right or wrong. In fact, we believe that the study of language and literature has always been inclusive and has changed over the years; we also believe that different students learn in different ways and therefore benefit from a variety of approaches and teaching practices. The MLA's proposal expressed the hope that the departments participating in the project would develop different exemplary programs appropriate to their departmental and institutional missions, faculty commitments, student needs, and state and local requirements concerning the preparation of secondary school teachers.

Baseline Study for English Departments

COURSES

As a first step in preparing your baseline report, we ask that you and the members of your team generate a list of the English department courses taken by students who are preparing to be secondary school teachers. Please group the courses in the following categories:

1. Courses students must take because of state certification requirements
2. Courses required by the department (repeat courses from category 1)
3. Courses frequently recommended by English or education faculty advisers
4. Elective courses students commonly take
5. Elective courses students rarely take

Once you and your colleagues have compiled a list of the relevant courses in your department that prospective English teachers take, we ask you to consider how the following questions apply to each group of courses. In responding to these questions, you will want to consult the teachers of these courses, and you will want to consider teachers' stated objectives as well as the possible unintended consequences of the various ways these courses are organized and taught, individually and as groups of courses.

1. How does each group of courses introduce students to the discipline?
2. What does each group of courses convey about the nature of the discipline?
3. What are the organizing principles in each group of courses?
4. Which works of literature are regularly assigned in each group of courses?
5. What is the role of coverage as an organizing principle in literature courses?
6. What is the role of historical connections as an organizing principle in literature courses?
7. Which texts and theories are regularly assigned in language and writing courses?
8. How much writing and reading are students doing in each group of courses?
9. What do these courses convey about the teaching of writing, literature, and language?
10. What do these courses convey about grades, tests, and other forms of assessment?
11. What do these courses convey about rhetorical, linguistic, and literary theories?
12. What role do oral language, drama, film, and technology play in these courses?
13. Do any of these groups of courses prepare students to meet the needs of students whose first language is not English?

AN INVENTORY OF TEACHING PRACTICES

When students become teachers, they often imitate their teachers. Therefore, we ask you to give special consideration to the range of practices, models, and attitudes toward teaching that students encounter in the department's required and elective courses. The question of modeling is particularly pertinent, because the education reform movement, drawing on research emphasizing more and less effective classroom practices, encourages the active engagement of students as learners. To encourage consistency among departments' reports, we set forth the following terms and definitions. If the members of your department use practices not described here, please name and describe them.

Classroom Practices

Lecture. The instructor presents material for an entire class period, leaving perhaps five or ten minutes for questions, quizzes, or a writing activity.

Discussion. The instructor and students engage in dialogue for an entire class period. We ask you to distinguish between two types of discussions:

Teacher-directed discussions, in which discussion most commonly starts from questions posed by the instructor and most conversation occurs between the instructor and individual students by turn. Socratic questioning often provides examples of teacher-directed discussions.

Open-format discussions, in which students and instructor assume a variety of roles. Open-format discussions are distinctive in their reliance on improvisation. Discussion may begin either from the instructor's questions or from students' questions or presentations; for example, students might read journal entries written outside class or short pieces of writing done in class. Instructors manage open-format discussions in various ways, and it will be important to note differences—how the instructor organizes and moderates such discussions, how time is apportioned between instructor and students, the degree to which the instructor serves as an interlocutor, and whether students sustain conversation among themselves with minimal teacher support or intervention. Because of the element of improvisation, open-format discussions bring to the fore issues of how discussion is serving learning. If students are talking largely among themselves, who or what ensures that the talk is educationally productive? How are the goals of such discussions described, and how does the instructor judge whether those goals are being achieved?

Lecture and discussion. The instructor presents material in one or two minilectures, of perhaps ten to fifteen minutes each, and the remainder of a given class period is devoted to either teacher-directed or open-format discussion. Of special interest in this format is how instructors use the two activities in relation to each other. One instructor might lecture at the beginning and end of class, using the lecture format to introduce a topic and summarize conclusions and questions. Another might ask two or three students to read excerpts from their journals, listen to what members of the entire class say to one another in an open-format discussion, and watch to see if a theme or issue or occasion emerges in relation to which a minilecture is appropriate.

Small-group activities. The instructor divides the class into groups of, say, four to six students. We ask you to distinguish small-group activities that are based on an assignment prepared by the instructor from groups that engage in less structured, open-topic conversations. If small groups are used in a given course, are the groups given specific activities to do or problems to solve? And are the assigned activities or problems designed to give students experience with specific ideas or concepts that the course is intended to convey?

Student reports and oral presentations. It will be useful to know the length of class time individual student presenters take.

In-class writing. We ask you to distinguish between two types of in-class writing:

Half-sheet responses: one-minute writings done at some point in full or minilectures (usually at the end), in which students quickly note the main point they took away from a presentation and any questions they have

Free writing: timed, nonstop writings, in which students write with as little concern as possible for such features as spelling, grammatical correctness, or other mechanics. Free writing may be directed to a specific topic, or the topic may be open.

In-class dramatic presentations or readings, whether by teachers or students

Computer classroom, lab, or instruction

Audiovisual materials (especially film, video, or recorded voice) in class and field trips (to theater, etc.)

Student-teacher conferences. Are conferences held with individual students or with groups of students? Are conferences used for specific purposes in various courses (for example, to supplement or replace teacher comments on written work)?

Assignments

Group projects, in which small groups of students are assigned to work together on an out-of-class project

Writing assignments. We ask you to distinguish among three types of writing assignments:

Journals, either focused on a particular task or subject or open in topic

Learning logs, in which students state the date of starting and completing an assignment; describe the steps taken, problems encountered, and mistakes made in the course of their work; and say what they would do differently, giving their level of satisfaction with the task

Peer editing, in which groups of students read and comment on one anothers' written work

Teacher Evaluation We would like to learn about how faculty members and departments are evaluating and grading student work. Examples would be:

Midterm and final examinations written in a class period. Please distinguish among essay exams, short-answer exams, and mechanically scored tests.
Papers. Please distinguish among papers of fewer than five pages, papers of five to ten pages, and term papers (ten to twenty pages).
In-class quizzes
Portfolios of students' written work

In evaluating these or other performances and projects, what uses do faculty members make of written comments and letter grades? How frequently do faculty members assign writing that is (1) read but neither graded nor commented on; (2) read and commented on; and (3) not read? Are comments used without letter grades in some circumstances? Or are letter grades used without comments? Are students ever asked to respond to comments prior to the assignment of a letter grade? Finally, if staff-graded essays or exams are used in the department, is holistic or analytic scoring used?

Student Evaluation

Early-in-term course evaluations, in which students comment on how a course is going near the beginning of a semester, with the aim of allowing the instructor to make adjustments if appropriate
End-of-term course evaluations

Finally, we ask that you collect and review the following information:

1. Mission statements for your institution and department
2. Your state's teacher-certification requirements
3. Your state's framework for secondary school study in English (if such a framework exists)
4. The catalog description of your English education program (or English major) and its requirements

Baseline Study for Foreign Language Departments

COURSES

As a first step in preparing your baseline report, we ask that you and the members of your team generate a list of the foreign language department courses taken by students who are preparing to be secondary school teachers. Please group the courses in the following categories:

1. Courses students must take because of state certification requirements
2. Courses required by the department (repeat courses from category 1)
3. Courses frequently recommended by foreign language or education faculty advisers
4. Elective courses students commonly take
5. Elective courses students rarely take

Once you and your colleagues have compiled a list of the relevant courses in your department that prospective foreign language teachers take, we ask you to consider how the following questions apply to each group of courses. In responding to these questions, you will want to consult the teachers of these courses, and you will want to consider teachers' stated objectives as well as the possible unintended consequences of the various ways these courses are organized and taught, individually and as groups of courses.

1. How does each group of courses introduce students to the discipline?
2. What does each group of courses convey about the nature of the discipline?
3. What are the organizing principles in each group of courses?
4. To what degree is each of the four skills (listening, speaking, reading, and writing) emphasized at each level in these courses?
5. What do these courses convey about the teaching of each of the four skills?
6. Is the teaching of language integrated with the teaching of literature in each group of courses?
7. How are the sequences in each group of courses organized?
8. Are the levels of linguistic competence required in literature and culture courses in keeping with students' abilities?
9. What is the role of assessment at entry and exit points in the language sequence?

10. What do department courses convey about tests, grades, and other forms of assessment?
11. Do language and literature courses in each group reflect current research in second language acquisition and reading?
12. Are students introduced to cultural concepts and authentic materials at each level of the language sequence and in each group of courses?
13. Are students taught to manage their own language learning effectively and efficiently at all levels and in all courses?
14. How is technology used in each group of courses?
15. Are the needs of students who are studying their home languages addressed in constructive terms, and what do department courses convey about the study of heritage languages?
16. How are language-across-the-curriculum, study-abroad, and immersion programs integrated with other department offerings?
17. What role do courses in translation play in the department and what do these courses convey about the nature of the discipline?

AN INVENTORY OF TEACHING PRACTICES

When students become teachers, they often imitate their teachers. Therefore, we ask you to give special consideration to the range of practices, models, and attitudes toward teaching that students encounter in the department's required and elective courses. The question of modeling is particularly pertinent, because the education reform movement, drawing on research emphasizing more and less effective classroom practices, encourages the active engagement of students as learners. To encourage consistency among departments' reports, we set forth the following terms and definitions. If the members of your department use practices not described here, please name and describe them. Throughout your descriptions you will want to keep in mind the attention paid to language, literature, and culture at all levels and to the interplay of speaking, listening, reading, and writing in the development of linguistic and cultural competence.

You may find it useful to organize your report around the categories and examples listed below.

For Language Courses

Teacher-student dialogue
Peer-group activities
Grammar and vocabulary drill
Balance between explanations and applications

Listening exercises
Reading and responding to authentic materials from daily life
Reading and responding to literature
Oral presentations
Writing in class
Uses of technology

For Assessment

Classroom quizzes
Exams
Writing assignments
Oral presentations
Oral proficiency interviews
Portfolios
Computer driven individualized tests

For Advanced Courses in Literature and Culture

Attention to language skills through the study of texts
Emphasis on textual analysis, with limited regard for developing language skills
Teacher-directed discussions
Small-group activities
Emphasis on writing
Use of the target language and the use of English for lecture, discussion, and writing assignments

EXAMPLES OF SOME GENERAL CHARACTERISTICS OF CLASSROOM TEACHING

Classroom Formats

Lecture. The instructor presents material for an entire class period, leaving time for questions.
Teacher-directed discussion. The class is guided toward a conclusion.
Open format. Improvising, students and instructor can assume a variety of roles, such as interlocutor, respondent, or a part in a play or story.

Student Activities

Small-group activities in class. Groups of two to four students either work on an assignment prepared by the instructor or engage in less structured discussion.

Student reports and oral presentations. What length are they? How often are they given?

In-class dramatic presentations or readings by students or teachers

Writing, in class or for homework: literary analysis, journals, creative work. How often is it assigned? What length is it? Who evaluates these exercises? Faculty members? Peers?

Self-evaluation. Learning logs, in which students state the date of starting and completing an assignment; describe the steps taken, problems encountered, and mistakes made in the course of their work; and say what they would do differently, giving their level of satisfaction with the task

Group projects on research. For example, interviews of a certain local language group, or the establishment of Internet ties with students in another country

Materials

Textbooks, literature, authentic materials from the target culture like newspapers, periodicals, advertisements

Films, videos, TV programs, recordings

Computer classroom or language lab instruction using writing programs, hypertext, the Internet, or other formats. Are the programs written by faculty members, or is existing software used?

Teacher Evaluation of Students

Student-teacher conferences. Are they held in the middle or at the end of the course? Do they supplement or replace teacher comments on written work?

Tests: in-class quizzes, midterms, and finals written in a class period. Please distinguish among essay exams, short-answer exams, mechanically scored tests, individual computer tests.

Papers. Please distinguish among papers of fewer than five pages, papers of five to ten pages, and term papers (ten to twenty pages). Is the paper in the target language or in English?

Portfolios of students' written and oral work

Oral proficiency interview or the adaptation of such a test

Grading. What uses do faculty members make of written comments and letter grades? Are comments used without letter grades in some circumstances? Or are letter grades used without comments? Are students ever asked to respond to teacher comments prior to the assignment of a letter grade? Finally, if staff-graded essays or exams are used in the department, is holistic or analytic scoring used?

Student Evaluation of Teaching

Early-in-term course evaluations, in which students comment on how a course is going, with the aim of allowing the instructor to make adjustments if appropriate

End-of-term evaluations. Are these shared with the department chair? With other administrators?

Finally, we ask that you collect and review the following information:

1. Mission statements for your institution and department
2. Your state's teacher-certification requirements
3. Your state's framework for secondary school study in foreign languages (if such a framework exists)
4. The catalog description of your foreign language education program (or foreign language major) and its requirements